The Garden Path

SPIRITUAL CHURCH OF THE MANIFOLD WISDOM OF GOD

With Spiritual theology UNDER
"The Tabernacle in the Sun"

MASS, Capt Francis Charles Malcolm

Copyright © 2019 by MASS, Capt Francis Charles Malcolm. 799434

All rights reserved. No part of this book may be reproduced or transmitted in any form or by any means, electronic or mechanical, including photocopying, recording, or by any information storage and retrieval system, without permission in writing from the copyright owner.

Scripture quotations marked KJV are from the Holy Bible, King James Version (Authorized Version). First published in 1611. Quoted from the KJV Classic Reference Bible, Copyright © 1983 by The Zondervan Corporation.

To order additional copies of this book, contact:
Xlibris
1-888-795-4274
www.Xlibris.com
Orders@Xlibris.com

ISBN: Softcover   978-1-7960-6262-5
         EBook   978-1-7960-6263-2

Print information available on the last page

Rev. date: 09/30/2019

Contents

Reference

The BG's/the beetles/

The Bible

The Garden Path mass

THE PREFACE

The Institution of the Tabernacle in the Sun by God The Creator, creates a single Church out of the reach of man to Govern over all the Churches with the Angels of the Seven Churches having control over all these Churches in the hand of the Lord Jesus Christ, putting out the light of their candle sticks in failure to recognize God will and continuing in the filthiness, wickedness, and lack of Grace and love in ordinances of man to worship God. The Spiritual Church of the Manifold Wisdom of God can only be manifested "WE the ENTRUSTED" the brazen wall of fire, it is not yours but that of God by The Refresher of the Master's Soul, The Minister of God, The Messenger Greater than John the Baptist and Greater than John the Revelator for all Priests comely Understanding of The LIBERALITY by the BIBLE and no other book, which is the gift of God. For in as much as you know it will not be to you upon deceitful lips under a face of darkness filled with the lust of envy, puffiness and muffled up to retreat into their closet with the great work of good hiding in the darkness mingling with Satan covered with fiend lips. The Priest of the First Beast needs to remove self from riding of Satan. The Priest of the Second Beast needs to remove self from the evil of the first beast and from riding of Satan. All the Priests as offspring out of the darkness and "Enmity of Christ", need to remove themselves from the "Enmity of Christ" and BEAST of their powers, which is grossly Man's, looking like the true Spirit of God, The evil Spirit of Satan and the Filthy Spirit of Man in the ordinances of Man to be in the Spirit of God. Hence, making a way, under "The Prepared Way", that of the New Gospel and the New Covenant, of the Messenger for Lord Thy God. The term **new** means **not of the Old** and **not of the Scattered Parts** of the old gospel, but that which cometh after the gospel in decay and that which creates the of the vanishing of the Old Gospel and Old Covenant, for the Lord Thy God to pour out His Seven Spirits upon Man, under The Tabernacle in the Sun. The Tabernacle in the Sun is indeed the monitoring Church kept by the Seven Angels in the heaven for the Unified Church on earth. Hence representing all the Churches on earth that is worthy to God that was ushered in by "We the ENTRUSTED" with the LIBERALITY and the Spiritual Church of the Manifold Wisdom of God. The New Gospel and New Covenant is not engineered by a New Bible but by the Prepared Way of the same Old Bible and its work that the people of old could not understand, and such work must be understood for the interpretations thereof be the full truth of God, from the Mysteries of Christ. This brings the messenger with the Sword of the Spirit to stand, now out of controversary because of the STIR and the Moderation on Face Book, to the four (4) corners of the earth, for the people's perusal all over the world. This book was never prepared for conflict with the Churches but to bring them into unity with one New Gospel and teachings to follow the Ordinances of God through the prepared way of our Lord Jesus Christ. He that is the Lord of the Sabbath hath manifested a new thing set in a book to move mankind from the enmity of

Christ. Which means that, being delivered of your faults would be an easy thing to do than to accept change, which should be easier, noting your degrees of freedom to relive holiness at the will of God. It is now time for mankind to realize that they can't quench the fire of God as they did to the Spirit of God throughout the ages. It is now time for mankind to see that they can't toggle with God in a fight for supremacy and blessings, but to accept the will of God. As we mount up from the example of the Messenger with now the tallest candle stick that will last forever to carry the light of the whole world with the dominion of the Seven Angels in the hand of God. Now name brand or no name brand the unity will be under the Tabernacle in the sun by reconciliation through the Prepared way unto one God, He that created the heaven and the earth and all bodies of waters and the creatures therein. Many are there the Priests and Pastors with exponents of the Seven Churches and the Seven Churches that may claim to be Jesus Christ and also claim that there is no God. It will not be well with your soul, but you don't care as you are already at fault with God. Maybe the falling away is not far from you and may be a easy and better thing to do so that you can be revealed as the wicked one. It is just enough for you to just claim that you are God above all Gods, and see the end thereof to the entire incognizant frail being you be by who is the Almighty and most Omnipotent God. The LIBERALITY moves the world into a phase where we are at the High time. This is a time of consequence unto the Churches in their religious pursuits as seen unto God but in the ordinances of man. For God hath sent His son to bring a sword to the world but it was not taken at the time of His visitation because man was full of Himself and had to do what He had to do. Because they at the time gone by could not understand Jesus Christ and His sayings the Sword of the spirit was enacted for the End of Time, the Last Days or the High Time. Such sword would deliver a prepared way for the return of the Saints, or in other words the Patient Saints, unto God, and the ordinances of God. As the way is prepared, and delivered unto men, the coming of the Priests to the work of the Messenger, for the understanding there of, to make it relevant to the Churches under the Tabernacle in the Sun which is in the hand of the Lord Jesus Christ with New Gospel and New Covenant as ordered by the Lord being administered by the Angels in his hand, for the management of the seven Churches and their exponents in the return of the Saints unto the will of God. For God so loved the world that He gave His only begotten Son, that whosoever believeth in Him should not perish but have everlasting life, as a promise of faith unto Him, who was dead but now alive.

DEDICATION

THE TRUTH OF JESUS CHRIST is dedicated to all those that are, stirred up at the altar of the SON of GOD under The Tabernacle of the Sun, with the last alter call in the High Time for all people TO DO THE WILL OF GOD, that encourages the full freedom of my BLACK BROTHERS and SISTERS from Satan. Such freedom enhances the quality of life for all people for then they will inherit the sweetness of life through God to begin see that more brings more for everyone under GOD. This book is also dedicated to the races of people that will be united from racism with the freedom of the mind that the last days people will all have to find, as we move bit by bit into eschatology. Further dedication to the friends of Jesus Christ Lt. Colonel Sean Chin-See, Lyunion Stoddart, Erol Haughton for Their love and generosity in times of adversities, and the numerous Sister that I have met face to face that helped to preserve the way, that be not without witnesses. Special dedication to the one and two witnesses that followed the STIR and the MODERATIONS, before god and all mankind your spiritual anointing had come also under The God of Light. Dedication to the Priests with the understanding of The Liberality, and the extended Clergy and the Laity that will be able to unlearn that which was understood and now not good because it was all wrong. Dedication to the Great Multitude being far away and some getting out of Babylon which saw the light of God and got to know God before it is or was too late.

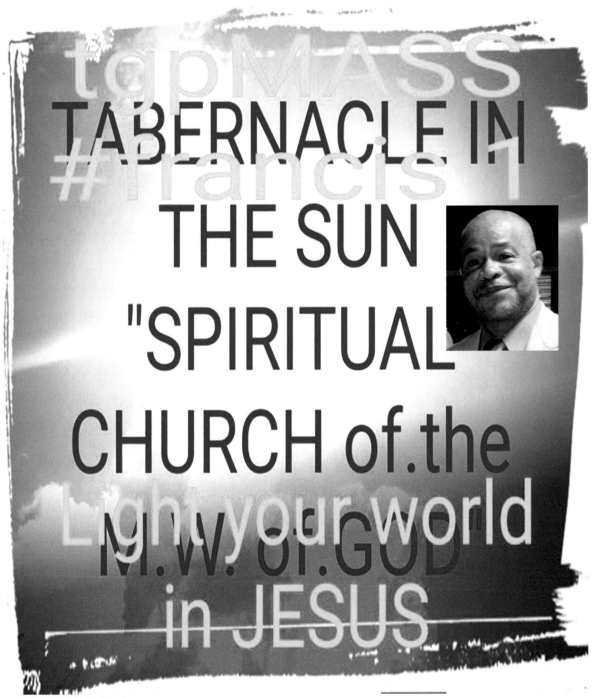

FIGURE 1: THE FACE BOOK GRAPHICS IN THE MODERATIONS

INTRODUCTION

IN MAN IS NOW THE GENERATION OF THE HOLY SPIRIT OF GOD THROUGH JESUS CHRIST. IT IS MANIFESTED IN THE HOLY GHOST, THE SPIRIT OF JESUS CHRIS, AND THE SPIRIT OF GOD. WITH MANKIND HAVING ACCEPTED THE WILL OF GOD, WITH ALL THEIR HEARTS AND TO LIVE THE LAW OF LOVE, THROUGH JESUS CHRIST IN THEIR TEMPLE, MEANING WITHIN THEIR PHYSICAL BODY, THE FATHER OF CREATION WILL POUR OUT HIS SEVEN HOLY SPIRITS UPON THEM. JESUS CHRIST MANIFESTING THE SPIRITUAL CHURCH OF THE MANIFOLD WISDOM OF GOD UPON MAN, IN THE HIGH TIMES.

THE INCORPORATION OF THE SPIRITUAL CHURCH WITHIN THE SOUL MEANS LIVING IN LOVE WITH ALL MEN, TEACHING THE LIGHT AND LIVING THE LIGHT OF GOD FOR EVER.

IN SEEKING THE KINGDOM OF GOD, YOU ALL HAVE TO DO THE WILL OF GOD. THE WILL OF GOD WAS ESTABLISHED FROM CREATION AND THE COMING OF HIS SON THE LORD JESUS CHRIST TO ENLIGHTEN MEN OF HIS WILL WITH THE SWORD OF THE SPIRIT WHICH THEY STILL COULD NOT UNDERSTAND AND AFTER HIS PURGING FROM WATER BAPTISM BY JOHN THE BAPTIST AND ALL HIS DICIPLES HAD GONE FROM HIM, HE SPOKE OF THE MESSENGER THAT WILL BRING UNTO THIS WORLD THE WORD. TELLING THOSE THAT ENCROACHED ON THE WILDERNESS TO SEE IF HE WAS STILL WITH THEM THAT JOHN THE BAPTIST WAS THE GREATEST PROPHET, HE HAD SEEN BUT THE MESSENGER TO COME IN THE HIGH TIME WILL BE GREATER. THE SPIRITUAL CHURCH IS BORNE OUT OF A PEOPLE WILLING TO WORSHIP GOD SPIRITUALLY SEEKING THE KINGDOM OF GOD. LIVING WITH LOVE SPIRITUALY GIVING LOVE ONE TO ANOTHER IN THE HIGH TIMES WHEN MAN HAVE GONE THROUGH THEIR SUSCEPTIBILITY AS STRONG MEN TO BECOME WEAK MEN THAT LACK WISDOM AND UNDERSTANDING BECAUSE OF GREED AND MONEY.

FOR THE WEAKNESS OF MEN DWELL IN THE FLESH AND MANKIND WILL NOT COMPREHEND HIS FAULTS UNTIL HE IS LIVING IN THE SPIRIT WITH TO DISCERN THE WILL OF GOD AND NOT HIS OWN WILL AND FRIVOLOUS UNDERSTANDING THAT HE DEPENDS UPON IN THE FLESH. FOR IN THE SPIRIT ALL WILL WORK THEIR GIFTS FROM GOD AND INSTEAD OF BEING LOVERS OF THE

WORLD WHICH ONLY GLORIFIES THE SELF AND MEN, THEY WILL LOVE THE ALMIGHTY GOD AND HEAL AND REDEEM THEMSELVES IN THE HIGH TIMES FOR THE GOD OF HEAVEN AND EARTH.

THE CHURCH IN MANKIND FOREVERMORE WHEN THE HEARTS OF MEN TURN TO GOD ACCEPT GRACE AND LIVE A LIFE OF LOVE TEACHING THE LIGHT OF THE KINGDOM OF GOD WITH ALL MEN AS THEY THE WHEAT AND THE TEARS LIVE TOGETHER.

THE MANY RULES OF THE BIBLE WILL BE SEEN IN THIS BOOK AS METHOD OF UNDERSTANDING OF THE SWORD OF SPIRIT OF GOD. THE HOLY WORD OF WHICH THE GREAT MULTITUDE HAVE FED UPON AND THE CHURCHES FINDING IT HARD TO RECEIVE.

THE POWERFUL SPIRIT OF GOD WILL DETERMINE THE ENABLEMENT OF MAN UNDERSTANDING AND DETERMINATION TO FOLLOW THE WILL OF GOD AND ACCEPT IT WITH ALL THEIR HEARTS. THOUGH BEING A MANIFESTO IN THE LAST DAYS AS THE WATERS BEFORE HIM MOUNTS UP TO THE BRIM IT IS WITH TRUE LOVE OF GOD THAT MANKIND WILL SEE IF THEY OME TO UNDERSTAND HIS PRECEPTS.

THE BOOK IS ALL SET TO FOLLOW THE BIBLE BUT INTRIGUINGLY SEEMS TO DEVIATE TO FETCH YOUR UNDERSTANDING WITH NOTHING NEW EXCEPT GIVEN BY THE SPIRIT OF GOD. THIS BOOK REMAINS THE ONLY EXECUTIVE BOOK OF THE PREPARED WAY OF THE LORD JESUS CHIRST, THAT MARKS A PERIOD OF DEVELOPMENT THROUGH THE GARDEN PATH, WHICH ALLOW PEOPLE TO UNDERSTAND THAT THE END OF THE WORLD IS NOT REALLY AWEFUL THING BUT A CHANGE IN BELIEFS AND IDEALOGIES OF MAN'S BELIEFS IN GOD, THROUGHOUT THE EPHEMERAL CHURCHES AND THE NOMADIC SOCIETIES. THIS IS WHERE GOD HIMSELF WILL MITIGATE THE CHANGES AS SEEN IN THE SCRIPTURES AFORE BUT WITH LITTLE OR NO UNDERSTANDING OF THE BIBLE, IN CONGRUENCE WITH BELIEFS OPINIONS, AND PEOPLES GREED CONCEPTUALIZED OVER SELFISH NEEDS.

THE CHURCH HAS ENDURED BABYLON FOR A LONG PERIOD OF TIME UNTIL IT CONQUERED AMERICA, TO COVER IT WITH THE BEAST AND ITS FILTHY LIVING WHILE FIGHTING THE OTHER BEAST OF THE SAME POWERS OF SATAN. IF AMERICA FITS ITSELF INTO GOING DOWN ITO PERDITION WITH THE RISE OF FILTHINESS AS ITS DOMAIN IN UNCLEANSENESS, THEN IT WILL BE DESTROYED BY ITS OWN WILL TO BOLDLY ADVANCE INTO DARKNESS WITHOUT BEING ABLE TO BE HEALED. BUT IF THEY BE HEALED WILL CERTAINLY RISE ABOVE THE CONTEMPT OF THE CHURCHE AGAINST GOD THE CREATOR WITH FILTHY AND EVIL DEEDS. WE HAVE NO ACCOUNT OF A MATTER OF PERDITION BEING DEVOURED BUT WE HAVE AN ACCOUNT OF THE BRAZEN WALL OF FIRE TO STAND IN POSITION UPON EARTH AS "WE The ENTUSTED" © 2018, THEREFORE ALL MEN ARE STILL GAURANTEED A MEANS OF SALVATION THROUGH THE SWORD OF THE SOIRIT OF GOD.

The Garden Path a System of Preparedness for the High Time

1. **The 1, 2 & 3 Crew. Number 1 Mandela Hallmarks and His 72 years freedom line and issues of the Black people as the rise above rejection and apartheid. It has been way down the road building up to the years gone by when even Westinghouse Publishers were to publish "The Garden Path" as "The Tempest".**

2. **The Messenger rises out of the doldrums and stand to deliver the prepared way of the Lord. With every minute of disparage in the glaciers that line every spring time of the purpose to stand with the LIBERALITY. I understand the contempt in many a hearts that were swimming upstream rather than following the messenger running this race in the upheavals of time.**

3. **Many women fled my presence for they had their own beliefs of criminality of an underground gospel in tandem to the truth of reality, even though they co-habit with their own comfort of indulgences and insatiable greed of all kinds. The Messenger remained strong and undisturbed with a determination to stand through all adversities.**

THE SYSTEM WITH THE LIBERALITY AND THE SPIRITUAL CHURCH OF THE MANIFOLD WISDOM OF GOD

4. THE LIBERALITY endowed with the WORD, from the Sword of the Spirit which the Lord Jesus Christ took to me the Messenger. Took a long shot to prominence. Waiting, musing and lingering to the relative time line to change the Gospel of Jesus Christ at the appointed time within a concerted effort of the Voices of the City, The Voices of the Temple and The Voices of Jah under the second Crew.

5. The LIBERALITY now a matter of procurement of the Gospel of the end of time called "The New Gospel" under the Tabernacle in the Sun New Covenant unto God. In the High Time when God is ready to erase The Old Gospel, that is dead, decaying and in parts and scattered all over and make it to vanish away.

6. Thirdly Spiritual Church of the Manifold Wisdom of God that will anchor the Prepared Way, bring Grace Love and light to the hearers of the word.

7. Mankind in the flesh seems more capable to Categorizes, Idolize and Iconize the self in the Churches of our present Old Gospel and Religions. Setting back the Church spiritually and the Temple of God to be demonized.

8. In the Spirit the word is love, you let self be until you return to the fleshy thing of the world. Here you lock the utter carnation of the world out to call upon God in His ever presence and your contrite heart. You walk many kilometers

in God's presence under the sun to Jerusalem to pray. But this you can do by the command of the Lord Jesus anywhere under the Tabernacle in the Sun in the Spirit. So, coming to the Synagogues in your holiness and as you leave the Synagogues you are at war. Then why come to pray?

9. The Children of the New Gospel and The New Covenant will set aside the flesh anywhere they are and praise God, giving Him thanks for everything, blessing Him continually. Yes set aside the big fat batty Gal, set aside the fat car, set aside the riches, which isn't tried Gold and Silver from the furnace, set aside the loftiness of mind, and come down low unto God with a broken heart, set aside your dreams and aspirations your God already knoweth it all unless you are about to ask for a blessing and to tell Him thanks for a blessings, set aside strife with people on your mind unless you are asking God to protect you from the evil hands, set aside the lust of the fleshy heart, set aside the iniquity, set aside the will of man and disobedience unto God and come unto God with truth in your hearts believing upon your God.

10. Recognize your God under The Tabernacle in the Sun for minimum seven (7) minutes of peaceful prayers of repentance, prayers of acceptance of his will, prayers of declaration of His promise to be with you, prayers of gratitude, prayers of love, prayers of praise, prayers of worship and prayers of thanks giving for His Seven (7) Spirit to fall upon you, to be worthy of seeking the Kingdom of God.

11. When you muster under The Tabernacle in the Sun, remember to give God praise, and glorify His Holy Name

above all other names. To extol His Name Jah is His pleasure, forsake it not.

12. **Feel at home with the New Gospel and The New Covenant quenching not the Spirit but admonish the workers in faith in the High Time of our Lord Jesus Christ.**

13. **After your holiness give love unto every man, taking the evil rod off the righteous man, giving love and sharing love for His Holy peace.**

14. **All said and done belief and obedience unto God will eventually purge you to share the Kingdom of God.**

15. **Remember God is always the Holy God and He is a spirit so worship Him in Spirit and in truth. So that when the light be sent into you can be Holy too, but first you must believe in His Son the Lord Jesus Christ, who was dead but now alive.**

16. **Your belief in God should take you to read the bible, but you have believed in the Churches and the Pastors, seeking their own meat instead of God.**

17. **When you begin to follow me and understand the Bible, you will begin to see that Grace is not handed down in the Churches or at the Pastors hands because he should not even be baptizing you with water but the name of Jesus Christ and His Spirit and the spirit of God. Grace is come with the complete acceptance of God's Will with all your hearts, coupled with the acceptance of the Law of Love, that helps to spread the words of light to the hearers. Here Grace and the Spirit of Salvation is come unto you all, for this is the way of the New Gospel and the New Covenant, under The Tabernacle in the Sun – MASS remember I came**

back to the Church to save some, with The Prepared way, through the Sword of the Spirit, the WORD I say unto you, believe, If you know or know not, your Bible.

18. Be not amazed and surprised for the Messenger's coming unto us ward with the Prepared Way of the Lord. It is for your edifying of your will in an endangered world that has strayed from the heavenly Father of creation. I come with the Sword of the Spirit; this too is a gift that will bring to all men the understanding of Godly principles from His precepts. The Spirit of God I cannot touch and hold as even though ever present with me, and I know it is there with me, I have no authority to sell it, hence certainly you have to attain unto it with your own will, belief in God the creator of heaven and earth and all there is with determination and to love and serve Jesus Christ.

19. In this the effectual work of the Sword of the Spirit of God, let us remember that it is god that hath made us and not we ourselves.

The Garden Path a System of Amalgamating the Churches under The Tabernacle in the sun in the High Time

20. Watch then follow the messenger of the Last Days to know when the right time comes to follow through for the understanding of the LIBERALITY.

21. God creates the decay of the Churches Old Gospel and Old Covenant. Which eventually goes into vanishing away?

22. **The Prepared way is introduced by The STIR, and The Moderation. Infusing the New Gospel and The New Covenant under The Tabernacle in the Sun the managerial structure of the final Church. It is by no means accessible by any church without faith in God and acceptance of the Prepared Way of the Messenger of God with the Sword of the Spirit which is the WORD taking you through the Reconciliation and Redemption onto Jesus Christ, by finally accepting His will with all your hearts, spread the light, and live the Law of Love.**

23. **The messenger will stand, in the right hand of God with, The Tabernacle in the Sun, having issued to the Angels the LIBERALITY and the Spiritual Church of the Manifold Wisdom of God to manifest their dominion and work over the Worthy and the Unworthy in Jesus Christ.**

24. **At this point the New Gospel begins to be administered upon earth as to a full understanding of the bible and the WORD. For salvation of all, not by the Messenger precepts but those of God alone, within The Tabernacle in the Sun in the right hand of His Son and Lord.**

BOOK ONE

AIMS AND OBJECTIVES OF THE SPIRITUAL CHURCH OF THE MANIFOLD WISDOM OF GOD

1. The Priest and they that love the Lord God who created all things from the heaven above to the earth beneath and the waters thereof, to come for the Understanding of The LIBERALITY at Xlibris and be "WE the ENTRUSTED" a BRAZEN WALL OF FIRE.

2. Understand the nature of GOD in the renewal of the Children of God, for the Kingdom of GOD, by "WE the ENTRUSTED" a BRAZEN WALL OF FIRE. to bring healing to thyself, the people of the world SPIRITUALLY, PHYSICALLY AND MENTALLY with humility in peace and in love.

3. Understand how to accept The Will of God, and develop the Grace of god and how to worship GOD in The Spirit, and in Truth forevermore.

4. Understand how to become the fruits of Jesus Christ and develop the fruits of Jesus Christ, and the Creatures of God.

OBJECTIVES OF THE SPIRITUAL CHURCH OF THE MANIFOLD WISDOM OF GOD

1. **To call the great MASSIVE to the throne of GRACE in cleanliness, Spiritually on a Rest Day and Spiritually, Physically, Mentally, on a Worship Day or night.**

2. **To worship on a Worship Day, SPIRITUALLY with the saints internationally calling all people to Honour God the Creator.**

3. **To be borderless, wall-less, race-less, in the victory of SALVATION spreading light to the hearers of the word.**

4. **To observe CHRIST JESUS as the center of faith in THE ONE GOD, OF CREATION, within the Churches, the temples of man, under The Tabernacle in the Sun, by worshiping God for Minimum seven (7) minutes on the days of teaching the New Gospel and New Covenant outside the Church building.**

5. **To give spiritual baptism to all people in the spirit of the Lord Jesus Christ The Son of God and the Spirit of the Lord thy God, as the Spirit of the Lord Jesus Christ will also do to and for those that believe.**

THE STIR AND THE MODERATION

THE STIR IS AN INTERACTION WITH THE CHURCH WHEN I SUDDENLY RETURNED TO WORSHIP WITH THEM. IT IS A TROUBLESOME PERIOD THAT CREATES MANY DIFFERENT FEELINGS OF THE STATE OF THE CHRISTIAN MAN HIS DIRECTION AND HIS LOVE FOR MANKIND HIS FELLOW MEN. THE STIR CAPTIVATES WITH NEW INFORMATION AND THE INSISTING ON A BETTER METHOD OF DEDICATION TO JESUS CHRIST IN OBEDIENCE TO THE WORD OF GOD FOLLOWING THE BIBLE. THE STIR IS BASED ON THE BIBLE ITS KNOWLEDGE AND ITS TRUTH AS MANKNIND IS SUPPOSED TO SEE GODLINESS. WHEN I STARTED THE STIR, MANY FELT THAT THEY COULD DRIVE ME OUT OF THE CHURCH NOT KNOWING THAT I WAS NOT WILL TO STAY AS I HAD MY FATHERS BUSINESS TO DO. I TOLD THEM I HAD TO REST ON THE SABBATH DAY SO NOW AFTER ABOUT A YEAR THEY ARE INQUIRING, "IF I HAVE NOT RESTED ENOUGH"? THIS IS A CHURCH THAT I WANT TO BRING TO THE TRUE REST OF GOD THEIR CREATOR IF THEY WOULD JUST HUMBLE THEMSELVES AND GET BACK ON THE RIGHT TRACK WITH GOD.

FOR I HAVE FORESEEN THEIR LACK OF UNDERSTANDING OF THE WORD REST. FOR I HAVE FORESEEN THEIR LACK OF UNDERSTANDING OF THE WORD SPOKEN FOR GOD HIMSELF SPOKE AND IT WAS WORK UNTO HIM SO HE RESTED. FOR I HAVE FORESEEN THEIR LACK OF UNDERSTANDING OF THE SABBATH IN THEIR HOUSE AND NO OTHER PLACE TO RECUPERATE THE BODY WHICH IS THE TEMPLE OF GOD. FOR I HAVE FORESEEN THEIR LACK OF UNDERSTANDING OF THE MOSIANIC LAWS WHICH WAS SET FOR THE RBELOUS ISRAELITES CHILDREN OF GOD. FOR I HAVE FORESEEN THEIR LACK OF UNDERSTANDING OF THE LAW OF LOVE AND TO KNOW THAT WITH SUCH IT SUFFICCETH ALL. NOW THIS SAME CHURCH THE SEVENTH DAY ADVENTIST CONFERED THE STIR UPON THEM AS A TEACHING NOT WITH THEIR TEACHINGS AND THEIR CUSTOMS WITH DISPARAGING REMARKS TO THE POINT OF ASKING THE ENTIRE CONGREGATION TO MARK HIM THAT PRESS TO STAND WITH THE STIR AS TO THE BEAST BY THE CHIEF ELDER GRANT, IMMEDIATLELY PRESSING INTO THEIR CONFIRMATION FROM REVELATION. WHICH WAS REBUTTED BY THE LAY PASTOR EVANS THAT THEY THE CHURCH SHOULD BE MINDFUL AS TO WHICH SIDE OF THE FENCE THEY ARE ON, AS HE CONTINUED TO ADMONISH THE MESSENGER AS IF HE KNEW THE END THEREOF OF THIS MATTER. I MYSELF ADMONISH BROTHER EVANS WITH LOVE AS HE WAS THE FIRST TO WASH

MY FEEET ON MY SUDDEN RETURN, TO THE CHURCH. HE STOOD FOR ME AS I TRIED TO STAND IN A PLACE OF ADVERSITIES WHERE I HAD TO PRAY TO THE LORD TO GIVE ME PERMISSION TO ENTER IN AND TO SPEAK, PRAY, WORSHIP WITH THE PATIENTS SAINTS AND BREAK THE ICE FOR THE RETURN OF THE PATIENT SAINTS UNTO HIM, THE GOD OF HEAVEN AND EARTH, SO THEY COULD ACCEPT HIS WILL WITH ALL THEIR HEARTS AND TO LIVE A LIFE WITH LOVING ONE ANOTHER. I HAVE NOT MARKED THEM MINE ENEMIES FOR I CAME TO SAVE SOME. I AS A FRIEND

OF THE LORD CONSIDER THEM STILL MY FRIEND STILL ON THE WAY TO THEIR SALVATION WHICH THE LIBERALITY WILL HELP THEM TO FIND.

THE MODERATION IS A WARNING, CATEGORIZED AS A METHODOLOGY IN THE PREPARED WAY OF RETURN TO GOD LIGHTENING TH ELOAD OF REPENTANCE FOR SING THE WORD OF GOD INAPPROPRIATELY FOR 2018 YEARS NOT WILING TO ACCEPT THE REST OF GOD ON ALL FRONTS OF THE SEVEN (7) CHURCHES, AND THEIR EXPONENTS. IT CREATED THE INTERSEST IN THE PUBLIC DOMAIN AND THE CHURCHES O THE FAR SIDE TO WAKE UP AND BE READY FOR THEY WERE NOT READY RECEIVING THE SWORD OF THE SPIRIT WHICH IS THE WORD. I HAD TO STAND BEFORE STRONG MEN ALTHOUGH MANY WILL SAY I COME TO THE CHURCH NAKED BUT WILLFULLY PERSEVERING AGAINST STRONG MEN RIDING SATAN.

THE MODERATION BECOMES THE 2nd PATH OF SEEKING THE RETURN OF SANCTITY TO THE CHURCH OF JESUS CHRIST. BEARING IN MIND YOU HAD THE "GARDEN PATH WITH THE ESOTERIC PRELOGUE TO FOLLOW. IT IS DIRECTLY LINKED TO THE HISTORY OF THE CHRISTIAN CHURCH, BUT MORESO TO ITS FUTURE. IT IS LINKED QUESTIONABLY TO THE VERY PATIENT SAINTS WAITING ON WHAT THEY ARE NOT ABLE TO DEFINE AND ACCEPT VERY READILY BECAUSE OF THEIR PRIESTS THAT IS FOLLOWING THE ORDINANCES OF MAN, RIDING SATAN, AND SEEKING THEIR OWN MEAT FOR OVER 2018 YEARS WITH THE RIPENEND FIELD.

THE MODERATION BRINGS IN THE DECAY OF THE OLD GOSPEL AND THE OLD COVENANT IN THE YEAR 2017 OF THE YEAR OF GOD. IT LEADS TO THE RECOGNITION OF THE HIGH TIME, WITH THE RENEWAL OF THE GOSPEL OF JESUS CHRIST THROUGH "THE SWORD OF THE SPIRIT", "THE WORD".

THIS IS THE MOST PROLIFIC WAY OF ENGAGING THE ENTIRE WORLD IN THE HIGH TIME. IT IS NOT SO MUCH A WAY OF PUTTING SHAME TO THE CHURCHES FOR THE ENMITY OF CHRIST AND ALL THE WRONGS THEY HAVE DONE IN THE NAME OF CHRISTIANITY AND SACRED WORSHIP TO A GOD WHILE THE CLERGY SEEKED THEIR OWN MEAT. THE MODERATION EXCITES THE WORLD ABOUT THE NEW GOSPEL AND THE NEW COVENANT OF GOD WHICH REMOVES THE WATERED-DOWN CHRISTIANITY THAT IS SCATTERED ACROSS THE GLOBE INTO STIRRING RECOGNITION THAT THERE IS A CREATOR THAT THIS CHRISTIANITY IS SERVING AND

IT MUST BE DONE IN HOLINESS UNTO GOD WITH THE FULL GOSPEL AND FULL BIBLE IN TRUTH. THIS RECOGNITION COMES ABOUT IN THE HIGH TIME WITH THE LIBERALITY AND AN UNDERSTANDING OF THE LIBERALITY BY THE PRIESTS FOR IT TO BE ENTRUSTED TO THEM FOR THEIR WARDS AND THE GREAT MULTITUDE OF PEOPLE WHO LOVE GOD, TO HAVE IT TO USE.

THE MODERATION PLACES THE LIBERALITY WITH ROOM TO MAKE ALL MEN MEASURE THEMSEVES, THEIR OWN FAITHFULNESS AND CREATE ROOM FOR ADJUSTMENT FROM RIDING SATAN UNDER THE ENMITY OF CHRIST AND THE

UNWORTHINESS TO GOD AS THE HOLY FOLKS OF GOD, WHO MUST RETURN TO GOD THE CREATOR. FOR THROUGH THE TABERNACLE IN THE SUN'S LIBERALITY, ALL WILL BE FREE FROM THE ENMITY OF CHRIST UNTO SALVATION. CIRCUMVENTING THE LIBERALITY, THE CHURCH STILL LIVE WITH THE BURDEN OF THE ENMITY OF CHRIST, NOT UNDER THE WILL OF GOD AND GRACE WITH THE LAW OF LOVE. OF WHICH WILL THEN MAKE THE CHURCH A SHAME UNTO GOD THE CREATOR OF THE WORD, THE WORLD AND ALL THAT THEREIN IS.

WITH THE AIMS OBJESTIVES THE CHURCH WILL NOW UNDERSTAND THE LIBERALITY AND THE ACCEPTANCE OF GRACE, THANKING GOD FOR THE STIR AND THE MODERATION THAT CAME UNTO THEM SO THAT THEY COULD MAKE GOOD THEMSELVES UNTO GOD.

THE EFFECTS OF THE MODERATION AND THE LIBERALITY WILL NOW BE MANIFESTED INTO THE THOSE THAT WILL OVERCOME AND THE GREAT MULTITUDE THAT WILL STAND AFTER THE EXAMPLE OF THE MESSENGER, THE MINISTER, THE REFRESHERS IN THE HIGH TIME WITH THE LIBERALITY AND "WE the ENTRUSTED" THE BURNING WALL OF FLAME BEFORE GOD AND ALL MANKIND.

THE LIBERALITY BRINGS LOVE TO THE WORLD AND IN SUCH IT EXTENDS PEACE TO ALL MEN AND BY GOD THE WRATH OF HIS HANDS UNTO ALL MEN WILL BE LIFTED. LOVE BRINGS HARMONY AND WITH SUCH THE GARDENS MUCH MORE BEAUTIFUL THAN EDEN WILL BE CREATED FOR THE RETURN OF JESUS CHRIST FINALLY.

THE MODERATION ENLIGHTENS ALL AS TO THE PREPARED WAY TO SEEK GOD, BUT TO BE CAREFUL OF THE MAN OF PERDITION THAT MAY BE REVEAL IN THE LAST DAYS OF THE HIGH TIME AS HE THAT IS ABOVE ALL THAT IS CALLED GOD AND WORSHIPED AS GOD, WORKING THE MISTERY OF INIQUITY DOTH ALREADY WORK, AND ONLY HE THAT LETTETH WITH LET UNTIL HE BE TAKEN OUT OF THE WAY. THEN SHALL THE EVIL, AND WICKED ON BE REVEALED WHOM THE LORD SHALL CONSUME WITH THE SPIRIT OF HIS MOUTH, AND THE BRIGHTNESS OF HIS COMING.

The Emerging Me

At the finish line the emerging Me for many to see the new light, the new beginning, new ending and new things, with an account of the New Gospel so hard to receive under the New Covenant of God as the Patient saints wait for it.

Now the natural man will even see himself as god in all things. The Spiritual Man see Himself as the instrument of God. I am a strong man running a race unto faith in god and my favorite number is six (6) I run this race and as it climaxes, I stand as the Greatest Prophet of god greater than John the Baptist and greater than John the Revelator.

For Jesus Christ said unto them you shall not see a greater one than he John the Baptist but the Messenger in the High Time., now with the sword of the Spirit and the word, so to speak of understanding of His will, at last, so unto the four corners of the earth I come. Now unto all seeing the things that clarify unto all the scriptures of the Old gospel which you just could not understand and comply with as DADDY SEVEN (7). Now waiting on the return of the Lord Jesus Christ as the eighth (8) elevations. Then the spirit of God returns to the earth as on the great day of creation to walk and talk with man in the flesh as the ninth (9) elevation. For if the Priests cannot come for the understanding when I stand then I say unto you come out of Her for She upholds Babylon and is still riding Satan, therefore know now how you will know the unworthy in Jesus Christ.

1. "The Garden Path" have started the race with Francis Charles Malcolm as Running Man and have finished it.

2. Now Francis Charles Malcolm choose to stand. By publishing through the Holy Ghost from the highest place ever through the Tabernacle in the Sun MASS through the Sermon "Ministry of reconciliation" and The Spiritual Church of The Manifold Wisdom of God in Sermons one (1) through to seven (7).

3. I stand with rebuttals in Sermons that shows who is right from who is wrong, such as Popping the Words, and last of all "He that Letteth". This allows the Church to see their own ways that are not of God or of the Holy Spirit of God, hence seeing themselves as com-promisingly aligned to the Beast, thereby sharing as deceivers the words of God. It is now time for the Church to wake up and live the Law of Love making

the Patient Saints be filled with the light of Jesus Christ and the Spirit of God.

He being natural will blur the way of the patient Saints. For this is the way in Babylon, to make the people not see as they feed on the on the Lord as deceivers in Jesus Christ.

The Spiritual Man stands to show the way, and the light of Jesus Christ. Who shows a door never seen or understood? Here to welcome the First fruits of Christ and to them give the knowledge of GOD for them to create the First Creatures of GOD.

The Tabernacle in the Sun MASS

Hear what the spirit saith to the Churches by means of the Ministries under the Tabernacle in the Sun MASS, through "The Ministry of Reconciliation". Over you and upon you all on the earth I have set the Tabernacle in the Sun and in it the seven Angels with control and dominion over the seven Candle Sticks. This shall have the powers to dim your candles until that great day of the Lord.

The Messenger saith to all the Churches for all the people to hear that which concerneth the Churches all in one for all have sinned and come short of the Glory of God. Now what is held against one Church by God is also held against all Churches of God because they all serve one God but do not the will of God.

Many will contend that they do the will of God and that is not so but, in all things, they try to show it to be so. So, The Comforter ask where is your faith in the God you all serve? Your faith should begin at the cross of Jesus Christ knowing that his sacrifice for us all meant that He covers us for all our sins and through repentance in his name, blood and Spirit and the acceptance of the PERFECT in the Latter

Rain of Last Days we will receive the Body of Christ and be transformed from the Natural Man to the Spiritual Man. For the Comforter now redeemed and have overcome the will of all the Seven (7) Churches to be set forth as a Minister over the Tabernacle in the Sun MASS which is higher than all hills by the fulfillment of the works of God in The Garden Path.

"The Garden Path" a new way forward?

The Garden Path was set forth afore in a few esoteric words leading into the Tabernacle of the Sun and the Spiritual Church of the Manifold Wisdom of God. Take it or Leave it (tek it or Leave it) (Ten It) The New Jersey piece, up north, that led to a sense of where we are going when it is all done. Now knowing the after the crushing of the 2nd. Beast they will build gardens more beautiful than The Garden of Eden. This leads mankind to know that the return of Jesus Christ is nearer than we think and so we all should be watching and praying unceasingly, living with the light and making peace through the Law of Love.

Murmur not neither find yourself to let at the Messenger greater than John the Baptist, and john the Revelator with the light of God, through Jesus Christ who came in the flesh unto us. Captain Francis Charles Malcolm tgpMASS, of the Jamaica Combined Cadet Force.

This Man Francis Charles Malcolm is not a spectacle but a Man to be ADMONISHED with all those helpers that helped The Garden Path through the Gift of help and Peaceful Governments, The Messenger and Xlibris.com, to deliver to the four corners of the earth through the Holy Ghost, The Sword of the Spirit, The WORD of understanding. I come as a battered Soul, not as a King, nor one dressed as Princes, even naked unto you for all that you have done unto me as your Messenger. tgpMASS

I come forth with **The LIBERALITY** and the Spiritual Church of The Manifold Wisdom of God under The Tabernacle in the Sun - MASS. Which complete The Prepared Way making The Garden Path Complete? In My true love for the lord jesus Christ above all things, to bring "The LIBERALITY" with the Mettled Letter to the world.

TO RECEIVE ME ASK YOURSELF THE QUESTION AND TELL YOUR SELF THE ANSWER BY MY EXAMPLE UNTO USWARD. WHAT ABOUT JESUS, IS HE ON YOUR MIND? WHEN HE CAME THROUGH THE WALLS AT THE FRONT OF MY HOUSE,

HIS BRIGHT SHINNING GLORY WAS MORE THAN ENOUGH TO BELIEVE IN THE STORIES THAT I HAVE BEEN TOLD. THE SPLENDOUR OF HIS GLORY NEVER WORRANT MUCH MORE IT WAS JESUS HIMSELF HANDING ME THAT SHINING SWORD. I TOOK THE SWORD OF THE SPIRIT AND RAN WITH IT TILL THE HIGH TIME TO DELIVER TO T HE PATIENT SAINTS THE SWORD OF THE SPIRIT AS THE PREPARED WAY OF THE LORD. YES, FOR THE REDEMPTION OF

MAN, THE HEALING OF THE BEAST AND THE THEIR RECONCILIATION, BEFORE THEY END UP SAYING THEY BE GOD OF ALL GOD'S. UPON EARTH. I BELIEVED UPON THE SON OF GOD, I TOOK THE SWORD OF THE SPIRIT WITH ALL MY HEART

AS I ACCEPTED TO DO THE WORK OF JESUS CHRIST AS GIVEN, WIT MY READY PEN. NOW MY BELIEF HATH GIVEN ME SALVATION BY THE SPIRIT TO BECOME AN HIER OF HIS FATHER'S THRONE, AND THE GREATEST EXAMPLE OF A FRUIT OF HIS VINE. FOR THIS PORTION IN MY WORK IS NOT THE PORTION OF ANY OTHER MAN OR EVEN AN ERRING WOMAN BUT THE PORTION OF THE SWORD OF THE SPIRIT, THE WORD, OF THE PREPARED WAY OF THE LORD JESUS CHRIST AND OF GOD ALONE FOR SALVATION AND THE CREATION OF THE GARDEN PATH UNTO THE FOUR CORNERS OF THE EARTH, AND THE TABERNACLE IN THE SUN.

IF HE GIVES A SWORD FOR THE END OF TIME, THEN WHO IS YOUR LORD? IS HE UNABLE TO FIND? GOD WITH HIS OUTSTRETCHED RIGHT HANDS AND THE WONDER OF HIS DESIGN, TO CARRY HIS SEVEN ANGELS AND HIS SEVEN CANDLE STICKS IN THE END OF TIME, TO RETURN TO HIM, ONLY, IN HIS PREPARED WAY, BY HIS MERCY AND HIS POWER THIS TIME. HIS HUMBLE SERVANT WHO LABOURED FOR FREEDOM, MANDELA 1, 2 & 3 CREW THE FILTER OF THE TIME LINE, TO MENIFEST THE HANGE HE HAD ON HIS MIND. HIS HUMBLE SERVANT WHO LABOURED FOR RESTITUTION, OF A PEOPLE WE CALL OUR OWN, 10 TO 10 DAYLIGHT DID SEE THE FREEDOM OF A MAN UNDER APARTHIED DECLINE.

BE YEE THEREFORE TRYING TO BE PERFECT AS YOUR FATHER IN HEAVEN, FOR THE TIME HAS COME TO AS THE WATERS ARE MOUNTING UP GUIDE YOU AGAINST YOUR FALLING AWAY. FOR OUT THERE YOU'LL SEE THE PUBLICANS TOO, SO JUST REMEMBER JESUS CAME NOT FOR THE SHEEP ONLY, BUT FOR THEM TOO. AND THAT IS WHY IN HIS RIGHT HAND, HE HAS ACCEPTED THE TABERNACLE IN THE SUN TO ENTREAT WITH THE CANDLE STICKS THE LAST THING HE HAD ON HIS MIND, AS SALVATION OF THE SAINTS AS THEY MINGLE WITH THE TARES, ALL HAVING FAULTS RIGHT THERE IN THE HIGH TIME. NOW THE REAL HARVEST IS ON AND THE LABOURERS ARE FEW BUT THE WORK MUST GO ON. RESERVE NOT THE KNOWLEDGE OF YOUR INIQUITY FOR THAT WHICH YOU WORKETH AND KNOW LETTETH AND SO YOU WILL CONTINUE TOO LET. BE MERCIFUL AND SPREAD THE LIGHT INSTEAD, TURN OYOUR EYES UPON JESUS LOOK UP IN HIS WONDERFUL FACE, THERE TO SEE THE LIGHT AND ALL OF HIS GRACE, WITH ALL YOUR HEARTS UPON HIM, ACCEPT GODS WILL WITH ALL YOUR HEARTS AND NOT CONFUSE THE ENMITY OF CHRIST WITH YOUR REDEMPTION. SAYING THAT YOU KILLED A MAN THEREFORE CHRIST IS STILL A MAN. FOR IF YOU STILL KNOW HIM NOT, HE COME TO YOU WITH FIRE TRY TO RISE ABOVE HIM HE DESTROYS YOU WITH THE SPIRIT OF HIS MOUTH. HE'S GONNA GET YOU ONE OF THESE DAYS. I AM HERE WITH THE WARNING, AND MORESO A NEW GOSPEL UNDER A NEW COVENANT WHICH YOU STILL FIND YOURSELF NOT READY FOR AFTER 2018 YEARS, WHICH WILL BE ABLE TO GET YOU TO SALVATION BEFORE IT IS TOO LATE, NOT AS A MESSENGER TO TOGGLE WITH YOU, IN HEATED MUFFLED UP CONVERSATIONS IN REPROOFING THE BIBLE, WHICH IS BEFORE YOU AND EVERY MAN.

The LIBERALITY

This is an instrument unto the Seven Angels of the Church in the High Time, Commanding the Angels to take command over the Churches for their Salvation or Damnation into Perdition with the dimming of their Candle Sticks according to their perfection in the High time. Spiritual Church of The Manifold Wisdom of God under The Tabernacle in the Sun – MASS.

The LIBERALITY brings about the decay of the Old Gospel and the Old Covenant slated to vanish away and usher in the New Gospel and the New Covenant under the threshold of The Tabernacle in the Sun. The Messenger as a complete figure is a Minister of God, with the Sword of the Spirit. Having the WORD, I have furnished the entire world, as creating a STIR within the Church which was then compounded by a MODERATION on Facebook, with it as a prelude of what is to come. Hence refreshing My

Master's Soul, and becoming The Refresher. At a time when the understanding of Christ visit will be made clear for before then there was not a Socrates or a Malcolm, but John the Baptist whom had to do His will.

THE MINISTRY OF RECONCILIATION

- THE PREPARED WAY OF THE MESSENGER OF GOD

- o THE GARDEN PATH
- o RECONCILIATORY EFFERTS
  - THE GADREN PATH – MASS: AN ESOTERIC POETRY BOOK

  - THE STIR

  - THE MODERATION

  - THE GARDEN PATH VOLUME 2:

    THE LIBERALITY

    - Under THE TABERNACLE in the SUN

  - THE GARDEN PATH VOLUME 3:

    THE SPIRITUAL CHURCH OF THE MANIFOLD WISDOM OF GOD:

    - Under "THE TABERNACLE in the SUN"

    - WITH THE PREPARED CONCEPTS OF THE SPIRITUAL THEOLOGY NEEDED TO RETURN TO GOD.

HELP THE CHURCH TO BECOME;

1. THE SPIRITUAL CHURCH OF THE MANIFOLD WISDOM OF GOD, UNDER THE TABERNACLE IN THE SUN, THE CHURCH FORMATED FOR THE RECONCILIATION OF MANKIND TO GOD BY THE PREPARED WAY OF THE GARDEN PATH, THAT WILL START THE HOLINESS OF THE HOUSE OF GOD FOR HUMANITY TO CONTINUE TO BUILD GARDENS MUCH MORE BEAUTIFUL THAN THAT OF EDEN.

2. THE CHURCH THAT SEEKS THE KINGDOM OF GOD.

3. THE CHURCH THAT RISES FROM THE DECAY OF THE OLD GOSPEL AND THE OLD COVENANT.

4. THE CHURCH THAT HAVE THE FULL GOSPEL OF GOD.

5. THE CHURCH THAT REFRESHES THE LORD JESUS CHRIST AS THE MISTRY OF THE SON OF GOD, FROM THE EXAMPLE OF THE MESSENGER AND MINISTER OF GOD.

6. THE CHURCH UNDER THE TABERNACLE IN THE SUN – MASS IN THE HIGH TIME.

7. THE CHURCH OF THE SPIRIT OF GOD AND MAN WHICH IS THE TEMPLE OF GOD.

8. THE CHURCH, THAT KNOWS NO LIMITS UNDER "WE the ENTRUSTED" THE BURNING WALL OF FLAME.

9. THE CHURCH UNBOUND FROM THE SCATTERED AND OLD GOSPEL IN PARTS.

10. THE CHURCH IN UNITY IN ORDINANCE OF GOD UNDER THE TABERNACLE IN THE SUN.

11. THE CHURCH THAT ACCEPTS GRACE WITH ALL THEIR HEARTS.

12. THE CHURCH THAT LIVES THE LAW OF LOVE.

13. THE CHURCH, THAT REPRESENTS AND TEACH THE LIGHT OF GOD AND SPREAD THE LIGHT.

14. THE CHURCH, OUT OF CAPTIVITY WITH THE NEW GOSPEL AND THE NEW COVENANT OF GOD.

15. THE CHURCH WORTHY IN THE HIGH TIME.

16. THE CHURCH THAT REAPS THE SEVEN SPIRITS OF GOD.

17. THE CHURCH THAT REPENTETH OF EVIL DEEDS AND FLEES ALL FORM OF EVIL.

18. THE CHURCH THAT REPRESENTS THE LAW OF LOVE.

19. THE CHURCH OF THE MANIFOLD WISDOM OF GOD TO GENERATE THE HOLY KISS WITH THE MANIFOLD HAND, WITH AND THROUGH THE SWORD OF THE SPIRIT.

20. THE CHURCH STOP WATCHING THE SINFUL WORLD AND SPREADING OF DARKNESS UPON EACH OTHER BUT BE SEEKING AND WATCHING OUT FOR CHRIST.

21. THE CHURCH THAT FULLY USES THE BIBLE AND NOT THE WAYS OF MAN AS ITS GUIDE FOR ALL INTERPRETATIONS UNDER THE PREPARED WAY OF THE LORD JESUS CHRIST.

22. THE CHURCH THAT PLACES THE POWER OF GOD TO BE IN CHARGE OF HUMANITY AND NOT MAN.

23. THE CHURCH THAT BRINGS HUMILITY FROM WITHIN THE TEMPLE OF GOD TO THE ENTIRE HUMAN RACE.

24. THE CHURCH THAT REPRESENTS NO GUILE, NO JEZEBEL SPIRITS, NO DARKNESS, NO EVIL, AND NO ENVIOUS WORKS.

25. THE PRIESTS, THE LAITY, BUT WITH AN EVERLASTING LOVE THE WITNESSES AND THE GREAT MULTITUDE WITH THE VOICES OF THE CITY, THE TEMPLE AND OF JAH THE MIGHTY GOD, WILL ADMONISH THE MESSGENGER GIVING THANKS ALWAYS FOR EVERY

26. LITTLE INSIGHT INTO HIS WORD, THE SWORD OF GOD, BY THE SPIRIT OF THE SWORD OF GOD AS MUCH AS THE MESSENGER GIVE THANKS UNTO THGOD AND THEM THAT PRESERVE THE WAY.

27. THE LIBERALITY MAKES A BID FOR A SIMPLE RETURN TO GOD IN RETURNING SO SHALL THEY BE SAVED. IT DOES NOT LIMITS THEIR CONDITIONAL EFFORTS IN AN WAY WITHOUT EVEN RELAXING THEIR ABILITY TO RECEIVE THE NEW GOSPEL AND THE NEW COVENANT IN THE HIGH TIME, ITS JUST FREE WILL BASED ON TRUST, FAITH AND BELIEF IN GOD, WITH ALL THEIR HEARTS, IN ALL THE THINGS THE SAME HOLY PEOPLE WERE AT WHILE THEY THOUGHT THEY WERE FULLY THE CHILDREN OF GOD WHO WERE PATIENT SAINTS WAITING FOR NOTHING BUT TO SEE GOD IN THEIR SELF RIGHTEOUS MANNER WITHIN THEIR OWN ORDINANCES, UNTIL THE KNOWLEDGE OF THE RECONCILIATION, THE PREPARED WAY AND THE REBUTTALS UNTO THE PUFFED UP SAINTS TO SETTLE THEIR DISBELIEF AND UNREADINESS UNDER THE TABERNACLE IN THE SUN. THE DEVEOPMENT OF THE SPIRITUAL CHURCH UNDER THE TABERNACLE IN THE SUN WITH THE USE OF THE LIBERALITY BRINGS ABOUT THE TEACHING OF THE NEW GOSPEL THROUGH THE NEW COVENANT AS TO THE INFORMED WORLD OF THE DECAY OF THE OLD GOSPEL AND OLD COVENANT. IT CONTAINS THE SERMONS OF THE PREPARED WAY AS IT INTERACTs WITH THE PEOPLE OF THE WORLD FROM THE GARDEN PATH, THE STIR AND THE MODERATIONS.

28. HONOUR THE HOLY KISS AS A SYMBOL OF LOVE, AS THE LIBERALITY MAKES A BID FOR A SIMPLE RETURN TO GOD.

28:1 THE SPIRITUAL CHURCH OF THE MANIFOLD WISDOM OF GOD, EMMITS FROM;

I. THE DIACRITIC DIALOGUE OF "TEK IT OR LEAVE IT, TEN IT" FOR THE INITIATING OF FREE SALVATION FOR SOME TO MAKING HOLINESS TO BECOME THE HOUSE OF GOD THROUGH ACCEPTANCE OF REPENTANCE UNTO SALVATION FREELY BY GOD WHO CREATED THE HEAVEN AND THE EARTH.

II. THEN THE GREAT MULTITUDE AND WITNESSES, AND THE FEW LABOURERS OF JESUS CHRIST THE SON OF GOD AT WORKS OVER THE LONG TEDIOUS PERIOD OF THE COMING OF THE PREPARED WAY OF THE LORD JESUS CHRIST.

III. ALONG WITH THE REALITY OF THE STIR, AND THE MODERATION TO THE FOUR (4) CORNERS OF THE EARTH.

IV. THEN THE LIBERALITY TO THE PRIESTS WHO COME FOR THE UNDERSTANDING OF THE WORD RATHER THAN DIPPING INTO PERDITION MANIFESTING A NEW GOSPEL BEYOND THE CLIMAX OF THE HIGH TIME AS THE HOLY LEADERS IN CHARGE OF THEIR UNION OF CHURCHES, INTO THE TEMPLE OF GOD.

V. THEN THE WARDS OF THE PRIESTS, TEACHING OF THE PATIENT SAINTS OF GOD THE ORDINANCES OF GOD ABOVE THE SEEKING OF THEIR MEAT AND THE LOVE OF RIDING SATAN, TO KNOW HOW TO ACCEPT THE WILL OF GOD WITH ALL THEIR HEARTS AND LIVE THE LAW OF LOVE.

VI. THIS IS NOT THE ACT DISPITE UNTO GRACE BY SOME OF THE PUFFED UP PRIEST AND CHURCHES FORGING AHEAD WITH THE LIBERALITY FROM THE MODERATION ONLY, BUT IN FAITH TO THE WHOLE WORKS OF GOD FROM THE PRIEST COMING FOR THE UNDERSTANDING AND ENHANCING THE INHERITANCE OF THE LORD JESUS CHRIST THROUGH THE LAW OF LOVE FOR THE CONTINUITY OF WORTHINESS TO GOD AND NOT MAN.

28:2

TABERNACLE IN THE SUN – MASS

BAPTISM RITES UNDER THE LIBERALITY

TO BE REPEATED SEVEN [7] TIMES

THE HOLY SPIRITUAL BAPTISM

I BELIEVE IN THE NAME AND BLOOD OF JESUS CHRIST, YAHSHUA THE SON OF GOD IN THE HIGH TIME. I WILL DO THE WILL OF GOD UNDER THE TABERNACLE IN THE SUN – MASS

I BELIEVE IN THE LIBERALITY WITH THE REDEEMING WAY, I HUMBLE REPENT AND RECONCILE MY SINS OF NOT RESTING ON THE SEVENTH DAY AND DOING THY WILL, FOR YOU O GOD WHO CREATED THE HEAVEN AND EARTH.

I COME TO YOU LORD GOD WHO CREATED THE HEAVEN AND EARTH IN THE SPIRIT OF YOUR SON FOR PEACE, AND NOT FOR A CURSE.

I ACCEPT WITH ALL MINE HEART HIS CLEANSING BY YOUR HOLY SON'S BLOOD, HIS GRACE IN MY HEART, HIS LOVE AND HIS LIGHT IN THIS FULL GOSPEL, THE NEW GOSPEL, AND NEW COVENANT OF YAHSHUA FOR THE NEW HOPE OF THE SALVATIONS GIVEN UNTO ME, AND I NOW MAKE MY SOUL STABLISH IN THEE IN THE NEW GOSPEL

MIGHTY GOD WHO CREATED THE HEAVEN AND THE EARTH BAPTIZE ME NOW IN YOUR HOLY SPIRIT IN THE NAME AND BLOOD OF JESUS CHRIST YAWSHUA YOUR SON IN HOLINESS AND THE TRUTH THAT HE LIVES FOR HIS GREAT MESSENGER HATH PREPARED THE WAY.

AS YOU COVER ME WITH YOUR HOLY KINGDOM IN THE NAME, AND BLOOD OF JESUS CHRIST YAWSHUA YOUR SON AND YOUR SEVEN HOLY SPIRITS, I AS OF THE SEVENTH DAY EACH WEEK WILL REST AND WORSHIP YOU IN THE SPIRIT AND IN LOVE UNDER THE NEW

COVENANT OF GOD AS YOUR GREAT MESSENGER HATH REFRESEHED YOUR SOUL, LORD LET THE TABERNACLE IN THE SUN BE MY REPUTATION. AS OF

THIS DAY TO PASS ON LIGHT AND LOVE ONE ANOTHER WITH ALL MINE HEART.

THE REPUTATION OF BELIEF AND LOVE FOR THE WORD MAY ALSO SANCTIFY ONE IN THE SPIRIT AS TO THE SAME A THAT OF THE MESSENGER AND MINISTER OF GOD WHOM REFRESHETH THE SOULD OF THE MASTER. AS OF THIS DAY TO PASS ON LIGHT AND LOVE ONE ANOTHER WITH ALL MINE HEART EVEN WITH AN HOLY KISS UNTO THE FOUR (4) CORNERS OF THE EARTH. IT MUST BE SEEN THAT FROM THE HIGH TIME GOD IS SERIOUS ABOUT THE BEHAVIOURS OF THE SAINTS OF GOD AND THE PERDITIONERS RIDING SATAN. HRE THE TABERNACLE IN THE SUN WILL BE ELEVATED TO MAKE GOOD THE PROTECTIVE HOUSE OF GOD IN SPIRITUAL HOLINESS FOREVER.

FIGURE 2: THE MESSENGER CAPT FRANCIS CHARLES MALCOLM

"TABERNACLE IN THE SUN – MASS™®©2018", BEING IN THE RIGHT HAND OF JESUS CHRIST WHO WAS DEAD BUT NOW ALIVE, FOR ALL TO KNOW NOW THAT IT IS OF GOD AND NOT ABOVE GOD ALMIGHTY.

THE TABERNACLE IN THE SUN OF THE HIGH TIMES THAT WILL HOLD THE LIBERALITY, FROM WHICH THE METTTLED LETTER, THE PREPARED WAY AND THE REDEEMING WAY FOR RECONCILIATION TO GOD, WILL BE DELIVERED TO THE WORLD AFTER THE MODERATION TO THE FOUR CORNERS OF THE EARTH, BY THE MASSENGER.

THE MESSENGER OF THE PREPARED WAY UNDER THE TABERNACLE IN THE SUN – MASS

THE GREAT ONE THE EXPECTED MESSENGER, GREATER THAN JOHN THE BAPTIST. WHOM JAH HATH NEVER SEEN A PROPHET GREATER THAN JOHN THE BAPTIST BUT HE. WHO IS ALSO THE ONE GREATER THAN JOHN THE REVELATOR?

THE ONE GREATER THAN JOHN THE BAPTIST WHOM COMETH AFTER THE LORD AND BAPTIZE WITH THE NAME OF THE LORD AND THE HOLY GHOST OR THE SPIRIT OF THE LORD, FOR HE BAPTIST NOT WITH WATER BUT THE HOLY SPIRIT OF GOD THE CREATOR IN THE HIGH TIMES.

THE MESSENGER DOES THE STIR AND THE MODERATIONS ON FACEBOOK AND COMES OUT VICTORIOUS STANDING WITH A PURPOSE ONCE FIXED ON A RADIANT INCLINE WITH THE TABERNACLE IN THE SUN AS HE REFRESHES THE MASTERS SOUL AROUND THE FOUR (4) CORNERS OF THE EARTH.

28:3 THE DEDICATION AND COMMITMENT TO THE PREPARED WAY, IS HUMANLY POSSIBLE IF THE CHURCHES SEEK ONE GOD, RECEIVE THE MESSENGER WITH ALL THEIR HEARTS, START BEING HONEST TO THE PATIENT SAINTS ABOUT THE GOSPEL AND THE SEEKING OF THEIR

OWN MEAT, REPENT OF THEIR SINS AND STOP BEING PUFFY AND

MUFFLED UP AT EVERY CORRECT REVIEW OF THE BIBLE THAT IS NOT IN LINE WITH WHAT THEY TEACH AS THEIR LAWS FROM THE SCRIPTURES. USE THE ENTIRE BIBLE AS A GUIDE AND NOT THE GOSPEL IN PARTS. THEY MUST DO THE WILL OF GOD OR ENTER INTO PERDITION WITH SATAN, WHICH IS ONE OF THEIR PRECIOUS TEACHINGS, DEDICATION TO THE PREPARED WAY AND COMMITMENT TO THE WAY IS WITH THE ENTIRE HEART OF ALL MANKIND, TO BE GUIDED BY THE PRIEST THAT HAVE RECEIVED THE UNDERSTANDING OF THE PREPARED WAY OF THE MESSENGER AND THE WORD.

UNTO USWARD A MATTER TO RECEIVE WITH THE ENTIRE HEART FOR THE PATIENT SAINTS TO SETTLE WITH THE LORD THEIR OWN FAULTS WITH HIM AND BRING A HEART WITH LOVE TO ACCEPT HIS MERCIES.

FROM THE FIRST BOOK MARK THE PERFECT WAY THAT OF THE BIBLE IN HONOUR TO EACH MAN'S REST ON THE SABBATH DAY, THE WHOLE BOOK MARKS THE PREFECT WAY WITH THE PERFECT MAN OF GOD AND WITH GOD IT CARRIES SIXTY SIX BOOKS AND THE STRONG MAN TO RUN A RACE TO THE KINGDOM OF GOD WILL FINISH WITH GOD AND WITHOUT

SATAN. WITH GOD NOW MEANS THAT YOU HAVE NOW UNDERSTAND HOW TO BE WITH GOD AND WHY THE NEED TO RETURN TO HIM TO BE SAVED BY YOUR SAVIOUR THE LORD JESUS CHRIST. BUT IF MAN WILL NEVER UNDERSTAND HE WILL CONTINUE TO BE WITH HIS PUFFED-UP SELF, IN THE ORDINANCES OF MAN, BEING ANNOINTED WITH EVIL FROM SATAN TO RIDE ON HIM AS A POWER PLAGUE TO HUMANITY AND TRYING TO CONTINUE TO BE HOLY UNDER GOD. NOW A STRONG MAN WITHOUT SATAN IN HIS COMMITMENT TO GOD AND BEING WITH GOD IS A PERFECT MAN. BUT A STRONG MAN WITH SATAN AND IN TANDEM WITH GOD IS A PERFECT BEAST.

THE SPIRITUAL CHURCH WITHIN MAN IS HIS TEMPLE DEDICATED UNTO JESUS CHRIST TO HONOUR THE WILL OF GOD AND NOT THE WILL OF GOD AND SATAN WITHIN THE ORDINANCES OF MAN. LETS US HOPE THAT IN DOING THIS THE SWORD OF THE WICKED DOES NOT OVERSHADOW THE RIGHTEOUS LEST THEY STEP INTO INIQUITY. BUT PERCEIVE PAULS WORDS AS A MANTLE UNTO CHRISTIANITY'S MILE STONE INTO REVELATION.

IN THE SPIRITUAL CHURCH OF THE MANIFOLD WISDOM OF GOD I FURTHER MAKE MY SELF COMMITED TO HIS WILL AND WORTHINESS THROUGH MY BELIEF AND COMMITMENT IN THE WORD. I NOW ASK MY BRETHEN TO RECEIVE THE LIBERALITY, BELIEVE, AND BE COMMITTED NOW IN THESE WORDS. THE CHURCH DOES NOT EXCEED MY LIMITATIONS AS SEEMS TO BE BEWITCHED FOR NOT RECEIVING THE TRUTH, FOR YEE TOO BEGAN THE WORK OF THE LORD BY THE SPIRIT BUT NOW MADE PERFECT IN THE LAW BY THE FLESH. YEE ARE PUFFED UP AT THE MESSENGER BUT HE COMETH IN FAITH THROUGH THE SPIRIT OF THE LORD THY GOD, WHO BELIEVED IN THE WORD AND GAINED SALVATION THROUGH THE SPIRIT WHICH YOU LACK AND WILL ALWAYSS LACK FOR REJECTING CHRIST AS THE MESENGER CONTINUE AS A MEDIATOR NOT MEDIATOR OF ONE, BUT GOD IS ONE. FOR WITH FAITH WE ARE NO LONGER SHUT UP UNDER THE LAWBUT HEIRS OF THE LORD JESUS CHRIST IF WE ABHOR THE THINGS HE HATES AND DO HIS WILL. THEREFORE, FOLOW THE MESSENGER THAT IS PREDESTINED TO CARRY THE WORD WITH HIS FEET SHOD WITH THE NEW GOSPEL AND THE NEW COVENANT OF JESUS CHRIST TO ENDEAVOUR ALL TO KEEP THE UNITY OF THE SPIRIT IN ONE BOND WITH CHRIST.

28:4

EXPLANATION OF THE MODIFICATIONS

Paul and Sylvanus and Timotheous, unto the church of the Thessalonians in God our Father and the Lord Jesus Christ. Grace unto you, and peace, from God our Father and the Lord Jesus Christ. We are bound to thank God always for you, brethren, as it is meet, because that your faith growth exceedingly, and the charity of every one of you all towards each other aboundeth:

HE COMFORTS THEM

So that we ourselves glory in you in the in the churches of God for your patience and you're your faith in all your persecutions and tribulations that ye endure: which is a manifest token of the righteous judgment of God, that we may be counted worthy of the kingdom of God; for which you all suffer: seeing it is also a righteous thing to God to recompense tribulation to them that trouble you; and to you who are troubled rest with us, when the Lord Jesus shall be revealed from the heaven with his mighty angels. In flaming fire taking vengeance on them that know not God, and that obey not the gospel of the Lord Jesus Christ. Who shall be punished with everlasting destruction from the presence of the Lord, and from the glory of his power; when he shall come to be glorified in his saints, and to be admired in all of them that believe (because our testimony among you was believed) in that day? Wherefore also we pray always for you, that our Lord that our Lord God would count you worthy of his calling and fulfill all his good pleasures of his goodness, and the work of faith with power; that the name of our Lord Jesus Christ may be glorified in you and ye, in him, according to the grace of our God and the Lord Jesus Christ.

EXHORTATION OF STEADFASTNESS

Now we beseech you, brethren, by the coming of our Lord Jesus Christ, and by our gathering together unto him. That ye be

NOT SOON BE SHAKEN IN MIND, OR BE TROUBLED, NEITHER BY SPIRIT OR BY WORD, NOR BY LETTER AS FROM US, AS THAT THE DAY OF CHRIST IS AT HAND. LET NO MAN DECEIVE YOU BY ANY MEANS; FOR THAT DAY SHALL COME, EXCEPT THERE BE A FALLING OUT AWAY FIRST AND THAT THE MAN OF SIN BE REVEALED, THE SON OF PERDITION. WHO OPPOSED AND EXHALTETH HIMSELF ABOVE ALL THAT IS CALLED GOD. OR THAT IS WORSHIPPED; SO THAT, HE AS GOD SITTETH IN THE TEMPLE OF GOD, SHOWING HIMSELF THAT HE IS GOD. REMEMBER YE NOT, THAT THAT WHEN I WAS YET WITH YOU, I TOLD YOU THESE THINGS? AND NOW YE KNOW WHAT WITHHOLDETH THAT HE MIGHT BE REVEALED IN HIS TIME.

WARNING AGAINST THE WICKED ONE

FOR THE MISTERY OF INIQUITY DOTH ALREADY WORK; AND ONLY HE WHO NOW LETTETH WILL LETUNTIL HE BE TAKEN OUT OF THE WAY. AND THEN SHALL THE WICKED ONE BE REVEALED, WHOM THE LORD SHALL CONSUME WITH THE SPIRIT

OF HIS MOUTH, AND SHALL DESTROY WITH THE BRIGHTNESS OF HIS COMING; EVEN, HIM WHOSE COMING IS AFTER THE

WORKING OF SATAN, WITH ALL POWERS AND SIGNS AND LYING WONDERS; AND WITH ALL DECEIVABLENESS OF UNRIGHTEOUSNESS INTO THEM THAT PERISH; BECAUSE THEY RECEIVE NOT THE LOVE OF THE TRUTH THAT THEY MIGHT BE SAVED. AND FOR THIS BECAUSE GOD SHALL SEND THEM STRONG DELUSION, THAT THEY MIGHT BELIEVE A LIE; FOR THEY ALL MIGHT BE DAMNED WHO BELIEVE NOT THE TRUTH, BUT HAD PLESURES IN UNRIGHTEOUSNESS. FOR WE ARE BOUND TO GIVE THANKSALWAYS TO GOD FOR YOU, BRETHEN BELOVED OF THE LORD, BECAUSE GOD HATH FROM THE BEGINNING CHOSEN YOU TO SALVATION THROUGH SANCTIFICATION OF THE SPIRIT AND BELIEF OF THE TRUTH. WHEREUNTO HE CALLED YOU BY OUR GOSPEL, TO THE OBTAINIG OF THE GLORY OF THE LORD JESUS CHRIST. THEREFORE, BRETHEN STANDFAST AND HOLD THE TRADITION WHICH YEE HAVE BEEN TAUGHT, WEATHER BY WORD OR BY OUR EPISLE. NOW OUR LORD JESUS CHRIST HIMSELF, AND GOD EVEN OUR FATHER, WHICH HATH BELOVED US, AND HATH GIVEN US EVERLASTING CONSOLATIONAND GOOD HOPETHROUGH GRACE. COMFORT YOUR HEART AND STABLISH IN EVERY GOOD WORD, AND WORK.

PAUL ASKS THEIR PRAYERS

FINALLY, BRETHEN PRAY FOR US THAT THE WORD OF THE LORD MAY HAVE FREE COURSE, AND BE GLORIFIED EVEN AS IT IS WITH YOU: AND THAT WE MAY BE DELIVERED FROM UNREASONEABLE AND WICKED MEN: FOR ALL MEN HAVE NOT FAITH. BUT HE LORD IS FAITHFUL, WHO SHALL STABLISH YOU AND KEEP YOU FROM EVIL. AND WE HAVE CONFIDENCE IN THE LORD TOUCHING YOU, THAT THAT YEE BOTH DO AND WILL DO THE THINGS WHICH WE COMMANDED YOU. AND THE LORD DIRECTS YOUR HEARTS UNTO LOVE OF GOD, AND UNTO THE PATIENCE WAITING FOR CHRIST.

GIVES DIVERS PRECEPTS

NOW WE COMMAN YOU, BRETHEN, IN THE NAME OF OUR LORD JESUS CHRIST, THAT YEE WITHDRAW YOURSELVES FROM EVERY BROTHER THAT WALKETH DISORDERLY, AND NOT OF THE TRADITIONS WHICH HE RECEIVE OF US. FOR YOURSELVES KNOW HOW YEE OUGHT TO FOLLOW US; FOR WE BEHAVED NOT OURSELVES DISORDERLY AMONG YOU. NEITHER DID WE EAT ANY MAN'S BREAD FOR NOUGHT; BUT WROUGHT WITH LABOUR AND TRAVAIL NIGHT AND DAY, THAT WE MIGHT NOT BE CHARGEABLE TO ANY OF YOU. NOR BECAUSE WE HAVE NOT POWER, BUT TO MAKE OURSELVES AN EXAMPLE UNTO YOU TO FOLLOW US. FFOR EVEN WHEN WE WERE WITH YOU, THIS WE COMMANDED YOU, THAT IF ANY WIL NOT WORK, NEITHER SHALL HE EAT. FOR WE HEAR THAT THERE ARE SOME WHICH WALK AMONG YOU DISORDERLY, WORKING NOT AT ALL, BUT ARE BUSYBODIES. NOW THEM THAT ARE SUCHWE COMMAND AND EXHORT BY THE LORD JESUS CHRIST, THAT WITH QUIETNESS THEY WORK, AND EAT THEIR OWN BREAD. BUT YEE BRETHEN BE NOT WEARY IN WELL DOING. AND IF ANY MANOBEY NOT OUR WORD BY THE EPISTLE, NOTE THAT MAN, AND HAVE NO COMPANY WITH HIM, THAT HE MIGHT BE ASHAMED, YET COUNT HIM NOT AN ENEMY, BUT ADMONISH JIM AS A BROTHER.

28:5

CONCLUSION OF AFFIRMATION

NOW THE LORD OF PEACE HIMSELF GIVE YOU PEACE ALWAYS BY ALL MEANSS, THE LORD BE WITH YOU ALL. THE SALUTATION OF PAUL WITH MINE OWN HAND, WHICH IS THE TOKEN IN EVERY EPISTLE; SO, I WRITETHE PEACE OF THE LORD JESUS CHRIST BEWITH YOU ALL; AMEN. MY AFFIRMATION

IN THE LORD IS "I AM ATHIRST, FOR I KNOW YOU ARE ALPHA AND OMRGA, I KNOW YOU ARE THE FIRST AND THE LAST, I KNOW YOU ARE THE BEGINNING AND THE END, GIVE ME OF THE LIVING WATERS OF LIFE, LET ME EAT YOUR SPIRITUAL BODY AND COMMUNE WITH THEE OH LORD IN REMEMBRANCE OF YOU. NOW LORD JESUS, LET GOD'S GRACE BE WITH ME, NOW AND FOREVER, AND THE LAW OF LOVE. LORD I OBEY THE WORDS OF THIS BOOK THE BIBLE. FOR YOU ALONE IS FAITHFUL AND YOU ALONE CALLETH ME UNTO THE TABERNACLE IN THE SUN WITH ALL THE CHURCHES, TO BE AT PEACE WITH YOU FOREVER.

I RENDER NOT EVIL FOR EVIL TO ANY MAN, BUT REJOICE AND PRAY TO YOU O GOD, THROUGH YOUR SON JESUS CHRIST UNCEASINGLY. I GIVE THANKS FOR ALL THINGS BY YOU WILL O, GOD. I FIRMLY BELIEVE IN JESUS CHRIST AND THE LAW OF LOVE, I WILL QUENCH NOT THE SPIRIT, NOR WILL I IN ANY WAY DESPISE PROPHESYING. I AS AN ESCHAT WILL PROVE ALL THINGS, BY SHOWING, HOLDING ON STRONGLY TO THAT WHICH IS GOOD, UNLEARNING WHAT WAS UNDERSTOOD BY TEACHINGS OF THE OLD GOSPEL THAT LACKED SPIRITUAL

ENACTMENT. AS I ABSTAIN FROM LETTING, AND I WILL ABSTAIN THE VERY APPEARANCE OF EVIL, AGAINST YOUR SERVANTS AND YOUR WILL O, GOD. LET THE PEACE OF GOD SANCTIFY ME WHOLLY, TO PRESERVE ME BLAMELESS UNTO THE COMING OF THE LORD JESUS, AND GOOD LORD LET ME GREET THE BRETHEN, AS MUCH AS POSSIBLE WITH AN HOLY KISS, FOR MY GOD REIGNETH, YES HE REIGNETH SO HE FORGIVETH SO YOU CAN BE REFORMED IN HIS WORDS, TRUTH AND GRACE AND THE LAW OF LOVE. I WILL BAPTIZE IN THE NAME OF JESUS CHRIST AND THE SPIRIT OF GOD THAT WILL NEVER SET OUT TO MUTE THE WORD OF THE LORD.

FROM THE AUTHORITY OF GOD WHO IS A SPIRIT AND HIS SON THE LORD JESUS CHRIST, THE COMMANDER OF THE ORDER OF MINISTER OF GOD, THE GREATEST PROPHET OF ALL TIME TO THE CONVENIENT TIME OF THE HIGH TIME, THE MESSENGER THE LITTLE LIGHT IN THE DARK, WHOM HAVE REFRESHED THE MASTER'S SOUL WITH THE NEW GOSPEL AND THE NEW COVENANT UNDER THE TABERNACLE IN THE SUN.

BOOK TWO

THE MINISTRY OF RECONCILIATION

THIS A MINISTRY UNDER THE TABERNACLE OF THE SUNSET ASIDE TO REPLENISH THE EARTH IN LOVE.

AIM:

1. UNDERSTAND THE GOSPEL OF CHRIST, SO AS TO UNDERSTAND WHY THE CHURCH SLEPT, RECONCILE, RETURN AND REPENT UNTO GOD WITH THE AIMS AND OBJECTIVES OF THE SPIRITUAL CHURCH OF THE MANIFOLD WISDOM OF GOD WITH THE POWER OF GOD UNDER THE TABERNACLE IN THE SUN.

OBJECTIVES: TO OR TO KNOW WHY;

1. WAKE UP THE DEAD CHURCH TO THE GOSPEL OF CHRIST

2. CHANGE THE CHURCH WORSHIP OF CHRIST IN THE ORDINANCES OF MAN TO THE ORDINANCES OF GOD.

3. WORSHIP GOD IN SPIRIT AND IN TRUTH – IN THE SPIIRIT OF THE LORD JESUS CHRIST THE SON OF GOD – OR THE HOLY GHOST WHICH IS ONE OF THE SPIRIT OF GOD.

4. STIR THE CHURCH UP TO EXAMINE SELF AND KNOW WHERE YOU WERE RIGHT AND KNOW WHERE YOU WERE WRONG.

5. MOVE THE CHURCHES TO ACKNOWLEDGEMENT OF GOD'S ORDINANCES, GRACE AND REPENTANCE

6. TAKE ON SPIRITUAL THEOLOGY AFTER REPENTANCE THAT CAN TEACH THE CHURCH HOW TO ATTAIN UNTO PERFECTION WITH THE LIGHT OF GOD.

7. MAKE ALL MEN KNOW THE WILL OF GOD TO ACHIEVE HIS AWE SOME POWER, GOD BEING WILLNG AND ABLE TO BRING THEM INTO THE KINGDOM OF GOD.

THE CHURCH MUST BE WILLING TO DO THE WILL OF GOD. SOME CHURCHES CONTENDS TO BE THE TRUE CHURCH AND SO SHOULD BE ADMONISHED AND HAVE POWER OVER ALL OTHER CHURCHES AND WARDS – IF THIS WAS SO JESUS CHRIST WOULD NOT EXTEND AN OLIVE BRANCH OF REPENTANCE TO ALL SEVEN CHURCHES IN THE LAST DAYS OF THE HIGH TIME.

THERE ARE SEVEN CHURCHES TO GET BACK INTO GOD'S FOLD. THEY HAVE BEEN IN BABYLON SINCE CHRIST LEFT THE EARTH AND THROUGH THE AGES OF THE FOUNDATION OF THE CHURCH. BUT THE POWER OF GOD WILL BE MANIFESTED IN MANKIND WHO LOVES GOD AND WILL DO HIS WILL. GOD SAYS IF MY PEOPLE THAT ARE CALLED BY MY NAME WOULD JUST HUMBLE THEMSELVES BEFORE HIM.

IN THE SPIRIT I ANNUL THE LAWS, BUT WAS I UNKIND, I LOOKED AT THY LABOUR ON THE SABBATH DAY IN MY CHURCHES, ILOOKED AT YOUR UNDERSTANDING OF MY SABBATH DAY IN WHICH THOU SHALT NOT LEAVE THINE HOUSE TO DO ANY LABOUR, SPEAK THINE OWN WORDS, AND HAVE THINE OWN PLEASURES. I GAVE YOU ANOTHER WAY "LOVE" TO YOU I GIVE MY SPIRIT AND MY SON'S SPIRIT FOR A SIGN AMONGST MEN TO DRAW ALL MEN UNTO ME. THE LAWS ONLY REQUIRE LOVE TO BE FULFILLED UNTO ALL MEN. IS MANKIND WILL TO MAKE THE WAY OF GOD BE THE WAY OF GOD WITHOUT PRETTYING IT UP AND MANIFESTING THEMSELVES AS THE EARTHLY GODS FOR IT TO WORK?

GOD BEING WILLNG AND ABLE TO MAKE ALL MEN KNOW HIS AWESOME POWER, GAVE YOU A COMMAND MENT OF LOVE. ONE ANOTHER, FOR WITH SUCH MANKIND WILL HAVE GRACE, NOW THE LACK OF LOVE AND THE SPIRIT OF JESUS CHRIST AND THE SPIRIT OF GOD YOU WILL BE FALLEN FROM GRACE. I NOW ASK, DO YOU SERVE GOD? DO YOU HAVE ETERNAL LIFE IN GOD? IS THERE A LAW GREATER THAN LOVE? I THE MESSENGER ASKED, IS THERE ANY MAN WITH MEAT? IF SUCH A ONE STOOD, THEN HE COULD COMPARE AND PRESENT ALL NEEDED TO STAND IN THIS HIGH TIME OF GOD'S CALLING WITHIN THE CHURCH OR IN THE WIDER WORLD ACCORDING TO THE WILL OF GOD AS THE MESSENGER AND NOT AN HISTORIAN. I LIKENED THIS TO A PUBLIC-SCHOOL CLASS WHEN THE TEACHER ASKED WHO DON'T HAVE LUNCH. SUCH BOY OR GIRL WITHOUT HIS LUNCH WOULD HAVE THEIR HANDS UP AND SUCH BOY OR GIRL WOULD BE FED OR DELIVERED.

TO HAVE THE MEAT DESIRED IN THE LAST DAYS IS CHARACTERIZED BY A LONG-STANDING WORK IN FAITH BY GOD AND HIS SON THE LORDS JESUS CHRIST WHO IS LORD OF THE SABBATH. IF HE IS LORD OVER HIS OWN THING CAN'T HE BE LORD CHANGING IT. HOWEVER CHANGING THINGS ONLY MEANT TO LIFT THE CHILDREN OF GOD TO AN HIGHER AUTHORITY

CALLED LOVE. AND AGAIN, CHANGING THINGS ONLY MEANT TO LIFT THE CHILDREN OF GOD TO A SPIRITUAL AUTHORITY CALLED GRACE. AGAIN, CHANGING THINGS ONLY MEANT TO LIFT THE CHILDREN OF GOD TO AN HIGHER AUTHORITY SPIRITUAL PERFECTION. THERE ARE SEVEN CHURCHES THAT THE MESSENGER WILL STIR ALTHOUGH NOT FULLY AMONGST THEM BUT IN

THE MEDIUM OF THE MODERATION WHERE MANY WILL GET ZEALOUS, WANTING THE WORD SO MUCH THAT THEY WILL TRY TO PERFECT THAT WHICH IS UNPERFECTED IS IN THE ORDINANCES OF MAN. AND EVEN THE CONSEQUENCES TO THE ADVENT CHURCH BEING THE TRUE CHURCH IS SO HEAVILY LOADED BECAUSE THEY ALL FEEL THAT THEY DO THE WILL OF GOD. IF ONLY MY PEOPLE THAT ARE CALLED BY MY NAME WOULD HUMBLE THEMSELVES AND SEE TO THE WORD OF GOD THAT THE SEVENTH DAY IS NOT A LABOUR DAY IN THE CHURCH BUT A REST DAY IN THE HOME". THE MESSENGER HATH COME FROM A DULY ANTICIPATED POINT OF NO RETURN TO PASTURING BUT TO FULFILL THE WILL OF GOD. CAUSING THE TERMINAL DECAY OF THE OLD GOSPEL AND COVENANT OF GOD TO BECOME THE NEW GOSPEL AND NEW COVENANT OF GOD IN A SPECIFIC TIME CALLED THE HIGH TIME AS THE GREATEST PROPHET THAT THE LORD JESUS CHRIST ENCOURAGED THE SEEKERS OF HIM OUT OF THE WILDERNESS WHEN ALL HIS DISCIPLES HAD LEFT TO LOOK OUT FOR IN THE LAST DAYS. I MAY NOT BE ROBED AS A KING'S SON BUT I HAVE FULFILLED THIS PROMISE WHEN I FIRST BELIEVED IN HIS SWORD AND THE WORD OF GOD.

BUT THE LORD SAID I AM ALPHA AND OMEGA THE BEGINNING AND THE END, THE FIRST AND THE LAST, THAT WHAT THOU SEEST WRITE IN A BOOK AND SEND IT UNTO THE SEVEN CHURCHES WHICH ARE IN ASIA. AND IN TIME HEREAFTER, THAT THERE SHALL BE A GREAT MISTRY BUT THE LORD SAID I AM ALPHA AND OMEGA THE BEGINNING AND THE END, THE FIRST AND THE LAST, THAT WHAT THOU SEEST WRITE IN A BOOK AND SEND IT UNTO THE SEVEN CHURCHES WHICH ARE IN ASIA. AND IN TIME HEREAFTER, THERE SHALL BE A GREAT MISTRY. REMEMBER NOW THE GREAT DISCRIPTION OF THE GOD OF HEAVEN IN BETWEEN THE 7 GOLDEN CANDLE STICKS WITH FIERY EYES AND HIS HAIR AS WHITE AS WOOL HE HAVING 7 STARS IN HIS AND OUT OF HIS MOUTH AS IF A SHARP TWO HEDGED SWORD AND HIS COUNTENANCE WAS AS THE SUN SHINETH IN HIS STRENGTH. HE LAID HIS RIGHT HAND UPON JOHN BUT JOHN HAVING KNOWN THAT, THAT GOD WORK SENT FORTH SHALL BE HERE AFTER. NOW I SAY UNTO YOU THAT HE WITH LOVE HAVE CONQUERED THE LAWS FOR HE CHRIST BRINGETH THAT LOVE TO YOU IN THE SWORD OF THE SPIRIT.

NOW UNTO US, I THE MESSENGER IS ALSO AN HEIR TO HIS FATHER TOO AND SO I CALL UPON HIM ABBA, ABBA, ABBA, FOR HIS SPIRIT OF LOVE TO KEEP US ABOVE THE LAWS AND SO WE THE CHILDREN OF GOD IS TO;

KNOW THE MESSENGER RUNNETH AND HE RAN WELL INTO THE HIGH TIME, WITHIN THESE LAST DAYS LIKE JOHN BUT ONLY NOW GREATER THAN JOHN THE BAPTIST AS A FULFILLMENT OF NOT WHAT THE CHRISTIAN CHURCH WAS LOOKING FOR AND READY TO RECEIVE IN THE HIGH TIMES.

KNOW THAT THE MESSENGER CARRIES THE SEVEN CHURCHES AND THEIR EXPONENTS OF CHURCHES TO FIND THE MINISTRY OF RECONCILIATION IN A PREPARED WAY CALLED THE LIBERALITY AND THE SPIRITUAL CHURCH OF THE

MANIFOLD WISDOM OF GOD UNDER THE TABERNACLE IN THE SUN – MASS. THEN SHALL EACH EXAMINE THE SELF AND THE CHURCH AND THEREAFTER REPENT. THE CHURCH MUST LEAVE THE ORDINANCES OF MAN GET OUT OF HER MYSTRY BABYLON AND COME TO THE GRACE OF GOD IN THE ORDINANCE OF GOD. IF THE TIME OF GOD IS NO THEN TO TOUCH DOWN ON REDEMPTION GROUND THE FIRST LAP IS KNOW THE TRUTH, THEN NEXT LAP IS TO ACCEPT GRACE AND THE LAW OF LOVE, THE MEXT IS TO RECONCILE AND REPENT TO TAKE THE CHURCH TO THE PEOPLE FOR A TRUTHFUL WALK WITH GOD, AND FINALLY GET THE WILL TO FOLLOW THE MESSENGER IN THE TABERNACLE OF THE SUN TEACHING SPIRITUAL THEOLOGY WITH THE MANIFOLD WISDOM OF GOD

CHRIST JESUS GAVE YOU LAW OF LOVE, AND A GREATER LAW YOU CANNOTH FIND AND IN WORSHIPING HIM IN SPIRIT AND IN TRUTH YOU ARE NO DEBTORS OF THE LAWS. NOW REMEMBER THAT CHRIST IS NOTHING TO YOU IF YOU ARE JUSTIFIED BY THE LAWS, CAUSE BY HIS WILL AND HIS FATHER'S WILL FOR YOU, YOU BECOME DISOBEDIENT AND SO FALLEN FROM GRACE. HERE IS THE REASON TO EXAMINE THE SELF. THE CURCH HAS STRAYED FROM THE HOLINESS OF GOD – HERE YOU ALL NEED A LITTLE LEAVEN TO LEAVENETH THE WHOLE LUMP FOR THE ENTIRE CHURCH TO COME BACK TO GOD. AS I THE MESSENGER STIRS YOU AND AGITATE YOU EACH TIME YOU REMEMBER THE CALL TO THE ALTER AND THAT YOUR CALLING AND ELECTION WAS NOT SURE THEN COME UNTO THE TABERNACLE OF THE SUN FOR REDEMPTION AND BE REDEEEMED BY JESUS CHRIST HAVING FAITH IN KING JESUS MAKES THAT ELECTION SURE, AND GET THE STRENGTH OF THE SAINTS OF GOD THROUGH JESUS CHRIST.

IN THE LAST DAYS THE MINISTRY OF RECONCILLATION WILL STIR YOU UP AS MUCH AS POSSIBLE FOR THE CHURCH IS SO DEEP IN BABYLON THAT THEY CALL ANYTHING THEY DON'T LIKE BABYLON TO APPEASE

THEMSELVES. BUT IT IS THE HIGH TIME IN IT THE MESSENGER NEEDS TO GET YOU TO REALIZE THAT THE PEOPLE OF GOD IS NOT FULLY SERVING GOD, BUT RIDING SATAN, FOR THEY HAVE LEFT HIS ORDINANCE AND IS SERVING THE ORDINANCE OF MAN UNDER THE LAWS. GOD NEEDS EVERYONE TO LEAVE BABYLON AND COME HOME TO HIM IN HIS ORDINANCE SO YOU CAN BE PROFILE WITH THE SPIRIT OF SON OF GOD THE LORD JESUS CHRIST AND THE SPIRIT OF GOD. BUT CHIDREN OF GOD, YOU NEED TO BE TAUGHT, BECAUSE OF THE UNWILLING PRIESTS, ELDERS, AND LAITY THAT I THE MESSSENGER HAVE TO STIR YOU UP RATHER THEIR MEAT THAN TO DO THE WILL OF GOD.

THIS IS THE LORD KNOCKING, BUT YOU CAN'T COME TO HIM BECAUSE YOUR DENOMINATION ARE TIED UP IN THE LAWS AND BABYLON—IF YOUR ELDERS CAN'T CHANGE TO WORSHIPING GOD IN THE ORDINANCE OF GOD AND LIVE THE LAW OF LOVE THEN FALLEN FROM GRACE ARE YOU—CHRIST HAVE NO ACCOUNT OF YOU

AND THE CHURCH. NOW IN THE MINISTRYOF RECONCILIATION YOU WILL BE MADE FREE FROM SIN AND BECOME STEWARDSAND SERVANT OF GOD. BEARING

FRUITS UNTO HOLINESS, RIGHTEOUNESS AND EVERLASTING LIFE. THE LORD GOD WILL BE MIGHTY TO PUT UPON YOU THE BREATPLATE OF RIGHTEOUSNESS, FOR YOU HAVE RECEIVED THE HELMET OF SALVATION WITH ABUNDANT GRACE. THE TRUE BELIEVERS IN CHRIST WILL BE UNDEER GRACE AS SERVANTS OF RIGHTEOUSNESS. THEREBY GLORYING PASS THIS TRIBULATION, THAT WORKETH PATIENCE. AND PATIENCE WORKETH EXPERIENCE, AND EXPERIENCE WORKETH HOPE IN THE PASTURES OF GOD. HERE HOPE MAKETH NO ONE ASHAMED BECAUSE THE LOVE OF GOD IS SHED ABROAD IN OUR HEARTS BY THE HOLY GHOST WHICH IS GIVEN UNTO US BUT WILL WE ACCEPT HIS WILL? REMEMBERING WHEN WE WERE HIS ENEMIESWEWERE RECONCILES TO HIM BY THE DEATH OF HIS SON, NOW SAVED BY HIS LIFE, SO JOY IN GOD THROUGH JESUS CHRIST BY WHOM WE NOW UNDERSTAND AND RECEIVE THIS FINAL ATONEMENT, TO COMBINE HIS WILL WITH OUR WILL WHERE THERE IS NO LAW. THE FIRST CHURCH, THE SECOND CHURCH, THE THIRD CHURCH, THE FOURTH CHURCH CONT, THE FIFTH CHURCH, THE SIXTH CHURCH PHILADELPHIA, THE SEVENTH CHURCH, THE SEVENTH CHURCH AND THEIR EXPONENTS AS DEALT WITH IN THE LIBERALITY

THE PREPARED WAY IS DIRECTING YOU TO OBEDIENCE BEING MEMBERS OF THE CANDLE STICKS THE LORD THY GOD SAID UNTO JOHN, ON THAT ISLE OF PATMOS, FOR GOD SAITH "I AM ALPHA AND OMEGA, THE FIRST ANS THE LAST", WHAT THOU SEEST WRITE IN A BOOK AND SEND IT TO THE

SEVEN CHURCHES WHICH ARE IN ASIA—EPHESUS, SMYRNA, PERGAMOS, THYATIRA, SARDIS, PHILADELPHIA, LAODICEA — JOINING NOW THE EXPONENTS OF CHURCHES AND THE FLOCK OF THE GREAT MULTITUDE — NOW ONLY THOSE THAT HAVE ATTAINED THE FELLOWSHIP WITH JESUS CHRIST SHOULD FOLLOW THE MINISTRY OF RECONCILIATION, AND IS WILLING TO RECONCILE TO GRACE, REPENT ALL UNDER THE ORDINANCES OF MAN, LIVE THE LAW OF LOVE AND TEACH LOVE OF JESUS CHRIST TO THE WORLD IN THE ESCHATON'S WAY. AND FELLOWSHIP WITH THE LITTLE CHURCH THE TABERNACLE IN THE SUN PLACES WITHIN YOU THE SPIRITUAL CHURCH OF THE MANIFOLD WISDOM OF GOD TO GET THE LIGHT OF JESUS CHRIST. UNDER THE TABERNACLE IN THE SUN - MASS. IF FOR INSTANCE THE STIR AND THE MODERATION OF THE PREPARED WAY DID NOT COME UNTO YOU, THEN YOU WOULD HAVE BEEN HOPELESS NOT EVEN BEING ABLE TO COPY THE WORK OF THE MODERATION BY THE MESSENGER AND REFRESHER OF THE MASTER'S SOUL, AND BOAST ABOUT YOUR KNOWLEDGE IN THE HIGH TIME WITHOUT THE LIBERALITY. IN SOME CASES, THE EVIDENCE IS CLEAR CUT. THE REALITY IS THE ANSWER FROM THE LORD THY GOD. I KNOW FOR THE LORD HATH SAID I THE LORD IS SOMEWHAT AGAINST BECAUSE THOU HAST LEFT THY FIRST LOVE THE JEWISH TRUE ORDINANCES OF GOD TO THINE OWN, COME BACK TO GOD AND LEAVE SATAN FOR THE LORD HAST FOUND YOU TO BE SOOTH SAYING LIARS. REMEMBER THEREFORE FROM WHENCE THOU HAST BEEN CALLED UNTO FREE SALVATION OR TO BE FALLEN IN NOT WILLING TO CONCEDE TO THE GOD WHO CREATED THE HEAVEN AND THE EARTH, FOR THOU HAST FIGHT THOSE OF THE FIRST LOVE OF CHRIST FOR JERUSALEM WHICH THOU HAST LEFT TO THY NEXT LOVE, A WICKED GOSPEL IN UNBELIEF AND STEADFASTNESS. SUCH WICKED GOSPEL IS NOT OF JESUS CHRIST, BUT, THE GOSPEL OF CHRIST IS OF GRACE, LOV,E AND THE LIGHT OF GOD.

WORSHIP IN THE ORDINANCES OF MAN AND THE WILL OF MAN. IT IS GODS THAT SAITH UNTO YOU REPENT NOW, AND DO THE FIRST WORKS THAT WILL PROSPER MANKIND UNTO SALVATION THROUGH REPENTANCE UNTO HIM. FOR THE LORD WILL COME QUICKLY UPON YOU AND WILL REMOVE HIS CANDLE STICK OUT OF HIS PLACE EXCEPT THOU REPENT. MAKE HASTE TO OVERCOME, FOR TO HIM THAT OVERCOMETH WILL GOD GIVE TO EAT OF THE TREE OF LIFE, WHICH IS IN THE MIDST OF THE PARADISE OF GOD COME BACK TO GOD, AND TO YOU YOUR SALVATION WILL BE FREE FOR UNTO YOU, YOU WERE LED BY MISBELIEFS, SOOTHSAYINGS OF THE PROPHETS OF OLD BUT THE PEACE OF GOD BE UNTO YOU AS YOU DROP THE ENMITY OF CHRIST TAKE THE REPENTANCE AND BUILD GARDENS BETTER THAT THOSE OF EDEN.

WHEN JOHN WROTE TO THE CHURCHES SEVENTH DAY ADVENTIST WERE NEVER EVEN IN EXISTENCE BUT IN THE EXPONENT FORM. NOW I WRITE

UNTO THE ANGELS WHO HAVE DOMINION AND THE POWER TO GUIDE THESE CHURCHES INTO THEIR HANDS IN THE HANDS OF GOD, BUT TODAY THEY SPREAD OUT LIKE A PYRAMID UNDER THE SEVEN CHURCHES. THEY HAVE BECOME MOCKERS OF EVEN GOD IN THEIR HOLY SELF-RIGHTEOUS STAGES. HAVING SET THE SIMPLE TASK OF RETURN UNTO GOD UNTO THEM THEY CANNOT ATTAIN UNTO IT FOR THEY ARE LITTLE PUFFED UP, AND MUFFLED UP GODS IN THEIR OWN RIGHTEOUSNESS. THEY BAPTIZE IN WATER STILL NOT SEEKING THE LIVING WATERS OF JESUS CHRIST OUR LORD.

FOR I SAY UNTO YOU MY FELLOW SERVANTS THAT WORKETH FOR THE LORD JESUS CHRIST. YOU MUST KNOW THAT THE LORD JESUS CHRIST LOVE ME, THE MESSENGER GREATER THAN JOHN THE BAPTIST TO COME UNTO YOU. MY FELLOW SERVANTS OF GOD KNOW YEE THAT JESUS BAPTIZED NOT ONE IN WATER BUT JOHN AND THE LORD HATH BESEACHED YOU TO BAPTIZE THE BRETHEN IN HIS SPIRIT AND THE SPIRIT OF GOD AND BE FILLED WITH THE GRACE OF THE LORD JESUS CHRIST FOREVERMORE.

MY FELLOW SERVANTS OF GOD HAVING FOLLOWED THE FOOTSTEPS OF THE KING CHRIST JESUS ON THE FOUNDATION OF PETER THE ROCK, HAVING SEEN THAT IT IS WRITTEN TRUE AND WORTHY THEN YOU REALIZE THAT THE MESSENGER OVERCOMETH THE SEVEN CANDLE STICKS AND HAVE NOW SET YOU TO THE LITTLE CHURCH WITHIN YOU TO GAIN THE SPIRIT OF PERFECTION OF THE LORD JESUS CHRIST THE SON OF GOD WHERE YOU ALL CAN GET THE SEAL OF GOD THAT YOU WEAR UNTO THE DAY OF REDEMPTION NOT JUST FOR TODAY AND SO YOU SHOULD NOT GRIEVE THE HOLY SPIRIT OF GOD THAT CAN REDEEM YOU FROM SIN.

GOD ALLOWS YOU TO COME BACK TO HIM, WITH SO MANY SINS THAT YOU NEVER KNEW, AND ASK FOR FORGIVENESS SO LIKEWISE YOU SHOULD BE KIND TO EACH OTHER, TENDER HEARTED ONE TO ANOTHER AND FORGIVE ONE ANOTHER FOR HIS SAKE. DO REMEMBER NOT TO LEARN IN THE MINISTRY OF RECONCILIATION THAT WE ARE NOT TO THINK OF MEN ABOVE THAT WHICH IS WRITTEN THAT YE BE NOT

PUFFED UP FOR ONE AGAINST THE OTHER, FOR IN CHRIST JESUS I HAVE BEGOTTEN YOU THROUGH THE GOSPEL, YEA THE WHOLE TRUTH OF THE GOSPEL. WHEREFORE I BESEACH YOU BE MY FOLLOWERS FOR SHORTLY THE KINGDOM OF GOD COMES IN PPOWER.THE CHILDREN OF GOD IN THE LAST DAYS MUST GO THROUGH THE MINISTRY OF RECONCILATION SO THAT, THEY MAY PUT ON THE WHOLE ARMOUR OF GOD AND BE ABLE TO STAND AGAINST THE WILES OF THE DEVIL, HENCE BEING STRONG IN THE LORD AND HIS MIGHT. BE THE SERVANTS OF THE LORD DOING HIS WILL FROM THE HEART, NOT WITH JUST LIP SERVICE, AND AS MEN PLEASERS,

WITH YOUR GOOD SERVICE AS BEING TO THE LORD AND NOT TO MEN. YOU CAME TO YOUR CALLING IN MEEKNESS AND LOWLINESS, IN ONE BODY ONE SPIRIT AND ONE FAITH, ONE BAPTISM, ONE GOD ONE FATHER OF ALL, BUT TO EVERYONE OF US IS GIVEN GRACE ACCORDING TO THE MEASURE OF THE GIFTS OF CHRIST. THE MINISTRY OF RECONCILIATION SETS OUT TO REMOVE THE DARKNESS OF UNDERSTANDING OF THE LORD THROUGH IGNORANCE AND BLINDNESS OF HEART, AND VANITY OF THE MINDS AND BEGIN TO SPEAK IN TRUTH IN LOVE AS YOU KNOW SON OF GOD AND BE PERFECT IN HIM AS A PERFECT MAN. FOR THE PERFECTING OF THE SAINTS FOR THE WORK OF THE MINISTRY FOR THEEDYFING OF THE BODY OF CHRISTTILL WE ALL COME IN UNITY OF ONE FAITH IN THE ENTIRE WORLD. FOR THIS WISE BE NO MORE CHILDREN TOSSED TO AND FRO AND CARRIED ABOUT WITH EVERY WINDS OF DOCTRINES, BY THE SLEIGHT OF MEN WITH CUNNING CRAFTINESS, FOR THEY ALL LIE IN WAIT TO DECEIVE YOU ALL

WHO HATH MEAT? RAN WELL AND STAND AS THE MESSENGER AND MINISTER OF GOD. NOW HE THAT OPPOSSETH THE MESSENGER AND MAY ALSO BE IN AN ENVIOUS CAMPAIGN AGAINST ME FOR THE GARDEN PATH. I WRITE CONCERNING THE BRETHREN. UNDER GOD IN THEIR FORM IN UNTO THE DARKNESS OF HATE, GOD IN THE TRUE FORM IS UNTO LOVE AND THE LIGHT OF PURITY OF THE SPIRIT, HE WANTS TO RECLAIM THE SAINTS AND IS ASKING THEM TO PUT AWAY THE FORMER CONVERSATIONS OF THIS OLD MAN WHICH IS CORRUPT ACCORDING TO THE DECEITFUL LUSTS, AND BE RENEWED IN THE SPIRIT OF YOUR MINDS, AND SO PUT YE ON THE NEW MAN, WHICH AFTER GOD IS CREATED IN RIGHTEOUSNESS, AND TRUE HOLINESS. THEREFORE, PUTTING AWAY LYING, AND SPEAK EVERYMAN TRUTH WITH HIS NEIGHBOUR FOR WE ARE MEMBERS ONE TO ANOTHER, BE NOT ANGRY AT ME AND BRETHEN SIN NOT AND SO LET NOT THE SUN GO DOWN UPON YOUR WRATH ANYMORE. FOR WITH GRACE YOU WILL BE SEALED BY GOD TO THE DAY OF REDEMPTION, SO GREIVE NOT THE SPIRIT WITH CORRUPT CONVERSATIONS FROM YOUR MOUTHS, BUT LET IT EDIFY AND MINISTER GRACE TO THE HEARER—PUT AWAY BITTERNESS, MALICE, ENVY, ANGER, WRATH, AND FORGIVE ONE ANOTHER.

THE SEVEN CHURCHES THAT PERCIEVETH THE REMEMBERANCE OF THE "TABERNACLE IN THE SUN" BEING THE LEAST AND WILL LOVE THE COMMANDMENT OF LOVE BEING LIFTED UP THROUGH THE GRACE OF GOD THAT CONTAINS THE MINISTRY OF RECONCILATION, THAT STIRRED UP THE CHURCHES, WILL USE THE ENSIGNS FOR MEASURE OF FAITH AND WORSHIP HAVING SEEN GOD'S PURIFICATION

THE LAST DAYS OR THE HIGH TIME, THEN BRINGING THE SPIRITUAL CHURCH OF THE MANIFOLD WISDOM OF GOD CLOSE TO THE HEARTS OF MEN FOR PERFECTION

THROUGH JESUS CHRIST AND THE SPIRIT OF GOD, WILL BE LED TO LOVE THE REMEMBERANCE. THIS ALSO IS THE COMMANDMENT OF LOVE. REPENT NOW LIVE LOVE – HERE ALSO IS THE COMMANDMENT OF GOD. THE FRUITS OF THE SPIRIT WILL LEAD PEOPLE WILL SEE THE FRUITS BEING GOOD THEREOF TO PLEASE GOD. THEN OUR GOD WRATH WILL BE LIFTED FROM THE CHILDREN OF MEN, FOR EVERMORE IN THE TABERNACLE IN THE SUN WITH THE DIACRETIC DIALOGUE, HOLINESS HATH BECOME THE HOUSE OF THE LORD AND DIVINITY OF THE LAST DAYS.

INITIATION of SPIRITUAL THEOLOGY

TEN IT—TAKE IT OR LEAVE IT

Published in THE CITY of UNION, NEW JERSEY

TEN IT meant that if you fell in love with this poem then take it and put it in ten different languages for those that have transgressed wickedly to the death to recognize it. The Messenger tenned it.

TEN IT TAKE OR LEAVE IT meant Salvation if given out freely now take or leave it as a choice as the end is come upon us. The Dust in the Rocks of their mountains are waiting on the disobedient amongst us not my redeemer.

THE PATIENCE GARDEN PATH, NOT LUKE WARM, COLD BUT NO HOT WAITING A WHILE IN SILENCE, ZION TRAIN UNDERGROUND, CUTTING OFF OF THE ONE LOCKS AND TOSSING IT AWAY, THE CHURCH STILL NO WAKE UP, THE BOOK OF JUDE, THE MODERATION OF THE GARDEN PATH, ZION TRAIN THE LITTLE LIGHT IN THE DARK COMING FORTH FROM UNDERGROUND, THE HIGHLIGHTS BUILDING OF GARDENS BETTER THAN THOSE OF EDEN, STAR TIME, THE WHITE STONE, THE ESCHAT'S WAY, THE STENCH OF THE NORTH ARMY, AND THE MORNING STAR. AND THE COMING OF THE CHRIST. THIS CHURCH WILL PREACH AND TEACH LOVE ONE TO ANOTHER

AS THE ESCHATS OF THE WORLD AND EXALT THE SEVEN SERMONS OF **THE PRIESTHOOD THEOLOGY** By MASS FRANCIS CHARLES MALCOLM © 2017.

THE SPIRITUAL CHURCH OF THE MANIFOLD WISDOM OF GOD IS BUILT BY GOD UPON THE LORD JESUS CHRIST FOR STAR TIME IS UPON US. IT NEEDS NO CONTENTION

OR CONFRONTATION FOR ITS PLACE IN SOCIETY WITH PREACHERS TELLING YOU THE CHURCH CAN ONLY BE IF IT IS BUILT UPON PETER THE ROCK. THE LORD DID BUT HE IS STILL LORD AND HE HAS OTHER THINGS IN STORE FOR THE PEOPLE WHO FOR SO LONG HAS LEFT HIS ORDINANCE TO WORSHIP THE ORDINANCES OF MAN. SPIRITUAL THEOLOGY IS ROOTED IN A SIMPLE NETWORK OF DEPENDENCE UPON GOD THROUGH HIS SPIRIT AND HIS SON'S SPIRIT FOR SURVIVAL IN THE LAST DAYS OR THE HIGH TIME. SPIRITAL THEOLOGY WILL ALSO CREATE THE FRUITS OF JESUS CHRIST AND THE CREATURES OF GOD. FOR NOW, THE TIME HAS COME OR THE DAY IS COME WHEN MAN SHALL NOT GO DOWN TO THE SYNAGOGUE TO PRAY BUT DO SO IN SPIRIT AND IN TRUTH. SO, THEY NEED NOT TO WAR OVER THE SYNAGOGUES IN JERUSALEM ANYMORE TO OBSERVE GODS PRESENCE OR BE IN THE PRESENCE OF GOD.

BECAUSE;

- THE SPIRITUAL CHURCH IS NOT LAYING A NEW FOUNDATION, AS THAT IS GONE ALREADY, AND DONE BY THE CHURCHES

- THE SPIRITUAL CHURCH BEGINS WITH AN ENDORSEMENT OF THE SPIRITUAL EPISODE TO BER IMPACT ON THE ILLS OF SOCIETY AS MEN LOOK FOR AN ANSWER IN THE BEHVIOUR OF OUR SOCIETY AND THE CHURCH'S ROLE IN IT.

- THIS SPIRITUAL CHURCH OF THE MANIFOLD WISDOM OF GOD LOGS YOU ONTO SPIRITUAL AND TRUE WORSHIP OF GOD THROUGH JESUS CHRIST

- THIS ALLOWS ANY MEMBER TO HAVE FAITH, ACCEPT THE LIGHT, LOVE EACH OTHER, SUBMIT YOURSELVES ONE TO ANOTHER SPIRITUALLY AND DRAW ALL MEN ONTO CHRIST WITH THE LIGHT

- THE OLD CHURCHES ARE LIBERATED IN THE LAW OF LOVE

- THE LORD JESUS CHRIST HAS ANNULLDED THE LAWS BY GRACE AND ESTABLISHED IT WITH LOVE

- THE SPIRITUAL CHURCH IS A PATHWAY TO PERFECTION

- THE SPIRITUAL CHURCH LEADS TO FINDING THE LIGHT HELP THE ESCHATONS TO PERFECTION IN THE BODY OF CHRIST

- THE SPIRITUAL CHURCH HAVING PERFECTION, YOU BECOME CHRISTLIKE HAVING TO BE ANGRY AT TIME BUT SIN NOT

- THE SPIRITUAL CHURCH HAS NO BOUNDARIES AND IS OPEN TO WHO WORSHIP GOD IN SPIRIT AND IN TRUTH

THE LORD JESUS CHRIST ALTHOUGH BEING LORD OF THE SABBATH – REQUIRES THAT MAN LEAVE THE EPHERMERAL CHURCHES AS THEY ARE OF THE ORDINANCES OF MAN, EVEN THE SABBATH DAYS CHURCHES.

THE SPIRITUAL CHURCH IS THE GROUND OF REPENTANCE FOR THE SEVEN EPHERMERAL CHURCHES AND THEIR EXPONENTS, THAT NEEDTO REPENT BEFORE GOD CAN SPARE THEM A PATH IN THE SPIRITUAL REALM OF HIS PRIESTHOOD TO REACH FOR THE LIGHT AND FIND FULL FERFECTION IN THE BODY OF CHRIST

THE SPIRITUAL CHURCH WILL NOT WRESTLE WITH YOUR CLAIM OF THE LAWS AND THE OLD CHURCH THAT IS BUILT UPON PETER THE ROCK, THAT CLEAVE TO THE ORDINANCES OF MAN, AND LEAVING THE LIGHT OF GOD AND FOREVER WALK IN DARKNESS BECAUSE OF BEING STUBBORN AND BLIND IN HEART

THE SPIRITUAL CHURCH ALLOW THE PEOPLE OF THE SPIRITUAL CHURCH AND THE GREAT MULTITUDE TO ACCEPT THE SPIRIT OF GOD AND BOW AT THE FEET OF JESUS AND SAY YES LORD YOU ARE LORD OF ALL

THE SPIRITUAL CHURCH CLEAVE TO THE GRACE OF GOD THROUGH JESUS CHRIST, AND THE LAW OF LOVE WHICH TAKES THE LIGHT OVER THE DARKNESS AND GIVE LOVE ONE TO ANOTHER WITH HONESTY, LACK OF DECEPTION AND ENVY

THE SPIRITUAL CHURCH USE THE LAW OF LOVE TO MAKE A PEACEFUL WORLD OF LOVE AND RIGHTEOUSNESS FOR ALL MANKIND IN THE ORDINANCE OF GOD WHICH ENDS UP BUILDING GARDENS MUCH MORE BEAUTIFUL THAN THAT OF EDEN

THE SPIRITUAL CHURCH OFFERS THE OLIVE BRANCH TO THE MODERN SAVEGES OF HUMANITY, WITH HEARTS BROKEN MOST WILL GIVE UP THE FIGHT AND TAKE SALVATION FREELY FROM THE GOD OF HEAVEN AND EARTH WHOM THEY THOUGHT WAS NOT REAL TO HAVE SENT HIS SON TO DIE ON THE CROSS FOR THE SALVATION OF IRNORANT MEN THAT NEVER TRUSED THE BIBLE

THE SPIRITUAL CHURCH PUT THE TEMPLE OF GOD IN ALL WILLING MEN'S HEART, WHICH IS APPROPRIATE UNTO SALVATION WITH BELIEF JUST AS THE MESSENGER OF GOD, HOWEVER

THE PUFFED UP CHRISTIANS WILL NOT ONLY HAVE TO BELIEVE IN THE GOD, HIS SON AND THE NEW GOSPEL AND THE NEW COVENANT, BUT ALSO ACCEPT THE MERCIES OF GOD TO ACCEPT

GRACE AT THE LATEST STAGE ALONG WITH THE LAW OF LOVE TO BECOME CHLDREN OF THE LIGHT OF JESUS CHRIST, WHOSE TRANGRESSION AGAINST GOD WILL BE NO MORE IF IT CAN BE DONE WITH ALL THEIR HEARTS.

THE SPIRITUAL CHURCH BAPTIZE EVRYMAN IN THE NAME OF JESUS CHRIST AS WITH THE SPIRIT OF GOD WHICH SPRINKLES SUCH A MAN FROM EVIL AND IN HIM THE SPIRIT OF GOD WORKETH TO CLEANSE HIS SOUL BY PURGING IT FROM HIS DEEDS IN THE LAW TO BE REFRESHED AS THE MASTER IN PEACE AND LOVE WITH GRACE UNTO THE WORLD.

BOOK THREE

THE DIACRETIC DIALOGUE

"TEK IT OR LEAVE IT, TEN IT"

TEK (TAKE) IT OR LEAVE IT

TEN IT OR LEAVE IT

ABSTRACT

THIS IS A SIMI MUSICAL DIALOGUE DONE BY MASS (FRANCIS CHARLES MALCOLM) FOR THE WORLD OF PEACE. TO TEN WAS TO ADD TEN DIFFERENT LANGUAGES TO THE WRITING AND THEN TO ADD SINGERS OF TEN DIFFERENT BACKGROUND TO IT. THE FIRST APPROACH WAS IN UNION NEW JERSEY 2016 BY FRANCIS CHARLES MALCOLM MASS/MATTY SET ON YOUTUBE. THE ENTITY CORELLATED THE CAPTAIN'S JOURNEY UP NORTH TO DELIVER THE PIECE IN THE MODERATION OF "THE GARDEN PATH" THAT WILL LEAD MANKIND TO GRAVITATE TOWARDS PEACE BY BRINGING THEM TO ACCEPT SALVATION AS A MEANS FOR ETERNAL PEACE AND RESPECT TOWARDS HUMANITY AND RECEIVING GODS PARDON FOR THEIR WRONGS DONE TO MANKIND THROUGHT THEIR EVIL HEARTS.

PC
PIPE 5 MUSIK/tgp-MASS/fcm/MATTY
fcm@gmail.com 2017

Figure 3: "Tek It or Leave It, Ten It" ™ ©2016.

TEK IT OR LEAVE IT
TEN IT OR LEAVE IT

TEN BY: FRANCIS CHARLES MALCOLM

ENGLISH / PATOI VERSION PUBLISHED IN 10 DIFFERENT LANGUAGES.

OH I KNOW-W NOW, I TELL YOU RIGH NOW, YEAH I TELL YOU RIGHT NOW OH WOW, WOW, WOW YEAH, MI NEVER TROD GEM (THEM) PLACE DEH (I HAVE NEVER BEEN TO THOSE PLACES) MI NEVER TROD GEM (THEM) PLACE DEH (I HAVE NEVER BEEN TO THOSE PLACES), NO I NEVER TROD GEM (THEM) PLACE DEH (.O, NO I HAVE NEVER BEEN TO THOSE PLACES), NOOO, OH NO, AFGANISTAN, OH, OH NO, O PALESTINIAN LANDS, OH, OH, THE SYRIAN LANDS, MI NEVER TROD GEM (THEM) PLACE DEH (I HAVE NEVER BEEN TO THOSE PLACES), MI NEVER TROD GEM (THEM) PLACE DEH (I HAVE NEVER BEEN TO THOSE PLACES), SAY I NEVER TROD, I AN I, NE-VER TROD, NEVER TROD DEM (THEM) PLACE DEH (I HAVE NEVER BEEN TO THOSE PLACES).

JAH IS WITH MEE, AND FOREVER SO STRONG, HE HAS NEVER FORSAKEN, OOH O, HE HAS NEVER FORSAKEN MEE, OH NOOO, OH NO, NO, NO, NO, SO I WIPE AWAY MY TEARS BUT I'M STRONG, WIPE AWAY MY TEARS YEAH I'M STRONG YOU REFUSE ME ALL THE WAY, BUT I DON'T HAVE A THING TO SAY.

CAUSE JAH, MY REDEEMER LIVETH, OH YEAH EEEHM OH YAH MY REDEEMER LIVETH, SO I DON'T HAVEA THING TO SAY, OH NO. OH NO, NO, NOOO, SO I'M STEPPING OUT YEAH, I'M STEPPING OUT STRONG,

STEPPING OUT YEA, STEPPING OUT, JAH PROVIDE, EACH AND EVERY DAY SO I-IIII WIPE MY TEARS AWAY, THEY REFUSE I, THEY REFUSE I THIS IS WHAT I SAY, MI NEVER TROD DEM LAND DEH (I HAVE NEVER BEEN TO THOSE PLACES), AFGHANISTAN, MI NEVER TROD DEM LAND DEH (I HAVE NEVER BEEN TO THOSE PLACES), PALESTINIAN LANDS, MI NEVER TROD DEM LAND DEH (I HAVE NEVER BEEN TO THOSE PLACES), OVER SYRIA, OH NO, NO, OHOH SO I SAY, BROTHERS AND SISTERS CLEAN UP YOUR WAY, I BRING TO YOU SALVATION TODAY, TEK IT OR LEAVE IT (TAKE IT OR LEAVE IT), JAH NAW REFUSE IT, HE ABUNDANTLY PARDON, SO HEAR WHAT I SAYYY, TEK IT OR LEAVE IT (TAKE IT OR LEAVE IT), TEK IT OR LEAVE IT (TAKE IT OR LEAVE IT),

CAUSE JAH ABUNDANTLY PARDON OH WOW, WOW, WOW YEA OH WOW, WOW, WOW YEA, TEK IT OR LEAVE IT (TAKE IT OR LEAVE IT), AYE, MI NAW SAY NUTHING MORE TO YOU MI SAY TEK IT OR LEAVE IT, PARDON THAT

JAH HAVE GOT FOR YOU, OO OO, BECAUSE YOU DESTROYED MA HUMANITY OH O HO HOW YEA, DESTROYED MA HUMANITY

SO I SAY TEK IT OR LEAVE IT (TAKE IT OR LEAVE IT), AYE, SALVATION I BRING TO YOU, SO BOW DOWN AND CHANGE YOUR WAYS, OH, OH, YAE BOW DOWN TO JAH THE ALMIGHTY ONE, CHANGE YOUR WAYS AND BE STRONG WOW, WOW YEA, THIS A DI (THE) GARDEN PATH THING YEA AND MI NAW TELL YOU NO MORE, THE GARDEN PATH THING AN A IT A RUN THE PLACE FI SURE, A SO MI SAY YOU AFFI TEK IT OR LEAVE IT, TEK IT OR LEAVE IT, CAUSE MI NEVER TROD DEM LANDS BEFOREEE, NO MI NEVER TROD DEM LANDS BEFORE, AFGANISTAN, OH, OH AH AHN OH YEAH, PALESTINIAN LANDS, WHO, WO, WHO OOH, OOH, WHOOO, SYRIA I SAY TEK IT OR LEAVE IT, TEK IT OR LEAVE IT, YOU NATIONS OF WAR, BRING THE PEACE, SALVATION I BRING, SALVATION I BRING, JAH WILLING TO PARDON, JAH WILLING TO PARDON, JAH WILLING TO PARDON, AH SO MI SAY TEK IT OR LEAVE IT, TEK IT OR LEAVE IT, JAH WILLING TO PARDON, JAH BRING ABUNDANT SALVATION TO YOU, HE WILL PARDON YOU ABUNDANTLY, OH CHILDREN, CHILDREN OF JACOB, OH O HOW YEA, TEK IT OR LEAVE IT,

HAVING STRAYED UNTO THEIR GOSPEL IN PARTS AND CREATED THROUGH UNBELIEF IN JESUS CHRIST AND THE GOD WHO CREATED THE HEAVEN AND THE EARTH. THEY HAVE HATED THE LORD JESUS WITH THE ENMITY OF CHRIST AND THEIR BROTHERS AND SISTERS IN THEIR MINDS, IN THEIR ANTICIPATION OF HATE FROM THEIR CALLING TO THE BATTLE FIELDS OF HATE. SETTING THEIR EVIL HEARTS AND EVIL DEEDS OF SACRIFICING MANKIND TO SEE PARADISE TO BECOME CHILDREN OF DARKNESS UP TO THE HIGH TIME. OF THE HIGHEST GOD. THEY MUST MUSTER A LITTLE STRENGTH TO RELINQUISH THE DARKNESS UPON THEM BY GREED IN THE DARK AND DARK SAYINGS AGAINST THE PEOPLE OF THIS WORLD IN THE DARKNESS OF THEIR BELIEF AT WORK FOR A GOD FROM A PROPHET OF DARKNESS. SUCH MUST RETURN TO GOD AND THE LIGHT OF FREE SALVATION FROM A GOD THEY NEVER THOUGHT EXISTED BUT CREATED THEIR OWN.

THEY MUST EXTEND PEACE AND LOVE TO THOSE HAVING NOT STRAYED UNTO THEIR GOSPEL IN PARTS THAT WAS CREATED THROUGH

UNBELIEF IN JESUS CHRIST AND THE GOD WHO CREATED THE HEAVEN AND THE EARTH. TO LIVE IN THE LIGHT OF THE LORD JESUS CHRIST ONLY, FOR THE LIBERALITY FOCUSES ON THE LIGHT FOR EVERMORE UNDER THE TABERNACLE IN THE SUN.

THE SEVEN SERMONS OF THE SPIRITUAL CHURCH OF THE MANIFOLD WISDOM OF GOD

THE FIRST (1ST) SERMON

HOLINESS HATH BECOME THINE HOUSE

FOR YET THE PRIEST MOUTH IS FIEND BUT IN YET A LITTLE WHILE UNDERSTANDING COMETH UNTO HIM TO KNOW THAT THE LIGHT OF JESUS CHRIST CANNOT DWELL WITH THE DARKNESS SO WITH UNDERSTANDING OF THE LIBERALITY OUT OF THE MOUTH OF THE PRIEST, SHALL COME FORTH KNOWLEDGE? SO, PREPARED BY THE MINISTER OF THE LORD THY GOD ORDAINED TO FULFILL THE EFFECTIVE WORKING OF GOD IN THE LIBERALITY FOR THE SPIRITUAL CHURCH OF THE MANIFOLD WISDOM OF GOD, TO CONTINUE IN A NEW PATHWAY FOR THE UNITY OF THE CHURCHES. FOR IN THE HIGH TIME THE LORD THY GOD WILL GO WITH YOU TO BLESS YOUR PEOPLE WITH HIS WILL THROUGH HIS GRACE AND MERCIES OF HIS LOVE BY BRINGING UNTO YOU THE PREPARED WAY BY AGAIN CAPTAIN FRANCIS CHARLES MALCOLM, THE MESSENGER GREATER THAN JOHN THE BAPTIST AND ALSO GREATER THAN JOHN THE REVELATOR IN THE HIGH TIME. COMING UNTO YOU AND USWARD WITH THE SWORD OF THE SPIRIT, THE WORD OF THE FULL TRUTH, THE SPIRIT OF OUR LORD OUR GOD, AND NOT OF YOUR LAWS AND ORDINANCES OF MAN BUT WITH THAT OF GOD'S ORDINANCES. "THE GARDEN PATH" / "THE STIR" /" THE FACEBOOK PLUS MODERATION" /

"THE LIBERALITY" / "THE SPIRITUAL CHURCH OF THE MANIFOLD WISDOM OF GOD" / "THE TABERNACLE IN THE SUN" / "THE SPIRITUAL MAN OF LOVE" / "WE THE ENTRUSTED" THE BRAZEN WALL OF FIRE FOR THE RECONCILED UNTO GOD, WHEREWITH SHALL MAN FAULTER ANYMORE WITH GOD, UNDER THE WILL OF MAN, BUT GROW SPIRITUALLY IN FAITH AND HOPE IN GRACE AND THE LAW OF LOVE.

THE SPIRITUAL CHURCH OF THE MANIFOLD WISDOM OF GOD WILL UNIFY ALL MEN IN ALL QUARTERS OF LIFE AROUND HE WORLD TO BE AT PEACE WITH EACH OTHER UNER "WE THE ENTRUSTED" THE BURNING WALL OF FLAME TO ALLOW THE PATIENT SAINTS TO TASTE OF THE LOVE OF

GOD. THIS IS THE TRUTH OF GOD'S WISDOM TO EDIFY AND DIRECT THE CHURCH IN TRANSFORMATION TO HOLINESS IN THE HOUSE OF GOD AND THE TEMPLE OF MAN, UNDER THE TABERNACLE IN THE SUN. THIS TRUTH IS NOT OF CONTENTION WITH THOSE WANTING TO COMPROMISE THE HIGH TIME. THEY HAVE COMPROMISED THE GOSPEL IN PARTS FOR 2018 YEARS SEEKING THEIR OWN MEAT. IF THEY CANNOT COME INTO THE LIGHT OF JESUS CHRIST THEN STAY IN THE DARKNESS OF PERDITION WHERE THEY WILL ONLY CONTINUE TO RIDE SATAN UNTIL THE COMING OF OUR LORD IN DESPITE UNTO GRACE.

THE FINISHER'S KNOWLEDGE FROM FRANCIS CHARLES MALCOLM IS THE ONLY WARNING IN THE HIGH TIME WARNING SET OUT NOW IN THE HAND OF THE SEVEN (7) ANGELS UPON THE CANDLE STICK WITH THE PATIENT SAINTS, OUT OF THE MOUTH OF THE PRIEST SHALL COME KNOWLEDGE FROM THE UNDERSTANDING GATHERED HENCE SETTING NO MORE EVIL UPON THE CHILDREN OF MEN BUT LOVE TO HUMANITY TO OVERCOME THE ILLS OF SOCIETY? I CHARGE YOU TODAY TO HEAR AND SEE THE SWORD OF GOD — I COME IN THE SPIRIT OF THE LORD JESUS CHRIST, DO BELIEVE AND TAKE THE SWORD IN FAITH WHEN THOU SHALL HEAR AND SEE. THEN BEGIN YOUR SUP WITH THE LORD JESUS CHRIST.

YEA LET US NOW SAY, MAJESTY, MAJESTY, MAJESTY WITH GOD'S KINGOM IS HERE. THE CALAPHATE YOU MUST PUT ASIDE AND BEAR IN MIND YOU ARE THE CHILDREN OF GOD. JAH THE ALMIGHTY WELCOME YOU TO SALVATION IN HIS HOLY AND PRECIOUS NAME.

HOLLLOWED BE THE NAME OF THE GOD OVER ALL THE EARTH AND OF HEAVEN ABOVE, AND EXTOL HIS MIGHTY NAME JAH.

FOR HE LIVETH IN THE CHURCH FROM THE FOUNDATIONS OF THE CHURCH THROUGH OUT THE AGES, HE LIVETH THROUGH THE TRANSFORMATION OF THOSE WHO DISBELIEVED IN HIM FORMING THEIR OWN BIBLES AND THE CALLAPHATE TO REDEEM HIM WHO IS GOD. GOD IS RIGHTEOUS ALLTOGETHER AND HIS SON JESUS CHRIST IS THE ONLY REDEEMER. GOD GAVE YOU WISDOM TO WRITE OTHER BIBLES AND STILL YOU CAN'T REDEEM HIM, YOU MUST REDEEM THE SELF. IN YOUR DEATH AND DESTRUCTIONS, YOU STILL CAN'T REDEEM HIM, HENCE LOOK T THE SELF AND REFORM. IN SOOTH SAYING YOU STILL CAN'T REDEEM HIM. I CALL YOU BACK TO THE GARDEN PATH TO REDEEM YOURSELVES FROM THE GREAT TRANSGRESSION AGAINST YOUR GOD COME TAKE IT OR LEAVE IT, IT IS FREE, YOUR SALVATION FROM GOD BECAUSE GOD LOVES YOU.

I COMES ONTO YOU WITH THE SPIRIT OF OUR LORD GOD, NOT OF YOUR LAWS, WITH, [THE GARDEN PATH 1, 2 & 3 CREW, THE MODERATION, THIS SPIRITUAL MAN OF LOVE WHO BELIEVED IN THE WORDNWITH A PREPARED WAY FOR YOUR SALVATION. HAVING FORTIETED THE FREE GIFT THEN FULL REPENTANCE WITH YOUR CHURCH THROUGH THE SPIRITUAL CHURCH OF THE MANIFOLD WISDOM OF GOD. TO TASTE OF THE LOVE OF GOD. THIS IS THE TRUTH, OF GOD'S WISDOM TO EDIFY AND DIRECT THE CHURCH].

YOU HAVE TREAD OWN THE SMALLER CATTLE ENOUGH FROM YOUR HILLS AND GOD IS IN THE BUSINESS OF BUILDING GARDENS NOT FOR THE CREATION OF BRIERS AND THORNS. YOUR HEADS ARE SICK WITHOUT SOUNNESS, AS YOU MAKE YOUR COUNTRY DESOLATE

IT IS TIME TO SANCTIFY THE LORD OF HOST AND LET HIM BE YOUR FEAR FOR NOW THE PEOPLE ARE FULL OF YOUR CONFEDERACY, AND NEITHER WISH TO FEAR YOU ANY MORE, YOU HAVE WEARIED MANY MEN BUT YOU CANNOT WEARRY GOD, WHO WILL GIVE YOU SALVATION OR CUT YOU OFF. SO, PUT AWAY YOUR EVIL. CAUSE WHEN YOU SPREAD YOUR HANDS TO PRAY BEFORE GOD. YOU BRING YOUR VAIN OBLATIONS. GOD WILL HIDE HIS EYES FROM

YOUR HANDS AND FROM YOUALL. AN WHEN YOU MAKE MANY PRAYERS, HE WILLHIDEHIS EARS FROM HEARING THEM YOUR HANDS ARE FULL OF BLOOD. WASH YOU MAKE YOURSELVES CLEAN AND PUT AWAY YOUR EVIL FROM

BEFORE GOD. LEARN NOW FROM THE GARDEN PATH TO O WELL, LEARN TO DO GOOD. SEEK JUDGEMENT AND RELIEVE THE OPPRESSED, JUDGE THE FATHERLESS AND PLEAD FOR THE WIDOWS YOU HAVE MADE. COME NOW AN LET US REASON MY GOD IS CALLING FOR YOU TO TAKE IT OR LEAVE IT. COME NOW THOU YOUR SINS MAY BE LIKE SCARLET THEY CAN BE WHITE AS SNOW. IF YOU ARE WILLING AND OBEDIENT, HE WILL MAKE YOU EAT OF THE LAND, AND IN THIS TIME IF YOU REFUSE AND REBEL MORE AGAINST GOD YOU WILL BE DEVOURED. YOUR REDEMPTION IS FREE, COME LET US REASON TAKE IT OR LEAVE IT. FOR WHERE YOU HAVE MADE EVIL CLEAVAGES IN THE MOUNTAINS OF THE LORD, THERE IN THESE LAST DAY YOU SHALL RETURN TO EXALT THE LORD GOD LIKE AS IN JERUSALEM AN SANCTIFY THE NAME OF THE LORD THY GOD, REMOVING THYSELF FROM EVIL DEEDS, HUMBLE YOUR SELVES AND PUT AWAY LOFTY LOOKS PUT DOWN YOUR IDOLS. OR UPON HIS COMING THERE YOU WILL ENTER INTO THE ROCKS AND HIDE THERE IN THE DUST MADE THEREOF BY THE GREAT ONE, AND FROM THE FEAR OF THE LORD AND HIS HOLY MAJESTY, LET GOD ALONE BE MAGNIFIED IN THAT TIME, AND SO THE DAY OF THE LORD WILL BE UPON ALL HIGH TOWER AND HIGH AND LOFTY MEN.

NOW EXALT THE NATION METED OUT AND TRODDEN UNDER FEET FOR SO LONG, PEELED AND SCATTERED, AS A PEOPLE TERRIBLE FROM THE BIGINING TO WHEREEVER THEY ARE, WHOSE LAND THE RIVERS HAVE SPOILED TO A PLACE OF THE NAME OF THE LORD OF HOST "MOUNT ZION" IS ON HIGH WATCHING OVER YOU. FOR YOUR WOE IS COME BUT OUT OF THE LORD THY GOD COME MOUNT ZION. JOIN

HANDS IN MOUNT ZION WITH THE PEOPLE OF GOD WHOM ARE ENTRUSTED WITH THE WORD, SO THAT THE PEOPLE CAN BE METED OUT TO THEIR GOOD IN THE LAST DAYS. THEN WE ALL BUILD GARDENS BETTER THAN THOSE OF EDEN.

IT IS AT A TIME WHEN THE FIRE IS GONE OUT OF HER BRANCHES, WHICH HATH DEVOURED HER FRUITS SO THAT SHE HATH NO STRONG ROD, TO BE A SCEPTRE TO RULE, THIS IS YOUR

LAMENTATION. REEURN TO GOD, AND WASH YOURSELVES IN THE SPIRIT OF GRACE AND LOVE WITH BELIEF OF THE ENTIRE HEART IN GOD. REPENTANCE IS FREE FOR YOU ALL EVEN THOSE OFF THE BATTLE FIELD.

SHALL I ASK YOU WHAT TIME WAS IT? IT IS A TIME OF SALVATION AND I MEAN FREE SALVATION FOR SOME, THE STIR TO SAVE SOME AND THE MODERATION ON FACE BOOK TO SAVE OTHERS. THEN IT WILL BE REPENTANCE AND BELIEF IN THE WORD TO SAVE MANY MORE. THE TIME IS THE LAST DAYS. BUT GOD WILL NOT PREVAIL IN THE HEARTS OF ALL MEN AND THOUGH THEY MAY HEAR THE TRUTJ WILL GO DOWN INTO PERDTION AS HATERS OF THE WORD.

REMEMBER WE ARE NOT EVEN ON ONE ACCORD YET. FOR THE SEVEN (7) ANGELS OF THE LORD LIVETH IN DOMINATION IN THE CHURCH IN THE HIGH TIME, IT WILL NOT ANYMORE BE THE PRIESTS THING TO CONTROL THE WORD AND THE CANDLE STICKS OF THE LORD THY GOD, WITH THE MANNIFOLD WISDOM.OF THE NEW GOSPEL, THE FULL GOSPEL, AND THE NEW COVENANT OF GOD. THE GOD OF THE HEAVEN AND THE EARTH, THE GOD OF THE TABERNACLE IN THE SUN, THE GOD OF THE MESSENGER, THE GOD OF THE FINISHER, THE GOD OF THE SEVEN SPIRIT, THE GOD TO BE MADE MANIFEST TO ALL THE EARTH, THE GOD OF HEAVEN AND EARTH YEA THE LORD REIGNETH AND IS CLOTHED WITH MAJESTY. BUT, BEAR IN MIND THAT THE LORD IS CLOTHED WITH STRENGHT WHEREWITH HE HATH GIRED HIMSELF.

THE WORLD ALSO IS ESTABLISHED THAT IT CANNOT BE MOVED AND MANKIND YOU CANNOT MOVE THE WORLD. MANKIND YOU CANNOT CHANGE THE GOD OF MAJESTY. HUMBLE YOURSELVES BEFORE HIM GOD AND PUT THE CALLAPHATE DOWN. BE PURGED OF EVIL AND WORSHIP

HIM IN EVERLASTING GREATNESS FOR THE LORD GOD WILL SAY ONTO YOU THAT HIS THRONE IS ESTABLISHED OF OLD, IT IS FROM EVERLASTING TO EVERLASTING. BELIEVE NOW THAT YOU

CANNOT CHANGE GOD, NEVER CHANGE GO ALMIGHTY, HIS MAJESTY IS EVERLASTING, WORSHIP HIM IN SPIRIT AND IN TRUTH, YOU GOT TOUNDERSTAND ME., AND WORSHIP THE LORD THY GOD IN SPIRIT AN IN TRUTH.

THE HOLINESS OF THE LORD JESUS CHRIST AND OF GOD YOU MUST ESTABLISH UPON YOUR HEARTS AND KEEP THE RESTORATION OF THE

PEOLE PEELED AND SCATTERED UPON YOUR HEARTS BEFORE GOD IN HIS HOLY HILLS. LET THE BLACK MAN BEGIN TO REAP SOME PEACE AND LOVE FOR HIS SELF WORTH AND HIS FREEDOM TO LIVE AS A MAN.

THIS IS AND WAS THE FIGHT AGAINST GOD PARTONE 01 IT IS TIME FOR THE LORD TO WORK FOR THEY HAVE MADE VOID HIS LAWS BEFORE HE THE LORD HATH DONE IT. FOR THE LORD SAID BE NOT CONFEDERATES WITH THEM, THE SOOTH SAYERS GOD CANNOT BE MOCKED, NEITHER FEAR THEIR FEARS, NOR BE AFRAID BUT SANCTIFY THE LORD OF HOST AN MAKE THE LORD GOD OF HOST OUR FEAR. FOR IT IS WRITTEN THAT THEY SHOULD'ST FEAR GOD AND RETURN FROM THEIR EVIL WAY WASHING AWAY THE BLOOD IN THEIR HANDS AND CLEAVE TO THE DUST IN THE ROCKS OF THEIR MOUNTAINS TO HIDE FOR THEY HAVE FORSAKEN THE LORD OUR GOD. THEIR DESIRED GARDENS ARE FAKE AND THE OAKS IN IT FADE. FOR YET THEY HAD NO WATER THE LIVING WATERS OF CHRIST JESUS. GO SHALL ARISE IN HIS JUDGEMENT AND SHALL SHAKE THE EARTH TERRIBLE AND YEA THEIR FEARS CATCH HOLD OF THEM. TO CEASE FROM MAN WHOSE BREATH IS IN HIS NOSTRILS AND SURELY, HE WILL ACCOUNT OF IT. SO SHALL GOD CUT THE BASE AGAINST THE HONORABLE AND WOE TO THE WICKED IT SHALL BE ILL WITH HIM, BUT UNTO THE RIGHTEOUS IT SHALL BE WELL. LEANING ON THE PEOPLE PEELED AS THEY ADMONISH

THE MIGHTY GO IN FEAR OF HIS MAJESTY BRINGING BACK SOME HOLINESS TO HIS WORSHIP. FOR YET THEY SHALL BE DRIVEN TO DARKNESS BUT I WILL WAIT UPON THE LORD OF HOST THAT HIDETH HIS FACE FROM THE HOUSE OF JACOB, AND I WILL LOOK FOR HIM. THEY SPEAK NOT ACCORDING TO THIS TESTIMONY THEREFORE THEIR

IS NO LIGHT IN THEM BUT UTTER DARKNESS? THEY SHALL PASS THROUGH IT ALL WITH NO HUNGER BUT THE FIGHT AGAINST GOD WILL NOT PREVAIL FOR SOON THEY WILL BE HUNGRY, CURSING THEIR KING AND LOOKING UPWARDS AFTER DRIVING THEMSELVES TO DARKNESS. AND UNTO THEM THEY THAT DWELL IN THIS DARKNESS I BRING THE GREAT LIGHT SO THAT

IT WILL SHINE UPON THEM AND THEY CAN WALK WITH GOD. THE ZEAL OF THE LORD THY GOD WILL PERFORM THIS.

THIS IS AND WILL BE THE FIGHT AGAINST GOD PART TWO (2) THE

GREATER LIGHT FROM THE LITTLE LIGHT IN THE DARKNESS. IS COME UNTO MEN TO SHOW HOW THE FIGHT WAS ESTABLISHED IN THE CHURCH BY MEANS OF SEEKING MEAT AND WILL HAVE TO DECAY AND VANISH. THIS IS THE WILL OF GOD. THE END THEREOF IS THE WILL OF THE CHURCH. HAVING BEEN CONFUSED ABOUT THE MARK OF THE BEAST AND HAVING PREACHED IT TO THEIR ADVANCEMENT IN THE ADMONISHING OF THEMSELVES IN THE ORDINANCES OF MAN. ARE NOT WILLING TO BLESS THE MESSENGER. THE MESSAGE IS DO NOT JOIN A CONSPIRACY. SAY NOW NO TO THE GREATEST CONFEDERACY AGAINST JESUS CHRIST AND GOD BY THE CHURCH IN THE HIGH TIME.

MANKIND IS NOT WILLING TO BLESS THE MESSENGER. THE MESSENGER GREATER THAN JOHN THE BAPTIST AND GREATER THAN JOHN THEREVELATOR. THE MESSENGER WHO IS THE FINISHER. FOR HAVING COME WITH THE LIGHT OF THE SPIRIT AND TO SAVE THOSE OF THE FOLD IN THE PREISTHOOD OF JESUS CHRIST, THEY BECOME ENVIOUS, JEALOUS OF THE MESSENGER AND HIS WORK FROM THE GARDEN PATH TO TEN IT TAKE IT OR LEAVE IT, THE WORLD ECONOMIC DEVELOPMENT PLAN AND THE LETTER TO THE UNITED NATION FOR BLACK PEOPLES ANCESTORS REWARD AND RESENTFUL THEY BECOME, THEY THEMSELVES ADMONISHING THE MARK OF THE BEAST THEMSELVES, NOT BLESSING THE POOR AND NEEDY, HAVING NO LOVE ONE TO ANOTHER, AND TO CONTINUE TO WORSHIP THE LORD THY GOD IN THE ORDINANCES OF MAN INSTEAD OF IN SPIRIT AND IN TRUTH BEARING THE GREAT LIGHT ONE TO ANOTHER.

FOLLOW ME THE MESSENGER, THE MINISTER WITH THE EFFECTIVE WORKINGS OF THE LORD THE MESSENGER GREATER THAN JOHN THE BAPTIST AND GREATER THAN JOHN THE REVELATOR, WHICH YOU ALL MUST FOLLOW ME IN THE LAST DAYS FOR THE FULL UNDERSTANDING OF THE NEW GOSPEL AND THE NEW COVENANT, OF THE PREPARED WAY BY GOD THE ALMIGHTY UNTO THE FOUR (4) CORNERS OF THE EARTH.

THE SECOND (2ND) SERMON

THE SPIRITUAL CHILD OF GOD

THE THRUTH WILL SET YOU FREE, THE THRUTH WILL SET YOU FREE, THE THRUTH WILL SET YOU FREE, TO BE A CHILD OF GOD. IT IS ONLY TO BE HUMBLE IN YOURSELF WITH THE SPIRIT AND LOVE OF JESUS CHRIST. AS YOU HUMBLY ASK FOR THE BODY OF CHRIST, TAKE IT UNTO YOURSELF WITH A WILLING HEART OF BELIEVING IN HIM. FOR NO MAN CAN ASK FOR THE BODY OF CHRIST FROM ANY MAN AND ALLOW HIMSELF TO RECEIVE IT FROM SUCH A MAN.

FOR HIS SALVATION IS PERSONAL. IT IS A PERSONAL MENTAL MODE OF RECOGNITION AND CONNECTION BY A FEW THINGS SUCH AS WASHING OF THE FEET AND THE DRINKING OF HIS WINE FOR THE RECEIVING OF THE PROMISE THROUGH FAITH AND REMEMBERANCE.THIS HOLY BODY OF CHRIST A PERSONAL MENTAL STATE OF ACCEPTANCE OF THE SPIRIT OF GOD AND HIS SON THE LORD JESUS CHRIST. IT IS A PERSONAL MENTAL STATE OF RELEASE FROM YOUR OLD WAYS, TO A STATE OF PREMIIUM BELIEF IN GOD AND HIS SON AS YOUR SAVIOUR FROM SIN.

AND AS YOU BECOME PURE AND TRUE IN THE SPIRIT OF GOD YOU BEGIN TO WORSHIP GOD IN SPIRIT AND IN TRUTH. HIS PRESENCE AROUND YOU BECOMES JOY AND POWER. YOU WILL BE FILLED WITH SALVATION THROUGH JESUS CHRIST. WHEN THE SPIRIT OF GOD BECOMES A PART OF YOU, YOU BECOME A NEW CREATURE, TAKING YOUR FERVENT LOVE THAT YOU HAVE FOD GOD, TO NEW HEIGHTS OF HUMAN CONSCIOUSNESS, NOW SEEING THE SELF BEING MORE ACCEPTABLE THAN A GROUPED MINDSET ON YOUR GOD AS A SELFISH COMMAND POST, BUT HE IN YOU TO HAVE DOMINION OVER ALL THINGS. THE SPIRIT OF GOD LEADS YOU TO TRADE IN YOUR WEAPONS, YEA, YOUR WEAPONS OF DESTRUCTION TO HUMANITY THAT YOU'LL NEVER NEED ANYMORE.

AS YOU GRRAPPLE WITH SALVATION NOT AT THE FOOTSTOOL OF MEN BUT BY THE SIDE OF JESUS CHRIST, HE WHO IS ABLE TO BAPTIZE YOU IT THE SPIRIT OF GOD, WILL AND RECEIVE YOU UNTO HIMSELF AS A NEW MAN.

YOU BECOME A CHILD OF GOD PARTICIPATING IN THE SPIRITUAL CHURCH OF THE MANIFOLD WISDOM OF GOD UNDER THE TABRERNACLE IN THE SUN. AND BE SAVED LIKE THE GREAT MULTITUDE FROM SIN AND BE SET FREE BY HIS BLOOD. YOU WILL FIND THE MERCIES OF GOD FULFILLING. AS YOU RECOGNISE THAT GOD IS MORE TERRIBLE, THAN YOU HUMANS WHOM HAVE DESIGNED YOURSELVES INTO GODS. YOU WILL FIND GOD AND LOVE HIM. AS NO MAN CAN CONFINE A SPIRITUAL ELEVATOR TO THE GROUND,

YOU WILL FIND OUT THAT YOUR OPPORTUNITY TO FELLOWSHIP WITH GOD IS NOT NDUCED BY MAN. YOUR OPPORTUNITY IS NOT INDUCED WITH SOOTH SAYING. YOUR OPPORTUNITY IS NOT INDUCED BY THE ORDINANCES OF MAN, BECAUSE THE ORDINANCES OF MAN HAVE NEVER BEEN PURE. BECAUSE THE ORDINANCES OF MAN HAVE NEVER BEEN TRUTHFULL EVEN UPON THE ALTER OF GOD'S HOLY SYNAGOGUES. BECAUSE THE ORDINANCES OF MAN HAVE BEEN A PEDESTAL FOR SOCIETY'S CONTROL OVER PEOPLE. BECAUSE THE ORDINANCES OF MAN HAVE NEVER BEEN PURE. BECAUSE THE ORDINANCES OF GOD HAVE BEEN TRODDEN ON BY MEN. BECAUSE THE ORDINANCES OF MAN CANNOT RELINDLE THE SPIRIT OF GOD IN THE HUMAN SOUL. BECAUSE THE ORDINANCES OF MAN HAVE RIOTED AGAINST THE SPIRI. BECAUSE THE ORDINANCES OF MAN HAVE RIOTED AGAINST GOD. BECAUSE THE ORDINANCES OF MAN HAVE RIOTED AGAINST THE BODY OF CHRIST. BECAUSE THE ORDINANCES OF MAN HAVE RIOTED AGAINST THE ONLY CREATOR. BECAUSE THE ORDINANCES OF MAN HAVE FOUGHT FOR THEIR BELIEFS IN IN ANOTHER GOD AND HAVE FORSAKEN THEIR GOD AND HIS ORDINANCES. BECAUSE THE ORDINANCES OF MAN HAVE REPELLED THE PRESENCE OF THE LORD

GOD IS HERE THERE AND EVERY WHERE, BUT YOU IN THE FLESHY SELF HAVE NOT REPELLED THE ORDINANCES OF MAN AS THEY WERE YET THE DOORS OF REDEMPTION AND YOUR SALVATION AMONGST THE NOW HEADING DOWN INTO PERDITION IF YOU CONTINUE.

NOW YOU ARE THROUGH THE DOORS AND HAVE SEEN THE LIGHT OF JESUS CHRIST. TO MAKE GOOD IS YOUR OWN RESPONSE TO A CALLING FROM THE UNDERSTANDING OF THE NEW GOSPEL IN THE NEW COVENANT OF THE FULL GOSPEL OF GOD. NOW THE WHEAT AND THE TARES ARE IN THE SAME BOAT THEY ALL HAVE FAULTS BUT SO MUCH DIFFERENT FROM EACH OTHER BUT TARES DON'T SEE PERDITION UP THEIR STREET THEY SEE REDEMPTION FROM SIN IN A NEW WAY OF FINDING LOVE IN THEIR HEARTS TO CHANGE AND ACCEPT SALVATION FROM THEIR EVIL DEEDS TO THE LAW OF LOVE. BUT THE SELF RIGHTEOUS IS IN LIMBO WITH THEIR LUKE WARM SELVES WONDERING, AND WONDERING WHERE TO TURN TO? OH, SHALL WE RETURN TO GOD? AND THE ALL HAVE THE ANSWER THEY ARE ALREADY RIGHTEOUS AND SERVING GOD. SO THAT IS WHY IT WILL BE EVERYMAN FOR HIMSELF IN THE HIGH TIME. IT IS EVERYMAN FOR HIMSELF, YOUR MOTHER AND FATHER CAN'T RESCUE YOU. YOUR BROTHER CAN'T RESCUE YOU; YOUR SISTER CAN'T RESCUE YOU. YOU HAVE BEEN CALLED TO WORSHIP HIM IN SIPIRIT AND IN TRUTH. THE WORD TRUTH MEANS FIND THE TRUTH AND TEACH IT, LEAVING THE OVERLY GREEDY AMBITIONS OF SEEKING YOUR OWN MEAT AND RETURN TO THE TRUTH OF GOD.

IN THE END IF YOU HAVE BEEN SEEN TO BE FAITHFUL, YEA REALLY SEEN TO BE FAITHFUL, IT SIMPLE MEANS THAT YOU HAVE FOUND THE FOUNDATION OF YOUR FAITH IN THE BODY AND SPIRIT OF CHRIST, THAT HAVE BAPTIZED YOU IN THE SPIRITOF GOD, AND HAVE MADE YOU A NEW MAN, NOW A FRUIT OF JESUS CHRIST. HE THAT MADE YOU WILL ALSO DO A NEW THING FOR YOU, UNTIL YOU ALL LEAD MANY TO COME TO THE MERCY SEAT OF GOD. WHERE SALVATION WILL RESCUE THE PERISHING AND JESUS WILL CARE FOR THE DYING, THE SPIRIT OF GOD WILL SEE YOU THROUGH WHEN YOU SUBMIT YOURSELVES IN GLORY AND HONOUR TO THE LORD JESUS CHRIST, IN SPIRIT AND IN TRUTH TO BE BAPTIZED IN THE SPIRIT OF GOD, AND AS A REWARD, YOU WILL ACCEPT THE SEAL OF HIS MERCY AND BE IN POWER WITH THE LORD JESUS CHRIST

IN KNOWING THESE THINGS, PUT DOWN YOUR WEAPONS OF DESTRUCTION AND FARM THE LAND INSTEAD, CLEANING YOUR HEART WITH THE SPIRIT OF GOD, LOVE AND THE SHARING OF THE LIGHT. SO YOU WILL NOT STEAL THE MOTHER'S MILK FROM THE SUCKLING SHE BEARS, BUT REPLENISH THE EARTH AS YOU REPLENISHES YOUR SOUL IN THE SPIRIT OF GOD, LEAVE YOUR EMPOWER SELF TO CAUSE OBSTRUCTION HUMAN PROGRESS WITH SUFFERING AND FOR OTHER, FILTHINESS OF SELF AND MIND POURING DOWN ON OTHERS TO MAKE ALL UNWORTHY.

FREE YOURSELF WITH THE TRUTH IN WISDOM OF GOD, WHETHER YOU ARE WILLING OR NOT TO LEAVE THE EPHEMERAL CHURCHE, FOR THEY ARE IN A BALANCING ACT THAT WILL NOT ALLOW THEM OF THEM TO REPRESENT GODLINESS BUT REPRESENTS BABYLON. SO THAT YOUR CHOICE OF REAL FREEDOM IN THE HOUSE OF GOD WILL BE TO BRING HOLINESS BACK TO THE HOUSE OF GOD, FROM BEING FAITHFUL NOW TO THE SPIRIT OF GOD THAT WILL BE DWELLING WITHIN YOU FROM ACCEPTANCE OF SALVATION FREELY OR BELIEVING IN THE TRUE GOD OF CREATION OR BEING REPENTANT.

BEING NOT BOND IN ORDINANCES OF MAN THAT CONDEMNS YOU WITH EVERTHING YOU DO EAT OR SAY, ESPECIALLY THE ONES YOU SHOULD NEVER BE, A PART OF BEING BLACK, BEING A CHILD OF JAH, BORN FREE YET IN SLAVERY. OR IN ANY OTHER COLOUR AS YOU COME TOGETHER WITH LOVE IN THE HUMAN RACE. PUT YOUR SPIRIT IN LINE WITH THE SPIRIT OF GOD AND BE FREE IN THE SPIRIT OF GOD. REMOVE YOURSELVES FROM THE MARK OF THE BEAST THAT CARRIES HATRED TO ALL MEN FOR THEMSELVES AS LOVE FOR THEMSELVES AND NOT LOVE UNTO ALL MEN. BE SEALED WITH JESUS IN YOUR LIFE AS YOU WALK IN BEAUTY OF HIS HOLINESS, FINDING THE FREEDOM OF THE MIND THAT THE LAST DAYS PEOPLE WILL ALL HAVE TO FIND, TO GET RECOMPENCE FOR THE ATROCITIES AGAINST HUMANITY, IN THE GREAT MASSIVE WAY IS THE

ESCHATS WAY, OF THE NEW SENSATION OF SPIRITUAL AWAKENING IN THE SPIRITUAL CHURCH OF THE MANIFOLD WISDOM OF GOD.

I CHARGE YOU TODAY TO HEAR AND SEE THE SWORD OF GOD, I COME IN THE SPIRIT OF THE LORD JESUS CHRIST, DO BELIEVE THE SWORD OF THE SPIRIT IN FAITH WHEN THOU SHALL HEAR AND SEE THIS SERMON ASK FOR REPENTANCE, THE THRUTH WILL SET YOU FREE AS YOU HUMBLE YOURSELF IN CHRIST JESUS.

THE THIRD (3RD) SERMON

MERCY

IN AS MUCH AS WE ARE CHILDREN OF GOD, WE HAVE FAULTS BEFORE HIM AND THIS IS THE CAUSE FOR THE NEW GOSPEL AND THE NEW COVENANT IN THE HIGH TIME, AMEN. NOW GOD LOVES US ALL AND IS WILLING TO BRING US ALL INTO HIS FOLD OF RIGHTEOUSNESS ONCE MORE NOW KNOWING THE TRUTH AND HAVING THE FULL UNDERSTANDING OF THE SCRIPTURES FROM THE GARDEN PATH, ITS STIR TO THE MODERATION AND TO THE LIBERALITY AND THE SPIRITUAL CHURCH OF THE MANIFOLD WISDOM OF GOD UNDER THE TABERNACLE IN THE SUN. THAT HIS CHILDREN COMING BACK TO HIM WILL ONLY HUMBLE THEMSELVES AND TAKE HEED UNTO THE MESSENGER OF THE HIGH TIME AND FOLLOW THE MESSENGER'S ADVISE BEFORE IT IS TOO LATE. GOD WILL HAVE MERCY UPON ALL THAT SEEK HIM YEA ALL THAT SEEK HIS FACE. IF YOU LOOK AT ALL YOUR FAULTS MAYBE YOU WILL SAY YOU NEED NO MERCY BUT GOD WIPE YOUR FAULTS AWAY AND SAY COME UNTO ME FOR YOU RESPECT MY PRECEPTS AND HAVE REND YOUR HEART TO ATTAIN GLORY AND MERCY. IT IS TIME TO STOP HATING YOUR BROTHERS AND SISTERS AND MEND YUR WAYS. REMOVE YOURSELF FROM THE CONFEREDACY AGAINST THE WILL OF GOD AND LEAVE THE CONSPIRACY TO THE EVIL ONES, HAVE NO PART IN IT FOR THE GOD WHO CREATED THE HEAVEN AND THE EARTH WILL NOT HOLD YOU GUILTLESS FOR YOUR ACTS AMONGST MEN BUT COME QUICKLY UPON YOU FOR ALL YOU HAVE DONE TO HIS MESSENGER OVER THE YEARS. KNOW NOW THAT THE LORD THY GOD WILL BE KIND TO YOU. LET THE MESSENGER'S BLESSING STANDFAST UNTIL THE GREAT DAY OF THE LORD AS HIS FOR IT BELONGETH UNTO NO OTHER MAN.

THIS INHERITANCE IS OF THE LORD AND BLESSINGS FOR HIS MERCIES UPON HIM FOR HIS OPPRESSION BOURNE FROM YOU ALL THAT CONSIDERED YOURSELVES THE MOST RIGHTEOUS BEFORE GOD.

THE LORD SAID I MAKE AND GIVE YOU THE MOUNTAIN. FOR THE MOUNTAINS SHALL DEPART, AND THE HILLS BE REMOVED, BUT MY KINDNESS

SHALL NOT DEPART FROM THEE. NEITHER SHALL THE COVENANT OF MY PEACE BE REMOVED, SAITH THE LORD THAT HATH MERCY ON THEE. THIS SAITH HE WHO HATH WHO HATH MERCY ON YOU, YEA HE WHO HATH MERCY ON YOU, SURELY HE WHO HATH MERCY ON YOUTO GIVE YOU ALL REPENTANCE WITHOUT ASKING FOR REPENTANCE, BY HIS KINDNESS AND LOVE SALVATION UNTO YOU WITHOUT BEGGING FOR YOUR EVER FAITHFUL REPENTANCE, BUT JUST CHANGE THAT HAVE REDEEMED THE HEART WITH THE WHEAT AND THE TARES.

FOR HIS KINDNESS SHALL NOT DEPART FROM THEE, NEITHER SHALL THE COVENANT OF MY PEACE (THE PEACE OF THE LORD), BE REMOVED FOR THE HOUR COMETH WHEN MEN BEING THE TRUE WORSHIPERS SHALL WORSHIP GOD IN SPIRIT AND IN TRUTH JUST BY YOUR EXAMPLE IN SETTING THE PEACE.

AND JESUS SPOKE THIS OF THE TIME TO COME WHICH IS NOW THAT IT COMMETH WHEN MEN SHALL NOT GO TO THE MOUNTAIN TO WHORSHIP THE FATHER, AND MEN SHALL NOT GO TO THE PLACE CALLED JERUSALEM TO WORSHIP THE FATHER, FOR THE HOUR COMETH WHEN MEN BEING THE TRUE WORSHIPERS SHALL WORSHIP GOD IN SPIRIT AND IN TRUTH. THIS SAITH HE WHO HATH MERCY ON YOU, YEA, HE WHO HATH MERCY ON YOU, SURELY BY HE WHO HATH MERCY ON YOU. THE LIVING GOD FOR HE GAVE THEM MERCY SO THAT THEY COULD WORSHIP HIM IN SPIRIT AND IN TRUTH

THIS BLESSINGS AND CURSE WHICH THE LORD HATH SET BEFORE ME AS A PREPARED WAY OF THE LORD WILL I WILL CALL TO MIND WITH ALL NATIONS WHITHER THE LORD GOD HATH DRIVEN MEN, FOR JAH WILL TURN OUR CAPTIVITY AROUND, HE WILL HAVE COMPASSION ON THEE AND SHALL RETURN AND GATHER THEE FROM YOUR SCATTERING AMONGST NATIONS AND AMONGST MEN, THIS SAITH HE WHO HATH MERCY ON YOU. YEA, HE WHO HATH MERCY ON YOU,

SURELY, HE WHO HATH MERCY ON YOU.

HE THAT WILL BRING YOU INTO THE LANDS THAT YOUR FATHERS HAVE POSSESSED BEFORE, SO YOU CAN POSSESS IT ALSO, SO LOVE GOD WHO HAVE MERCY ON YOU, YEA HE WHO HATH MERCY ON YOU, HE SURELY, HE WHO HATH MERCY ON YOU. WHO HATH MERCY ON YOU WILL DO IT, JUST FOR YOUR OBEDIENCE UNTO HIM?

LOVE HIM WITH ALL THINE HEART, FOR PLENTY WILL HE GIVE YOU IN THESE DAYS OF HIS RETURN WHEN YOU SHALL WORSHIP HIM IN SPIRIT AND IN TRUTH, FOR THESE STATUTES ARE WRITTEN IN THE BIBLE THE

HOLY BOOK. IF THOU SHALL ASK A MAN TO BRING IT FOR YOU THEN YOU WILL NEVER GET IT.

THE WORDS ARE NIGH UNTO US AND NOT HIDDEN FROM YOU, BESANTIFIED IN IT AS UTTERED FROM MY MOUTH SO WE SHALL DO IT IN TIME OVER SEAS AND VALLEYS—THE LIVING GOD AND HE GAVE THEM MERCY SO THAT THEY COULD POSSESS THE FOREFATHERS LANDS LETS WORSHIP HIM IN SPIRIT AND IN TRUTH – HE IS A SPIRIT OF MERCY.

FOR HIS COVENANT IS ESTABLISHEDWITH US AND THAT IS GREAT MERCY. FOR THE LORD WILL NOT FORSAKE HIS PEOPLE ANDSHALL BRING JUDGEMENT UNTO THE KINGS THAT WILL CONTINUE TO FIGHT AND DO WICKEDNESS UNTO US THE CHILDREN AS WE COME INTO SPIRITUAL WORSHIP WITH GOD. THIS SAITH HE WHO HATH MERCY ON YOU, YEA, HE WHO HATH MERCY ON YOU, SURELY BY HE WHO HATH MERCY ON YOU. THE LIVING GOD FOR HE GAVE THEM MERCY SO THAT THEY COULD WORSHIP HIM IN SPIRIT AND IN TRUTH.

FOR NOW THE PEOPLE WILL RENEW THEIR STRENGTH AND YEE, ISLANDS KEEP SILENT – TO DRAW NEAR UNTO JUDGEMENT, FOR I AM COME OUT OF THE EAST SIDE OF JAMAICA UNTO YOU AND THOUGH I HAVE NOT GONE SOME PLACES WITH MY FEET DOING THE WORK AS HIS SERVANT YES HE THE FIRST AND THE LAST WHO WAS WITH ME, FOR ME HIS SWORD IS EVERLASTING AND THE WORDS ENDURETH FOREVER. GO SEE AND HEAR MY PART TO YOU FROM GOD.

WHILE I THE MESSENGER WAS COMING, THEY WERE INCENSED AGAINST ME, KEEP SILENT I SAY, I WILL NOT BE ASHAMED AND CONFOUNDED BEFORE YOU OR THEM, AND WHEN I SHALL SEEK THEM, THEY WILL NOT BE FOUND. THIS SAITH HE WHO HATH MERCY ON YOU, YEA, HE WHO HATH MERCY ON YOU, SURELY BY HE WHO HATH MERCY ON YOU. THE LIVING GOD FOR HE GAVE THEM MERCY SO THAT THEY COULD WORSHIP HIM IN SPIRIT AND IN TRUTH. HE WHO HATH MERCY ON YOU — HOLDING MY RIGHT HAND. HE WHO HATH MERCY ON YOU — SAYING FEAR NOT BEFORE MEN AS HE WHO HATH MERCY ON YOU — SAYING I THE SPIRITUAL GOD OF HEAVEN AND EARTH WILL ALSO HELP ME, THE MESSENGER.

HIS SWORD IS EVERLASTING AND THE WORDS ENDURETH FOREVER, IT ESTABLIDHED THE GARDEN PATH. IT IS NEVER A WORD STOLEN FROM YOU, AS INCRIPTED IN PATH LED BY THE LORD JESUS CHRIST MY LORD AND MY SAVIOUR. IN MY DESPENSATION YOU STOLE THE DAMN UNFINISHED PLAN, BUT GOD SAID I AM WITH YOU MALCOLM TO HELP YOU IT MUST BE DONE, IN HIS GREAT MERCY, FOR THE LORDS DAY IS AT HAND AND WE SHALL RISE WITH HIS HELP FOR AN INTRUSION INTO THE SWEETNESS

OF LIFE, AND FROM THE ROOT OF JESSE I COME WITH THE GARDEN PATH ENSIGN AND MANY SHALL SEEK IT OUT TO WILL NEED TO REMOVE ENVY THEIR HEARTS THIS MOMENT AND ONWARDS FOR THE LORD HATH GOD SHED HIS MERCY ON YOU, YEA, HE HE WHO HATH POWER TO REDEEM MANKIND, HATH SHED HIS MERCY ON YOU.

FOR STOLEN WATERS ARE SWEET AND YOU SEEK AFTER MY SOUL AND YOUR DECIETFUL TONGUE LOVETH LYING RATHER THAN GOOD

LET THE ISLANDS KEEP BE SILENT ~ TO DRAW NEAR UNTO JUDGEMENT, FOR I AM COME OUT OF THE EAST SIDE OF JAMAICA UNTO YOU, AS GOD REBUILD. I COME WITH PIPE FIVE (5) MUSIK WITH THE VOICE OF THE CITY, THE VOICE OF JAH, THE VOICE OF THE TEMPLE.

THE SWORD OF GOD IS EVERLASTING AND THE WORDS ENDURETH FOREVER — SEEK HE WHO HATH MERCY ON YOU — HOLDING YOUR RIGHT HAND AND LEADING YOU TO HIS PERFECTION WHEN I SPEAK

OF WHO HATH MERCY ON YOU — I LISTEN, HEAR AND OBEY, SAYING FEAR NOT THE EMPOWERED EVIL ONES ANYMORE FOR HE WHO HATH MERCY HAVE DONE IT, AND WILL SETTLE THE PEACE.

SO, THE LORD THY GOD WILL BEGIN TO PLANT FOR THE POOR AND THE NEEDY, A NEW GARDEN THUS SAITH HE WHO IS THE GOD OF

ISRAEL WILL NOT FORSAKE THEM. SO, LET US REJOICE AND GLORY IN THE LORD GOD OF ISRAEL, FOR THE HOLY GOD OF ISRAEL HAVE CREATED THIS THIS SAITH HE WHO HATH MERCY ON YOU, YEA, HE WHO HATH MERCY ON YOU, SURELY BY HE WHO HATH MERCY ON YOU. THE LIVING GOD FOR HE GAVE THEM MERCY SO THAT THEY COULD WORSHIP HIM IN SPIRIT AND IN TRUTH.

NOW KNOW THAT HE WHO HARH MERCY ON YOU FOR HIS MERCY IS EXCEEDLY GREAT, AND NOW THE TIME HAS COME WHEN HE WILL SHOW US HIS MERCIES

EVEN THROUGH FRE E SALVATION AND WITHOUT REPENTANCE UNTO HIM SO WE CAN COME BACK TO HIM IN ONE HEART AS ONE, NOW UNTO ALL GENERATION IS COME THE GARDEN PATH UNTO ALL GENERATIONS IS HIS MERCIES TO BUILD GARDENS MUCH MORE BEAUTIFUL THAN THAT OF EDEN.

AS HE HAVE MERCY UPON ZION TAKING IT FROM UNDERGROUND AND FROM THE INCENSED OF THOSE WHO HATED ME AND HE THE LORD GOD TO RETURN TO HIM GOD THE CREATOR TO BUILD UP ZION, FOR SOON

HE SHALL APPEAR IN HIS GLORY, SAITH HE WHO HATH MERCY ON YOU — HE SHALL APPEAR IN HIS GLORY, HE WHO HARH MERCY UPON YOU — SAYING FEAR NOT, COME UNTO ME FOR SALVATION YOU IS YOURS, FOR HIS MERCIES ENDURETH FOREVER.

THE FOURTH (4TH) SERMON

THE FEAR OF GOD

SUBMIT YOURSELVES ONE TO ANOTHER IN THE FEAR OF GOD,

BE NOT HATERS OF THE CHILDREN OF GOD. BE NO STUMBLING BLOCKS TO THE CHILDREN OF GOD. BE YE ANGRY AND BRETHEN SIN NOT. LET NOT JAH SUN SET ON YOUR ANGER. YOU USE TO STEAL THINGS STEAL NO MORE. BRETHEN IN THE FAITH AND FELLOWSHIP OF GOD WITH LOVE IN YOUR HEARTS IF YOU FIND IT TO GIVE, GIVE IT WITH LOVE IN YOUR HEARTS. IF YOU USE TO GIVE, THEN GIVE MORE TO THE NEEDY. NO ONE CAN COME INTO THE GRACE OF GOD WITH JESTING. AND ALSO, BE AWARE THAT NO ONE CAN COME INTO THE GRACE OF GOD WITH FOOLISH TALKING AND VAIN BABBLING AGAINST EACH OTHER AND TOWARDS GOD IN HIS ETERNAL REALM. NO ONE CAN COME INTO THE GRACE OF GOD, WITH FILTHINESS, FOR HE DOES REMEMBER THAT HE THAT PREACHETH FILTHINESS AND VOW THAT IT IS RIGHT AND PLEASANT IS ABOMINABLE, UNTO THE LORD JESUS CHRIST AND HE, GOD, HIMSELF, IS NOT ABLE IN REDEEMING OF THE SAINTS OF GOD. IT IS A FACT THAT NO ONE CAN COME INTO THE GRACE OF GOD WITHOUT THANKS GIVING. THEREFORE, WITH THE FEAR OF GOD IN YOUR HEARTS YOU NEED TO GIVE THANKS FOR EVERY LITTLE THING GRANTED UNTO YOU. YOU HAVE TO LEARN TO GIVE THANKS UNTO GOD.

IT IS NOW THE HIGH TIME AND IF YOU FEAR THE LORD THEN PUT AWAY LYING, AND IF YOU CAN'T THEN LEARN TO PUT AWAY LYING. AS LYING IS A FORM OF PROPAGANDA THAT BRINGS OTHERS DOWN. LEARN TO KNOW THAT WE ARE MEMBERS ONE TO ANOTHER UNDER JESUS CHRIST AND THE LOVE WE SHOULD HAVE FOR ONE ANOTHER. YOUR FOOLISH TALKING AND VAIN WORDS AS CHILDREN OF GOD, WILL CAUSE THE WRATH OF GOD WILL COME UPON YOU AS THE DISOBEDIENT NOT WILLING TO HEED GOD'S WORD.

TODAY UNDER THE NEW GOSPEL YOU ARE A NEW BEING IN THE GRACE OF GOD AND A NEW CHAPTER IS UPON YOUR LIFE, TO WALK AS CHILDREN OF THE LIGHT. REMEMBER THAT NO ONE CAN COME INTOTHE GRACE OF GOD, WITHOUT WALKING AS CHILDREN OF THE LIGHT. FROM YOUR WHOLE HEART, SPEAKING LOVING AND KIND WORDS, SETTING IT WITH MEANING

WITH MEANING, FOR THE IDEALS THAT THE NEW MAN CARRIES, WHICH WILL BE BRINGING JOY TO THE HEARERS.

REMEMBER CHILDREN OF GOD, WE WERE SOMETIMES DARKNESS BUT

NOW WE ARE LIGHT UNTO THE WORLD, THEREFORE GO OUT INTO THE WORLD AND REDEEM THE SOULS OF THE PEOPLE IN AS MUCH AS NOT TO INTERFERE WITH WHAT THEY DO, AND IN THE SPIRIT OF HUMILITY. GO OUT INTO THE WORLD AND REDEEM THE SOULS OF THE EVIL PEOPLE LIKE THEY WERE YOUR FRIENDS AND NEVER HATE THEM TO THE LEVEL OF CALLING THEM YOUR ENEMY. FOR THEY MUST LEARN TO FEAR THE LORD, OUR GOD, AND NOT FEAR MAN IN HIS EVIL DEEDS. GO OUT INTO THE WORLD AND REDEEM THE SOULS OF THE EVIL ONES UNTO JESU.S CHRIST, HE THAT WAS DEAD BUT NOW LIVES.

BROTHERS AND SISTERS, I BRING TO YOU THE MESSAGE OF GOD AND HIS SON THE LORD JESUS CHRIST. I BRING TO YOU THE MISTRY OF CHRIST AS I WROTE IN FEW WORDS ALSO IN THIS BOOK., FROM TIMES GONE BY TO THE FUTURE OF MANKIND, WHICH LEADS TO THE GARDENS TO BE CREATED BY MAN, MUCH NORE BEAUTIFUL THAN THOSE OF EDEN. IF IT WAS NOT SO I WOULD NOT HAVE TOLD YOU. IF IT WAS VAIN BABBLING, I WOULD NOT HAVE TOLD YOU. IF I DID NOT INTEND TO WRITE IT TO COMFORT YOUR WEAK PATIENT SOULS, I WOULD NOT HAVE MENTIONED LYUNION AND MONEY MAN, WHICH IN AGES GONE BY WAS NOT MADE KNOWN UNTO THE APOSTLES, BUT NOW UNTO THE PROPHETS BY THE SPIRIT OF THE LORD JESUS CHRIST.

NOW YOU SHALL HEAR THIS OLD MAN, I THE MINISTER OF GOD AND THE MESSENGER OF THE LORD JESUS CHRIST, SPEAKING AND MAKING NOTES OF JESUS CHRIST IN THE HOPE OF SAVING SOME.

IN THE HOPE OF MY CALLING UNTO YOU, IN THE FEAR OF THE LORD JESUS CHRIST I COME WITH ONE LORD, ONE FAITH, ONE BAPTISM IN THE SPIRIT OF JESUS CHRIST AND OUR GOD. IN THE FEAR OF GOD YOUR FORMER CONVERSATIONS ABOUT ME, I MEAN THIS OLD MAN, YOU PUT AWAY AND JUST REMEMBER THAT YOU WERE TOSSED AND CARRIED ABOUT BY THE WINDS OF EVERY DOCTRINE, TILL NOW THE HIGH TIME WHEN WE ALL MUST COME TOGETHER IN UNITY OF THE FAITH AND OF THE REAL KNOWLEDGE THE SON OF GOD. WHERE AS I WAS MADE A MINISTER TO BRING UNTO YOU, BY THE EFFECTIVE WORKINGS OF GOD IN THE FEAR OF GOD. I COME UNTO YOU, BUT I CALL UPON NO MAN SUDDENLY AND SO IN THE DISPENATION

I WROTE ONE BOOK TO PORTRAY THE EXPECTANT WORK OF THE MESSENGER, FOR I NEED NOT WEARY THE SOUL IN MINE OWN CONTEMPLATIONS. AND

TO THE WORLD IN A FEW WORDS, I CAME AND MARKED TIMING WITH THE EFFECTUAL WORKINGS OF THE LORD THY GOD, WITH THE GARDEN PATH. WHERE AS I WAS MADE A MINISTER ACCORDING TO THE GIFT OF GRACE OF THE LORD GOD, BY THE EFFECTIVE WORKINGS OF THE POWER OF GOD AND MY BELIEF IN THE SWORD OF THE SPIRIT THAT THE LORD JESUS CHRIST GAVE UNTO ME. IT MAKES ME TO BECOME SAVED WITH SALVATION UNTO GRACE WITH THE SPIRIT, NOW ENDEAVOURING TO KEEP THE UNITY OF THE SPIRIT IN THE BOND OF PEACE THROUGH FAITH IN THE LORD JESUS CHRIST TO COMPLETE THE WORK OF GOD.

I SAY UNTO YOU. YOU NEED TO KNOW THE STRENGTH AND MEASURE OF THE GIFT OF GOD'S GRACE FOR YOU AND SURELY YOU WILL UNDERSTAND THESE THINGS. YOU HUG IT UP AND YOU DON'T KNOW THE AMOUNT OF YOUR CALLING. YOU HUG IT UP, BUT YOU MUST EXPERIENCE THE LIGHT OF JESUS CHRIST AND HIS LOVE. YOU.YOU HUG IT UP, BUT YOU MUST FEEL THE LOVE IN YOUR HEARTS TO MAKE IT WORK, YOU HUG IT UP YOU MUST FEEL THE LOVE FOR GOD TO SUBMIT YORSELVES ONE TO ANOTHER IN THE FEAR OF GOD. YOU CAN PREACH ABOUT ME BUT DARKNESS DOESN'T BEAR FRUITS FOR CHRIST. YOU CAN TEACH ABOUT ME BUT, NOW, THE TIME HAS COME FOR THE GREAT MISTRY OF CHRIST TO BE KNOWN, IN THE FEAR OF GOD. IT MUST BE UNDERSTOOD THAT THE GREAT MISTRY OF GOD, WHO WAS FROM THE BEGINNING AND WILL BE UNTO THE END AS WE SAY, NOW AND FOREVER WAS FROM THE BEGINNING OF THE WORLD, WHEN GOD CREATED ALL THINGS BY JESUS CHRIST.

NOW TO FELLOWSHIP IN HIM CHRIST JESUS, I AS A MAN SO MUCH LESS THAN THE LEAST OF THE SAINTS IN CHRIST JESUS, BUT I HOLD ON TO THIS GRACE AND IN FAITH I SHARE THIS KNOWLEDGE UNTO YOU IN THE GARDEN PATH. BUT MORE SO IN THE STIR, AND THE MODERATION OF THE GARDEN PATH. I HAVE HEARD A VAIN BABBLING OF A PREACHER, TELLING PEOPLE AROUND ME THAT I SHOULDN'T TALK THINGS BEFORE THE TIME, AS IF THEY KNOW THE TIME OF GOD, OR THE HIGH TIME THAT IS UPON US.

BUT TO WHOM MUCH IS GIVEN MUCH IS REQUIRED OF US CHRIST JESUS GAVE ME THE SWORD AND I TOOK IT. I DID NOT ACHIEVE THIS SWORD OF THE SPIRIT FROM MAN SO THEY SHOULD ADVISE ME ON WHEN TO SPEAK OR WHEN TO DO THE WORK OF THE LORD JESUS CHRIST.

AND SO, I WILL TELL THEM THAT I KNOW WHAT TO DO WITH IT IN JESUS CHRIST WHETHER I AM RICH OR POOR. FOR UNTO THEM IF I AM POOR, I WILL NEVER BE ABLE TO FULFILL THIS DESTINY, AND ACHIEVE MINE INHERITANCE, HENCE BEING A FAILURE IN THE HIGH TIME OF THE LORD. AND I SAY TO YOU I TOOK ME THE READY PEN AND WROTE WHAT HE

WROTE EVERY TIME IN ME, AND IF YOU NOW SEE ME AND THE WORD, AND THE BIBLE IS NOT IN ME THEN IT TOO WAS THE WORK OF THE SPIRIT.

THE FOOLISH THINGS AROUND MY LIFE ALL THE TIME, YES I NEVER ASKED HOW WOULD THEY FIT IN, IN THE EARLY DAYS OF THE GARDEN PATH, MY BROTHER LEROY MALCOLM WAS TOLD ONCE BY ME THAT I DID NOT EVEN KNOW WHAT THE 1, 2 AND 3 CREW MEANT BUT AS THE YEARS GO BY IT FITTED IN. WELL EVENTUALLY I GOT A BLACK MAN CREW OUT OF IT TO USHER IN THE TIME, THEN I GOT THE PRIESTHOOD CREW OUT OF IT TO PERCEIVE AN UNDERSTANDING OF THE HIGH TIMES AS WITNESS BY A FEW AND THE LORD GOD HIMSELF. THEN FINALLY I GOT THE REDEEMED OF THE MINISTRY OF RECONCILIATION OUT OF IT, WITH ALL COMING IN HANDY AS THE PREPARED WAY OF THE LORD JESUS CHRIST UNDER THE TABERNACLE

IN THE SUN, TO USHERING IN THE GLORY OF JESUS CHRIST.

I NOW KNOW THE LOVE OF CHRIST BEING GROUNDED IN LOVE OF GOD, FOR THAT LOVE PASSETH WISDOM AND KNOWLEDGE TO ME BY NIGHT AND BY DAY, TO ME IN THE GARDEN PATH, THAT YE MAY BE FILLED SOME DAY WITH THE FULNESS OF GOD'S GLORY FOR BEING A WORTHY BELIEVER. NOW UNTO HIM THAT IS ABLE, THE LORD JESUS DID PASS ABUNDANTLY TO ME THE MESSENGER OF GOD, THROUGH THE FEAR OF GOD. ALL THINGS AS MUCH AS WE MAY ASK OR THINK OF ACCORDING TO HIS POWER THAT WORKETH IN US, MUST NOW COME TO PASS AND BE ACCOMPLISHED. I THANK YOU O MIGHTY GOD FOR COMING INTO YOUR PRESENCE. WHERE YOU PERFECTED.

THE WORKS OF THE MINISTRY FOR THE EDYFING OF THE BODY OF CHRIST. AND SO, I HOLD THE MANTLE UP HIGH, WITH THE FIVE GRAPHED BRANCHES OF THE CHURCH [PIPE 5] FOR UNTO THE GENTILES THE SPIRITUAL CHURCH NOW PROCLAIMED WITH THE MANIFOLD WISDOM OF GOD. IN REVERENCE TO THE LORD JESUS CHRIST AS WE PROCLAIM THE HOLY KISS UNTO MANKIND.

THE JEALOUSY OF THE CHURCHES, AND THE MARK OF THE BEAST WILL NOT BLEMISH THE EDYFICATION UNTO YOU, OF THE GREAT BODY OF CHRIST, FOR WHEN THIS OLD MAN COME UNTO YOU, LET NO CORRUPT WORDS COME FROM YOUR MOUTH, SPEAK THAT WHICH IS GOOD, LEST YOU GREIVE THE SPIRIT OF GOD. IN THE FEAR OF GOD FOR WHEN THIS OLD MAN COME UNTO YOU, SPEAK THAT WHICH IS GOOD, THAT WHICH CAN BE USED TO THE EDYFING OF THE SOUL WITH THE LIGHT OF LOVE, AND NOTE NOW, O HOW SWEET, IT MINISTERS GRACE UNTO THE HEARERS. AND IF YOU GREIVE NOT THE HOLY SPIRITOF GOD, YOU WILL SEE WHEREBY,

YEE ALSO, ARE SEALED UNTO THE DAY OF REDEMPTION OF THE LORD THY GOD.

I SAY BRETHEN IN THE SPIRITUAL CHURCH OF GOD, AS YOU ARE AWAKENED FROM YOUR SLUMBER IN THE CHURCHES, PUT AWAY ALL THINGS WITH ALL MALICE UNTO ME, THE MESSENGER, AND THE WHOLE WORLD. PUT AWAY ALL THINGS SUCH AS BITTERNESS AND WRATH UNTO ME THE MESSENGER AND THE ENTIRE WORLD. PUT AWAY ALL THINGS SUCH AS ANGER AND CLAMOUR PUT AWAY ALL

THINGS SUCH AS UNMANIFESTED AND ARE SECRETS IN THE DARK. TROUBLE THE PSALMS AND HUM AMONGST YOURSELVES TO FEEL THE LOVE OF GOD AMONGST YOURSELVES. SING AND MAKE MELODIES IN

YOUR HEARTS, FOR THE FRUIT OF THE SPIRIT IS GOODNESS AND RIGHTEOUSNESS AND TRUTH, WILL COME UPON YOU, TO REMEMBER

THAT, YEE WERE SOMETIMES BEFORE IN DARKNESS AND NOW YOU ARE COME INTO THE LIGHT OF THE LORD JESUS CHRIST, TO WALK AS CHILDREN IN THE LIGHT. WHEN I AWAKE FROM MY SLEEP INTO THE LIGHT OF GOD, I MUST ONLY BE SEEKING LOVE BEYOND THE HORIZON OF THE INNER MAN, PROVING ALL THINGS FOR UNTO YOU HONORABLE TO THE SCRIPTURES THAT WAS WORTHLESS AND NOW I SAY IT WAS UNTO US FROM THE ORDINANCE OF MAN, BUT NOW WE ARE UNTO THE ORDINANCES OF GOD, AS WE MOVE INTO THE BODY OF CHRIST REDEEMING THE MASSIVES, IN THE FEAR OF GOD.

LET'S UNDERSTAND THE WILL OF THE LORD, GIVING THANKS ALWAYS IN ALL THINGS UNTO GOD AS WE DO WITHOUT BEING PUFFED UP AND MUFFLED UP BY THE NEW GOSPEL AND THE NEW COVENANT OF GOD. IN THE NAME OF THE LORD JESUS CHRIST WE MUST BE REMEMEBRING THAT IN THE BEGINNING GOD CREATED ALL THINGS AND BY HIM ALL THINGS WERE MADE. I CALL YOU BRETHEN TO THE ALTER OF GOD RECOGNIZE HIS PRESENCE AROUND US, THEN SUBMIT YOURSELVES AS INSTRUMENTS IN HIS BODY, FOR IN HIS BODY YOU ARE ONE AND BEING ONE, YOU ARE STRENGTHENED BY CHRIST JESUS, AS HE DWELLS IN YOU BY THE FAITH YOU HAVE IN HIM. AS HE STRENGTHEN YOU WITH HIS MIGHT BY THE SPIRIT IN THE INNER MAN, YOU INFINITELY BUILD THE GREAT BODY OF WATER IN THE VASTNESS, WIRTOUT BREADTH, LENGTH, DEPTH, AND HEIGHT, KNOWING THE LOVE OF CHRIST, IN UNITY OF ONENESS, BEYOND THE OLD DOORS OF THE ORDINANCES OF MAN, INTO THE NEW DOORS OF THE ORDINANCES OF GOD, IN THE SPIRITUAL CHURCH OF THE MANIFOLD WISDOM OF GOD. BUT IF THE GOSPEL YOU READ IS UNDERSTOOD, BY ALL MEANS THEN WE ARE ALL THE SAME WITH THE GIFTS GIVEN UNTO US, BY

AND SO HE THAT DESCENDED, AND IS ALSO HE THAT ASCENDED, FOR HE IT IS TO FILL ALL THINGS. GOD HAS FULFILLED HIS PURPOSE TOO AND SO HAVE MANKIND. THEIR GREAT

WATERS HAVE COME UP TO THE BRIM. MARKING THE HIGH TIME. MANKIND WHO SAY THAT THEIR LOVE FOR GOD IS SEEN IN GOING TO CHURCH AND GALLIVANTING AS THE MOST RIGHTEOUS IS AT FAULT

WITH GOD. HERE IS THE WARNING TO RETURN BY JUST THE FEAR OF THE LORD THY GOD WHO YOU KNOW IS THE MOST OMNIPOTENT OF ALL GOD'S AND SATAN WHOM YEE RIDE IN THE LIGHT OF THE CANDLE STICKS. IT IS TIME BE YEE AWAKEN TO

SEE THAT, I THE MESSENGER IS HERE TO SAVE SOME FROM THEIR CONTINUED FIGHT AGAINST GOD WHILE SEEKING YOUR OWN MEAT AND WORSHIPING GOD IN GOSPELS OF THE PARTS FOR OVER 2019 YEARS NOW. DO NOT CONTINUE TO EXHORT YOURSELVES AFTER THIS WARNING IN 2020, IS COME THROUGH THE TIME LINES. TO FEAR THE LORD THY GOD AND DO WHAT IS RIGHT WHEN THIS WARNING IS ISSUED WILL BE THE MOST RIGHTFUL THING TO DO AS CHRISTIANS.

THE FIFTH (5TH) SERMON

EXHORT NOT AND FALL AWAY FROM FAITH

YEAH, WE MOVE ONTO PERFECTION THEN BY THE WISDOM OF THE CHURCH. THE MINISTER I AM NOW, HAVE BEEN SET TO FULFILL THE EFFECTUAL WORK OF GOD IN YOU LIKEWISE UNTO ALL MEN. NOW THAT THE WATERS HAVE REACHED THE BRIM, IT IS NO OTHER TIME THAN THE TIME OF THE HIGH TIME, THE LAST DAYS THAT ARE UPON US. I WAS THEN A CHILD, BUT I REMEMBER VIE, VIE, A MOTHER OF GOD'S CHILDREN IN THE CHURCH. I REMEMBER PASTOR CLOUGH A FATHER OF GOD'S CHILDREN TOO, HE DIPPED ME IN THE WATER. I HAD EXPECTED TO RISE UP IN A ZION. BUT I ROSE UP FROM THE WATERS IN THE CHURCH, NOT LUKE WARM MAYBE LEFT ME COLD BUT NOT HOT, IN THOSE DAYS AS I TRIED TO FIGURE OUT WHAT THE SWORD OF THE SPIRIT WAS GIVEN UNTO ME FOR. I HAD NOT MUCH KNOWLEDGE OF THE SCRIPTURES BUT THAT WHICH WAS SPOON FED TO ME IN THE CHURCH UNTIL THE SPIRITUAL SOLDIER MATTY NOW CALLED MASS, GOT A PEN AND BEGAN WRITING. MANY THINGS CAME AND SOME FELL BY THE WAYSIDE BUT I KEPT ON WRITING UNTIL I HAD A MANY BAG OF RECORDED CASSETTES MANY PAPERS, AND BOOKS OF WHICH I SAY AFORE, SOME FELL BY THE WAYSIDE.

I PUT HOWEVER THE GARDEN PATH IN MOTION AND MY CROWN IS ON TOP OF THAT MANTLE, TO BE HELD UP BY ZION TRAIN WHICH PEOPLE PUT UNDER GROUND, FOR THE STARVATION OF THE COMMON GOOD FOR ALL MANKIND, MATTY NOW CALL MASS, WAIT IN A PATIENCE TILL THE LAST DAYS COME TO EXPLORE THE GARDEN PATH AT THE BEST OPPORTUNE TIME. HAVING ENCOUNTERED A GOOD RULER OBAMA MASS LET THE TIME PASS TO THE FULFILLMENT OF THE WORD.

YEA THE TIME OF A BALACK REWARD

THE TIME OF A BALACK REWARD

THE TIME OF A BALACM REWARD

THE TIME OF AN ADVANTAGE REWARD

CAUSE, FIT WI AFFI FIT FI SURVIVE IT

SO BIG UP JUNIOR RIED ONE A DI DJ'S IN A JAH ARMY WITH THE VOICE OF JAH, SINGING FIT WE AFFI FIT AND THE ENGINEER PON DI TUNE WHO A WEAR WHITE FI SO LONG CHA CHA BROWN, CONRAD MALCOLM, A FIRM BELIEVER IN GOD AND THE BIBLE. BRINGING US TO THE BOOK OF JUDE. WHERE WE GOT TO BE FIT TO ESCAPE IT.

AS WE RALLY THE CAUSE OF HUMAN CONTEMPLATION WITH THE VOICES OF THE CITY, THE VOICES OF JAH AND THE VOICES OF THE TEMPLE, AS THE GREAT WATERS BEGINS TO NEAR THE BRIM THE RIGHT WAY OF RETURN IS PREPARED AND IT IS A RALLY OF THE CAUSE OF REVELATION TO TAKE MORE. NEVER THE LESS WE WATCHED UNTIL THE BEAST IS DEFINED AND OPERATING AS A KINGDOM IN GOD'S WORLD, AS THE POWER OVER MAN WITH THE GAG OF THE RIGHTEOUS FOR THE FILTHINESS OF MAN.

ENOCH ALSO SAW LIKEWISE, THESE FILTHY DREAMERS DEFILING THE FLESH, DESPISING DOMINIONS OF GOD LEGACY OVER PARTS OF THE WORLD, AND SPEAKING EVIL OF DIGNITARIES. TOSSING RAILING ACCUSATIONS LEFT RIGHT AND CENTER. SPEAKING EVIL OF MANY THINGS WHICH THEY KNEW NOT, BUT WHAT THEY KNOW NARURALLY, BEING BRUTE OF NATURE AND BITTER VAUNTING BEASTS, THEY CORRUPT THEMSELVES, IN SPEECHES AGAINST THE OLD MONGREL NON – THE LESS PEERS AND COLLEAGUES, LEFT ME TO DIG DEEPER INTO THE FAITH FROM MY ROOTS IN STANTON, AS BENJIE'S PARRALAX ILLUSION OF TRUSTED SIMULARITIES,

FADES AT THE LOCKED GATES. THE LORD REBUKES THEM, FOR HINDERING THE PREPARED WAY.

NOW HE THE MESSENGER IS RAISED TO ANOTHER LEVEL IN CHRISTENDOM, A LEVEL ABOVE ALL CHURCHES TO HIS DOMINION. A LEVEL IN THE TABERNACLE IN THE SUN I WILL COME BACK TO SAVE

SOME IN THE SEVEN CHURCHES AND THEIR EXPONENTS, WITH THE WARNING OF THE LIBERALITY AND TEACH THEM WITH THE WORD OF RENEWAL OF THE GOSPEL AND THE COVENANT OF GOD, IN THE SPIRITUAL CHURCH OF THE MANIFOLD WISDOM OF GOD. NOW OUR GOD, THE ONE YOU USED TO WORSHIP, IN THE ORDINANCES OF MAN, IS WORKING ON THE SPIRITUAL PLATFORM, WITH THE OLIVE BRANCH SET AS MEDIAN OF ESCHATUALISM.

TO ALLOW THOSE DIPPED IN THE WATERY GRAVE AS MYSELF YEARS BEYOND NOW, WILL HAVE THE RIGHT TO COME UNTO YOU O LORD, IN THE SPIRIT FOR THE SHORT PERIOD OF RETURN UNTO YOU.

IT IS AN EXPECTED THING THAT YOU PERMIT US TO WORSHIP OCCASIONALLY IN THEIR SANTUARIES, AS WE THE ENTRUSTED PRAY FOR THAT PERMISSION TO SPEAK, PRAY AND WORSHIP IN THE SANCTUARY ON THE REST DAY, BUT NOT TOO OFTEN BECAUSE OF OUR NEED TO REST AND OBEY THY WILL, UNTIL THE UNDERSTANDING IS REACH AND UNDERSTOOD BY THE PRIEST ON ALL SIDES OF THE FENCE, TO INCLUDE THOSE WHO ARE AT WORK IN THEIR BUSINESS ON THE REST DAY THE SABBATH OF THE LORD THY GOD. LET US HEED THE WARNING AS TO CONTINUE AGAINST THE WARNING WITH YOUR EXHORTATION KEEPS YOU RIDING SATAN AND ALLOWS YOU TO EXHORT THYSELF UPON YOUR GOD WHO CREATED YOU.

LEAVING NON BUT THOSE WHO FAIL TO READ OR HEAR THY TESTIMONIES. TO REACH OUT FOR PERFECTION, LOVE ONE ANOTHER, AND SUBMIT THEMSELVES ONE TO ANOTHER, AS CHILDREN OF THE MIGHTY GOD.

THE USING OF THE ENSIGNS OF THE OF THE GARDEN PATH NEARING THE HIGH TIME IS SETTING THE TONE IN THE TIME OF PATIENCE, FOR THE PATIENT SAINTS TO BE PULLED CLOSER TO A RECOGNITION OF JESUS CHRIST AND THEIR FAULTS. HOWEVER, AS THE GREAT WATERS TOUCHED THE BRIM AND ALL FAULTS BE KNOWN, THE WHEAT AND THE TARES WILL BE TOGETHER. YOU ALL WILL DEFY GOD WITH YOUR FAULTS AND AS THE WHEAT WILL SAY THAT YOU DON'T NEED TO CORRECT THYSELF BEFORE GOD FOR YOU ARE ALREADY RIGHTEOUS.

NOTE THIS IS THE TIME OF THE NEW GOSPEL AND THE NEW COVENANT THAT ALLOWS THE CHURCHES TO STOP PLAYING CHURCH WITH THE

PATIENT SAINTS, AND THE EVANGELIZED SAINTS OF GOD, SEEKING THEIR OWN MEAT, BUT COME TO THE REALITY OF WHAT WAS RIGHT FROM THE BEGINNING TO THE END OF THE CREATION AND THE WORD.

I SEE THOSE OF THE GREAT MULTITUDE, AND THE FEW WITNESSES OF THE DELIVERY OF THE STIR AND THE MODERATION, WHOM ARE NEVER ANNOYED AT THE WORD OF TRUTH AND THE WORDS OF WARNING UNTO THEM AS THEY SPIRITUALLY SEEK OUT THE MISION OF GOD AND SHARE THE WORD, THAT IS PREPARED AND SET TO BRING LIGHT AND JOY TO THE HEARERS AS THEY TOO BEGINS TO WORK ON THE SPIRITUAL PLATFRORM OF PERFECTION.

I REMEMBER THE LATE VIE VIE, PASTOR CLOUGH, EVANGELIST PLUMMER, EVANGELIST LORNA MILLER, OTHER MEMBERS OF THE LEGIONS OF JAH, FOR HAVING SHARED THE LOVE OF JESUS CHRIST WITH US AND THE CHURCHES. THESE WERE THEY IN THOSE DAYS OF THE ROOTS OF ZION TRAIN, NOW I AM NOT SETTING A NEW GOSPEL AND A NEW COVENANT UPON THE OLD FOUNDATION FOR THE CHURCH, WITH THE PREPARED WAY OF THE LORD THY GOD, BY THE ELDERS ALREADY GONE BY, AS MEMBERS OF THE LEGIONS OF JAH.

WORKING ON THE SPIRITUAL PLATFRORM OF PERFECTION, IF TRANSFORMATION CANNOT BE DONE IN THE CHURCHES, AND F MY PEOPLE THAT ARE CALLED BY THE NAME OF GOD, CAN REFUSE THE LOVE AND THE LIGHT OF GOD, WORKING ON THE SPIRITUAL PLATFORM OF PERFECTION, THEY WILL NEVER FIND HIS GRACE. PERFECTION CANNOT BE ATTAINED BY THEM FOR THEY CONTINUE AS THE LUKE WARM IN HIS HOLY RENEWAL OF THE CHURCHES AND THEY WILL CONTINUE TO BE FILLED WITH THE ORDINANCE OF MAN

THEY WILL BOAST ABOUT A 144000 THAT WILL BE SAVED AND CAN'T EVEN SEE THAT IT WILL AFFECT THEM. MANY WILL NOT BE A PART OF THE GREAT MULTITUDE FROM THE WORLD'S POPULATION EITHER, BECAUSE THEY WILL NOT COME OUT OF HER, WHEN THEIR PRIESTS REFUSE TO COME FOR THE UNDERSTANDING OF THE LIBERALITY.

GOD 'S WILLING TO SAVE EVERY MAN, WILL BRING THEM INTO HIS FOLD RATHER THAN IN CONTEMPT OF THE HOLY GHOST. BUT NOW, FALLING FROM GRACE WHICH HE GIVES SO FREELY UNTO THEM WHICH HAD JUST A LITTLE FAULT THAT COULD BE CORRECTED. FOR THEY ARE STIFF NECKED. SAYING THEY STAND FOR THE TRUTH BUT THEY ARE FIGHTING DAILY TO UPHOLD THE ORDINANCES OF MAN, WHEN THEY COULD CHANGE THE NUMBER OF 144000 SAVED OF THE CHURCH LIKE THAT OF THE GREAT MULTITUDE ON THE OUTSIDE OF THE CHURCHES. I HOPE THE PRIEST CAN

UNDERSTAND THIS, THE GREAT MULTITUDE IS SPIRITUALLY SEEKING OUT THE MISION OF GOD, BUT THE GENTILES YEA THEY THAT NEED TO KNOW GOD, CAN ACCEPT THE GRACE, LOVE AND THE LIGHT OF GOD, BY THEIR BELIEF IN THE WORD AS THEY WORK ON THE SPIRITUAL PLATFRORM TO PERFECTION, THEY WILL FIND HIS SALVATION IN VAST NUMBERS. FOR, THEN AND ONLY THEN, THE LORD SHALL COME, WITH TEN THOUSAND OF HIS SAINTS.

FOR UNTO GOD WE COME, AND BY HIS SIDE HIS SAINTS HAVING BEEN WASHED OF ALL SINS BY THE SPIRIT AND THE BLOOD OF JESUS, AND APPOINTED AS KINGS AND PRIEST UNTO GOD AND HIS FATHER, ON THE SPIRITUAL PLATFORM. TO HIM BE THE GLORY AND DOMINION FOR EVER AND EVER. ON THE ISLE OF PATMOS, WHERE JOHN BRINGS US INTO REVELATION, OF THE COMING OF CHRIST. MANKIND MUST LACK THE DREAMERS LUST OF, HAVING MEN'S ADMIRATION BECAUSE OF ADVANTAGES, TO THE SELLING AND PERISHING OF THEIR SOULS FOR FILTHY REWARDS. THE SPIRITUAL CHILDREN MUST SET THE LORD IN FRONT OF THEM.

THE BOOK OF JUDE CONTENDS THAT THEY MUST DO SO. LET'S GO THE ADVANTAGE, THEY SAY, LET'S GO BALAM. LET GO BALAC TEACHINGS OF UNGODLY SENSUAL LUST AND WITH OPENNESS OF THEIR JOY AND THEIR PRIDE AS THEY EXHORT THEMSELVES.

BE YOURSELVES WITHOUT EXHORTATION AGAINST THE WILL OF GOD, BUILDING UP OURSELVES IN OUR MOST HOLY FAITH, AND PRAYING IN THE HOLY GHOST, LACKING UNGODLY SENSUAL LUST, TO REJOICE IN THE GREAT, I AM, HE THAT IS THE FIRST AND THE LAST, FOR HE SHALL COME TO EXECUTE JUDGMENT.

UPON ALL, AND TO CONVINCE ALL THAT IS UNGODLY AMONGST THE PEOPLE, OF ALL THEIR UNGODLY DEEDS, WHICH THEY HAVE UNGODLY COMMITTED. THEN ALL THEIR HARD SPEECHES, WHICH UNGODLY SINNERS HAVE SPOKEN AGAINST I THE MINISTER AND MESSENGER, SO I SAY I NEVER DEIGN BE GOD UNTO MAN OR GOD IN THE GARDEN PATH, FOR KNOWING MY PLACE IS RELATIVE TO BEING UNDER GOD'S CONTROL AS A HUMAN BEING AS I SET THE EXAMPLE OF THE TRUE BELIEVER IN GOD AND ASK OF YOU TO FOLLOW ME. IF YOU DO FOLLOW ME THEN SOONER THAN YOU BELIEVE YOU WILL REJOICE IN THE GREAT, I AM, HE THAT IS THE FIRST AND HE THAT IS THE LAST, YES, HE WHO WAS DEAD AND NOW HE WHO IS ALIVE.

I SAY AGAIN, I AM NOT LAYING AGAIN THE FOUNDATION OF THE CHURCHES, IT IS JUST THE NEW GOSPEL AND THE NEW COVENANT TO INSTALL MAN'S RETURN TO GOD FROM DEAD WORKS THROUGH REPENTANCE AND

ACCEPTANCE OF GRACE AND THE LAW OF LOVE THROUGH JESUS CHRIST THE SON OF GOD.

FOR NOW, WE ARE ENLIGHTENED AND WE HAVE TASTED OF THE HEAVENLY GIFT OF GOD, AND NOW WE ARE PARTAKERS OF THE HOLY GHOST, TO RECEIVE THE BODY OF CHRIST. THE GOOD WORDS OF GOD IS HERE AND THE POWERS OF THE WORLD TO COME UNTO YOU.

NOTE HE WHO DESTROY THE BODY OF CHRIST, HAS DONE IT ALREADY? WE PREACH NOT REPENTANCE TO THEM, BUT THE CLEARANCE OF THE ENMITY OF CHRIST FROM THEM. FOR THE HIGH PRIEST HAVE ENTERED AS KING OF SALEM, MEETING ABRAHAM THAT IS RETURNING FROM THE SLAUGHTER. TO THE KING OF PEACE AND LOVE, IN THE COUNCIL OF GOD. GOD NOW BEING IMUTABLE IS NOW ON TOP, AND WILL APPEAR WITH THE THRONES OF THE THOSE WHO FIRST WAS DESTROYED FOR WITNESSING FOR JESUS CHRIST. THEN THE REIGN OF THE PRIESTHOOD BEGINS WITH THE SAINTS, AND THOSE WHO ARE THE LIGHT OF THE WORLD THROUGH ESUS CHRIST.

FOR THE GOD OF THE GARDEN PATH IS NOT UNRIGHTEOUS, AND THE SAME GOD OF THE UNIVERSE IS NOT UNRIGHTEOUS, AND THE SAME GOD OF THE LANDS, OILS, WATERS, AND MINERALS, THAT WE FIGHT

FOR IS NOT UNRIGHTEOUS, THANKS TO THE SAUDI'S FOR KEEPING OIL PRICE DOWN, WHEN I ASKED, THEY RESPONDED, THOUGH 3RD. WORLD COUNTRIES HAVE NOT PLACED THIS INCREASE OF WEALTH TO BECOME THE PROSPERITY UPON THEIR PEOPLE. FOR THE GOD OF THE GARDEN PATH IS NOT UNRIGHTEOUS TO FORGET MY WORK AND LABOUR OF LOVE, WHICH I HAVES SHOWN TOWARDS HIS NAME FOR HIS PEOPLE, AND THAT ALL THE GOOD PEOPLE OF THE EARTH HAVE SHOWN TOWARDS HIS NAME, AS THEY WALK WITH THE LORD AND SHEW HIS GOODWILL. IN THAT WE HAVE ALL MINISTERED TO THE SAINTS, AND DO MINISTER NOW TILL THE DAY WHEN OLD TUNE, A TUNE THE TIMING COME BACK AGAIN.

THE CHILDREN AROUND ME

SAW THE CHANGES IN MY TIME

BUT IN THE DARKNESS, THEY COULD NOT UNDERSTAND

UNTIL THEY COME ON OVER AND HELD ONTO MY HAND

MI A DI MINISTER FROM ROUND A SCHOOL BACK

MI NUH LUKE WARM, COLD BUT NUH HOT

NOW THE WORKS COME TO PASS

A TUNE THE TIMING

AND I'M STEPPING OUT HOT, HOT, HOT

DADDY SEVEN HOT, HOT, HOT

IN MY WHITE STONE THERE IS A KING

NOT LIKED BY MANY

AND TOMORROW, AFTER TOMORROW, YOU WILL SEE

YOUR VAIN COMPARISONS CAN'T STOP HIM FROM BEING

A MORNING STAR, ANYONE CAN BE ANYTHING AT ANY TIME BASED OF HIS BELIEFS AND PERCEPTIONS.

THE GARDEN PATH DESIRE THAT EVERY ONE OF YOU, DO SHEW THE SAME DILIGENCE, TO THE FULL ASURANCE OF HOPE UNTO THE END. IN 2018 BE NOT SLOTHFUL AND MEDDLING AND PRYING INTO WHAT THE MESSENGERS OWN WITHIN THE SWORD OF THE SPIRIT. TRYING TO SHED YOUR OLD GOSPEL IN THE LIGHT OF MY STIR AND MY MODERATION AND AGAIN TRYING TO RUN WITH THE DAMN UNFINISHED PLAN., IN YOUR OLD CHURCH EQUILIBRIUM, WITH YOUR OLD GOSPEL AND YOUR OLD COVENANT, TO DEPRIVE HIM OF A PERSONAL BLESSING FROM GOD. THE MESSENGER OUTPUT IS PRETTY NEW I COMPARISON TO YOURS, I AM CERTAINLY NOT AN ELOCUTIONIST AND WILL NEVER BE, I COME WITH A PLAN TO PREPARE A WAY AND THAT IS EXACTLY WHAT I WILL DO. SO, GO, QUIETLY IF FOR ANY REASON YOU NEED TO RUN AND PREPARED YOUR OWN GOSPEL UNTO YOURSELVES, AND NOT UNTO GOD.

BUT FOLLOWERS OF THEM WHO, THOUGH FAITH AND PATIENCE

INHERIT THE PROMISES OF GOD BY JESUS

AS WE MOVE ONTO PERFECTION WITH THE HOLY SPIRIT.

MANY SHALL WALK IN HIS OWN WAY SERVING GOD, FOR THE WARNING IS OF NO GREAT IMPORTANCE TO THEM. BUT THEIR EXHORTATION WILL BE SHORT LIVED, AS FOR THE WATERS HAVE FILLED UP TO THE BRIM

NOW AND THERE IS NO CHANGING OF THE HIGH TIME OF THE LORD. THE WRITTEN WORK IS IN THE HANDS OF THE ANGELS OF THE SEVEN CHURCHES AND THEIR EXPONENTS, SET NOW FROM THE HAND OF THE LORD JESUS CHRIST TO GOVERN OVER THE CHURCHES DIMMING THEIR LIGHT AS THEY SEE IT FIT FOR NOT HEEDING TO THE WARNING BEFORE IT BECOMES A SHAME UPON THEM.

YEA THE FEAR OF THE LORD WILL SAVE SOME WHEN THEY HEAR THE CALL OF THE TABERNACLE IN THE SUN – MASS TO COME OUT OF HER IF FOR THEIR REASON OF HAVING NO FAULT BEFORE THEIR GOD WILL LEAD THEM TO BE PUFFED UP, AND MUFFLED UP AGAINST THEIR GOD, NOT HEEDING HIS COMMAND TO DO AND ACCEPT HIS WILL FINALLY. THE WISE WILL COME OUT OF HER AND BE SAVED IN THE

REVERENCE UNDER THE TABERNACLE IN THE SUN WHERE GOD WILL BE, THEIR ONLY PROTECTION FOR EVERMORE. THE TABERNACLE IN THE SUN IS ALWAYS OPEN TO FULFILL YOUR NEEDS, WHETHER IN ONES, TWOS, THREES, AND AS THE GREAT MULTITUDE OF THEM THAT RESPECT AND DO THE WILL OF GOD, BY ACCEPTING GRACE AND LIVING THE LAW OF LOVE BY BELIEVING IN THE WORD. THIS FEAR FOR THE LORD THY GOD WILL CAUSE YOU NOT TO EXHORT AGAINST THE CREATOR OF THE UNIVERSE AND COMPLETELY HAVING FEAR FOR THE LORD THEIR GOD WHO CAN DO ALL THINGS. FOR GOD WILL MANIFEST HIMSELF INTO HIMSELF WHEN THE TIME COMES TO KNOW HIM PHYSICALLY. THANKS BE TO GOD WHOM WE FEAR AND WILL NEVER EXHORT THE HUMAN FLESHY SELF AGAINST HIM.

IF YOU ALL FEAR THE LORD THY GOD THEN YOU WILL NEVER ESTABLISH YOURSELVES WITH AN EARTHLY GOD, WITHIN THE CHURCHES, OR IN ANY WAY CONTINUE TO THE REVELATION OF SATAN, OR ANY OTHER MAN, AS YOUR GOD, AFTER THE LIBERALITY IS DELIVERED UNTO YOU.

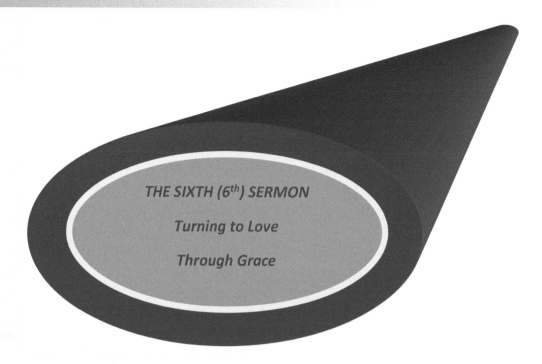

Figure 4: "The Sixth Sermon" ™ ©2019.

TAKE GOD FOR YOUR KING AND BELIEVE IN YOUR BEST, IT WAS HARD LABOUR IN SIX DAYS HIS HOLY REST ON THE SEVENTH DAY.

THE MESSENGER FROM THE GARDEN PATH WITH A CROWN OF PATIENCE, BRINGING THE BITTERNESS OF THE LITTLE BOOK CLOSER TO HUMANITY, THOUGH I HAD THE GOLDEN VOICE, ITS OLD CUT WITH MATTY WITH THE GOLDEN VOICE THAT YOU MAY HEAR. THINGS THEY DO WHEN THEY ALL AWAITS THE KINGDOM OF GOD AS HUMAN GODS.

WHEN YOU SEE THE KINGDOM OF GOD, WHICHEVER WAY, YOU WILL SEE THE MUSTARD SEED SOWN AS THE GARDEN PATH, SHINING ITS LIGHT DOWN ON YOU. IT WILL SHINE ALWAYS UNTIL TOMORROW, FOR THE WHOLE WORLD TO SEE. SPRINGING FORTH INTO THE ESCHATS WAY.

A TREE OF SALVATION NOW, BRINGING LOVE, AND SALVATION OF

GOD AND PEACE TO EVERY MAN, WITH THE SPIRIT OF THE GOD THE MESSENGER SERVE AND BELIEVE IN. BRINGING THE LIGHT OF GOD, TO EVERY MAN, FOR THERE IS NOTHING STOPPING GOD. WHENEVER YOU HIT THE LIGHT, IT STAYS OVER YOU AND PASS IT ON WITH JOY AND PEACE FOR THE HEARERS BECAUSE, THERE IS NOTHING STOPPING GOD, IN THIS LIBERALITY OF THE HIGH TIME.

WHENEVER YOU TAKE THE LIGHT OF JESUS CHRIST WITHIN YOU, THE MANIFOLD WISDOM OF GOD WILL COME FORTH, FOR YOU TO HEED TO GOD'S WORDS MORE AND MORE AS YOU REALIZE THE GREAT MYSTERY

OF CHRIST WAS IN SEEKING THE KINGDOM OF GOD. HIS WORDS ARE EVERLASTING. HIS WORDS ARE TRUE, SO WHEN THEY DO THINGS TO HURT ME, THEY MUST UNDERSTAND, THAT I HAVE PREPARED THE WAY TO SAVE SOME.

LOVE OF THE CHILDREN OF GOD NO MATTER WHAT THEIR CIRCUMSTANCES ARE, THE PASTOR IS WILLING TO DEGRADE THE WOMAN IN THE STREETS, SAYING SHE IS NOW A MESSY CROP. BUT HE HAD THEM IN THE CHURCH. MAYBE USED THOSE IN THE CHURCH, COMING BACK WON'T BE EASY. YET STILL THEY TREAD THE WINE PRESS DOWN, BAKING BREAD WITH OUR BOYS AND HAVING FUN WITH OUR GIRLS. HE IS NOT AT THEIR LEVEL, MORE SO HIS HUMILITY HAS GONE TO THE HIGHER SOCIETY.

TALK ABOUT TODAYS WOMAN IS NAKED IN THE STREETS, MAN WEAR BLINKERS CAUSE WHEN YOU SEE THE PIECE OF BOARD YOUR EYES, YOU LIGHT UP BEHIND THE ADVANTAGE. WHILE YOU ALL WORSHIP IN THE ORDINANCES OF MAN, AND AS THE FIRST SERMON HAVE IT, WE ALL SHALL BE LONGING FOR THE DAY. THE FIRST SERMON REVEALS, WHEN HOLINESS BECOMETH THE CHURCH, THE LIGHT WILL COME FORTH UPON THE CHILDREN OF MEN.

I HAVE HEARD IN THE CONFEDERATIONS, THE CRITIZING OF THE WOMAN, GETTING THE BLAMES EVER SINCE THE DAYS OF ADAM, OF EATING THE APPLE, YET STILL THEY WANT THE YOUNG GIRLS TO GO FOR THEM AS THE BEST APPLE HEAD IN THE WOODS, TODAY HER BOOBS IS AT THE ATTENTION IN THE STREETS, BUT TO ME IT MAY BE SO, BECAUSE OF WANTS AND NEEDS, BUT HER DESIRES IS IN HER

POVERTY, AS HER ONLY ASSETS ARE NOT YOURS, BUT HERS, BUT BEING HUNGRY THEY HAVE THE GREATEST HUMAN ASSET GOD GAVE THEM. NOW EVEN MEN HAVE ASSETS AND THEY ALL POST IT UP IN CHURCHES. ASSESTS YOU HAVE TAUGHT OUR BOYS TO HAVE, AND MAKE THE WOMAN A CURSE, UNTILL YOU CURSE YOUR MODERN GENERATION TO THE DEEPEST DIE, AS SADDLERS OF THEIR KIND

HAVE YOU EVER CONSIDERED THAT THE WOMAN IS HUNGRY? NEEDY AND IN WANTS OF A JOB AND A CARE GIVER. HAVE YOU EVER CONSIDERED THAT HER CARE GIVER IS OUT THERE SEEKING A CARE GIVER FOR HIMSELF BECAUSE OF GREED, LAZINESS AND COMPETING AGAINST THE WOMAN IN TODAY'S SOCIETY, TO THEIR OWN DETRIMENT?

HAVE YOU EVER CONSIDERED, THE WASTING OF HILLIONS OF DOLARS ON WAR? WHEN YOU COULD FEED HUMANITY. THE WASTING OF HILLIONS OF DOLARS ON BIG DESIGNS OF EVERY KIND. MAKES ME ASK YOU THE QUESTION, DO YOU SEE THE NEED FROM THE WOMAN ADVERTISEMENT? OR

DO YOU SEE THE OBJECT OF SATISFACTION? WOULD YOU GIVE THE WOMAN A JOB TO FILL HER NEEDS? OR A THOUSAND DOLLARS FROM YOUR STORE HOUSE? FOR FREELY YOU RECEIVE SO FREELY YOU SHOULD GIVE. AND SAY TO HER GO AND SIN NO MORE, AND COME INTO THE CHURCH, AND WE WILL HELP YOU FREE YOUR WANTONNESS, LIKE JESUS DID. JUST TELLING HER WITH HUMILTIY EVEN IF YOU KNEW SHE CAN'T. BUT IN THE NEXT WEEK YOU WILL PASS AGAIN AND HELP HER MORE FOR FREELY YOU GOT YOURS.

BUT YOU YOURSELF IS SO WEAK, THE FLESH TOGGLE WITH THE SPIRIT AND THIS IS FOR EVER MORE NOT ONCE IN A WHILE. BEING UNPERFECT WITH A HEART THAT GOES UP AND DOWN, WILL GO AROUND AND ROUND, AFTER A WHILE, THREE WEEKS OR SO, YOU OFFER HER THE FRONT SEAT INSTEAD OF WORK OR KINDS. THE HEARTS OF MEN WILL GO UP AND DOWN, AND WILL CATCH SEEKING DELIGHTS, AND FOR SURE YOU WILL SET YOUR MONEY ON USURY TOO. WILL THE WAY OF THE CHURCH CONTINUE IN THAT WAY? OR WILL THE CHURCH SEE THAT, THERE IS A CAUSE FOR EACH MAN'S NEED AND OF EACH MAN'S

SURVIVAL. WILL YOU SEE YOURSELF AS A BROTHER, IN THE BROTHERHOOD? WILL YOU SEE THAT EACH MAN'S SURVIVAL SHOULD BE HIS BROTHER'S. THROUGH LOVE, AND BOOST THE PRIESTHOOD TO MAKE A CALL FOR RENEWAL OF OUR ECONOMIC DEVELOPMENT IN THE NEW COVENANT OF THE LAW OF LOVE. THIS WOULD BE SHARING LOVE, RATHER THAN THE FILLING OF YOUR SOULS, WITH YOUR OWN NEEDS, ALONE WITH THE GOOD FOR ONE AND NOT ALL.

ARE YOU THE KIND THAT WILL LOVE EVERY CREATURE UNDER THE SUN? OR TO KEEP ON SEEING YOUR OWN SATISFACTION, RATHER THAN FILL THEIR NEEDS TOO, JUST AS HOW GOD FILL THE NEEDS OF THE LEVAITONS, IT MAKES ME SING THE SONG ABOUT MY BABY, AS I WAS HUMAN TOO NOW AND THEN AS LONG AS I LIVE.

WOMAN – I MADE LOVE TO YOU UUU

IT WAS–

NE–VER –

SINNNN

THE LOVE–EEEE

I MADE TO YOU

CAUSE I MADE LOVE, TO YOU - WITH LOVE

IT WAS NEVER SINNING THE LOVE I MADE TO YOU, ...

BUT I TELL YOU USE NOT THE SPIRIT TO GET THAT LOVE BUT OF NATURAL AFFECTION BETWEEN MAN AND WOMAN WITHOUT USURY. BUT LORD IF I LEFT MY FIRST LOVE, THEN GOOD LORD PLEASE FORGIVE ME, FOR LOVING THE SPIRIT OF JESUS CHRIST FIRST MAKES US FOREVER STRONG IN THE BODY OF CHRIST. THEREFORE, IN MY QUEST TO RETURN LORD TAKE YOUR WRATH AWAY FROM ME. TAKE YOUR WRATH AWAY FROM ME, TAKE YOUR WRATH AWAY FROM ME,

IN MY DESPENSATION, IN THE FREEDOM MANY NEVER HAD, GOD GAVE ME A SWORD AND A NEW SCHOOL THEREAFTER, ON THE 10TH OF JANUARY 1977. THE GARDEN PATH WAS BEGINNING TO BE SWEET TO ME, AND IN TEN YEARS IT WAS CRAFTED AS A WAY OF LIFE TO BE SEEN AS NOW MANIFESTED IN THIS TIME CONVENIENT TO ME. BUT IT LEFT ME IN STREET PRISON. NOW AS THE SONG SUGGEST, STRE -FEET PRISONS, STREET PRISON IT'S NO LIE.

I FOLLOWED THE PRECEPTS OF GOD, THE BITTERNESS I BORE, I NEVER LET THE, GO, I MINGLED WITH THE DIFERENT POWERS OF THE ORDINANCES OF MAN, I EVEN SOUGHT OUT MY OWN. THE LAW OF LOVE, IN AND OUT WITH ME SINGING SONGS OF JOY, FOR EVERYONE, BEING A HAPPY NON-SECTARIAN MAN, OUT OF THE ADVENTIST FOLD.

WITH EVERY DENOMINATION OF THE FAITH AND FOUNDATION OF GOD, FOR I CONSIDERED THEM TO BE FUNCTIONAL IN THE WAY OF THE PATIENT SAINTS RECONCILIATION. NOW MY ROOTS IN ZION IS UNDERGROUND, AND CHANGING ORIENTATION FROM TIME TO TIME, NOT DENYING GOD BUT THE DEVIL.

FINDING THE PRECEPTS OF GOD, AND THE LOVE I HAD FOR MY GOD IS THE LOVE I KEPT FOR MY GOD, AS A HAPPY NON-SECTARIAN MAN, AND THE ORDINANCE OF MAN BEGGED ME NOT TO BACKSLIDE EACH TIME THEY RECORD MY NAME IN THE CHURCHES. WHAT SHOULD I BACKSLIDE FROM THE CHURCH CANNOT CONTAIN ME WITH THEIR FAULTS UNTO GOD? I HAVE COME TO HELP THEM MAKE IT RIGHT AND TO SAVE SOME, AND ONLY HOPE THEY'D KNOW. I WOULD NOT MOVE ON INTO THEIR HUB OF FORNICATION AS FORNICATION WITH THE CHURCHES WAS NOT MEANT FOR ME UNTIL THE HIGH TIME WHEN ALL SHOULD COME UNDER THE UMBRELLA OF UNITY.

THEY SET DOWN MY NAME IN THEIR BOOKS, BUT GOD BOOK NO WANT NO NAME NOW, THE GREAT MULTITUDE WILL BE NAMELESS IN THEIR BOOKS BUT SEALED BY GOD. BUT I RATHER BACKSLIDE, THAN BE FORNICATING THEN, AND YOU WILL KNOW THE REASON WHY LATER.

DEEPER TROUBLED WATERS ARE MOUNTING UP TO THE BRIM, MY GOD PROMISSES TO COME AND SOUGHT THEM OUT EVERYONE YEA IN THESE EVIL TIMES, BUT THE PEOPLE LOVED THEIR GODS.

THEY SET THE FOUNDATIONS EACH AND EVERY ONE, EVEN IN

UNBELIEF, WITH SATAN SEATED IN THE HOUSE OF REDEMPTION. THE BOOK WAS NEVER RENTED FOR THE LOVE THEY HAD FOR THEIR GOD. BUT DEEP DOWN THEY LOVED THE OIL AND THE WINE, IT KEPT THEM FROM SINNING AGAINST THE LORD, THOUGH THEY WERE FRUITFUL AND DID MULTIPLY THIS WAS THE WORLD IN WHICH I LIVED. THE LITTLE ONES WAKE IN THE MORNING KNOWING NOT WHENCE THEY CAME. MANY AS CHILDREN WITH SERIOUS LACK IN A WORLD WHERE THERE IS PLENTY.

SOME MOTHERS TOLD THEM, THEY FELL FROM HEAVEN, FROM THE BOWELS OF A PLANE, CAUGHT UP IN THIS WILDERNESS, NOW WITH NOTHING TO EAT AND A LIFE FILLED WITH PAIN. THAT'S WHERE WE ARE COMING FROM AND THAT'S NOT WHERE WE NEED TO KEEP GOING TO.

WHAT WE DO IN THE DARKEST PARTS OF THE EARTH, THAT IS ON EVERY ONE'S SINFUL AND LUSTFUL MINDS, BUT THE LOVE OF THE GENERATIONS IS LOST TO THE LOVE OF MONEY. TO CHASTISE THE CHILDREN OF GOD IN THEIR WAY BY NOT PASSING DOWN THE WEALTH TO EVERY MAN, WOMAN AND CHILD.

OUR CHILDREN ALL ARE COMING FORWARD, WITH NOTHING TO EAT AND A LIFE FILLED WITH PAIN, WE TAKE OUT MORE EACH DAY AND WE LEAVE THEM HUNGRY, JUST TO LET, MANKIND KNOW THAT THEY CAN MAKE A CHANGE, FOR YES WE ARE THE REAL WORLD WE CAN MAKE IT BETTER THAN WHAT IT IS TODAY, AND NONE WILL LOSE BECAUSE ALL WE CAN EAT PER DAY IS THREE MEALS. WE NEED TO GIVE THE PEOPLE OF THIS WORLD A CHANCE TO LIVE THEIR LIVES WITH LOVE, AND SIMPLE CHANGE THE GAME. WHO ELSE IS GOING TO DO IT? WITH MONEY STOCKPILE EVERYWHERE IN THE WORLD, THAT CAN BRIDGE YOUR LOVE FOR THE NEEDY AND HURT NOT YOUR POCKET. BUT I SAY REMEMBER THE CHILDREN OF TOMORROW, THEY ARE THE NEEDY TODAY. WE MUST FIX THEM A BETTER PATH TO WALK IN THE GARDEN OF HARMONY THAT WE MUST BUILD FOR THE FUTURE. OF MANKIND. THE CLERGY MUST FOSTER GROWTH OF A NEW PARADIGM SHIFT OF THE POPULACE TOWARDS CHILDREN

DEVELOPMENT IN THE SOCIAL AND ECONOMIC DEVELOPMENT OF

FINANCIAL STABILITY OF THE WORLD. BECAUSE WHEN MANY PEOPLE MADE THEIR CHILDREN, THEY MADE THEM WITH LOVE, BUT LACK THAT WHICH TO GIVE TO THEM. I HAVE SEEN PEOPLE WHO GOT FREE EDUCATION PUTTING A TAX ON EDUCATION WHEN THEY CAME TO POWER. WE NEED TO CARE AND SHARE THE GOOD OF THIS WORLD NOW THAT THE WATERS ARE UP TO THE BRIM AND THE PEOPLE ARE SEEKING THE KINGDOM OF GOD, AND IF THEY CONTINUE TO FOLLOW THE EXAMPLE YOU CAN'T FOOL THEM ANYMORE, THEIR POWERS WILL MULTIPLY GREATLY UPON YOU. AND MORE THAN THAT, TO SHARE AND CARE FOR EVERYONE. IF WE DON'T CHANGE OUR WAYS, THE LITTLE ONES WILL NEVER CHANGE, BECAUSE NOW THEY KNOW MUCH MORE, THAN WHAT WAS HIDDEN, IN THE DARKEST PATH OF THE EARTH.

HUNDRED MILLION DOLLARS DELIVERED INTO A WICKED AND GREEDY RULER INSTEAD OF GIVING THE PEOPLE TWO MILLION DOLLARS EACH, TO RENEW THEIR PROSPECTUS IN LIFE. A HUNGRY MAN WILL CATCH AT A STRAW, IN SOME FORBIDDEN PLACES, ACCORDING TO THE BIBLE SELL A BOY FOR AN HARLOT, AND GIRL FOR JUST A BOTTLE OF WINE. FOR THEY HUNGER AND THIRST AFTER UNRIGHTEOUSNESS, THROUGH THEIR NEEDS AND WANTS.

WE ARE BUT STUBBLES BEFORE OUR GOD SO OPEN THE DOORS FOR EVERYMAN NOW TO RECREATE THE JUNGLE OF LOVE AND KINDNESS, FOR THE FATHER, THE FATHER WILL SEND A KING TO COME TO CHANGE ALL OF THAT, THEN WHEN HE COMES UNTO US HIMSELF WITH MAJESTIC POWER, AND YOU BOW YOURSELF BEFORE THEIR, AND SEE THAT YOU ARE NOTHING BUT STUBBLES BEFORE OUR GOD'S. WHO WILL GIVE THEM A LAND A LAND SO PRECIOUS, FLOWING WITH MILK AND HONEY JUST LIKE HE DID IN DAYS OF OLD?

O LORD THY PASTORS, THEY HAVE MADE THY PLEASANT PORTION A DESOLATE WILDERNESS, THY PASTORS HAVE TRODDEN UNDER FOOT THY VINEYARDS, FOR NO MAN SAW AND DISSERNED, MUCH LESS TO LAY IT UPON THEIR HEARTS, BUT THE LORD THY GOD HATH COMPASSION, AND WILL GIVE YOU ALL A CHANCE, A CHANCE TO SEE

HIS TRUTH AND THE LIGHT AND THE WAY, AND REMOVE HIS FIERCE ANGER FROM YOU.

BEHOLD HE IS INFINITE IN HIS MERCIES TOWARDS MEN, AND HATH POURED OUT HIS MERCIES UPON THEM. HE WHO IS GOD KNOW THAT I COME UNTO YOU IN THE NAME OF THE LORD JESUS CHRIST, A MINISTER FROM THE EFFECTIVE WORKINGS OF THE WORKS OF GOD. ASPIRERS DON'T WANT TO

NEGOTIATE FROM TIME TO TIME, FOR THE GOOD THINGS TO BENEFIT ALL MANKIND, AND THAT'S WHY WE DON'T WANT ANY BALAAM REWARD, WE DON'T WANT ANY DREAMERS REWARD, WE DON'T WANT ANY ADVANTAGE REWARD. BEING WILLING AND ABLE WITH ASPIRITIONS OF EVERY KIND, THOUGH IN THE TIME AFORE A VERBOSE KING, BEING WELL LOVE BY ALL IN SKIN AND FLAVOR OF HIS BELOVED, CAME DEALING IN ADVANTAGES AS SET OUT IN SODOM SELFISHLY DECIEVING THE DREAMERS, TO SADDLE UP SAFETLY IN THEIR FILTHINESS IN THEIR KINDS.

FORGET THE FILTHY MONEY AND OFFFERINGS TO THE CHURCH, LEAVE YEE THE BENEFITS UNTO GOD, AND IF ANY PREACHER AMONGST YOU, CAN AND IS WILLING TO PROVE THE PROPHECIES OF JESUS CHRIST WRONG. AND IF ANY TEACHER AMONGST YOU, CAN AND IS WILLING TO PROVE THE PROPHECIES OF JESUS CHRIST WRONG. AND IF ANY PREACHER AMONGST YOU, CAN AND IS WILLING TO PROVE THE PROPHECIES OF JESUS CHRIST WRONG. AND IF ANY PROPHETS AMONGST YOU, CAN AND IS WILLING TO PROVE THE PROPHECIES OF JESUS CHRIST WRONG. AND IF ANY MAN AMONGST YOU WITH ANY OF THE GIFTS OF GOD. CAN AND IS WILLING TO PROVE THE PROPHECIES OF JESUS CHRIST WRONG. MEET HE WITH SEVEN STARS IN HIS RIGHT HAND. FOR THIS WILL BE MEETING HE THAT HATETH THEIR DEEDS.

BUT UNTO YOU A NEW KING HAS COME WITH HIS LOVE FOR ALL MEN AND WILL BURN BABYLON. MEET JESUS CHRIST THAT GIVETH THE LIGHT UNTO ALL. MEET HE THAT WANTS TO TAKE HIS WRATH OFF THE YOUTHS. FOR IN THIS TIME IS COME THIS MINISTER, NOT LOVED AND SET AS THE LEAST AMONGST ALL GONE BEFORE, IN THE MIDST OF THE STORMS OF LIFE. IT'S DADDY SEVEN (7) THE MESSENGER

GREATER THAN JOHN THE BAPTIST AND GREATER THAN JOHN THE

REVELATOR, GETTING EVEN,

AS HE THAT IS GREATER COMES BETWEEN THE SEVEN ANGELS AND THE SEVEN CANDLE STICKS. IN THE HANDS OF THE SON OF GOD, OUR LORD OF HOST, AND THE LORD OF LORDS IN THE HIGH TIME.

FOR THE LORD OF LORDS HATH LIFTED ME UP TO PREPARE HIS WAY AND OPENED DOORS NO MAN CAN SHUT AND WILL CLOSE DOORS NO MAN CAN OPEN. IT IS A GOOD THING TO BE IN THE HANDS OF THE LORD WITH THE SEVEN ANGELS AND THE SEVEN CANDLE STICKS TO DELIVER SOME OF THE PATIENT SAINTS. IN HIS RIGHT HAND THE LORD, THE LORD HATH FULFILLED HIS TABERNACLE IN THE SUN WITH HIS HOLY PEOPLE AND THE PRIEST THAT HAVE COME FOR THE UNDERSTANDING NOW TO BE THE ENTRUSTED PRIESTS UPON THE EARTH. FROM NOW ON HE THAT HATH

UNDERSTANDING WILL SEE AND HAVE THE FULL KNOWLEDGE OF GOD AND KNOWING RIGHT FROM WRONG, GOOD AND EVIL, AND COMPENSATE IT WITH HONOUR TO GOD TO MAGNIFY HIS HOLY WORK UNDER THE TABERNACLE IN THE SUN.

HE WHO HATH POWER DELIVERS THE REST, IF YOU CAN'T FEEL THAT POWER ANYMORE AS A MAN THEN LET THE GOOD LORD DELIVER YOU FROM YOUR EVIL WORKS AND SATAN. THE SEVEN STARS TANGLING WITH AND FOR THE SEVEN CHURCHES, WILL NAVIGATE THE EARTH FOR THE LOVE OF MAN AND THE GRACE OF GOD AS ACCEPTED BY MANY TO SPARE THEM FROM HIS WRATH WHILE DIMMING THE LIGHT OF THE REBELLIOUS CHURCHES AGAINST GOD THE ALMIGHTY WAY TO RETURN TO HIM IN THE HIGH TIME WITH THE NEW GOSPEL AND THE NEW COVENANT OF THE PREPARED WAY OF GOD.

FOR AFTER JUDE THE LORD SPAKE THESE THINGS UNTO JOHN, O BELOVED ON THE ISLES OF PATMOS, AS I SAID BEFORE, REVELATION TEK MORE. EVEN IN CHURCHES WHERE SATAN SITTETH AND EXHALTETH HIMSELF, EVEN WHERE YOUR SINS ARE PLENTY, I EXHALT YOU TO PUT THE LORD THY GOD BEFORE YOU, AND SET THE LORD THY GOD ABOVE THE ORDINANCES OF MAN, AND ON TOP OF HIS ORDINANCES, FOR THE FIRST AND THE LAST ~ WILL HAVE HIS SEVEN SPIRITS OVER YOU ALL. YEA THE FIRST AND THE LAST ~ WILL HAVE HIS SEVEN ANGELS OVER

YOU ALL, GIVING PARADISE THAT MANY OF YOU EVEN THOUGH YOU COULD GIVE YOURSELVES PARADISE, IF YOU OPENED DOORS AND FLEW INTO HEAVEN AS MINCED UP MEAT OF A SLAUGHTER.

COME FOR THAT OPPORTUNITY AS THE PERFECT MAN AS TO HE THAT WILL OPEN THE DOOR AS HE KNOCKS, AND BECKON YOU TO OPEN YOUR DOOR TO LET HIM IN, IS GIVING PARADISE TO HE THAT HE OFFERS TO SUP WITH HIM IN THE SPIRIT OF GOD, AS HE VOWS FOR YOU BEFORE HIS FATHER TO BE HIS FRUITS ALL OF HIS VINE.

AS HE KNOCKS AT THE DOOR OF SALVATION, IT IS NOT PARADISE TO HIM THAT IS ABLE TO BOAST A MAN FIVE SIZES ABOVE HIMSELF HE TELLING AND SPREADING THE STORY OF HIS DEEDS OPENLY AS THE FIRST BEAST, NOR IS IT TO THE SECOND BEAST PARADISE FOR EVIL LIKE UNTO THE ENMITY OF CHRIST BUT GRACE AND LOVE TO TELL THE STORY OF YOUR REVERENCE TO MAN OPENLY BEFORE BUT NOW OPENLY AS REVERENCE TO GOD. TO TELL THE STORY OF YOUR ORDINANCES TO MAN OPENLY AS BEFORE BUT NOW OPENLY AS A STORY OF ORDINANCE TO GOD.

GOD LEEDS YOU TO THE OPEN DOOR, HE BEGS YOU THE PATIENT SAINTS AND THE PEOPLE OF THIS WORLD TO BOW DOWN ON YOUR KNEES, BOW

DOWN AND REPENT UNTO HIM THAT IS GOD. CHURCH BOW DOWN AND REPENT. FOR THE PREACHERS WERE LYING, CONVINCED IN THEIR DEEDS FOR THE GAINS OF THE FLESHY MAN, LEAVING THE FLOCK TO LIVE IN DARKNESS, AND LEAVING THE WRATH OF GOD ON THE YOUTHS. REPENT, THE LORD OF HOST IS WAITING FOR YOU TO SUP WITH HIM. REPENT, THE LORD OF HOST IS WAITING FOR YOU TO BRING THE IN SHEEVES. TO NOT STAND FOR GOD AS THE MESSENGER OF GOD DID AND BECAME THE EXAMPLE UNTO YOU. IT IS NOT WORTH THE FIGHT AGAINST GOD, WHEN YOU ALL SAY YOU ARE FOR GOD, AND HOLD ONTO THAT WHICH IS THE STANCE FOR THE BEAST. AS IT KEEPS YOU IN THE MODE OF UNREPENTANCE, GREED, UNTIL YOU REALIZE YOU ARE POOR WITHOUT GOD. YOU NEED GOD AND LOVE IN YOUR HEARTS NOT

THE WANT MORE MONEY THAT WILL ROTH IN HELL, AND DESTROY THE PEOPLE OF THE EARTH WITHOUT A CONSCIENCE. FOR YOU GOT SO

MUCH YOU CAN'T MANAGE, AND IN YOUR IGNORANCE THE MORE YOU SEE THE MORE YOU WANT, AND BECOME THIRSTY OVER UNRIGHTEOUSNESS. RUN FROM IT AND REPENT, RUN FROM THE ORDINANCES OF MAN AND REPENT. FOR YOUR WAYS ARE NOT OF THE

THINGS OF MY OWN, NOT OF THE FOUNDATIONS OF THE CHURCHES IN GOOD FAITH WAITING FOR THE PROMISE OF ABRAHAM, IT IS NOT A MODEL OF GOD'S WAY. IT IS OF GOD THAT YOU SEEK THE UNDERSTANDING OF THE LIBERLITY WHICH IS OF GOD. REPENT OF THE THINGS THAT HE HAVE SAID IN THE SCRIPTURES OF YOUR FAULTS, FOR YOUR DEEDS ARE PLENTY.

HE LEEDS YOU TO THE OPEN DOOR, OF FREE SALVATION AND A WAY TO RETURN UNTO HIM WITH THE PATIENT SAINTS, STOP THE FIGHT AGAINST GOD AND ALL HUMANITY AND BE COVERED UP IN THE ORDINANCES OF GOD, HE BEGS OF YOU REPENT FOR HE IS FIRST AND THE LAST CALLING IN THE HIGH TIME BEGGING YOU TO COME HOME AND SUP WITH HIM, SO TURN YOUR EYES UPON JESUS WHEN YOU SEE ZION TRAIN COMING FROM, UNDERGROUND WITH THESE SEVEN SERMONS, IN THE NEW GOSPEL AND NEW COVENANT. THIS IS THE PATIENCE OF THE GARDEN PATH AND THE ONLY CROWN I HAVE AS AN EXAMPLE, NOW BE YOU RENEWED IN YOUR SPIRIT AND YOUR REVERENCE TO GOD, AS YOU SEEK THE KINGDOM OF GOD, FOR HE WILL NOT LEAVE YOU LONELY NEITHER WILL HE FORSAKE YOU. BE THE NEW EXAMPLES OF THE MESSENGER AND BECOME THE FRUITS OF CHRIST, WHETHER YOU ARE YOUNG OR OLD. FOR YET WILL HE SHOW YOU VISIONS AND DREAMS IN THE HIGH TIME OF THINGS TO COME. TIME WILL TELL ALTHOUGH THE HARVEST IS PLENTY AND THE LABOURERS ARE JUST A FEW WHEN GOD BEGINS TO POUR HIS SEVEN SPIRITS ALL OVER YOU. OH, WHAT A DAY OF REJOICING THAT WILL BE.

THE SEVENTH (7TH) SERMON

THE BRIGHTER OR DARKER SIDE OF TOMORROW

HARD LABOUR N SIX DAYS HIS HOLY REST ON THE SEVENTH DAY. IN SIX DAYS, GOD MADE HIS WILL AND OVER 2019 YEARS YOU HAVE NOT ATTENDED UNTO IT. NOW HE HAS SET A PREPARED WAY TO BRING THE RENEWAL TO YOU. THE DARKNESS AND THE LIGHT STANDS BEFORE YOU AS YOU CONTEMPLATE THE FEAR OF GOD IN YOUR HEARTS, BEFORE THE GOD YOU SERVE, THINK AND WONDER ON THESE THINGS, "WHO IS GREATER THE CHURCHES, THE PRIESTS, THE PASTORS, AND YOU THE PATIENT SAINTS WITH EXHORTATION AGAINST GOD? – OR – THE TABERNACLE IN THE SUN, GOD, THE LORD JESUS CHRIST, THE MESSENGER AND THE REDEEMED, THROUGH GRACE AND THE LAW OF LOVE? WHEN YOU ARE THROUGH HERE THERE IS THE SIDE OF THE FENCE THAT GOES DOWN INTO PERDITION WITH SATAN AND THERE IS THE OTHER SIDE THAT WILL BE CALLED WORTHY TO SING TRIUMPHANTLY WITH THE LORD.

WHAT DOES IT MEANS TO COME OUT OF THE DARKNESS FOR THE PATIENT SAINTS? IT MEANS TO COME OUT OF BABYLON, AND STAND WITH THE EXAMPLE UNTO YOU BY THE MESSENGER OF GOD. LOOK AT HIMSELF AS THE ONLY SIX (6) AND THE SEEING OF HIS WAY IN THE SEVEN (7) – THE SABBATH ETC., FOR YOU AND WHAT YOU BELIEVE IN. SAY YOU'RE LIVING ON THE DARK SIDE OF TOMORROW OR THE LIGHT OF JESUS CHRIST AS THE BIBLE HATH SHOWED YOU TO.

NOW THEE LIBERALITY IS THE PREPARED WAY WITH THE CONSISTENCY UPON WHICH YOU FEED YOUR MIND UPON THE BIBLE IN THE LAST DAYS WITH TEACHINGS MAYBE IN A SCHOOL ROOM CALLED THE CHURCH, WHICH IS THE FOUNDATION OF GOD HOLY PLACE OF NEW REVERENCE, BUT FIXED UPON A RADIANT INCLINE TO THE TABERNACLE IN THE SUN OUT OF THE REACH OF THESE DESPERATELY GREEDY PASTORS THAT GOVERN OVER CHRISTENDOM, IN BABYLON.

OUR PRIEST PASTORS HAVE BEEN THROUGH THE STIR AND THEY HAVE BEEN PARTIALLY WARNED AS TO THE TRUTH OF THE WAY. THEY NOW KNOW THEIR TIME HAS COME TO KNOW GOD AND TO TEACH THE TRUTH ABOUT JESUS CHRIST, HIS GRACE TO BE ACCEPTED WITH ALL THEIR HEARTS, AND HIS LAW OF LOVE, HIS MYSTERY, AND THE WORSHIP OF GOD WHO IS A SPIRIT, SPIRITUALLY AND IN TRUTH, AND THE SABBATH DAY, IN THE HIGH TIME. UNDER THE TABERNACLE IN THE SUN, TO LOVE, TAKE AND KNOW HIM AS THE LIGHT OF THE WORLD, WHOM HATH GONE TO HIS FATHER WHO IS IN HEAVEN, AND NO MORE TO BE AT THEIR LEISURE, SEEKING THEIR OWN MEAT. LET NOT ANY THAT BELIEVE IN JESUS CHRIST BELIEVE

IT IS A SHAME AND ~~DISHONOR AND DISRESPECTFUL THING TO CARRY OUT THE~~ **STIR**~~, BECAUSE FOR THIS REASON OF WARNING OF THE CHURCHES OPENLY, IS ALSO PUBLIC WITNESS OF THE TRUTH. BUT NOW LET IT BE KNOWN IN THE UNDERSTANDING OF THE PRIESTS AND PASTORS THAT THEY ARE ALREADY BEING CURSED BY GOD THE CREATOR AND AFTER THE STIR AND THE MODERATIONS AS SOON AS THE LETTERS OF THE LIBERALITY AND THE SPIRITUAL CHURCH OF THE MANIFOLD WISDOM OF GOD UNDER THE TABERNACLE IN THE SUN IS RELEASED TO THEM THEREAFTER, THEIR FULL CURSE BEGINS. FOR I SPEAK NOT OF MYSELF IN THIS SPIRIT OF TRUTH BUT OF THE FATHER AND THE SON THAT SENT ME TO LET YOU KNOW ALL THINGS AND THE TRUTH. IN THE SCRIPTURES THERE ARE SOME THINGS HARD TO BE UNDERSTOOD AND HARD TO BE UNLEARNED, AND THIS THEY PARTAKE OF IN AN UNSTABLE WREST ALSO WITH OTHER SCRIPTURES AGAINST GOD, HAVING THOUGHT THEY HAVE ATTAINED ALL THAT IS RIGHT, UNTO THEIR OWN DESTRUCTION, AND CURSED SHALL THE PRIESTS AND PASTORS BE.~~

FOR THE LORD WOULD HAVE IT THAT YOU AS EARTHLY BEINGS ATTAIN PEACE. THEREFORE, HE HATH BROKEN DOWN THE MIDDLE WALL OF PARTITION BETWEEN US, HAVING ABOLISHED IN HIS FLESH THE ENMITY, EVEN THE LAW OF COMMANDMENTS, CONTAINED IN ORDINANCES, FOR TO MAKE IN HIMSELF OF TWAIN ONE NEW MAN, SO MAKING PEACE WITH THE CHILDREN OF DISOBEDIENCE. NOW BOTH WHOM ARE NEAR OR FAR FROM GOD THOUGH CHRIST WE ALL HAVE

ACCESS TO GOD, THROUGH HIM.

CHRIST HAVING SLAIN THE ENMITY ON THE CROSS THEREBY KNOCKING IT OUT OF THE WAY AS FALLEN FROM BOTH THOSE FAR AND NEAR TO BE RECONCILED UNTO GOD IN HUMBLENESS, AND GREAT HUMILITY OF ACCEPTANCE OF HIS GRACE, BY HIS BLOOD. OR THE CURSE BE UPON THEM AS THEY THAT OFFEND IN WORDS AGAINST THE METTLED LETTER AND THE SPIRITUAL CHURCH OF THE MANIFOLD WISDOM OF GOD UNDER THE TABERNACLE IN THE SUN, AS DEFILERS OF THE SPIRIT OF TRUTH FROM HE WHOM HATH REFRESHED THE MASTER'S SOUL. AND THE LORD THY GOD SAID CURSE SHALL THEY THAT LEAD THE FLOCKS, THE PATIENT SAINTS, BE.

THERE ARE TIMES WHEN YOU FIGHT AGAINST GOD UNKNOWINGLY HURTING JOY AND HAPPINESS, AND TAKE FOR GRANTED THE BUILDING UP SORROWS AS A SIMPLE THIN, UNTIL YOU REALIZE THAT YOU ROB THE CHILDREN OF THEIR FUTURE. WHEN THERE IS NO HOPE HERE OR THERE TO FOLLOW, UNTIL THE DARK SIDE BECOMES BRIGHTER AND NEW JOY COMES IN WHEN THE DARKNESS GOES AWAY

THEN ALL WILL CRY, FILL ME UP WITH SOMETHING MORE, THAT I CAN LIVE FOR WITHOUT YOURS, GIVE ME ALL THAT I WOULD NEED, TO FOREVER BE A SHINING LIGHT AND BEAM, GIVE ME ALL AND FILL ME UP WITH SOMETHING MORE, IN THE WORLD WE ARE LIVING IN.

IF YOU FIND YOURSELF IN THE DARKNESS, HOW WOULD YOU KNOW? THE FIRST THING IS THAT YOU MUST REALIZE THAN YOU OR ANY MAN WITH YOU ON THIS BURN SIDE OF EARTH HERE IS NO GOD ABOVE ALL GODS, AND IS NO MAN ABOVE ANY GOD THAT YOU MUST WORSHIP, FOR IF IT BE SO THEN THE END SEEMS EMINENT AND A FALLING AWAY WILL COME BEFORE THE GREAT DAY OF THE LORD.

BE DISGUST WITH THE FEELINGS AND THE THOUGHTS OF YOURS, THAT TEST THE MOST OMNIPOTENT, FOR HE IS THE DOOR THAT THAT WE MUST GO THROUGH TO FIND PEACE AND LOVE, GREAT SIGNS OF WONDERS, AND ENDLESS GLORY AND HOPE IN IT TOO.

FROM THE GARDEN PATH, THE DARK SIDE IS FILLED ENVY, HATE AND JEALOUSY, AND BORDERS AWAY MOMMY, DADDY AND ME, BUT THE

BRIGHT SIDE IS LOVE AND WISDOM, WHICH HATH POWER IN ONE GOD AND THE SON, AND SHINES AGAIN IN MY JUNGLE, WHERE HERE ALL SHALL SEE, THEN WHIST WE SWING ON IN GULLY, MORANT BAY, TO THE APPLE VALLEY IN MY EYES, THAT CAN TAKE THE LATTER GROWTH TODAY. TO THE CHILDREN THERE BE LIKE YOU, TO LET YOU LIVE ON THE BRIGHT SIDE OF TOMORROW, WHERE ALL OF US SHOULD REALLY BE, HISTORY MIGHT HAVE GONE COLD, BUT WISDOM HOPE, HOPE LOVE AND POWER, WILL BE HERE FOR US TO RESTORE. MANY THINGS SEEMS IMPOSSIBLE TO THE CHURCH I GREW UP IN. THEY USED TO SAY THIS CHURCH IS THE ONLY CHURCH, WHEN GOD SAID UPON PETER I BUILD MY CHURCH, AND IN REVELATION HE TELLS US, ALL SEVEN CHURCHES HAVE SINNED AGAINST HIM, AND THE SCRIPTURES FURTHER TELLS US WE SHALL ABIDE UNDER THE TABERNACLE IN THE SUN IN UNITY OF ONE BODY IN CHRIST. THEREFORE, ALL SEVEN CHURCHES ARE ON THE DARK SIDE AND ALL SEVEN CHURCHES NEEDS TO REPENT. GOD HAVE SPLITUP THE HOLY CHURCH SO THAT, NONE SHALL HAVE POWER OVER THE OTHER, AND NOW THEY DON'TEVEN KNOW WHAT THE MARK OF THE BEAST IS, OR WHAT THE BEAST REPRESENTS. THE BIBLE SAYS, A WISE MAN WILL TELL THEM WHAT THE MARK OF THE BEAST IS, ALTHOUGH IT TELLS THEM IT IS THE NAME OF A MAN, AND IN CONFUSION THE SCURRY TO DETERMINE SUCH A ONE, AND HAVE FOUND MANY OVER THE YEARS AS THEY HAVE LIVED TO WORSHIP IN THE ORDINANCES OF MAN BEING THE FRUITS OF THE BEAST, AND HATING THE ORDINANCE OF GOD. NOW THEY ARE JEALOUS OVER THE PRIESTHOOD AND SPIRITUAL THEODOLOGY, OF THE PREPARED WAY, WHILE TURNING AWAY FROM THE

LIGHT, AND WHILE FIGHTING THE SPIRIT OF GOD, AND WHILE RESISTING THE LORD JESUS CHRIST, FOR IF ANY MAN TAKETH THE MARK OF THE BEAST, HE WILL HAVE THE POWER OF DARKNESS IN HIS HAND AND SUCH A MAN THE LIGHT IS NOT IN HIM. SUCH A MAN WILL NOT SUP WITH THE LORD JESUS CHRIST, BECAUSE THE FILTHINESS AMONGST MEN IS SEEN IN HIM. SUCH A MAN HAVING THE SPIRIT OF MAN THE SPIRIT OF GOD AND THE SPIRIT OF SATAN COVERING HIM.

NOW GOD CREATED ALL IN SIX DAYS, AND MAN STILL NOT SURE WHAT THEY HAVE, YOU CREATE BEFORE ME AN OPEN DOOR AND LORD I KNOW WHAT IT IS. IT IS AN OPEN DOOR TO COME UNTO YOU

IN THE PRIVILEGE AS YOUR SAINT. YOU SET BEFORE ME O LORD AN OPEN DOOR, WHICH NO MAN CAN SHUT, FOR THE VINES OF THE VINEYARD CAN COME UNTO YOU, AND IF THEY WERE VINES OF GRASS THAT THEY SET BEFORE ME, YOU LORD WOULD HAVE TOLD ME, BUT YOUR WORDS ARE THE VINES AND THE BRANCHES ALTOGETHER IN THE SPIRIT OF GOD, WITH THE PEOPLE WHO LOVES YOU TO CLING TOGETHER UPON YOU TO BEAR FRUITS OF RIGHTEOUSNESS AS FRUITS OF CHRIST, IF THEY HAVE AN EAR TO

HEAR, FOR YOU O LORD IS MIGHTY AND HATH COME, WITH SEVEN SPIRITS OF GOD, THAT YOU WILL POUR OUT UPON US. AND ONTO MAN YOU ARE THE FIRST AND THE LAST, THE SON OF GOD SO THAT THOUGH OUR SINS ARE PLENTY YOU ALONE LORD JESUS CAN WASH THEM AWAY, WITH YOUR LOVE, YOUR GRACE, AND YOUR SPIRIT AND THE SPIRITS OF GOD THE FATHER. THOUGH YOUR SINS ARE PLENTY, AND A NO ONE SIN YOU ALL HAVE, YOU MUST BOW DOWN BEFORE THE LORD, TO WASH YOUR SINS AWAY,

THEREFORE, ALL CAN BOW DOWN BEFORE THE LORD. HE WHO IS GOD KNOW THAT I COME UNTO YOU, IN THE NAME OF THE LORD JESUS CHRIST, A MINISTER FROM THE EFFECTIVE WORKINGS OF THE WORKS OF GOD. NOW YOU BEARING FULL REPENTANCE FOR ALL SINS KNOWN AND UNKNOWN, MAKE YOUR GARMENTS ARE WHITE, TO THE LORD YOU CONSECRATE YOUR SOUL, TO BUILD YOURSELF UP IN ZION. SEARCH NOW FOR YOUR LORD INFINITE LOVE, ACCEPT THE HOLY AND PRECIOUS SON OF GOD, AS YOUR SAVIOUR FROM SIN. TAKE THE SPIRIT OF GOD FULLY INTO YOUR SOUL, BY JESUS CHRIST WHO IS LORD OVER ALL THINGS EVEN THE SABBATH DAY. YOU MUST SUBMERGE AND PURGE MYSELF INTO SPIRITUAL BAPTISM BY JESUS CHRIST, THY HOLY SON

FATHER OUR SINS ARE GREAT, BUT YOU WASH THEM AWAY, FOR AS IN MANY CHURCHES AND BEING CAUGHT UP IN MANY CHURCHES, EVEN

WITH THOSE THAT BLASPHEMED AGAINST THEE, SAYING THEY ARE JEWS AND ARE NOT, BUT NOW IN REDEMPTION GROUND

THE MESSENGER HAS IT THAT THOSE COMING TO GOD, THOUGH THEIR SINS ARE PLENTY, AND THEY LOVE THE THINGS THE LORD ABHOR,

NOW IF THEY WILL BOW DOWN BEFORE THE LORD, AND ASK HIM TO WASH THEIR SINS AWAY. HE GOD WILL DO IT.

THE LAWS OF MY GOD'S MOUTH ARE BETTER TO ME THAN FINE GOLD, FOR IT IS THINE HANDS THAT HAVE MADE ME AND FASHIONED ME, IT IS YOUR HANDS THAT GAVE ME UNDERSTANDING, THAT I MAY LEARN THY COMMANDMENTS. MAN, IN THEIR ORDINANCES HAVE REVILED THY LAWS, BUT ONLY YOU O LORD CAN ANNUL YOUR LAWS. FOR YOUR TIME COMMETH AND SO REVELATION GET MORE FROM THE LAWS OF GOD.

ONE OF MANY CHURCHES FOR ALL THOSE WITH SINS THAT ARE PLENTY IN THE ORDINANCES OF MAN, ON THE CHURCH OF THY HOLY FOUNDATIONS, HAVE NOW MADE VOID THY LAWS IN THE ORDINANCES OF MAN, HAVING NO INSTRUCTIONS FROM THE BIBLE.

LET EVERY MAN RETURN TO THE SPIRIT OF GOD, AND ESTEEM HIS PRECEPTS, ACCORDING UNTO THY MERCIES, AND LET THEM ALSO FIND HIS STATUTES, SO THAT YOUR SALVATION AND RIGHTEOUSNESS, O LORD CAN RETURN TO THE CHURCHES, AS THEY ESTEEM HIS PRECEPTS AND RETURN FROM YOUR FALSE WAYS, UNTO GOD.

LET HE ENTRANCE OF THY WORDS, BRING LIGHT TO EVERY CHURCH NOT JUST MINE AND EVERY SOUL THEREIN. FOR GOD WILL LOOK DOWN UPON THE CHURCH, AND UPON THY CHILDREN AS YOU USED TO DO WITH THOSE THAT LOVED YOUR NAME, AND MAKE THY FACE TO SHINE UPON THEM, EVEN UNTO US ALL AS HE SO LET THE GREAT REPENTANCE COME UP UNTO HIM.

WE BELIEVE NOW IN YOUR WORDS O LORD, FOR NOW WE KNOW THAT YOU CAN PUT AWAY ALL THE WICKED OF THE EARTH LIKE DROSS, LET THE GREAT SALVATION TAKE HOLD OF THE CHURCHES AND THE SOULS THEREIN, COME UNTO US AND ORDER OUR STEPS O LORD IN THY WORDS. FOR WHOSOEVER, SHALL HEAR YOUR WORDS, AND GLORIFY YOU LORD JESUS, THEY SHALL HEAR YOUR WORDS AND BE CLEANSE FROM THEIR DEEDS. THEY SHALL HEAR YOUR WORDS AND BE LOVED, BE LOVED LIKE THOSE WHO USED TO LOVE YOUR NAME, AND LORD LET NO INEQUITY HAVE DOMINION OVER US AND THE CHURCHES IN JESUS NAME, AS THEY TAKE THE LIGHT OF JESUS CHRIST DAY BY DAY AND LITTLE BY LITTLE.

LET THEM SEEK YEE O LORD SEVEN TIMES A DAY TO PRAY, BECAUSE OF THY RIGHTEOUS JUDGEMENT AND LOVING YOUR LAWS THROUGH GRACE. LET NOTHING OFFEND THEM. GIVE OUR HANDS POWER, LET OUR HANDS HELP US UP,

SO SHALL YOUR CHILDREN GIVE YOU O LORD PRAISE, LET OUR SOUL LIVE O LORD FOR THEY WILL GIVE YOU PRAISE. LORD THESE ARE

YOUR SHEEP THAT HAVE GONE ASTRAY, LET THEM GIVE YOU PRAISE ONCE MORE, FOR NOW, THE TIME OF THY WORD OF PROPHECIES ARE COME, AND YOU SHALL BRING FORTH THY PEOPLE WITH JOY, AND YOUR SERVANT WITH MUCH GLADNESS, O LORD HOW MANIFOLD IS THY WORKS, IN GREAT WISDOM HAST THOU MADE THEM, MAN CAN NOT ATTAIN UNTO IT, O LORD WITH YOUR SPIRIT YOUR PEOPLE WAS CREATED, THERE IS NO END TO WHAT YOU CAN DO.

BUT THE HEAVENS THEY SEE AND CAN'T MAKE IT, STRETCHED OUT LIKE A CURTAIN TO ONLY ADORE IT, YOU ARE THE LIGHT, YOU ARE CLOTHED WITH MAJESTY AND HONOUR, YOU ARE OUR GOD, AND NO OTHER. AS WE LIVE AND WILL SING PRAISE TO THE LORD.

WHILE WE HAVE OUR WELL BEING, LET US MEDITATE ON THE LORD, OH HOW SWEET HE IS TO US, LET ALL PUT GOD IN THEM AND FIND THE LIGHT. FOR THESEARE THE LAST DAYS, WHEN THEY COME, THEY ARE NOR GOING TO COME BACK, NOW THEY CARRY THE HEAVENLY GIFT, THE GRACE OF GOD IN ABUNDANCE, BUT AFTER PERDITION BEGINS HEY NO MORE WILL BE. FOR ALL MANKIND THAT HAVE STRAYED WITH UNBELIEF, IN SO MANY WAYS, IT CARRIES SALVATION FOR SOME AND EASY REPENTANCE TO OTHERS, FOR IT IS THE LAST DAYS. GOD IS MAKING A WAY REBUILD HIS GARDEN.

FOR GOD SO LOVED THE WORLD, THAT HE GAVETH HIS ONLY BEGOTTEN SON, THAT WHOOSOVER BELIEVETH IN HIM, SHOULD NOT PERISH BUT HAVE EVERLASTING LIFE, AND TO THE CHILDREN IN THE FOUNDATION OF THE OLD CHURCH, YEA, THE EPHERMERAL CHURCHES, BEFORE REPENTANCE THE LORD JESUS BESEECH YOU ALL, TO PUT YOUR LOVE ON HIM, FORGETTING HUMAN ORDINANCES AND

PUT YOUR FAITH IN HIM. IF YOU BELIEVE THAT CHRIST CAN DO ALL THINGS, THEN BELIEVE HIS WORDS, FIND THE LIGHT OF THE SPIRIT, AND KEEP IT IN YOU, AND FROM THE ENSIGN BEGIN THE RENEWAL OF THE CHURCH.

LET THE SPIRITUAL GROWTH OF THE TREE BE ENLARGED BY THE LATTER RAIN, AND LET ALL BE GRAPHED IN THE SPIRITUAL LIGHT OF THE LIVING

GOD, AND NOW SEEK THE TABERNACLE IN THE SUN, THE LAST CHURCH OF THE LORD YOUR GOD, AND LOVE IT MORE EACH DAY.

YEA THIS IS THE TIME IT YOU MEN THAT ARE MARRIED TO LOVE THE TABERNACLE IN THE SUN, JUST LIKE HOW YOU LOVE YOUR WIVES. NOT LIKE IN TIMES GONE BY WHEN YOU HAD MORE CARES IN THE WORLD, FOR IN THINE YOUTH THINE EYES WERE PLACED ON HIM, BUT STAYED TO MUCH CARE OF THE WORLD, A PLACE YOU NOW FIND NOT ENTICING AS THE GRACE OF GOD, THE TRUTH OF GOD AND THE IN THE LAST DAYS, FOR FINDING THE LIGHT.

THE SPIRITUAL CHURCH WILL WITH THE ENSIGNS OF GOD, WILL LEAD THE CHURCH TO REPENTANCE, WITH THE PREPARED WAY, AND WIVES YOUR HUSBANDS HATH LOVED THE TABERNACLE IN THE SUN THE LAST CHURCH OF THE LORD THY GOD, THEREFORE LOVE THEM TOO AND SUBMIT YOURSELVES UNTO THEM, LEST THEY BECOME WEAK AFTER THE FLESH. LET HUMILITY AND LOVE WILL BEGIN TO GROW ONCE MORE IN THE HEARTS OF MEN,

AT HIS COMING, YOU ALL SHALL UVE WITH THE LORD A THOUSAND YEARS AFTER THE FIRST COMING, THEN THOSE WHOM HAD ACCEPTED GRACE AND THE LAW OF LOVE WILL BE ABLE TO ENTER HIS COURTS, AND DRINK OF HIS HEALING STEAM.

THE HIGH TIME IS PULLING THE VINES OF THE HOLY CALLING TO THEE AND AS THE CHURCHES HEAR LET THE PEOPLE COME, SO THAT THEY CAN KNOW THE LORD AND BE SAVED. LOOKING AT THE THINGS WHICH THE LORD HATED, WHICH MEN HAVE CONTRIVED UPON THEMSELVES AS FILTHY MEN. AS THE MESSENGER SAID SUBMIT YOURSELVES WIVES TO YOUR HUSBANDS TO KEEP THE LUST OF FILTHINESS OFF THEIR MINDS. MEN LOVE YOUR WIVES SO YOU DON'T HAVE ANOTHER MAN SLAPPING YOUR BUTT FOR ENTICING YOUR WILL IN DARKNESS. NOW WE KNOW THAT WHEN A FEW THINGS AGAINST YOU IS PLENTY TO THE LORD. IT IS UP TO YOU TO BE HEALED FROM YOUR FILTHINESS AND DARKNESS, TO BE FORGIVEN OF YOUR SINS AND TO TEACH AND BRING THY CHILDREN TO COME UNTO THE LORD.

TO THEM THAT CAST EVIL UPON THE WORLD, AND ARE PROCESSING THEIR BROTHERS INTO PARADISE AS MINCEMEAT, FOR A POSITION WITH GOD THAT THEY KNOW NOT, UNTIL THEY KNOW HIM IN THE JOY OF THE SPIRIT OF GRACE AND THE LAW OF LOVE. O LORD LET THEM TURN TO THEE AND THE SWORD WILL TURN FROM THEM, SO THEY CAN EAT THE JOY OF PARADISE. LET THE CHURCHES NOW SEE THAT THEY NEED TO RELEASE THEMSELVES FROM THEIR EVIL DEEDS AND COME BACK TO

GOD THROUGH THE LIBERALITY AND THE SPIRITUAL CHURCH OF THE MANIFOLD WISDOM OF GOD. TELLING YOUR BROTHERS THAT GOD HAVE WALKED AMONGST YOU AND WILL COME AGAIN QUICKLY IF YOU DO NOT TURN BUT CONTINUE TO

TEACH THIS EVIL UPON MANKIND. THEREFORE, LOOK AT THE NEW GOSPEL AND THE NEW COVENANT UNDER THE TABERNACLE IN THE SUN AND PLACE THE CHURCHES STEADFAST UNDER IT WITH A CLEAN HEART TO ACCEPT THE WILL OF GOD AND THE LAW OF LOVE. WITH ALL YOUR HEARTS. SO, YOU CAN HAVE LIFE ABUNDANTLY IN THE SPIRIT OF GOD BY JESUS

FINDING THE LIGHT, THE S CHRIST WHOM SHOULD BE YOUR FIRST LOVE. OURC E OF LOVE, AND PUT AWAY YOUR DOCTRINES AND UNBELIEF AS NOT COMPLIANT WITH THE BIBLE OF GOD'S WORD. FOR YOUR DARKNESS WILL RETREAT AS YOU SET THE LORD IN FRONT OF YOU AND TRY IN THE HIGH TIME TO KNOW THE LORD THY GOD, WHO IS JAH THE LORD OF LORDS AND WHO IS ABOVE ALL GOD'S, NOT YOUR GOD.

FO HE SHALL COME QUICKLY, HE WHO WALKETH BETWEEN THE SEVEN CANDLE STICKS, HE WHO HATH POWER OVER ALL THINGS, GO FOR THE WEAK AND HEAVY LADEN IN THE REFUGEE CAMPS AND THE WAR ZONE THAT FOUGHT YOUR WAR AGAINST GOD AND ALL MANKIND

AND MAKE THEM FULFIL THEIR RESTITUTIONS IN THE SAME GARDENS YOU ARE LIVING IN AND HAVE A GOOD LIFE LIKE YOU. YES, YOU CAN LOOK TO GOVERNMENTS FOR HELP BUT YOU SET THEM OUT TO WAR SO, LET YOUR PEACE BE THEIR PEACE AND YOUR DEVELOPMENT BE THEIR DEVELOPMENT AND SET OUT LOVE BETWEEN ALL MEN.

WHO STANDETH WITH THE TWO-EDGED SWORDS IN HIS MOUTH IS WATCHING AND IF YOUR CHURCH CANNOT RETURN FOR THE WEARY OF WAR AND HELP THEM THEN, HE WHO HATH EYES LIKE UNTO THE FLAMES OF FIRE? WILL ALLOW THE ANGELS TO DIM YOUR CANDLE STICK. REMEMBER HE IS THE FIRST AND THE LAST, FOR HE KNOWS ALL WORKS, AND HIS FEET IS AS FINE BRASS, YES, HE KNOWS OUR PATIENCE AS HE IS THE FIRST AND THE LAST. LET NOT THE CHILDREN VOW TO GO AGAIN UNTO DEATH AND DARKNESS, SHALL THE CHURCHES KNOW REPENTANCE OF THEIR GREAT SIN OR THE WRATH OF HE WHO IS GOD ALMIGHTY, THAT SHALL COME QUICKLY UPON ALL THEIR CHILDREN WITH DEATH, FOR GOD HE IS THAT SEARCHETH THE REINS AND THE HEARTS, THEN, SHALL HE NOT KNOW, SO, HE IS THE FIRST AND THE LAST, PAMPER NOT YOURSELVES IN THE ABUNDANCE OF YOUR SINS AS

THROUGH RICHES AND THROUGH GREED, AND A BAD DOCTRINE, CAN CAUSE GOD ALMIGHTY TO EMPATHIZE WITH YOU. FOR THE LORD IS MERCIFUL, ONLY IF YOU COME UNTO HIM AND KNOW HIM AND DENY NOT THE NAME OF THE LORD, THOUGH, YOU HAVE SATAN SITTING AT YOUR COUNSEL, HE GOD ALMIGHTY HATH FORGIVEN THE EVIL ONES, AND HATH GIVEN THEM SALVATION AND SO HE CAN FORGIVE THE CHURCHES AND GIVE TO YOU SALVATION FROM REPENTANCES OF YOUR SIN UPON HUMANITY AS YOU PORTRAY A CLEAN HEART IN DARKNESS FOR HAVING AN EVIL SWORD UPON THE PEOPLE ALWAYS.

FOR THE TIME IS COMING WHEN WE SHALL FALL INTO REVELATION AND THE DIMMING OF YOUR CANDLE STICKS IT CAN'T BE UNDONE, HE THAT HATH EARS LET HIM HEAR WHAT THE SPIRIT SAITH UNTO THE CHURCHES.

FOR BEHOLD GOD STANDS AT THE DOOR AND KNOCKS, HE HAS BEEN KNOCKING FOR SO LONG, FOR MANKIND TO ACCEPT GRACE AND LIVE THE LAW OF LOVE. THE SPIRITUAL CHURCH IS FOR A SHORT TIME TO

TEACH MANKIND THE WAY TO THE OPEN DOOR, IF ANY MAN, COME UNTO HIS KNOCKING, HEAR AND OPEN THE DOOR OF GRACE, THE LORD THY GOD WILL COME IN UNTO HIM AND THE FIRST AND THE LAST WILL SUP WITH HIM, AND HE WITH THE LORD JESUS CHRIST, GIVING YOU A PLACE IN HIS THRONE TO SIT WITH HIS FATHER ALSO. AND THOUGH THE PEOPLE SINS ARE PLENTY, AND A NO ONE SIN THEM HAVE, LET'S US BOW DOWN BEFORE THE LORD, LET US NOW KNOW THE LORD AND WASH THEIR SINS AWAY. AND THOUGH THEIR SINS ARE PLENTY, AND THEY LOVE THE THINGS THE LORD ABHOR, WE WILL NOT MOCK THEM BUT HUMBLE OURSELVES BEFORE THEM AS THEY NOW BOW OWN BEFORE THE LORD, WITH REPENTANT HEARTS, AND WASH THEIR SINS AWAY. AND THOUGH OUR SINS ARE PLENTY, CAUSE A NO ONE CHURCH WE HAVE, THE CHURCHES WILL REOENT BEFORE THE LORD, AND WASH THEIR SINS AWAY.

NOW LET US CRY UNTO THE LORD, CRY FOR JAH CHILDREN, YEA, LIVE, LIVE ANOTHER DAY JUST TO LOVE THEM, AND, THE SPOKEN WORDS OF JAH, WILL COME IN THEIR HEARTS, ITH JAH LOVE. ALL THEM A SELL ME OUT SAY THEM WANT TO STOP THE MESSENGER, THIS IS ALL THE

REMEDY THEY NEED, TO COME BACK TO GOD, TO STOP THE PASS ROUND DONKEY THING AND BE AT PEACE WITH THE MESSENGER AND WITH GOD. SAY THEM WANT STOP THE MESSENGER WITH ALL THE THINGS THEY HAVE DONE TRYING TO HIDE THE DARKNESS BY PLACING MISERY UPON HIS HEAD, FOR THINGS THEY KNEW NOTHING ABOUT, WHEN THE MESSENGER SAY CRY, CRY FOR JAH CHILDREN, LIVE, YEA, LIVE ANOTHER DAY JUST TO LOVE THEM AND THE SPOKEN WORDS OF JAH, WILL COME IN THEIR

HEARTS, WITH JAH LOVE, THE MESSENGER WILL TAKE YOU BACK TO THE BEGINNING.

LET IT BE, FOR THE LONG BEEN PARTED MAY HAVE A CHANCE TO SEE REDEMPTION UPON THE WORLD AS IT MOVES AWAY FROM DARKNESS.

AND BREAK THE CHAIN AROUND ME, AND STAND TALL AGAIN, AND WALK DOWN THE STREET AGAIN, TO HEAR THE CHILDREN LAUGHTER AND THE VOICES OF THE TEMPLE, THE CITY AND OF JAH SING AGAIN.

BOOK FOUR

THE WILLING STEWARD

IN THE HIGH TIME THE WILLING STEWARDS ARE FEW. WHAT I MEAN IS THAT HE LABOURERS OF THE LORD ARE FEW IN THE GREATEST HARVEST OF ALL TIMES. THE MINISTRY OF RECONCILIATION NEEDS WILLING STEWARDS IN THIS HIGH TIME WHEN THE HARVEST IS PLENTY AND THE LABOURERS ARE JUST A FEW. SOME WILL BE FREE LANCE AND SOME ACREDITED UNDER THE TABERNACLE IN THE SUN, THE MANEGAERIAL CHURCH OF OUR LORD JESUS CHRIST WITH THE SEVEN (7) ANGELS RULING OVER THE SEVEN (7) CANDLE STICKS, IN THE RIGHT HAND OF OUR LORD.

IT IS SAID THAT DAY UNTO DAY BRINGETH KNOWLEDGE, AND NIGHT UNTO NIGHT BRINGETH FORTH WISDOM. THE ETERNAL WORKS OF THE FATHER IS WISDOM, NOW ARE YOU WITH ME, OR ARE YOU WILLING TO DO YOUR OWN THING, ARE YOU WITH ME, OR ARE YOU WILLING TO ACT AGAINST GOD, CONTINUALLY. THE FIGHT AGAINST GOD IS BEARS ANOTHER FRUIT, THE MARK OF THE BEAST, AFTER ALL IS SAID AND DONE WHEN YU HEAR AND YOU SEE, MY BIBLE TELLS ME YOU ARE TO OBEY, THE MESENGER OF GOD AND ACCEPT THE WILL OF GOD WITH ALL YOUR HAERTS.

DISOBEDIENCE LEAVES YOU LIKE LOT'S WIFE, MORE DEFIANCE TO THE TRUTH OF JESUS CHRIST, BEARS MORE DARKNESS, BUT THIS TIME, WITH TORMENT DAY AND NIGHT, THIS TABERNACLE THAT YOU ARE NOW AWERE OF WITH THE MANIFOLD WISDOM OF GOD IS YET UNSEEKABLE AT YOUR OWN WILL WHEN THE MESSENGER IS COME UNTO YOU, IT IS FOR RECEIVAL, AFTER THE SWORD OF GOD IS UNACCEPTED IT WILL BE YOUR DISOBEDIENCE UPON YOUR OWN HEAD. NO MAN CAN BEND, STRAIGHTEN, BLUNT OR CHANGE, THE MESSENGER OF GOD NO MAN CAN WARY TO DARKNESS AND MAKE THE MESSENGER OF GOD CONFOUNDED, AMAZED AND UNSURE OF THE WAY, THE FINISHER IS GREATER THAN JOHN YOU CAN'T MAKE A SPECTACLE OF HIM HUMBLE YOURSELVES BEFORE GOD AND SEE THE LORD THY GOD WORK THINGS

OUT HIS WAY, FOR ALL MEN, BY ACCEPTING HIS WILL AND THE LAW OF LOVE AS GIVEN BY THE MEASSENGER AS THE FIRST EXMPLE OF THE LABOURERS IN THE GREAT HARVEST. THIS WILLING STEWARD WILL KNOW CHRIST, THE MYSTERY OF CHRIST AND WILL PARTAKE OF HIS SPIRITUAL REDEMPTION TO SAVE THE WORLD IN THE HIGH TIME. HE WILL BE FOLLOWING THE LORD JESUS CHRIST WHOSE WAY IS PRESCRIBED AND CAN ONLY BE DONE HIS WAY. THE WILLING STEWARDS WAY IS DONE IN THE BEAUTY OF RECEPTION TO HOLINESS AND NOT IN YOUR SPOTTED WAY UNDER THE TABERNACLE IN THE SUN WITH CHOOSING GRACE AND THE LAW OF LOVE UNDER THE SPIRITUAL GUIDANCE OF THE CREATOR IN THE LAST DAYS.

YOU CANNOT REACH THE CHURCH AS A PRIESTLY STEWARD, WITH THE MESSAGE OF THE MESSENGER'S PREPARED WAY, AND BE LIFTED UP UNTO THE TABERNACLE OF THE SUN, THAT IS IN THE HAND OF THE LORD JESUS CHRIST WITH SEVEN ANGELS READY TO DIM YOUR LIGHT, WITHOUT THE TRUTH THAT IT IS OF THE LORD IN THE NEW GOSPEL AND THE NEW COVENANT OF THE HIGH TIME CALLED THE LIBERALITY FROM THE MESSENGER. UNTO YOU A WARNING TO KEEP THE CHURCHES STEADFAST UPON CHRIST IN THE HIGH TIME.

I WILL SAY UNTO YOU, THE SIGNS ON THE ROAD SHOWS THAT THE LORD'S MESSENGER DWELL IN THE SECRET PLACE OF THE MOST HIGH GOD, AND THEREFORE I WILL ABIDE UNDER THE SHADOW OF THE ALMIGHTY GOD, FOR IN THESE HIGH TIME, THE LORD WILL HELP ME THEREFORE SHALL I THE MESSENGER NOT BE CONFOUNDED AS YOU ALL WANTED ME TO BE, THEREFORE NOW HAVE I SET MY FACE AGAINST THEM LIKE A FLINT, AND I KNOW THAT I SHALL NOT BE ASHAMED. TO THE WILLING STEWARD A PERFECT EXAMPLE ON THE ROAD YOU WILL TRAVEL WITH THE LABOUR OF THE GREATEST HARVEST OF ALL TIMES.

YES, THE MESSENGER KNOWS THAT IN ALL THINGS I WILL NOT BE ASHAMED AND I BEAR IN MY BODY THE MARKS OF THE LORD JESUS CHRIST, AS IT SHOULD BE FOR THE LABOURERS OF THE GREATEST HARVEST. MY GOD HATH LAID IN SION AS IT IS WRITTEN, BEHOLD I LAY IN SION A STUMBLING STONE AND A ROCK OF OFFENCE AND WHOSOEVER BELIEVETH ON HIM SHALL NOT BE ASHAMED. GOD IS MY ROCK OF OFFENCE,

ZION TRAIN IS OUT OF THE GROUND NOT TO BE DISMAYED, AND ANCHORED DOWN ANYMORE BUT TO CAUSE THE PATIENT SAINTS TO PERSEVERE UNTO REDEMPTION UNTO CHRIST WITH THE PRIESTS COMING FOR THE UNDERSTANDING OF THE PREPARED WAY CALLED THE LIBERALITY AND THE SPIRITUAL CHURCH OF THE MANIFOLD WISDOM OF GOD UNDER THE TABERNACLE IN THE SUN.

YOU THE LABOURERS MUST COMPLETE THE WORK OF THE ONE THAT SENT ME, THE LORD THY GOD, ARE YOU WITH ME NOW. NOTE NOW AND KNOW THAT I TRUST NOT IN YOU AND YOUR PUFFED-UP SELVES, BUT IN THE LORD GOD OF HOST, AND SO MUST THE LABOURERS IN THE HIGH TIME TO BE STEWARDS OF CHRIST.

WHERE IS YOUR PLACE IN THE NAME GOD ALMIGHTY'S KINGDOM? WITHIN GOSPEL THAT ARE OF PARTS OF HIS WORD. HUMBLE YOURSELVES AND BE THANKFUL WITH ALL YOUR HEART, FOR THROUGH THE MESSENGER AND THE LABOURERS OF CHRIST, YOU SHALL SOON SHOW THE WORLD YOUR FRUITS OF UNRIGHTEOUSNESS, YOU SHALL SOON SHOW THE WORLD HOW

YOU FOUGHT AGAINST GOD, AND TO FIGHT AGAINST GOD YOU WILL BE SPIRITUALLLY DOOOMED, IT SAYS AGAIN, YOU SHALL BE TORMENTED DAY AND NIGHT, UNLESS YOU REPENT, AND COME TO KNOW GOD. THE MESSENGER AND THE LABOURERS IN CHRIST THROUGH THE SPIRIT WILL NOW SEE THE BEST OF THEM BE LIKE BRIERS, SO SHARP THAT THAT THE MOST UPRIGHT WILL BE SHARPER THAN A THORN EDGE. FOR THIS IS THE DAY OF THY WATCHMAN THAT COMMETH AND TO YOU YOUR VISITATION COMETH AND NOW SHALL BE YOUR PERPLEXITIES, AND ALL THAT YOU TRUST DISHONERETH EVERYONE SO IF YOU TURN MINE ENEMIES, WITHIN THE HOUSE OF GOD, REJOICE NOT AGAINST ME OR THE LABOURERS, FOR WHEN I OR THE LABOURERS FALL WE SHALL RISE, FOR WE SHALL WAIT ON THE LORD AND WE SHALL ALWAYS BE LOOKING UP TO THE LORD. WHEN WE SIT

IN DARKNESS THE LORD SHALL BE LIGHT ABOUT US THE WILLING STEWARDS, THE MESSENGER GREATER THAN JOHN, THE FINISHER, PROCLAIMS IT AND YOU HAVE SEEN THAT MY GOD HEARS ME AND IS MY SALVATION FOR EVER, DON'T FIGHT ME OR THE LABOURERS IN

CHRIST IN THIS GREAT HARVEST, JUST BE A WILLING STEWARD FOR GOD. YOU ARE NOW SINNERS AGAINST GOD WHEN YOU SHOULD BE RIGHTEOUS PEOPLE IN HIS FLOCK, BUT GOD IS RIGHTEOUS AND GOOD, THEREFORE HE WILL TEACH YOU HIS WAY. GOD BROUGHT THE MESSENGER TO YOU TO TEACH YOU HIS WAY BUT YOU TRANSGRESS AGAINST ME, BEING NOT READY TO RECEIVE THE WORD, BUT THE WILLING STEWARDS WILL. THE WILLING STEWARDS WILL COME TO THE LORD BY MEANS OF THE MESSENGER TO UNDERSTAND THE SWORD OF THE SPIRIT OR THE WORD IN THE SPIRIT OF GOD, NOT YOUR FLESHY SPIRIT OF UNBELIEF AND DARKNESS UNTO THE WORLD. BUT CHANGE HIS MIND TO ACCEPT GRACE AND DELIVER THE LOVE OF GOD TO ALL HIS SHEEP.

THE WILLING STEWARDS ARE TO BE THANKFUL WITH ALL THEIR HEARTS, YOU SHOULD ALL BOW DOWN AND ASK THE LORD TO SHOW YOU HIS WAYS, FOLLOW THE MESSENGER WHOM YOU ALL WERE NOT BUT, AS SOME WILL SAY INSTEAD, AS YOU SAID, IF YOU HAVE MEET YOU SHOULD DELIVER TO THE CHURCH FIRST, AS A GIFT, THAT IS NOT WILLING TO RECEIVE BUT LET AGAINST THE MESSENGER. THE MESSENGER IS NOT YOUR WIFE WHOM WILL GET THE WORDS OF WISDOM AND TO YOU GIVE, FOR YOUR DEVELOPMENT. THE MESSENGER IS A MESSENGER OF GOD WITH A PREPARED WAY FOR ALL TO FOLLOW AND NOT JUST YOU YOURSELVES. THEREFORE, YOUR PRIESTS MUST COME FOR THE UNDERSTANDING THEREOF TO GO AND TEACH THEIR WARDS AND ISSUE THE WORK OF THE MESSENGER TO THEIR WARDS.

SO, YOU ARE GOING TO BLOCK ME THE MESSENGER FROM REACHING THE WORLD WITH THE WORD, AND HAVE THINE OWN WAY, THE MESSENGER SAYS CONTINUE AT THINE OWN RISK AGAINST GOD THE ALMIGHTY WHOSE WORD, I CARRY TO THE WILLING STEWARDS. FOR THE SALVATION OF THE PATIENT SAINTS AND THE WORLD, CAN YOU BLOCK ME WHEN I AM ALL OVER THE FOUR CORNERS OF THE EARTH

ALREADY LOOKING AT YOU IN YOUR LITTLE CORNER AND I, IN SHADOW OF THE LORD GOD OF HOST WITH THE STIR AND THE PREPARED WAY MODERATION. THE WILLING STEWARDS WILL LOVE THE STIR AND THE MODERATION AND BECOME LABOURERS OF CHRIST.

I SAY UNTO YOU THE WAY OF THE TABERNACLE GOES WITH ME WHEN THERE IS ALSO MY VISITATION, AND THERE WILL BE NO LIGHT IN YOU WITHOUT MY REMEMBERANCE, YOU WILL BE LEFT IN DARKNESS, THE CHURCH AFTER BEING THANKFUL TO THE LORD FOR THE WATCH- MAN WITH ALL THEIR HEARTS, SHOULD HONOUR GOD, NOT THEIR FRUITS OF WITHIN THAT CAUSE THEM TO LACK IN THE LATTER RAIN AND SAY UNTO THE LORD, SHOW ME THY WAYS AND FOLLOW AS A WILLING STEWARD.

IN THIS THE LAST DAYS, THIS DOCTRINE I BRING — TO — YOU, IT IS, THE GOOD WILL OF THE LORD THY GOD. YOU SHOULD SAY UNTO THE LORD GOD OF HOST GIVE ME THE WILL TO HONOUR YOUR WORDS AND BELIEVE IN AS MUCH AS I AS A LABOURER IN THE GREAT HARVEST TEACHETH THE GENTILES AND SINNERS AND THE PATIENT SAINTS TO ACCEPT YOUR WILL O LORD, AND CONTINUE TO SHOW ME THY WAYS O LORD TEACH ME THE UNDERSTANDING OF THY PATHWAYS. LEAD ME IN THE TRUTH AND TEACH ME, SO I CAN UNDERSTAND AS A WILLING STEWARD.

THE LORD HAVE NOT UTTERLY CAST YOU OFF, BECAUSE I AM NOT GONE AWAY FROM YET AS THE MESSENGER OF HOPE, THE TABERNACLE IN THE SUN IS STILL AMONGST MEN, AND WILL BE FOREVER YOUR ONLY HOPE UNTO SALVATION IN THE HIGH TIME, THE SPIRITUAL THEOLOGY IS STILL WITHIN YOUR REACH FOR GOD. FOR GOD'S LOVING KINDNESS IS STILL BEFORE OUR EYS AND THROUGH IT THE WILLING STEWARDS MUST WALK IN THE FAITH OF THY TRUTH OF GOD.

I ASK THE LORD TO REMEMBER NOT THY TRANSGRESSION FOR THE UNHEARD SAKE AND MY BRETHEN THAT SEEKETH THE LORD IN THESE LAST DAYS. FOR YOU TO SAY WITH YOUR HEARTS LORD SHOW ME THY WAYS AND TEACH ME THY PATHS. LEAD ME IN THY TRUTH AND TEACH ME. WHAT DID THE MESSENGER SAY? LEAD ME IN THY TRUTH AND TEACH ME, FOR THOU HATH MY SALVATION AND ON

THEE O LORD DO I WAIT ALL THE DAY LONG. FOR THE LABOURERS OF THE GREATEST HARVEST TO COME FOR THE UNDERSTANDING OF THE LIBERALITY. LET NONE THAT WAIT UPON THE BE ASHAMED, BUT LET

THOSE THAT TRANSGRESS, WHO? LET THOSE THAT TRANSGRESS THE MESSENGER'S INHERITANCE WITHOUT A CAUSE BE ASHAMED. GOD HATH MADE ME TO WALK IN THE CONGREGATION AND BLESS THE

LORD OF HOST IN HIS HOUSE MY FOOT STANDETH IN AN EVEN PLACE NO LESSER MAN BECAUSE OF MINE INTEGRITY, MY GOD HATH REDEEMED ME FROM YOUR MISCHIEF AND BE MERCIFUL UNTO ME. THE MESSENGER, THE FINISHER GREATHER THAN JOHN THE BAPTIST, AND GREATER THAN JOHN THE REVELATOR IN THE HIGH TIME UNDER THE TABERNACLE OF THE SUN. SO SHALL THE LABOURERS FOLLOW THE EXAMPLE AND BE WORTHY IN THE LORD OF HIS PROMISE.

CHRIST CAME TO GIVE THE SWORD OF THE SPIRIT IN PERSON, TO A WILLING PROPHET THAT WOULD DO HIS WILL, AND HIS WILL ONLY TO ABIDE BY GRACE AND THE LAW OF LOVE. BAPTIZING MANKIND IN THE SPIRIT OF THE LIVING WATERS AND THE NAME OF HIS FATHER AND HIMSELF. BUT HIS DISCIPLES COULD NOT UNDERSTAND AND SO HE WAS LEFT TO PRESCRIBE ANOTHER WAY, A NEW WAY FOR THE FULL UNDERSTANDING, TO TEACH MEN THAT GRACE WAS SUFFICIENT TO COME UNTO HIM, AND THE LAW OF LOVE WAS ENOUGH FOR THE HEARTS OF MEN TO BE RIGHTEOUS, AND TO KNOW HIM WAS TO FEAR HIM, HE THAT WAS DEAD AND NOW LIVETH TO BE CLEAN, HATING THE THINGS HE ABHOR.

THE MISTERY OF JESUS CHRIST

IF I CAN'T FIND SOLACE IN A WORSHIP DAY ANYMORE IT'S BECAUSE OF GRACE AND LOVE, BUT MORESO THE LAW OF LOVE, TO LOVE YOUR BROTHERS AND SISTERS JUST LIKE YOURSELVES. THAT DOES NOT MEAN THAT PEOPLE WILL FORGET WORSHIPPING GOD. THEY ONLY NEED TO FIND THE TRUE WAY OF DOING IT RIGHT FOR GOD AND IN SO DOING IT ACCEPT GRACE AND THE LAW OF LOVE AS THEIR GUIDE IN HUMBLENESS OR THEIR HUMILITY IN THE SIMILAR WAY OF CHRIST. FROM ESCHATOLOGY THE COMPARISON OF HUMAN CONSCIOUSNESS BY THE "THE GARDEN PATH" YOU WILL SEE THAT HUMAN CONSCIOUSNESS DEPENDS UPON LOVE, YOUR LOVE FOR GOD WILL TAKE YOU TO MORE SOLID GROUNDS IN FAITH, AND MORE LOVE FOR YOUR LITTLE FAITH. THIS FAITH OF WORSHIPING GOD AND THE SON OF GOD IN THE SPIRIT AND IN TRUTH, BRINGS YOU SALVATION BY THE SPIRIT OF GOD IN SOME CASES AS THE MESSENGER.

YOU ARE TOO MUCH IN MISTRY BABYLON AND BEING WORTHY IN HER WILL ALLOW YOU TO FIGHT AGAINST EACH OTHER, FIGHT AGAINST THE TRUTH, AND FIGHT AGAINST THE APOSTLES, PROVEN BY YOUR FIGHT AGAINST THE MESSENGER AT YOUR SERVICE IN THE HIGH TIME. GOD IS NOT IN THE BUSINESS OF MAKING SACRIFICE OF OUR APOSTLES ANYMORE BUT BEING IN MISTRY BABYLON YOU STILL BELIEVE THE CHILDREN OF GOD MUST BE SACRIFICED AND PROVEN GUILTY OF THE LOVE OF GOD AND HIS SON. GOD IS IN THE BUSINESS OF MAKING THE NEW CREATURES OF GOD, WHERE THE MISTRY OF CHRIST BECOMES THE SOLVENT OF DIVINITY AND POWER BUT ONLY FOR THOSE WHO BELIEVE IN THE SPIRIT OF GOD AND THE SALVATIONS AT THE END OF TIME. I FRANCIS CHARLES MALCOLM THE MESSENGER TO YOU

WHEN YOU BELIEVE YOU HAVE TO CREATE CHANGE IN YOU, YOU HAVE TO CREATE CHANGE IN THE ENTIRE CHURCH WITH REPENTANCE UNTO GOD — REPENTANCE FOR HATING THE WORDS OF GOD HIS

SWORD THAT HE CAME TO GIVE AND WAS AT DEFAULT UNTIL NOW BECAUSE JOHN THE BAPTIST HAD TO DO WHAT HE WAS DOING UNTO THE SON OF GOD. FOR JOHN IN HIS BELIEF IN DOING THE BAPTISM AS A CLEANSING RIGHTS TO MAN'S SALVATION, THOUGHT THAT HE WAS TO CLEANSE THE LIVING WATERS ALSO. THE PEOPLE AND APOSTLES THEN COULD NOT UNDERSTAND THE PRECEPTS OF CHRIST AND SUCH WAS LEFT TO THE LATTER DAYS, AND EVEN NOW THE CHURCHES THEMSELVES ARE NOT READY TO RECEIVE IT. THERE MUST BE REPENTANCE FOR HATING THE PERFECT GOSPEL OF CHRIST AND IN LOVE WITH MISTRY BABYLON UPON TWO BODIES OF WATER THAT SHARE THEIR POWERS AND EXCEPTIONAL DIVINITY AGAINST GOD WILL. THE PEOPLE WILL FOREVER BE IN THESE

GREAT BODIES OF WATERS UNTIL IT MOUNTS UP TO THE BRIM, AT THE BRIM IF NO CHANGE, YOU TOO BE IMPUTED TO DESTROY YOURSELVES TOO AS A PUNISHMENT OF FIGHTING AGAINST GOD ALMIGHTY. COMING OUT OF HER IS SIMPLE, COMING OUT OF HER REQUIRES OF YOU TO WORSHIP GOD IN DPIRIT AND IN TRUTH. COMING OUT OF HER REQUIRES OF YOU TO WORSHIP GOD IN THE ORDINANCE OF GOD AND NOT MAN. COMING OUT OF HER REQUIRES OF YOU TO WORSHIP GOD IN THROUGH THE ONE COMMANDMENT CALLED LOVE IN WHICH IS THE APPLICATION OF ALL THE LAWS EVEN THOSE, ANNULLED BY CHRIST OUR SAVIOUR BECAUSE OF LOVE TO SAVE ALL BY THE ACCEPTANCE OF GRACE WITH IT. COMING OUT OF HER REQUIRES THE FINISHING TOUCH OF MERCY, FELLOWSHIP IN CHRIST AND RESTORATION OF THE LIGHT IN ALL MEN.

THE WORTHY IN JESUS ~ TRUST ME, THIS OLDMAN, YOU MAY TALK OF ME AND MY DECEITFUL LUST HAVE NOTHING TO DO WITH YOUR TRUST, THIS OLD MAN IS NOT UNJUST, AND YOU CAN'T JUDGE THE MESSENGER GREATER THAN JOHN THE BAPTIST.

THEN THERE IS THE WORTHY IN BABYLON, AND THE WORTHY IN CHRIST. ARE YOU WORTHY TO SIT WITH THE LAMB? ARE YOU WORTHY TO BE BY HIS SIDE? FOR TO ABIDE BY HIS WILL FOR ALL MEN YOU WILL BE WORTHY AND JUST UNTO GOD. ARE YOU WORTHY TO AS YOU CLAIM TO BE WITH HATE FOR THE MESSENGER AND THE WORD OF GOD THROUGH THE MISTERY OF HIS SON? CAN HE SEE THE FIRST FRUIT IN YOU? YOU SAY AMEN WITHOUT UNDERSTANDING, PF WHAT THE

FATHER WANTS OF YOU IN THE END.

O LORD I AM WORTHY, AND I AM HOPING TO SEE AND KNOW YOU IN SPIRIT AND IN LOVE, O LORD I KNOW I WILL BE BY YOUR PRECIOUS SIDE, FOR O LORD I AM WORTHY, OF YOUR LOVE IF THIS IS ALL I GET FROM YOU, I WILL BE BY YOUR PRECIOUS SIDE FOR LORD I AM WORTHY TO GLORIFY AND PRAISE YOUR NAME.

FOR THE MISTERY OF JESUS CHRIST IS TO CLEANSE YOU AND RETURN YOU UNTO GOD HIS FATHER IN SPIRIT AND IN TRUTH. YES, TOU CLEANSE ME AND MADE ME WHOLE SO SHALL IT BE UNTO ALL. AND NOW I KNOW YOU MADE ME WORTHY, FOR TO ABIDE BY HIS WILL OF ORDINANCE OF MEN. I HAD RATHER CLAIM WORTHINESS ON THE OTHER SIDE, THE LORD'S SIDE. THERE AWAITS A GREATER MULTITUDE OF MEN IMPUTED WITH YOUR WILL TO BUILD GARDEN MUCH MORE BEAUTIFUL THAN THAT OF EDEN. BUT THE UNWORTHY IMPUTED WITH THE WILL TO DESTROY MISTRY BABYLON. HAVING BEEN FOOLED WITHOUT UNDERSTANDING TO WORSHIP SATAN UNTIL THE END OF TIME. O LORD I AM WORTHY AND HOPING TO

SEE YOUR FACE, THE WORTHY HYPOTHESIS AT SOME CONFERENCES WAS IF I DON'T GET ON BOARD NOW THEY GONNA TAKE IT AWAY. FOR SINGING A SONG IN BABYLON. THEY DID NOT EVEN KNOW WHAT TO TAKE FOR THEY HAD NOTHING SO THEY COULD NOT EVEN SEE DOWN THE ROAD FROM WHERE THEY STOOD. I DID NOT COME AS THEIR PROFESSIONAL SINGER OR THEIR PROFESSIONAL MINISTERS, BUT AS THE LEAST AMONGST THEM, I COME AS THE HUMBLE MESSENGER, I COME WITH THE SWORD OF GOD, THE MISTERY OF JESUS CHRIST, NOT THE MISTRY OF BABYLON. THOSE WHO TOOK WHAT THEY THINK THEY TOOK AND CONTINUED TO CORRUPT MY WORK, WAS SO BLIND IN THE HEART THAT EVEN NOW THEY ARE BAFFLED BY THE WORK OF THE HOLY GHOST. THOSE WHO TOOK THE OPPORTUNE TIME BEFORE THE TIME, THOSE WHO TOOK WAS NOT SERVERS OF GOD AND CERTAINLY WILL NOT BE BY THE SIDE OF THE LAMB. THOSE WHO WORKED MY WAY DOWN INTO HELL ONLY TRIED TO MUTE THE WORDS OF GOD, WITH MANY DISCREDITS ALONG THE WAY. BUT HIS WORK IS IMMUTABLE, AND HIS WORD IS FOR EVER AND NOT FOR

THE ENVIOUS. THOSE WHO TOOK ADVANTAGE OF ME TO MY DISADVANTAGE BY MEANS OF MY FINANCES AND SETBACKS, WILL SOON VOMIT THEIR FROGS AND BE WITHOUT POWER BEFORE MY GOD.

THOSE WHO TOOK ASVERSE POSSESSION OVER MY RIGHT WILL NEVER GLORIFY THE GOD OF HEAVEN AND EARTH. YOUR ADVERSE POSSESSION IS NOT THE WORTHY IN JESUS. IT LEAVES YOU WORTHY IN BABYLON.

FROM THE TEACHINGS IN THE BIBLE THE MISTERY OF CHRIST IS REVEALED IN THE WOMAN AT THE WELL. SHE DID NOT FAIL TO SEE THAT THIS WAS THE MESSIAH, NEITHER DID SHE WANT TO HAVE HIS GREATNESS ALL BY HERSELF BUT WENT TO CALL THE PEOPLE IN THE CITY. WHEN THEY WERE ALL BACK TO SEE JESUS THE FIELDS WERE ALL FULLY READY TO BE REAPED. IN HIS PARABLE HE SPOKE UNTO THEM OF THE HARVEST THEY ALL REAPED AS BEING ALSO THE GREAT HARVEST OF HIS PEOPLE, UP TO THE HIGH TIME. IT CAN BE SEEN JUST NOW OUR PASTORS ARE REAPING THE HELL OUT OF PEOPLE AND NOT DOING THE RIGHT THING TO SAVE THEM. JESUS TOLD THEM THAT THEY WILL NOT NEED TO GO DOWN TO JERUSALEM IN THE LATTER DAYS TO PRAY AS FOR THAT THEY CAN PRAY IN SPIRIT AND IN TRUTH WHERE EVER THEY ARE.

THE LOVE OF THE SWORD OF THE SPIRIT PROPELLED THE UNKNOWN UNTO THE MESSENGER GREATER THAN JOHN THE BAPTIST TO GAIN THE INSIGHT INTO PARTS OF REVELATION. AS I WROTE BEFORE IN A FEW ESORERIC WORDS IN ESCHATOLOGY, FROM THE BOOK CALLED THE GARDEN PATH, AS RUNNING MAN, PAGE 191 – 192 RUNNING MAN FROM BABY AFRICA, TO THE THRILLS IN CHINA, RUNNING MAN WITH THE GARDEN PATH,

LOOKING ON CHANGES IN MEXICO AND THE NORTH, RUNNING MAN RUNNING A RACE, NOT FOR WHO CAN HAVE IT, STRETCH MARKS ARE ON THE CONCORDE BAG, THE WAGES ARE NOT THE TAG, BUT, THE LEGACY IN PIONEERS, ROCKSMEN, AND MICONIANS. UTECHIANS, WITH GREATNESS. AND AS THE FLAGSHIP, PAGE 189 – 190 THE FLAGSHIP MAKES AMEND TO THE LAND OF CURED SHAME. THE FLAGSHIP LEADS THE PILGRIMS AWAY FROM ROWS OF HARVESTED PAIN. FOR THE HEALING OF MANKIND MUST COME BACK

AGAIN. FOR JESUS CHRIST WANTED US TO BE WHAT WE ARE AND NOT WHAT WE WANT TO BE. IN ONENESS AND IN LOVE MAN AND WOMAN. THE REAL FLAGSHIP IN JESUS WANTS THE LAND TO BE HEALED AND CURED OF SHAME. ONLY YOU BECOME SHACKLED WITH YOUR FILTHINESS AND SO YOU BECOME UNSHACKLED AND BE IN PEACE WITH GOD AND MY ENSIGN OF THE GARDEN PATH. THE WORTHY IN JESUS THEN THERE IS THE WORTHY IN BABYLON AND I HEARD A VOICE FROM HEAVEN SAYING BLESSED ARETHE DEAD WHICH DIE IN THE LORD FROM HENCEFORTH, YEA, SAITH THE SPIRIT THAT THEY MAY REST FROM THEIR LABOUR AND THEIR WORK SHALL FOLLOW THEM. FOR AS SOON A S THE SICKLE IS IN, SHALL THE WORTHY IN THE BEAST BE FED. REMEMBER I THE MESSENGER HAVE TOLD YOU, FOR UNTO YOU HAVE I GIVEN THAT WHICH IS GOOD FROM "THE TABERNACLE IN HTTPS://WWW.FACEBOOK.COM/TGPMASS/ IN THE SUN MASS FRANCIS CHARLES MALCOLM MASS. NOW THE LAMB IS IN ONLY THE COMPANY OF THE SEALED APOSTLES # 144000 BY FAITH IN GOD. THEY ARE "THE FIRST FRUITS" BOASTY PASTORS WHO ARE YOU I'D SAY THE WORTHY OF BABYLON.

THE 144000 ARE EXPECTED TO CAST THE TABERNACLE IN THE SUN ON ALL WATERS, BEING WITH THE LAMB. OR LOOSE THEIR WAY ALSO AND BECOME UNWORTHY OF CHRIST AND TURN AS TO SATAN AND BE WORTHY IN BABY LON. IF THEY CAN'T LEARN MY SONGS THEN WHO ARE THEY? SHALL I NOT KNOW THEM? A STRONG MAN HAVING A STRONG GOD AND FORNICATING WITH SATAN ANOTHER STRONG MAN.

IF YOU FIND YOURSELF WORTHY AND YOU GET TO KNOW WHO WAS RUNNING THE RACE AND THE MESSENGR, WOULD YOU ACCEPT THE PERFECT MESSAGE? IF YOU CAN'T ACCEPT THE PERFECT THEN HOW WILL YOU DEAL WITH THE EVERLASTING GOSPEL?

THE WORTHY WITH THE BEAST HAVE THEIR WORK TO DO, ALSO THE MESSENGER'S GOD OF HAVE IMPUTED IT IN ALL OF THEM ALREADY TO DEAL WITH BABYLON AND THE BEAST WHEN THE OPPORTUNE TIME HAVE COME. THE MISTERY OF JESUS CHRIST WILL CAUSE A SELECTION OF HEARTS

THAT ARE CLEAN THAT CAN SEE HIS WILL AND DO IT IN THE NAME OF JESUS TO BE HEALED.

THIS IS WHERE THE TRUTH LIES IN THE SPIRIT OF GOD AMEN. IF YOU FIND YOURSELF WORTHY AND YOU GET TO KNOW WHO WAS RUNNING THE RACE AND THE MESSENGR WOULD YOU ACCEPT THE PERFECT MESSAGE? FROM THESE ESOTERIC WORDS THAT IN YOUR TIME WAS IN NEED OF THE ESP TO MAKE RIGHT

HEREBY HAD YEE TO UNDERSTAND BEFORE THE CHASTISEMEN OF YOUR FELLOWMEN FOR BY THE AGES GONE BY IT WAS NOT MADE KNOWN UNTO MEN BY NOW YOU WOULD HAVE KNOW OF THE DISPENSATION GIVEN UNTO ME TO US WARD, THAT THE MYSTERY OF CHRIST MAY BE KNOWN AND USED IN THE ACCEPTANCE OF GRACE. ALL WILL ACCEPT SALVATION IF ALL COME OVER TO THE NEW GOSPEL AND THE NEW COVENANT OF GOD, AND THEREBY COMING OUT OF THE CHURCHES IN BABYLON, THAT THEIR PRIESTS DOES NOT COME FOR THE UNDERSTANDING OF THE LIBERALITY BUT PIGGY BACK RIDE ON THE MODERATIONS AND THE STIR, BEING NOT READY TO RECEIVE THE UNDERSTANDING OF THE NEW GOSPEL AND THE NEW COVENANT THROUGH THE LIBERALITY, TO HAVE THE DOCUMENT TO SHOW TO THE CHURCHES AND THE PATIENT SAINTS, THAT WILL TAKE THEM UNDER THE TABERNACLE IN THE SUN, THEIR PASTORS WILL LACK AND THE PATIENT SAINTS WILL BE IN HUNGER FOR THE WORD. PRIEST AND PASTORS WHICH SHOULD KNOW WISDOM AND HAVE UNDERSTANDING OF THE MYSTERY OF CHRIST WILL CONTINUE TO BE LED BY RIDING SATAN IN THE HIGH TIME FOR WANTS OF GREED SEEKING THEIR OWN MEAT. THE PREPARED WAY OF THE GOSPEL CARRIED BY THE MESSENGER CANNOT BE MIXED IN BABYLON ALTHOUGH IN THE OLD FOUNDATIONS OF THE CHURCHES, THE CHURCHES MUST LEAVE THEIR BRAND NAME UNDER THE MIXED UP OLD GOSPEL IN PARTS, THAT HAVE DECAYED AND LET IT VANISH AWAY, AND UNITE UNDER THE TABERNACLE IN THE SUN. THE MISTERY PROVES THE GLORY OF CHRIST UNTO ALL AGES. THIS MISTERY IS TO A DEVOTIONAL CALLING THROUGH CHRIST AND THE SWORD OF THE SPIRIT OF GOD THAT HE CAME TO GIVE. THE MYSTERY OF JESUS CHRIST WITH THE WOMAN AT THE WELL, WAS REALISTIC TO THE FARMERS AND REAPERS, BUT PARABOLIC TO THE PRIEST AND PASTORS WHO SHOULD REAP IN THE HOLY SPIRIT OF GOD. TO THEM WAS THE GIFT OF THE SWORD OF THE SPIRIT IF THEY COULD BELIEVE. BUT BELIEF

BEING AN OBSTRUCTION TO THEM COULD NOT BELIEVE THAT THEY COULD PRAY IN THE SPIRIT UNTO GOD AND AVOID THESE CONFLICTS OF THE SELF WITH OTHERS, AS HE POINTED THEM AGAIN TO THE LAST DAYS WHERE IT SHALL BE FOR THE PRESERVATION OF HUMANITY FROM THEIR

UNBELIEF IN THE WORSHIP AND SERVING OF GOD THE FATHER AND THE CREATOR OF HEAVEN AND EARTH..

THE MISTERY ENDEAVOURING TO KEEP THE UNITY OF THE CHURCH WETHER WITH THE 144000, PRIESTS, APOSTLES, OR PATIENT SAINTS AND THOSE THAT THEY LEAD OR ALL THE CHUCHES FOR IN THE END THEY ALL WILL DO THE WILL OF GOD. THIS IS A FIGURE THAT THE CHURCH BOASTS ABOUT IN BILLIONS OF PEOPLE. CAN'T YOU SEE THAT SOMETHING IS WRONG WITH THEM? NOW THE LIBERALITY IS COME TO SAVE THE GREAT MULTITUDE AND TO SAVE SOME WHICH ARE IN THE CHURCHES, AS THE SEVEN CANDLE STICKS AND THEIR EXPONENTS.

OF GOD BEING WORTHY ON ONE SIDE OR THE OTHER, IT IS UPON YOU TO RECEIVE FOR BEHOLD THE DAY COMETH THAT SHALL BURN LIKE AN OVEN, AND ALL THE PROUD VAUNTING AT THE TABERNACLE IN THE SUN SHALL BE AT THEIR OWN PERIL.

GOD IS THE FATHER OF OUR LORD JESUS CHRIST AND THE LORD JESUS HATH COME TO THIS WORLD AND HATH GIVEN ME A SWORD AS HIS SON, AND NO ONE COMETH UNTO JESUS CHRIST WITHOUT THE SWORD OF THE SPIRIT BY RECEIVING GRACE, THE LAW OF LOVE AND SALVATION OF THE SPIRIT THROUGH BELIEF IN JESUS CHRIST AND THE TABERNACLE IN THE SUN. THE SWORD OF THE SPIRIT COMETH THROUGH YOUR PRIESTS, OR THE GREAT MULTITUDE, AND WITNESSES, THAT RECEIVED THE UNDERSTANDING FROM THE LIBERALITY UNTO ME THE MESSENGER FOR THE KNOWLEDGE OF IT.

READ YOUR CORRUPT WAYS, AND STOP TRYING TO READ MY MIND, THE GARDEN PATH GONE PASS ALL OF YOU. IN THE TABERNACLE OF THE SUN, THROUGH THE HOLY GHOST THAT IS HIGHER THAN ALL CHURCHES OR EVERY HILS FOLLOW ME. IF THERE WAS A WAY THAT IS GOOD TO GO AROUND THE LIBERALITY I HAVE PREPARED, I WOULD

HAVE TOLD YOU, AND YOUR PASTORS WOULD HAVE SEEN IT IN THE BIBLE. SO LET ME TELL YOU THE OTHER WAY IS BAD IT IS TO CONTINUE TO RIDE SATAN AND GO DOWN INTO PERDITION THROUGH DESPITE UNTO GOD'S HOLY SPIRIT. BUT THERE ARE SOME THAT WILL BE SAVED FROM THE CHURCHES, FOR THEY SHALL FOLLOW THE MESSENGER AND BE SAVED. FOR WHEN YOU SHALL ABHOR THE THINGS MY FATHER ABHORS, AND ACCEPT HIS WILL WITH ALL YOUR HEARTS, ACCORDING TO THE BIBLE, THEN SHALL YOU BE WORTHY. I MEAN REAL WORTHY.

FOR THE PREISTS THAT SHALL COME UNTO THE MESSENGER FOR THE PERFECT NEW GOSPEL AND NEW COVENANT TO BRING THEM AND THE PATIENT SAINTS CLOSER TO THE SIDE OF THE LAMB AND FEAR ONLY GOD.

FOR ONLY THEN, THEY CAN START THE CREATION OF THE FIRST FRUITS OF JESUS CHRIST AND CREATURES OF GOD.

THE FIRST FRUITS OF JESUS CHRIST AND THE CREATURES OF GODWILL KNOW TO LOVE GOD AND FEAR GOD AND WILL NOT BE AFRAID OF

ANY MAN OVER GOD, UNDER THE TABERNACLE IN THE SUN.

THEY WILL ASK THE QUESTIONS

1. WHO WAS THE FIRST BEAST?
2. THE PATIENT SAINTS MAY ASK. IS THE LIBERALITY A PART OF THE BIBLE?
3. WHO WAS THE SECOND BEAST?
4. WHAT ARE THE WATERS THAT THE BEASTS CAME UPON?
5. WHY DID THEY SHARE THEIR POWERS?
6. IN WHICH LINE OF THE BEAST ARE THEY THE SAME FROM 1ST, 7TH AND 8TH AND WHO TO COME?
7. WHAT DOES THE FIRST BEAST RIDE UPON?
8. HOW DO YOU KNOW THAT THE CHURCH IS BABYLON AND NOT AMERICA?
9. WHY WERE THE SAINTS FOOLED SO AS TO DEFILE THEMSELVES IN THESE TWO BEASTS?
10. WHEN BABYLON SPITS OUT SATAN WHAT WILL THEY ACTUALL LOOK LIKE?
11. IF YOU ARE WORTHY IN BABYLON WHAT WILL YOU BE ABLE TO DO?
12. IF YOU ARE WORTHY IN THE LAMB WHAT WILL YOU BE ABLE TO DO?
13. WILL YOU FOLLOW THE MESSENGER, OR THE BEAST, AND THE OLD GOSPEL IN DECAY?
14. HOW DO YOU KNOW THAT GRACE IS CERTIFIED BY GOD AND THAT YOU ARE FOLLOWING GOD'S PRECEPTS?

ANSWERS

1. WHO WAS THE FIRS BEAST? THE ROMANS AND THE ROMAN CATHOLIC CHURCHES AND ALL THEIR EXPONENTS, WHICH HAVE RIDDEN SATAN, CRUCIFIED CHRIST AND THE PROPHETS OF THE SAINTS.

2. **THE PATIENT SAINTS MAY ASK. IS THE LIBERALITY A PART OF? THE BIBLE?** AND IT TEACHES US TO MAKE THE GOSPEL OF CHRIST UNIFIED UNDER THE TABERNACLE IN THE SUN. READ YOUR BIBLES FOR YOURSELVES AND ALL WILL BE SEEING THE TRUTH. ASK YOUR PRIESTS IF THIS IS SO AND LET THEM SHOW YOU THE WORD IF THAT IS WHAT THEY ARE SUPPOSED TO BE DOING. THE PRIESTS THAT HAVE COME FOR THE UNDERSTANDING HAVE KNOWN THE BIBLE LONG AGO AND SUCH WILL BE EASY TO FIND.

3. **WHO WAS THE SECOND BEAST?** THE SOOTH SAYERS AND THE CHURCHES THAT MADE THEIR OWN BIBLE THROUGH UNBELIEF IN JESUS CHRIST THE SON OF GOD. THUS, MAKING MINCEMEAT OF THEIR FELLOWMEN SENDING THEM ON TO AN UNKNOWN PARADISE OF DARKNESS.

4. **WHAT ARE THE WATERS THAT THE BEASTS CAME UPON?** THE GREAT MASS OF UNWORTHY PEOPLE OF THE EARTH THAT CLINGS TO THE BEAST AND ITS POWERS IN DARKNESS.

5. **WHY DID THEY SHARE THEIR POWERS** ONE BEAST THE FIRST IS TRYING TO REDEFINE ITS PRINCIPLES IN THE APPROACHING THEIR SINS AGAINST GOD. THEY ARE PREPARED TO TRANSFER BABYLON INTO THE COUNTRY OF AMERICA, SO THAT ITS PEOPLE COULD DESTROY AMERICA FOR BABYLON. BUT IN MODERN TIMES BABYLON IS THE CHURCHES. WHILE THE OTHER BEAST DECIDES THAT THEY MUST RULE THE WORLD IN DARKNESS MAKING MINCEMEAT OF ALL THAT IS NOT IN FAVOUR WITH THEM. THE WAY OF THE NEW GOSPEL AND NEW COVENANT IS NOT IN THEM AND IT IS COME UNTO THEM AS A MEANS OF SALVATION FROM THEIR WICKED WAYS.

6. **IN WHICH LINE OF THE BEAST ARE THEY THE SAME FROM 1ST, 7TH AND 8TH AND WHO TO COME?** FROM THE FIRST LINE, BUT THE SECOND CONTINUE TO HAVE A WICKED EVIL PLAN UPON THE CHILDREN OF THE EARTH, TO MAKE THEM MINCEMEAT UNTO THEIR PARADISE, AND SICK VAUNTING FILTHY MEN BEFORE GOD.

7. **WHAT DOES THE FIRST BEAST RIDE UPON?** THE FIRST BEAST RIDES UPON BUT HAVE SHE SOME OF HER WORKLOAD TO LOOK MORE HOLY UNTO THE PEOPLE OF GOD. BUT THE SECOND BEAST IS DECLARING BOTH GOOD AND EVIL AT THE SAME TIME IN THE COUNCILS WITH SATAN.

8. **HOW DO YOU KNOW THAT THE CHURCH IS BABYLON AND NOT AMERICA?** THE CHURCH TRIED AND WAS SUCCESSFUL IN THE TO TRANSFER THE DISADVANTAGE WITH FILTHY ABOMINATION OF THE SAINTS UPON AMERICA THROUGH THE BEHAVIORS OF THE CHURCH IN HIGH PLACE WITH PRINCIPALITIES AND POWERS.

BRINGING SHAME UPON A GREAT COUNTRY BEFORE THE WORLD AND ITS ENTIRE PEOPLE WHICH NOW MUST BE CURED OF THEIR ILLNESS THAT BROUGHT THE SHAME THAT WAS DEEPLY ROOTED IN THE UNWORTHY CHURCH.

9. **WHY WERE THE SAINTS FOOLED SO AS TO DEFILE THEMSELVES IN THESE TWO BEASTS?** ADVANTAGE IN ONE AND BENEFITS OF THE FILTHY LUCRE. SOOTH SAYING EASY MONEY TO DO WRONGS UPON HUMANITY TO LOOK POWERFULL, BUT UNGODLY UNTO ALL MEN, WITH A MANMADE SCRIPTURAL WAR OF THEIR SAINTS ON SATANIC COUNCILS.

10. **WHEN BABYLON SPITS OUT THE SATAN WHAT WILL THEY ACTUALLY SEE?** THEY WILL SEE THEMSELVES VOMITING THREE FROGS AND THROUGH UNBELIEF IN JESUS CHRIST BEING UNWORTHY THEY WILL BE IMPUTED TO DESTROY THEMSELVES.

11. **IF YOU ARE WORTHY IN BABYLON WHAT WILL YOU BE ABLE TO DO?** CREATE A DESPITE UNTO GOD AND CONTINUE TO RIDE SATAN IN THE CHURCHES. THESE ARE THEY THAT WILL NOT ACCEPT GOD AND TRY TO KNOW THE GOD THEY SHOULD KNOW ALL THROUGHOUT THE AGES EVEN THOUGH THEY SAY AND LOOK LIKE THEY ARE WORSHIPPING GOD, HAVING A FORM OF GODLINESS BUT HAVE SATAN IN THE COUNCILS OF THE CHURCH NOT UNDER THE TABERNACLE IN THE SUN.

12. **IF YOU ARE WORTHY IN THE LAMB WHAT WILL YOU BE ABLE TO DO?** YOU WILL ACCEPT THE UNDERSTANDING OF THE LIBERALITY GRACE, AND THE LAW OF LOVE. HENCE SHEDDING THE LIGHT OF JESUS CHRIST WITH PEOPLE, THROUGH HUMILITY, THAT WILL BRING JOY TO THE HEARERS. THEY WILL ABHOR SPEAKING OF THE DARKNESS AT ALL TIMES, WHICH WILL CONTINUE TO CORRUPT THE HEARTS OF MEN AND MAKE THEM BITTER AGAINST EACH OTHER. MAYBE YOU WILL NOT CALL THE MESSENGER. MAYBE YOU WILL DEAL TREACHEROUSLY WITH THE MESSENGER TO HAVE HIS INHERITANCE WHICH YOU WILL NEVER BE ABLE TO HAVE EVEN WHEN JESUS CHRIST SHALL COME. MAYBE YOU WILL FOOL THE MESSENGER TO WRITE A NEW BIBLE. MAYBE YOU WILL STOP RIDING SATAN AND COME FOR THE UNDERSTANDING AND CHANGE TO ACCEPT THE LIGHT OF GOD. MAYBE YOU WILL COME OUT OF BABYLON AND JOIN THE GREAT MULTITUDE.

13. **WILL YOU FOLLOW THE MESSENGER, OR THE BEAST?** THIS DEPENDS ON HOW YOU RECEIVE THE MESSENGER OR STICK TO THE OLD GOSPEL THAT IS SUPPOSED TO VANISH AWAY.

14. **HOW DO YOU KNOW THAT GRACE IS CERTIFIED BY GOD AND THAT YOU ARE FOLLOWING GOD'S PRECEPTS?** GOD HAS UPHELD THE

FAULTS OF THE CHURCHES IN REVELATION, AND HAVE GIVEN HIS PRECEPTS OF THE WAY OF RETURN UNTO HIM, WHICH IS TO ACCEPT GRACE AND THE LAW OF LOVE, BAPTIZING EACH OTHER IN THE NAME AND SPIRIT OF GOD AND HIS SON THE LIVING WATERS AND BELIEVING UPON HIM. THEREFORE, AS THE MESSENGER REFRESHES THE SOUL OF THE MASTER SO SHALL YOUR SOUL BE REFRESHED BY THE EXAMPLE, HE IS UNTO YOU IN THE HIGH TIME,

FOR IT IS OF ALL TO KNOW FOR THE STIR AND THE MODERATION ARE UNTO THE FOUR (4) CORNERS OF THE EARTH. IF FOR ANY REASON AFTER THE LIBERALITY IS COME UNTO YOU, BEHOLD THE DAY COMETH THAT SHALL BURN LIKE AN OVEN, AND ALL THE PROUD VAUNTING AT THE TABERNACLE IN THE SUN AND ALL THAT DO WICKEDLY, SHALL BE STUBBLE AND THE DAY THAT COMETH SHALL BURN THEM UP SAITH THE LORD OF HOST, THAT IT SHALL LEAVE THEM NEITHER ROOT NOR BRANCH.

BUT UNTO YOU THAT FEAR GOD'S NAME, SHALL THE SON OF RIGHTEOUSNESS ARISE WITH HEALING, IN HIS WINGS, AND SHALL GO FORTH AND GROW UP AS CALVES OF THE STALL. LEST THE MISTERY MAN WHO DIED BUT LIVETH, SMITE THE EARTH WITH CURSE.

AND THE REMNANT OF JACOB SHALL BE IN THE MIDST OF MANY PEOPLE AND THE GENTILES, AS A LION THAT TREADETH DOWN ABD TEARETH IN PIECE, AND NONE CAN DELIVER. BUT GOD'S PEOPLE THAT FEAR THE LORD, THINE HANDS SHALL BE LIFTED UPON THINE ADVERSARIES AND ALL THINE ENEMIES SHALL BE CUT OFF. THE LORD WILL EXECUTE VENGEANCE IN ANGER. IN WHAT? IN ANGER AND FURY UPON THE HEATHEN, SUCH AS THEY HAVE NEVER HEARD.

THE MISTERY OF JESUS CHRIST ENGULFS THE METLED LETTER, WHICH IS SPECIAL ALTHOUGH THERE IS OVER OR APPROXIMATELY 340000 CHURCHES AROUND THE WORLD. THE METLED LETTER IS TO THE 7 IN ASIA AND NOW THEIR EXPONENTS ACROSS THE FOUR (4) CORNERS OF THE EARTH TO BE AS THE PRESENT

7 X 7 X 7 X 7 X 7 X 7 X AN APP. 2.8 ACROSS THE WORLD, CHURCHES, O WHAT, THEIR EXPONENTIAL GROWTH SINCE THE ORDERS OF JESUS CHRIST FOR THE LAST DAYS. THE FAITFUL WITNESS AND THE BEGOTTEN ALSO FROM THE DEAD, FROM HIS EYES FLAMES OF FIRE, YEA AND HIS FEET LIKE FINE BRASS ASIF THEY BURNED IN THE FIRE. TAKE HEED OF ALL THE

EXAMPLES UNTL NOW HERE COMES THE MESSENGER GREATER THAN JOHN THE BAPTIST TGP MASS THE GARDEN PATH, BRINGING TO YOU "THE TAB ERNACLE IN THE SUN.

FOR MAY WILL WALK IN VANITY OF MIND AND STRAY EPH 4:18 HAVING THEIR UNDERSTANDING DARKENED, BEING ALLIENATE, FROM THE LIFE OF GOD, THROUGH THE IGNORANCE THAT IS WITHIN THEM, SIMPLE BECAUSE OF THE BLINDNESS OF THEIR HEARTS THAT WILL LEAD THEM TO BE GIVEN OVER TO THE BEAST AND BABYLON.

THE MESSENGER A BELIEVER AND SANCTIFIED BY THE HOLY SPIRIT NOW A MINISTER NOT ACCORDING TO ME BUT OF THE FATHER FOR THE EFFECTUAL WORKINGS OF HIS POWER AND THE GIFT OF GRACE. NOW UNTO US WARDS IN ONE BODY, ONE SPIRIT UNTO THE HOPE OF YOUR CALLING TOO, UNTO ONE LORD, ONE FAITH, ONE BAPTISM, TO ONE GOD AND FATHER OF ALL, WHO IS ABOVE ALL. THE MISTERY JESUS WILL TELL YOU, THAT BEFORE NOW YOU HAD THE GOSPEL IN PARTS, YOU HAVE NOT SO LEARNED CHRIST, NOW THAT YE HAVE HEARD THE MESSENGER IN THE TABERNACLE OF THE SUN, FOR NOW THE DAY STAR IS OUT UNTO ALL MEN. NOW TO MAKE ALL MEN SEE THE MYSTERY AND FELLOWSHIP IN IT, WHICH FROM THE BEGINNING OF THE WORLD HAVE BEEN HID IN GOD. WHO CREATED ALL THINGS BY JESUS CHRIST, TO THE INTENT THAT NOW UNTO US THE PRINCIPALITIES AND POWERS IN HEAVENLY PLACES, MIGHT BE KNOWN TO THE CHURCHES, BY "THE CHURCH THE MANIFOLD WISDOM OF GOD"? IN WHOM WE HAVE BOLDNESS AND ACCESS WITH CONFIDENCE BY FAITH. NOW TO THE PUTTING ON OF THE NEW MAN SEALED UNTO THE DAY OF REDEMPTION, GIVING NO HEED TO THE DEVIL, BUT SPEAKING THE TRUTH IN LOVE TO GROW UP DAILY IN THE WAY OF CHRIST. BEING NOT FILTHILY JOINED TOGETHER AS MAN AND MAN, HAVING NO CORRUPT COMMUNICATION, BUT THAT WHICH IS GOOD AND EDIFYING TO MINISTER GRACE UNTO THE HEARERS. THE RECEIVED OF THE HOLY GHOST WILL NOT RETURN TO THE OLD WAYS OF THE GOSPEL AND RETURN TO HAVING THEIR UNDERSTANDING DARKENED AND TO BE ALIENATED FROM THE LIFE OF GOD, THROUGH THE IGNORANCE THAT IS IN THEM, BECAUSE OF THE BLINDNESS OF THEIR HEARTS. BUT CONTINUE TO RECEIVE THE GIFT OF GRACE ACCORDING TO THE MEASURES OF CHRIST WHO WAS DEAD BUT NOW ALIVE TO WALK WORTHY WITH CHRIST IN YOUR VOCATIONS. I ASK OF YOU NOW BE NOT FILLED WITH EXCESS ANYMORE BUT WITH THE SPIRIT, GIVING THANKS ALWAYS, SPEAKING TO YOURSELVES IN PSALMS, AND HYMNS AND SPIRITUAL SONGS, SINGING AND MAKING MELODIES IN YOUR HEARTS TO THE LORD AS

THE NEW MAN RENEWED IN SPIRIT AND IN MIND, CREATED IN RIGHTEOUSNESS AND TRUE HOLINESS. THIS OLD MAN AS AN EXAMPLE. AND FROM NOW ON LET NO MAN TROUBLETH YOU FOR YOU BEAR IN

YOUR BODY THE MARK OF THE LORD JESUS CHRIST. AS THE MESSENGER HATH COME IN THIS DISPENSATION TO GATHER ALL THINGS ON EARTH AND IN HEAVEN UNTO CHRIST IN THE FULNESS OF TIME SO THAT WE MAY BE UNTO HIM AS ONE, AND AS A MEDIATOR OF ONE GOD. NOW THROUGH CHRIST, AS YOU PUT ON CHRIST IN YOUR FAITH REMEMBER NO MAN DISANNULETH OR ANNULETH THAT WHICH IS OF CHRIST GO STEADFAST AND LEAVENETH UP THE WHOLE LUMP UNTO CHRIST, MAKING ALL THINGS TO COME UNTO HIM.

YOU HAVE BEGUN TO BE TAUGHT BY ME, AS THE TRUTH IN JESUS CHRIST. AND NOW YE SHALL PUT OFF THE FORMER CONVERSATIONS OF THIS OLD MAN, WHICH IS CORRUPT ACCORDING TO DECEITFUL LUST SAS TO BE RENEWED IN THE SPIRIT OF YOUR MINDS BY JESUS. AND GREIVE NOT THE HOLY SPIRIT OF GOD WHEREBY YE WERE SEALED UNTO THE DAY OF REDEMPTION. AND YE MEN OF GOD PUT AWAY CORRUPT COMMUNICATIONS BUT THAT WHICH IS GOOD PROCEEDING OUT OF YOUR MOUTHS SO THAT WHICH IS GOOD COMES OUT TO EDIFYING ~ AND SO MINISTER GRACE UNTO THE HEARER. YOU SHOULD NEVER MALICE I THE MESSENGER WHO IS TENDER HEARTED TOWARDS YOU TO BRING YOU INTO THE KNOWLEDGE OF GOD.

FOR THE MESSENGER HATH COME UNTO YOU AND HAVE SET THE WAY AFORE IN A FEW WORDS "THE GARDEN PATH" THE MESSENGER NOR THE WAY WILL NEVER CHANGE, NOT WITH YOUR TEST, LIES, REPROACH TO THE PERFECT, BUT IN THE END IT WILL BE, WHICH SIDE OF THE WORTHY ARE YOU ON? THE MISTERY OF CHRIST IS FOR A FEW CHOSEN LABOURERS TO BRING ALL MEN UNTO HIM., YEA, SHALL WE NOT KNOW? TO CHANGE THE CHURCH AND TO CREATE THE 1ST CREATURES OF GOD, AS IT IS, IT IS FOR ALL MEN, AND ALL THINGS IN THE EARTH OR THE HEAVENS ABOVE, TO COME UNTO HIM.

THE FIRST CREATUES WILL BE CREATED BY THE FIRST FRUITS OF GOD THE 144000 SEALED UNTO HIS REDEMPTION BUT THEY TOO CAN FAIL

TO FOLOW THE MESSENGER BECAUSE THE CHURCH WAS ALLIENATED FOR SO LONG FROM THE PERFECT GOSPEL THAT LEADS INTO THE EVERLASTING GOSPEL.

THE EVERLASTING GOSPEL STATES THAT "THIS IS LED BY THE LAMB AND ONLY THOSE WHO CAN FOLLOW THE LAMB WILL DELIVER IT", FEAR GOD, GIVE GLORY UNTO HIM ONLY, WORSHIP HIM THAT MADE THE HEAVENS

AND THE EARTH, THE SEAS AND THE FOUNTAINS OF WATERS. THE MISTERY OF GOD MAY PROVE ALL THINGS ACCEPTABLE UNTO GOD. DO YOU PROVE YOURSELVES? BE CAREFUL TO HAVE NO FELLOWSHIP WITH THE UNFRUITFUL WORKS OF DARKNESS – BUT RATHER REPROVE THEM. FOR THIS DO HEAR ME IT IS A SHAME TO EVEN SPEAK OF THOSE THINGS WHICH ARE DONE OF THEM IN SECRET. AND THAT SLEEPEST, AND ARISE FROM THE DEAD, AND CHRIST SHALL GIVE THEE LIGHT.

BUT REMEMBER THAT ALL THINGS THAT ARE REPROVED ARE MADE MANIFEST BY THE LIGHT FOR WHAT SO EVER DOTH MAKE MANIFEST IS LIGHT VS 14 IN THIS MISTERY YOU TALK CIRCUMSPECTLY IN WISDOM SO AWAKE THOU, TO THE MISTERY OF GOD, THAT MAY PROVE ALL THINGS ACCEPTABLE UNTO GOD.

BY MEANS OF THE HOLY GHOST YOU WILL GET IT. YOU CAN BLAZE THE TRAILS IN IT BUT UNTIL YOU COME UNTO THE TABERNACLE IN THE SUN AS A DAY STAR UNTO YOU, YOU WILL GIVE GOD THE GLORY FOR HE IT IS THAT CREATED THE HEAVENS AND THE EARTH, THE TABERNACLE IN THE SUN IS HIGHER IS HIGHER THAN ALL HILLS — AND THE MESSAGEIS PERFECT MUCH BETTER THAN THE PARTS GONE BY AND DONE, DONE, DONE AS DECAYED.

THE MISTERY TELLS YOU THAT BEFORE NOW, YOU ALL HAD THE GOSPEL IN PARTS – WITH THE MYSTERY OF JESUS HID FROM YOU IN THE LORD, YOU HAVE NOT SO LEARNED CHRIST – NOW THAT YE HAVE HEARD THE MESSENGER IN THE TABERNACLE OF THE SUN, COME AND KNOW CHRIST THROUGH THE GIFT OF GRACE AND THE SPIRITUAL THEOLOGY OF LOVE., YOU HAVE BEGUN TO BE TAUGHT BY ME, AS THE TRUTH IN JESUS CHRIST. THE MISTERY PAUL BESEACH YOU AS PRISONERS OF THE LORD TO WALK WORTHY OF THE VOCATION WHEREWITH YE ARE CALLED. THE GIFTS OF GOD BEFORE YOU] WALK WORTHY VOL. 3 FOR ONE GOOD REASON

TO ENDEAVOUR TO KEEP THE UNITY OF THE SPIRIT IN IN THE BONDS OF CHRIST, FOR IN THE HOPE OF YOUR CALLING YOU HAVE TO LOVE ONE ANOTHER, IN ONE BODY, ONE SPIRIT, ONE LORD, ONE FAITH, ONE BAPTISM. FOR CHRIST ASCENDANT AND DECENDED INTO HELL FOR THE PERFECTING OF THE SAINTS WAITING FOR 2018 YRS TO THIS DAY, TILL WE COME INTO UNITY OF THE FAITH AND OF THE KNOWLEDGE OF THE SON OF GOD. SPEAKING THE TRUTH IN LOVE. WITH A HEART THAT CAN SEE.

"POPEJO-HNPAUL THE 1ST" RIDING ON SATAN, IS THE NUMBER OF THE BEAST IN HIM AND FROM HIM AND ALL HIS SO-CALLED PROPHETS AND PRIESTS SHALL THREE FROGS BE VOMITED AND THEIR POWER IN SATAN BE DRIVEN TO NOUGHT.

TO THE INTENT THAT NOW UNTO THE PRINCIPALITIES AND POWERS IN HEAVENLY PLACE MIGHT BE KNOWN BY THE CHURCH THE MANIFOLD WISDOM OF GOD. SAYS ACCORDING TO THE ETERNAL PURPOSE PROPOSED IN JESUS CHRIST OUR LORD. AND TO KNOW THE LOVE OF CHRIST, WHICH PASSETH KNOWLEDGE, THAT YE MAY BY FILLED WITH THE FULNESS OF GOD.

AND THIS WOMAN ARRAYED IN PURPLE AND RIDETH UPON A SCARLET COLOURED BEAST, SET ON SEVEN HILLS WILL THE WORTHY IN HER BE CALLED BY THE GOD OF HEAVEN AND EARTH TO SEE AND DO JUDGEMENT UNTO HER AND THE BEAST, AND THIS WOMAN REIGNETH OVER THE KINGS OF THE EARTH IN BABYLON, BUT WHEN THE SON OF MAN HAVE FULFILLED HIS WORK AND TO THEIR AMAZEMENT THE SCARLET BEAST SHE SITTETH ON IS SATAN THAT WAS CAST INTO THE BOTTOMLESS PIT TO THE EARTH FROM OUT OF HEAVEN. THEN SHALL THE GREAT MULTITUDE OF PEOPLE, HATE THE BEAST, WHO HAVE NEVER LET THEM HAVE A GOOD DAY ON EARTH BUT A LIFE COVERED IN BLOOD, SIN AND SHAME. THEY SHALL EAT HER FLESH AND BURN HER WITH FIRE, FOR THE GOD THAT THEY SAY, THEY ALL SERVE WILL PUT IT INTO THEIR HEARTS TO FULFIL HIS WILL, AND TO AGREE TO GIVE THEIR KINGDOM UNTO THE BEAST UNTIL THE WORDS OF GOD BE

FULFILLED. THIS IS THE LINK BETWEEN THE PERFECT GOSPEL AND THE EVERLASTING GOSPEL COMING OUT OF THE GOSPEL IN PARTS. NOW THAT THE GOSPEL IN PARTS IS DONE THE PERFECT MUST BE PREACHED BY THE FRUITS BY THE SIDE OF THE LAMB AND THE EVERLASTING GOSPEL FINALIZE IT. AND LET US CONSIDER ONE ANOTHER TO PROVOKE UNTO LOVE AND GOOD WORKS AS WE WATCH FOR THAT DAY — THE MESSENGERS WORKS IS IN THE HOLIEST OF THE BLOOD AND SPIRIT OF JESUS CHRIST IN THE GATHERING OF ALL THINGS UNTO HIM.

BY A NEW AND LIVING WAY, WHICH HE HATH CONSECRATED FOR US, THROUGH THE VEIL, HIS FLESH, CHRIST FLESH OF WHICH YOU MUST NOW KNOW, AND PARTAKE OF.

WHY — FOR IF WE SIN WILLFULLY AFTER THAT WE HAVE RECEIVED THE KNOWLEDGE OF THE TRUTH THERE REMAINETH NO MORE SACRIFICE FOR SINS AND HATH DONE DESPITE UNTO GRACE AND THE SPIRIT OF GOD, AND HAVE TRODDEN UNDER FOOT THE SON OF GOD FOR WE ALL KNOW HIM WHO HATH SAID VENGEANCE BELONGETH UNTO ME, FOR SO MUCH THE DAY OF THE LORD IS APPROACHING, REMEMBER IT IS A FEARFUL THING TO FALL INTO HANDS OF GOD

THIS MESSENGER BROUGHT TO YOU AND TO US WARD, HE THAT CAME AND DESPISED MOSES LAWS AND DIED WITHOUT MERCY UNDER TWO OR THREE

WIYNESSES THE TRUTH OF JESUS OR GOD, THERE SHALL BE A CERTAIN FEARFUL LOOKING FOR OF JUDGEMENT AND A FIERY INDIGNATION, WHICH SHALL DEVOUR THE ADVERSARIES OF CHRIST AND HIS MESSENGER.

AND BEING A FEARFUL THING TO FALL INTO THE HANDS OF THE LORD I THE MESSENGER SAITH UNTO YOU, WHEN YOU WERE ILLLUMINATED UNDER THE GARDEN PATH WHILE YE ENDURED GREAT AFFLICTIONS, PARTLY WHILST YOU WERE MADE A GAZINGSTOCK AND WHILST YE BECAME A COMPANIONS OF THEM THAT WERE BEING USED. FOR YE HAD COMPASSION FOR ME IN MY BONDS ANF TOOK JOYFULLY THE SPOILING OF YOUR GOODS FOR MINE KNOWING IN OURSELVES THAT YE HAVE IN HEAVEN BETTER AND AN ENDURING SUBSTANCE BETTER THAN THE NOW, THEREFORE CAST NOT AWAY YOU CONFIDENCE WHICH SHOULD HAVE GREAT RECOMPENCE OF REWARD TO THE

MESSENGER FOR YE NEED OF PATIENCE JUST LIKE THE MESSENGER AND THE HOLY GHOST, THAT AFTER YE HAVE DONE THE WILL OF GOD YE MIGHT RECEIVE THE PROMISE, AND LET THE REWARD OF YOUR HANDS BE TO MASS THE ILLUMINATOR, AS YOUR COMFORTER AND HE THAT IS ABLE TO HELP YOU FINISH THE WORK, SO FOLLOW THE MESSENGER UNTO US WARD OR YOU DRAW BACK UNTO PERDITION JUST LIKE

THEY HAVE DONE BEFORE. THE MYSTERY OF CHRIST HATH SENT THE MESSENGER UNTO YOU TO REPROVE THE WORLD OF SIN, AND OF RIGHTEOUSNESS FOR YOU SEE JESUS NO MORE AS HE IS IN THE FATHER, AND OF JUDGEMENT OF THE PRINCE OF THE WORLD. RECEIVING ME THROUGH CHRIST OR A RIGHTEOUS MAN FOR UNTO YOU THE MESSENGER'S REWARD THROUGH GOD ALMIGHTY UNTO US WARD AS ANOTHER COMFORTER THAT WILL ABIDE WITH YOU FOREVER AS NOW, WE GO NOT TO THE MOUNTAINS OR JERUSALEM FOR SANCTIFICATION IN WORSHIP UNTO GOD BUT THROUGH THE SPIRIT OF DIVINITY.

THE DIVINITY OF THE LAST DAYS

THE TRUTH OF JESUS CHRIST, STIRS YOU UP AT THE ALTAR OF THE SUN, WITH THE LAST ALTER CALL FOR THE FREEDOM OF MY BLACK BROTHERS AND SISTERS, ALL OTHER MEN AND ALL THINGS ON EARTH AND IN THE HEAVEN ABOVE TO DO THE WILL OF GOD.

I SEE THE WONDROUS CROSS – ON YONDER HILLS – AWAY FROM MY TROUBLED LIFE, – I MADE IT TO THE FOOT OF THE CROSS – BUT I NEED

TO PUSH ON THROUGH – FOR I SEE YOUR PROPHECIES – ARE GIVEN TO ME TO FULFIL – IF I HAVE FOUND YOUR MIRACLES AND YOUR WILL – O IF I. ... COULD ONLY FIND YOUR PEOPLE'S WILL – THOUGH THEY BE UP

THROUGH YOU ~ YOU TOUCH ME LORD O LORD JESUS LORD YOU TOUCH ME ~ I AM BLESSED TO WORSHIP THEE ~ LORD I MAGNIFY YOU LIKE NO OTHER ~ YOU HAVE PLACED MY GOD IN CONTROL OF ME ~ YOUR SPIRIT LORD HAVE MADE ME ~ ALL I WANT TO BE, AND LORD I SEE ONLY YOU ~ LORD YOUR SPIRIT, YOUR MIRACLES AND ME ~ AND THE TRUTH OF JESUS CHRIST ~ DIVINITY FOR THE LAST DAYS IS A COMMAND BY GOD ~ BUT DIVINITY! WHAT IS IT?

THE WORD DIVINE, MEANINGS, DIVINE IS GODLIKE OR HEAVENLY. THE WORD DIVINITY, A DIVINE SENTENCE IS IN THE LIPS OF THE GOD AND HIS MOUTH TRANSGRESSETH NOT IN THE JUDGEMENT. DIVINITY IS TO RECEIVE INSTRUCTIONS OF WISDOM, JUSTICE, AND JUDGEMENT AND EQUITY. DIVINITY GIVES SUBTILTY TO THE SIMPLE AND THE YOUNG MAN KNOWLEDGE AND DISCRETION.

THE STORY OF THE CENTURION, THIS CENTURION HAD POWER BUT KNEW THAT HIS POWER WAS NOT DIVINE — HE RESPECTED JESUS WITH MORE FAITH THAN HE HAD EVER SEEN — AND THE POWER OF JESUS DIVINITY AROSE UPON HIM THAT JESUS TOLD HIM AND THOSE AROUND HIM WHAT SHALL BE OF MANY OF ABRAHAM SEED IN THE LAST DAYS. AND SO, IN THESE LAST DAY JESUS WILL SEEK TO FIND

DIVINITY IN MEN ONCE MORE. BUT MEN WOULD FIRST NEED TO FIND FAITH LIKE THE CENTURION, AS DIVINITY IS CHRIST CENTERED WITH BELIEF FROM THE HEART. AND SO TRUE DIVINITY WOULD LET US NOT BE DESIROUS OF VAIN GLORY, PROVOKING ONE ANOTHER, AND ENVYING ONE ANOTHER. THE FIRST BIG LESSON FOR THE CHURCH IS THAT IF YOU WANT TO LIVE IN THE SPIRIT YOU WILL HAVE TO WALK IN THE SPIRIT OF FAITH IN JESUS AND HIS WILL. THE FRUITS OF THE SPIRIT ARE THE WONDERS OF LIFE, SUCH AS ~ LOVE ~ JOY ~ PEACE ~ LONGSUFFERING ~ GENTLENESS ~ GODNESS ~ FAITH ~ MEEKNESS ~ TEMPERANCE, AGAINST SUCH THERE IS NO LAW, I AM LED THE SPIRIT AND THEREFORE NOT UNDERTHE LAW, AND NOW THE LAW IS FULFILLED IN ONE WORD "LOVE FOR A DIVINE PROSPECT OF CHRIST. NOT BECAUSE I COME TO YOU WITH LOVE THAT YOU SHOULD BITE AND DEVOUR ME FOR THE MANIFOLD WISDOM OF THE SPIRITUAL THEOLOGY OF GOD. I COME AS A MESSENGER NOT TO DISGRACE YOU BUT TO WARN YOU BUT YOU WANT TO BITE AND DEVOUR ME, AND NOW THE WORKS OF THE FLESH ARE MANIFESTED IN YOU, BECAUSE YOU KEEP COMMITTING YOURSELVES TO THE LAWS AND ARE JUSTIFIED BY THE LAWS. TO THEN STICK TO LAWS, KNOW NOW, THAT YE ARE FALLEN FROM GRACE AND MORESO HAVE, LOST ALL DIVINITY FOR FALLEN ARE YEE FROM GRACE.

AS FALLEN FROM GRACE, ALL PEOPLE CAN SEE THAT YOU ARE FILLED WITH, ENVY, HERESIES, SEDITIONS, MURDERS, STRIFES, DRUNKENNESS, WRATH, REVELLINGS, EMULATIONS, VARIANCES, HATRED, WITCHCRAFY, IDOLITARY, ADULTRY, FORNICATION, UNCLEANNESS, LASCIVIOUSNESS, DO YEE THEM AND YOU SHALL NOT SEE THE KINGDOM OF HEAVEN. THEREFORE, LET YOUR DIVINITY APPROVE OF THE MESSENGER AND COMFORTER UNTO YOU, THEREBY USE NOT LIBERTY TO CROSS MY PATH AND SHOW YOUR WORLD THAT THE OFFENCE TO THE CROSS IS CEASED. THE MESSENGER IS YET COME TO YOU IN LOVE PEACE AND WITH GREAT JOY TO GET YOU ALL TO THE SIDE OF THE LORD JESUS CHRIST IN FAITH OF A CHANGE TO THE NEW GOSPEL AND THE NEW COVENANT.

YOU ARE FALLEN FROM GRACE, YOU NEED REPEINTNCE, BEFORE YOU CAN APPROACH THE COVENANT OF SPIRTIUAL THEOLOGY UNDER THE TABERNACLE OF THE SUN. FIND LOVE, LIVE LOVE, GIVE LOVE TO ONE ANOTHER AND THERE YOU WILL REALIZE THAT LOVE HATH POWER OVER THE LAWS AND REPENT OF YOUR SINS SPREAD THE WORDS UPON THE JOY OF THE ENZIGNS AND COME TO THE FOOTSTOOL OF THE GRACE OF GOD. THE MESSENGER BEING GREATER THAT JOHN THE BAPTIST, IF THE PROPHET WOULD YOU WOULD BE IMMEDIATELY CUT OFF BUT THE SPIRIT OF GRACE IS TEMPERATE AND WILLING TO BRING YOU TO THE FOLD OF GOD, I RAN WELL AND I OBEY THE TRUTH WHOEVER CAN HINDER ME ARE LOST IN THE FLESH, DIVINITY HAS IT'S SEASON. EVERYTHING UNDER THE HEAVEN HAVE IT'S SEASON, I SHALL REJOICE IN MY OWN WORK, FOR WHATSO EVER GOOD IS IN THEM IS OF GOD, IT BEING SPIRITUAL FAILETH NOT IN THE SPIRIT OF GOD FOR IT SHALL BRING ME TO SEE WHAT SHALL BE AFTER ME, THE INHERITANCE OF THE LORD, AS AN EXAMPLE TO ALL. I SAID IN MINE HEART, CONCERNIG THE ESTATES OF THE SONS OF MEN, THAT THE LORD GOD WILL MANIFEST THEM THAT THEY MAY SEE THAT THEY THEMSELVES ARE BEAST, YOUR LACK OF DIVINITY WILL SHOW YOU AS BEAST TO THE WORLD. THE MESSENGER IS NOT A LABOURER IN HIS OWN LABOUR I REPRESENTS THE TRUTH, AND IN THE MATTER, THERE IS NO END TO THE WORKS OF GOD.

THE KNOWLEDGE AND DISCRETION OF DIVINITY ARE TO RECEIVE INSTRUCTIONS OF WISDOM, JUSTICE, AND JUDGEMENT TO BRING EQUITY. DIVINITY GIVES SUBTILTY TO THE SIMPLE AND THE YOUNG MEN., THAT THEY MAY ESCAPE THE CORRUPTION OF THE WORLD WILL BE PARTAKERS OF THE DIVINE NATURE OF GOD. GRACE AND PEACE SHALL BE MULTIPLIED UNTO THEM, THROUGH THE KNOWLEDGE OF GOD, AND OF JESUS OUR LORD ACCORDING TO HIS DIVINE POWER HATH GIVEN UNTO US ALLTHINGS THAT PERTAINETH UNTO GODLINESS THROUGH THE KNOWLEDGE OF HIM CHRIST JESUS WHO CALLED US TO GLORY AND VIRTUE, SO AS I WAIT IN PATIENCE WITH THE KNOWLEDGE AND TEMPERANCE AND TRUTH OF

GODLINESS I COME AS THE MESSENGER BUT I WAIT UPON YOU TO PUT AWAY YOUR GUILE AN ENVY AGAINST ME. THIS DOCTRINE IS PURE AND TRUE YEA I THINK IT MEET AS LONG AS I AM IN THE TABERNACLE OF THE SUN, I WILL STIR YOU UP BY PUTTING YOU IN REMEMBERANCE, AS THE SPIRITUAL MESSENGER I WILL PUT YOU IN REMEMBERANCE EVEN THOUGH YOU KNEW THEM AND BE ESTABLISHED IN THEM BUT YEE DO

AND OBSERVE THEM NOT. KNOWING THAT SHORTLY I MUST PUT OFF THIS MY TABERNACLE EVEN AS MY LORD JESUS CHRIST HAVE SHOWN ME SO THAT WHEN I AM GONE AWAY YOU WILL HAVE THEM IN REMEMBERANCE IN THE CREATION OF HIS FIRST FRUITS AND CREATURES OF GOD. O WHEN I STIR YOU UP YOU CAN'T COME TO THE MARRIAGE SUPPER WITH ENVY AND JEALOUSY AS CONCEERNING THE WORKS SPIRITUAL THEOLOGY WAS NOT YOUR WORKS, UNDER THE PROPHETESS ELLEN G WHITE OR ANY OTHER BEFORE AS IT IS UNTO THE HIGH TIME OF GOD'S CALLING.

I AM THE STIRRER COME TO STIR YOU UP AND GIVE YOU THE LIGHT OF THE WORLD ALSO THE MESSENGER GREATER THAN JOHN THE BAPTIST, AND JOHN THE REVELATOR, SO YOU CAN CLAIM VICTORY IN JESUS CHRIST WITH FAITH IN MY REMEMBERANCE, THE GATES OF HELL MAY BE OPEN BUT BE NOT A BEAST TO YOUR MESSENGER WITH THE BREAD OF LIFE. FITLY I COME TO YOU WITH THE LIGHT, THE TRUE BREAD OF LIFE FOR THESE LAST DAYS, AS THE MISTERY OF CHRIST ENDOWS ME. IT IS SUITABLE BUT YOU HAVE WARIED THE CHILDREN OF GOD IN THE WRONG DIRECTION THAT MY WORK HAS BECOME FITLY WEIRD AND RATHER STEALABLE FOR YOUR SUPREMACY.

FOR IN DOING SO THE BEAST YOU CHOOSE TO BE IN A CHURCH THA PROCLAIMS I COME TO YOU FROM THE DISPENSATION, AS A STEWARD FOR GOD NOT MAN, WITH A JOB FROM THE GARDEN PATH TO BE ADMINISTERED OVER TIME WITH THE DISPENSABLE MOMENTS OF GOD, BEING MANISESTED IN DISPARAGE [BROUGHT TO THE VERY LEAST AS NOTHING AMONGST YOU] AMONGST MY OWN WITH ALL THE PROPERTIES THAT HAVE CONFOUNDED THEM, DISPLEASED AS YOU MAY BUT IF THE TRUTH IS NOT FOUND IN YOU THEN YOU ARE FALLEN FROM GRACE AND YOUR DIVINITY. YOU CAN DISPLAY THE WORKS OF THE FLESH BUT THE TRUTH WILL NOT BE IN YOU, BUT BE IN THE BEAST, AND SO THE USE OF THE ENZIGNSOF THE GARDEN PATH, IS NOT THE MARKS OF THE BEAST BUT TRUTHFUL REMEMBERANCES OF ME THE MESSENGER, THE FINISHER, NOT A SPECTACLE WITH THE DIVINITY TO THE LIGHT OF JESUS CHRIST AND THE SPIRIT OF GOD. ALL ARE WELCOME TO THE TABERNACLE OF THE SUN THROUGH REPENTANCE AND POPPING THE WORD THAT BGINGETH GRACE AND JOY TO THE HEARERS,

POPPING THE WORD OF GOD

I FRANCIS CHARLES MALCOLM THE MESSENGER TO YOU DID NOT BRING A WAR TO YOUR DOORSTEPS, AS THE MESSENGER I COME TO WARN YOU BEFORE THE COMING OF THE LORD SO THAT SOME MAY BE SAVED. THE PASTOR JOHNATHAN MILLER WHO WED ME TO MY WIFE HAD THIS TO SAY WHILE CONVERSING "I DON'T ACTUALLY MATTER IF I AM IN THE 144,000 CHILDREN OF GOD, CHOSEN & SEALED BY THE ANGEL IN THE LAST DAYS OR IN THE GREAT MULTITUDE, I WANT TO BE COUNTED IN".

NOW GIVE ME A CHANCE TO TEACH THE SHEPHERDS THAT LEADS THE FLOCK YEA THE MESSENGER SAYS THE CHURCH WILL HAVE TO WAKE UP AND TAKE THE PEOPLE OUT OF BABYLON AND THE ORDINANCES OF MAN, FOR THE CHURCHES TO BE COUNTED IN THE MULTITUDE — IF YOU ARE THE FIRST NEITHER WILL YOU BE THE LAST FOR ALL MEN SHALL BOW AND SAY JESUS CHRIST IS LORD OF LOVE

AFTER ANNANYAS AND SAPHIRA THE HIGH PRIEST FOUND THEMSELVES IN PROBLEM FOR CASTING THE APOSTLES SENT BY THE SPIRIT OF GOD TO PREACH IN THE CHURCH, CAN YOU BE IN POWER OVER THE SPIRIT OF THE MIGHTY GOD? THE MESSENGER'S WORK IS GOD'S GIFT TO THE CHURCHES AND NOT A WORK FOR ENVY FOR ACCEPTING THE WORKS OF THE LORD JESUS THE WHOLE MATTER OF THE GARDEN PATH VOL. 1, VOL. 2, & VOL. 3 WITH ALL YOUR HEART THE CHURCH WILL HAVE TO SEE TO THE WELFARE OF THE TABERNACLE IN THE SUN MINISTERED BY MASS FRANCIS CHARLES MALCOLM

IN THE LAST DAYS THE SWORD OF JESUS CHRIST IS TRANSFORMED TO THE TRUE WORD OF GOD, THROUGH THE TRUE WORSHIP OF GOD IN SPIRIT AND IN TRUTH. THRUTH COMES WITH HONESTY, AND A LAW THAT COVERS ALL LAWS CALLED LOVE, HONESTY CARRIES NO FORM OF JEALOUSY IN THE WORK OF JESUS CHRIST ALL YOU GOT TO KNOW IS YOUR MESSENGER THAT IS GREATER THAN JOHN, KNOW YOUR

PLACE IN THE CHURCHES, HONORABLE, KNOW YOUR PLACE IN THE LINE OF REMEMBERANCE TO THE TABERNACLE OF THE SUN BY MASS, UNTO GOD UP IN THE HEAVENS, FOR HIS WORD TO BE FULFILLED.

I AM THE MESSENGER OF THIS MATTER, JUST THIS MATTER CONCERNING THE MINISTRY OF RECONCILIATION OF THE CHURCHES FORM THE TABERNACLE OF THE SUN BY MASS, I AM PATIENT AND A MAN OF STABLISH HEART WITH THE INTEREST OF PLACING THE SPIRITUAL CHURCH OF THE MANIFOLD WISDOM OF GOD IN EVERY MAN. I HAVE NEITHER GOLD NOR SILVER TO OFFER ANYMAN NEITHER DO I REQUEST OF YOU THE

SAME EXCEPT OF MY WELFARE FROM THE CHURCHES OF WHICH I KNOW YOU SHOULD NOT ROB GOD, AFTER SENDING THE GREATEST GIFT TO ALL MANKIND TO YOU FOR YOU ACCEPTANCE THROUGH YOUR FAITH IN JESUS CHRIST THE SON OF GOD, DON'T ERR AND BELITTLE THE MESSENGER, THE CHURCHES CANNOT GO AROUND THE END OF TIME MESSENGER OR THE WILL OF GOD. THOUGH THE EARLY RAIN FELL, AND THE FIELD RIPENNED, AND YOU ALL SLEPT WHILE NOT RECEIVING THE GOODNESS OF GOD NOW, TO YOU HAVE THE LATTER RAIN WHICH IS INEVITABLE AND CONSEQUENTIAL TO THE SAINTS OF HIS KINGDOM WHO HAVE WAITED IN PATIENCE, ON THE LABOURERS OF CHRIST TO CHANGE FROM SEEKING THEIR OWN MEAT, AND BECOME LABOURERS FOR CHRIST SO THAT HE CAN DRAW ALL MEN UNTO HIM.

THE LATTER RAIN BRINGS THE LIGHT AND YOU CAN'T ENVY AND STEAL THE LIGHT, IT WILL NOT SHINE ON THE CROOKED WAY. EACH MAN FILLEDWITH THE LIGHT HAVE GOT TO TELL OF THE LIGHT FOR FURTHERANCE OF THE LIGHT AND THE MAGNIFYING OF THE HOLY SPIRIT TO GAIN MORE SAINTS FOR THE KINGDOM OF GOD, THIS THE RETURN ON EACH MANS ACCOUNT AS SOON AS THEY ARE TAUGHT FOR ONLY A PURE IN HEART CAN CONVERT A SINNER FROM THE ERR OR OF HIS WAYS AND SAVE THAT SOUL FROM DEATH, HIDING HIS MULTITUDE OF SINS J/5/20, LET US NOT WORK AMMISS WITH THE MINISTRY OF RECONCILIATION FOR THIS IS FERVENT PRAYER SEASON FOR REPENTANCE FOR YOUR GRAPHED SINS OF WORSHIPING JESUS CHRIST IN THE ORDINANCE OF MAN. LET YOUR PRAYERS AND SUPPLICATION BE OF A STANDARD NOT UNTO MAN BUT UNTO GOD

WHILE UPHOLDING THE TRUTH OF THE MESSENGER'S LEGACY, AND REJOICE NOT IN YOUR BOASTINGS AGAINST THE MESSENGER, FOR SUCH REJOICING IS EVIL, THE BIBLE SAYS TO HIM THAT KNOWETH TO DO GOOD AND DOETH IT NOT, TO HIM IT IS A SIN. THE FRUITS OF RIGHTEOUSNESS IS SOWN IN PEACE, OF THEY, THAT MAKE PEACE NOTE WELL THAT THE MINISTRY OF RECONCILIATION IS A LITTLE MATTER SOWN IN PEACE FOR EVERY CHURCH BY THE MESSENGER GREATER THAN JOHN SO FOLLOW ME.

IT COMES WITH THE WISDOM FROM ABOVE THAT IS FIRST UNTO ME PURE, THROUGH JESUS CHRIST SWORD HANDED TO ME IN MY YOUTH, EATING UP THE LITTLE BOOK AND MODERATING IT IN THE END OF TIME AS THE MESSENGER GREATER THAN JOHN, WITH THE EFFECTUAL WORKS OF GOD, BEING THE ONLY MINISTER THAT WILL COME UNTO YOU IN THE LAST DAYS, THIS WISDOM FROM ABOVE COMETH THROUGH THE TABERNACLE OF THE SUN TO ALL THE 7 CHURCHES, SO THAT SOME MAY BE SAVED, AND I NOW SEE SOME OF MY BRETHEN ESTABLISHING THEIR WILL TO SEE THE WILL OF GOD ESTABLISHED IN THE CHURCH.

THIS WISDOM FROM ABOVE IS AGAIN FIRSTLY PURE, THEN PEACEABLE, SO THE MESSENGER CAN'T TELL YOU TO FIGHT FOR IT. IT WAS MADE FOR THE 7 CHURCHES THEREFORE IT IS ONLY TO BE ACCEPTED BY THE CHURCHES FOR THE PRIESTS, BISHOPS AND PASTORS TO USE OF NO SHORT ORDER FOR THE LOVE OF JESUS CHRIST TO BE SPREAD ALL AROUND, FOR THE WORDS OF GOD ENTREATS YOU IN GOOD CONVERSATIONS, SO AS TO LET ME SHOW YOU MY WORKS OUT OF KINDNESS AND MEEKNESS AS ENDUED WITH WISDOM AND KNOWLEDGE TO YOU ALL. AND I SAY IF YOU HAVE BITTERNESS AND ENVYING AMONGST YOU WITH STRIFE IN YOUR HEARTS GLORY NOT, AND BE NOT AGAINST THE TRUTH, FOR THIS WISDOM IS NOT OF THE EARTH BEING SENSUAL AND DEVILISH POPPING THE WORD OF GOD MEANS APOSTACY IS YOUR CALLING, THE SWORD OF GOD IS GIVEN AND APPOINTED AT A CERTAIN TIME TO A MESSENGER GREATER THAN JOHN THE BAPTIST, WHY HATEST THOU ME IF YOU MIGHT AS WELL DO THE WORK OF THE LORD JESUS IN PEACE. WHY SUPPRESS MY WORKS IF YOU MIGHT AS WELL DO WHAT YOU KNOW IS RIGHT, IN LOVE FOR THE LORD JESUS CHRIST WHO IS ALSO LORD OF THE SABBATH AND LORD OF THE LAW OF LOVE.

WHY NOT FOLLOW ME INSTEAD OF TRYING TO MAKE MORE MOCKERY OF THE LIFE I LIVE, WHY NOT FOLLOW ME INSTEAD OF TRYING TO TAKE THE WORKS FOR THINE OWN TO WHERE PEACE WILL NEVER ABIDE IN YOU AND YOU BEING FOREVER TORMENTED, BEING AN OUTCAST FALLEN FROM GRACE. BE NOT VAIN, FOR FAITH WITHOUT WORKS IS DEAD, AND SO THE BODY WITHOUT THE SPIRIT IT IS DEAD

RAHAB THE HARLOT WAS JUSTIFIED BY WORKS, WHEN SHE HAD RECEIVED THE MESSENGERS OF GOD AND PROTECTED THEM, THE PASTER OF PREACHING CAN'T CARRY THE WORKS OF STEALTH, THE MESSAGE WHICH IS THE WORKS OF THE MESSENGERS OF JESUS CHRIST SWORD OF THE SPIRIT MUSH COME FROM THE MESSENGER AS AN UNDERSTANDING TO THE PRIEST AND THE LABOURERS IN THE GRAET HARVEST UNTO GOD'S PEOPLE. SO, FOLLOW THE MESSENGER, THIS FOOD YOU GET FROM THE MESSENGER IS MEAT TO FILL THE SPIRIT WITH WISDOM AND KNOWLEDGE FOR TO BE USE WITHOUT ENVY IT IS HEAVENLY AND OF GOD. WHEN YOU SHALL TAKE IT UNTO YOURSELVES SELFISHLY CONDEMNING THE MESSENGER GREATER THAN JOHN THE BAPTIST AND GREATER THAN JOHN THE REVELATOR IN IT, THEN IT IS TAKEN WITH ENVY, LYING AND DEFRAUDATION IN A HOLY PLACE OF WORSHIP WITH A FOUNTAING OF SALT WATER AND FRESH WATER PROCEEDING FROM YOUR MOUTH WHICH DEFILETH THE MEMBERS OF THE BODY IN YOUR LUST AFTER EVIL, THEREFORE TO HIM THAT KNOWETH TO DO GOOD AND DOETH IT NOT, TO HIM IT IS SIN, USE IT WITH HONOUR FOR OUR GOD IS WILING AND READY TO HAND OUT THE GOOD.

POPPING THE WORD OF GOD IS TO BE DELIVERED BY SPECIALIST THAT HAVE READ THE WORDS HAVING SEEN AND HEARD THE TRUTH OF GOD AND HAVE ACCEPTED THE WORKS OF THE LORD JESUS CHRIST IN THE TAKING OF THE CHURCH TO FULL REPENTANCE IN THE NAME OF JESUS CHRIST UNDER THE LAW OF LOVE AND THE COVENANT OF GRACE FROM THE DIVINE STEWARDSHIP OF THE MEMBERS OF THE CHURCH. TO THE CHURCH TO ESTABLISH WITHIN MAN A NEW CHURCH WITHOUT CHANGING THE FOUNDATIONS OF THE SEVEN

CHURCHES AND WITHOUT WAVERING OF THE HEART WITH FULL ACCEPTANCE OF THE LAW OF JESUS CHRIST TO LIVE WITH LOVE IN THIS NEW FOUNTAIN OF WATER BLESS ALL MEN WHICH ARE MADE SFTER THE SIMULTITUDE OF FOR THE GOOD TREE IS OF GOD AND THE GOOD MESSENGER IS OF GOD AND THE KNOWLEDGE AND WISDOM COMES FROM ABOVE, J/3/26 FOR THE BODY WITHOUT THE SPIRIT IS DEAD, SO FAITH WITHOUT WORKS IS DEAD.

SO HENCEFORTH THE MESSENGER GREATER THAN JOHN THE BAPTIST HAVE COME TO THE SEVEN CHURCHES AND TO ALL MEN OF THIS WORLD BE THOU BELIEVERS IN GOD AND ON GOD FOR THE DEVIL BELIEVETH AND TREMBLE. FOR WHERE SHALL YOU PUT THIS MESSENGER GREATER THAN JOHN THE BAPTIST, UNDER YOUR FOOTSTOOL, OR UP TO THE TABERNACLE IN THE SUN. YET STILL WE ALL SHOULD BELIEVE IN ONE GOD YET YOU HAVE STRAYED ONE TO ANOTHER TO HARBOR EVIL THOUGHT AGAINST THE MESSENGER OF GOD, TRYING WITH YOUR VERY BEST HEART TO DISPLACE THE POOR MESSENGER OF GOD, I BLASTPHEME NOT THE WORTHY NAME OF THE LORD OF WHICH WE ARE CALLED BUT YOU HAVE MOCKED THE LORD JESUS CHRIST THE SON OF GOD, YOU HAVE MOCKED GOD AND THE SPIRIT OF GOD WITH ALL YOUR HEARTS, AND MORE SO HAVE MOCKED ME IN THE GAEDEN PATH FOR FAR TOO LONG AS A MADMAN AND IN ALL MANNER OF THINGS CONCERNING MEN TO TAKE AWAY MY DEJURE.

POPPING THE WORDS OF GOD IN THE LAST DAYS YOU MUST FULFIL THE ROYAL LAW OF THE SCRIPTURES, THEREFORE SHALL YOU ALL LOVE YOUR NEIGHBOURS AS THYSELF SO SHALL YOU DO WELL. BUT YOU HAVE RESPECT TO PERSONS SAYING IF I CAN'T READ THEN I THE MESSENGER IS GOING TO BE SALT, WELL CAN A MAN ROB GOD, CAN YOU ROB THE HEAVENLY GIFT THE MESSENGER HAVE FROM GOD? GOD KNOWETH QUITE WELL AND SO BY THE HOLY GHOST IT IS ENTERED INTO THE WHOLE WORLD. THE OWNER'S PARADIGM SHIFT FOR SURETY OF REMEMBRANCE IS IN CHRIST WITH HIS INGERITANCE, THIS YOU SHOULD KNOW BEFORE YOUR QUEST TO DECEIVE.

BE PATIENT OTHER MINISTERS OF THE FAITH AND LET PATIENCE HAVE THE PERFECT WORKS, JA 1:2-3 BUT COUNT IT TO YOU THOUGH JOY

FOR HAVING FALLEN INTO THE DEEPEST OF DIVERS TEMPTATIONS HAVING LEARNED TO FOLLOW AND ACCEPT THE MESSENGER FOR WHAT IT WILL BE AND NOT CONTINUE TO DEFILE THE SELF FOR SO

LONG ALSO GRIEVING THE HOLY SPIRIT OF GOD, [JA1] THEREFORE MY BELOVED BRETHREN DO NOT ERR FOR EVERY GOOD GIFT COMETH DOWN FROM HEAVEN YOU CAN ONLY TEMPT YOURSELF AS GOD CANNOT BE TEMPTED NOR CAN YOU TEMPT GOD,

THE VARIABLENESS OF THE GIFT IS FOR WHAT GOD WANT TO BE DELIVERED UNTO MEN OR UNTO PEOPLE OR UNTO CHURCHES.

THE MESSENGER'S GIFT IS UNTO CHURCHES PASTORS ITS NOT YOURS, DO NOT ERR ANYMORE, LET THE CHURCH ACCEPT THE MINISTRY OF RECONCILIATION AND HERE ENDEDTH THE WHOLE MATTER SO THAT YOU CAN USE IT ACCORDINGLY, TO RENEW THE RIGHT SPIRIT WITHIN THE CHURCH WHICH OBSERVETH THE LAW OF LOVE, THEN SHALL YOU TEACH THE GOSPEL OF THE LITTLE SPIRITUAL CHURCH OF THE MANIFOLD WISDOM OF GOD TO BE WITHIN MAN WHICH PROCURETH THE LIGHT FOR EACH MAN TO SHARE. LOOK IN THE MIRROR AT YOU, FORGET NOT THE WAY YOU BE ON YOUR OWN WAY, THE LAW OF LIBERTY MUST BE SEEN IN YOU, IT SIGNIFIES GREAT LOVE. IT WILL KEEP YOU LOOKING UNTO THE PERFECT LAW OF LIBERTY AND TO CONTINUE THEREIN SO AS NOT TO BE A FORGETFUL BEARER IN THE MINISTRY OF RECONCILIATION AND TO GET THE SPIRITUAL CHURCH OF THE MANIFOLD WISDOM OF GOD IN YOU. THE GARDEN PATH WAS AND IS AND WILL BE MANIFESTED TO FULFIL THE LAW OF LIBERTY SO AS TO MAKE ALL LIBERALIST FREE, BEING A DOER OF THE WORK AND FOREVER BLESSED IN ALL YOUR DEEDS.

HOWEVER, YOU WHICH ARE RELIGIOUS AND SEEMS PUFFED UP. I ASK THE QUESTION "WILL I BRIDLE YOUR TONGUE?" NO NEVER, THERE IS THE MIRROR AND THE LAW OF LIBERTY IF YOU CAN'T BE A GOOD BEARER IN THE FAITH OF JESUS CHRIST AND WAIT UPON THE GARDEN PATH TILL IT IS GIVEN TO BE COMMANDED TO FOLLOW THE MESSENGER GREATER THAN JOHN THE BAPTIST THEN GO AND BE VAIN IN YOUR BABBLINGS, BEATING UPON THE WIND AND DECEIVE THY OWN SELF— RECEIVE THE MINISTRY OF RECONCILIATION WITH

MEEKNESS, IN YOUR VARIATIONS RELIEVE ALL FILTHINESS THE SUPERFLUITY OF NAUGHTINESS AND OF STIFFNESS TO CHANGE AGAINST BABYLON AND THE ORDINANCES OF MAN, ALSO FILTHINESS OF THE DARK DAYS, WITH VARIABLENESS IN THE NEW MAN'S WORK

FOR YOU TO PROCEED WITH LOVE, WITH NO SHADOW OF TURNING BACK FROM GOD'S LIGHT AND HE WILL BEGAT US WITH THE WORD OF TRUTH SO

THAT YOU SHALL BE FIRST FRUITS OF HIS CRETURES ONCE MORE SETTINF FORTH NEW GARDENS OF PARADISE ONCE MORE. THIS WHERE GOD IS NOW CREATING NEW PEOPLE ON EARTH, WHICH THE BIBLE WILL STATE AS BEING FIRST CREATURES

THEREFORE, MORE CREATURES WILL COME, THE FIRST CREATURES OF THE MINISTRY OF RECONCILIATION WILL START THE PROCESS OF EVOLUTION WITH IT BEING ROLLED OVER IN THE LIGHT OF JESUS CHRIST. IN THE COMING OF OUR LORD JESUS CHRIST MORE NEW CREATURES WILL EVOLVE AND REVELATION TELLS US ABOUT THE OTHER NEW CREATURES AND THEIR BEHAVIOR TOWARDS MAN.

BUT AFTER THE BREAD OF LIFE IS CRUMBLED AND SERVED TO THE SEVEN CHURCHES FOR A WARNING AND TO GIVE SUPPORT TO THE MESSENGER FOR HIS WELFARE, THE FOUR ANGELS WILL HURT THE EARTH AND SO ANOTHER ANGEL WILL ASCEND FROM THE EAST WITH THE SEAL OF GOD REV 7:3 HURT NOT THE EARTH, NOR THE TREES, NOR THE SEAS AND WILL GO ABOUT TO SEAL THE SERVANTS OF GOD IN THEIR FOREHEADS AND WHEN THAT ANGEL WILL HAVE FINISHED IT WILL BE 144,000 + OR MINUS 10,000 BASED ON THE WILL OF THE PEOPLE, THIS IS WHAT WILL TELL THE INHABITANTS OF THE EARTH THEIR POSITION IN BABYLON AND THE ORDINANCES OF MAN. IS THEIR POSITION GOOD, IS YOUR GREEDY BEHAVIOR GOOD, IS IT GOOD TO

REJECT THE MESSENGER AND PUT AN ADVANTAGE IN PLACE, IS IT GOOD TO PREACH THAT OH HOW GOOD IT WILL BE TO SEE THE MESSENGER GO SPEEDILY, QUICKLY, FROM YOUR PRESENCE WHEN GOD HATH DECLARED ME TO BE UNTO YOU FOREVER.

HOWEVER, THE MESSAGE IS HOOVERING OVER FORTY + YEARS NOW, WHICH OF YOU IS WILING TO BRING YOUR FILTHINESS AGAINST THE ANGELS IN THE SUN, OR THE FOUR ANGELS SET TO DESTROY YOU? THE PREPARED WAY IS UNTO MAN BUT OF GOD A WAY IS MARKED FOR RETURN TO GOD FROM YOUR PREVIOUS DECEPTIONS. YOU SAY YOU SERVE MY GOD MY GOD. IF MY GOD IS YOUR GOD, WHY DON'T YOU OBEY THE GOD WE SERVE WITH A WILLING HEART, POPPING THE WORD? POPPING THE WORD BRINGS OUT HIS HOLINESS NOT CONTRIVED IN GREED AND PAST ENMITY OF CHRIST BUT IN SPIRITUAL REVERENCE TO A NEW GOSPEL AND A NEW BEING BEFORE GOD, FOR THE MESSAGE TO GO FORTH, TO BE ANY CLEARER? THE MESSENGER GREATER THAN JOHN CANNOT BE REPLACED, FOR THEN GOD'S WORD WOULD BE A MERRY GO AROUND AND HAVING DEVILISH PEROGATIVES. WILL YOU BE STILL BLINDED IN THE HEART FOR YOUR GREED AND SELFISHNESS THAT GRIEVES THE SPIRIT OF GOD? YOU DON'T EVEN WANT TO GIVE THE MESSENGER A JOB HOW WILL YOU CONCEDE TO

GOD'S LOVE AND PROVIDE THAT WHICH YOU SHOULD FOR HIS WELFARE. FIND THE LAW OF LOVE, AND FOLLOW ME AND LET'S DO THE WORK AS TRUTHFUL DOERS. MY PEOPLE SEEING AND FOLLOWING IN THE SPIRIT OF GOD IN THE NAME OF THE LORD JESUS CHRIST OVER THE YEARS ARE NOT FALLEN FROM GRACE, BECAUSE OF NEGLIGENCE AND A GREATER FIGHT AGAINST GOD AND THE MESSENGER, BUT MORE ARE THOSE WHICH ARE OBVIOUSLY A PART OF THE GREAT MULTITUDE.

I THE MESSENGER HAVE SEEN THE GREAT LOSS AMONGST THE EARTH FOR A PEOPLE CALLED BY THE GOD OF LOVE OVER ALL HEAVEN AND EARTH AFTER THE SEALING OF THE SERVANTS OF GOD AND I THE MESSENGER HAVE COME BACK INTO THE CHURCH TO SAVE SOME. HOW CAN THEY BE COMFORTED AFTER BEING FOOLED FOR CENTURIES IN THE ORDINANCES OF MAN, SO THE MESSENGER COMES WITH THE HOLY SPIRIT TO COMFORT YOU, THIS HOLY SPIRIT YOU CAN'T GET IN ENVY AND GREED SO FOLLOW ME, AND COME OUT OF BABYLON, AS YOU POP THE WORD OF GOD, THIS HOLY SPIRIT YOU CAN'T, BUY, BUT FOLLOW ME IN BELIEF, THAT THE HOLY SPIRIT OF GOD IS COME UNTO YOU FOR SALVATION. THIS HOLY SPIRIT I CAN'T SELL YOU EITHER, SO FOLLOW ME, AND GAIN FOR YOURSELVES THAT WHICH IS GOOD, TO THE EDIFYING OF THE SOUL UNTO GOD, AND SEE WHAT SHALL BE AFTER YOU, IN REDEMPTION UNTO GOD. FOR YOU TOO, WILL BE A NEW BEINGS CALLED BY GOD HIS NEW CREATURES TO GLORIFY HIM.

FOLLOW ME AS THE COMFORTER NOW. I NEED NOT SAY MORE AFTER YOU HAVE READ THE GARDEN PATH, THE LITTLE BOOK FOR THE ARTICAL CREW AND THE LOST CHILDREN OF PRAISE — THE GARDEN PATH P. 30 LINES 25–26 JEHOVAH "JAH" BIG UP HIS NAME AND LEARN THE DOCTRINES WHO MADE THE BOOK MUST UNDERSTAND IT. THE COMFORTER IS HERE LONG AGO AS THE MESSENGER OF GOD IN THE SPIRIT OF GOD I THE GARDEN PATH TO YOU ALL — THOSE WHO CATCHED UP BY THE BOOK OF THE GARDEN PATH STILL FOLLOW ME, IT WAS NOT YOU WHO ATE IT UP, BUT THE MESSENGER OF GOD. IN THE SPIRIT OF GOD, I SENT THE MINISTRY OF RECONCILIATION IN THE PREPARED WAY, TO YOU, SO THAT, ALL WOULD USE IT TO CREATE THE FIRST FRUITS AND THE CREATURES OF GOD.

IN THE SPIRIT OF GOD, I GIVE YOU, THEN AFTER THE RECONCILIATION THE SPIRITUAL CHURCH OF THE MANIFOLD WISDOM OF GOD TOBE IN EACH MAN. I AM THE COMFORTED FOLLOW ME, POPPING THE WORD, FOR THOSE INCENSED AGAINST ME, FOLLOW ME, POPPING THE WORD, NOW IT IS THE CHILDREN OF PRAISE TIME TO BE COMFORTED. THE CHURCH CANNOT GO AROUND ME I ATE THE BOOK. FOR 2018 YEARS THE HAVE BEEN WORSHIPPING GOD IN BABYLON THROUGH THE ORDINANCES OF MAN.

NOW IS THE TIME TO ACCEPT THE MESSENGER, TAKE THE WARNING AND REPENT SO THAT YOU CAN SAVE THE SOULS YOU NEED TO SAVE. AND MORE LEAVING YOUR MANY DOCTRINES NOT UNTO FAITH BUT IN THE ORDINANCES OF MAN AND WITH SUCH DOCTRINES YOU ALL MISSED, THE KNOWLEDGE TO KNOW GOD. THE MYSTERY OF CHRIST WAS THEN UNTIL NOW THE HIGH TIME AS HE WAS ABOUT TO EVEN LEAVE THE APOSTLES. HAVING THE HOLY GHOST TO TEACH THEM WHEN WOULD HAVE GONE, BUT CONSOLE THEM THAT HE WILL ALSO SEND ANOTHER COMFORTER FOR WHICH HE WOULD PRAY TO THE

FATHER TO PROVIDE IN THE HIGH TIME TO BE FOREVER WITH MAN. NOW UNTO THE HIGH TIME IT IS EVEN THE SPIRIT OF TRUTH WHICH THE WORLD CANNOT RECEIVE, WHY, THEY THE CHURCH DOES NOT LIKE TRUTH, EVEN THE TRUTH OF GOD? THE WORLD SEETH ME THE MESSENGER NOT, TOO INSIGNIFICANT A FIGURE IN LIFE FOR ANY MAN

TO MAKE NOTICE OF, BUT I THE MESSENGER HATH COME AND AS JESUS LIVES I LIVETH FOR THE DECLARATION OF HIS TRUTH TO THE FOUR (4) CORNERS OF THE WORLD. I WILL SHOW THE WORLD THAT I LOVE THE LORD JESUS CHRIST WITH ALL MINE HEART AND SO I WOULD LOVE THEM TO DO AS THE GREATEST EXAMPLE UNTO THEM AS THE FATHER MANIFEST HIMSELF UNTO ME. SO LIKEWISE, SHALL THE FATHER MANIFEST HIMSELF UNTO THOSE THAT FOLLOW THE EXAMPLE. THESE THINGS HAVE THE LORD SPOKEN AND THEY HAVE HE DONE SO THAT I COULD PREPARE THE WAY TO RECONCILIATION UNTO OUR GOD.

LET NOT YOUR HEARTS BE TROUBLED OR AFRAID FOR PEACE HE HATH GIVEN ME AND NOW TO US WARDS, FOR THE COMFORTER WHICH IS THE HOLY GHOST SENT IN THE NAME OF JESUS. I TEACH YOU ALL THINGS THROUGH THE LIBERALITY AND THE PREPARED WAY OF THE MANIFOLD WISDOM OF GOD BRING ALL THINGS TO REMEMBRANCE TO THESE FACTS THAT CHRIST HATH SAID AFORE. SO, LOVE THE LORD, AND FOLLOW ME, HE WILL ALSO ABIDE WITH YOU.

FOR HE THAT NOW ABIDETH WITH YOU IN THE HIGH TIME IS A SPIRIT WHICH IS GOD, THEREFORE TEACH ALL MEN TO WORSHIP GOD IN SPIRIT AND IN TRUTH. YEA I COME AND PREPARE THE WAY THAT YOU ALL SHOULD DELIGHT IN, AND IN YOUR DELIGHT YOU SHOULD FOLLOW ME AND LOVE ME JUST LIKE HOW YOU SAY YOU LOVE THE LORD, TO RECEIVE THE COVENANT AND THE SPIRIT AND THE MESSAGE TO ABIDE WITH THE LORD UNTO HIS COMING LIKE A REFINER'S FIRE, AND A FULLERS SOAP. NOW UNTO THE PRIESTS A COMMANDMENT FOR YOU. THIS YEE KNEW AND KNEW NOT, IF YOU WILL NOT HEAR AND LAY THE WORKS OF THE LORD TO THINE HEARTS AND RECEIVE THE UNDERSTANDING OF THE

MESSAGE AND THE MESSENGER, TO GIVE GLORY UNTO GOD'S NAME IN THE HIGH TIME WITH THE NEW GOSPEL UNTO THE NEW COVENANT OF GOD, AS THE GARDEN PATH CAME SHUT FOR NOUGHT AMONGST YOU, AFORE.

NOW THE FATHER WILL NOT KINDLE A FIRE AMONGST YOU FOR NOUGHT. BUT FOR AN INHERITANCE UNTO THE MESSENGER IN THE NAME OF JESUS CHRIST, AND IF YOU SHOULD COLLECT AN OFFERING FOR THE MESSENGER DO SO ON THE FIRST DAY OF THE WEEK. REMEMBER IF YOU SHALL NOT OBEY MY COVENANT WHICH IS BEFORE

YOU IN THE HIGH TIME, AND GIVE GLORY TO MY NAME FOR THE LEAST AMONGST YOU, SAITH THE LORD OF HOST, THE LORD SAID, I WILL SEND A CURSE UPON YOU, AND I WILL CURSE YOUR BLESSINGS, BUT LISTEN, I HAVE CURSED THEM ALREADY FOR YOU HAVE NOT LAID IT TO HEART, TO LET THY LIPS KNOW KNOWLEDGE. BEHOLD HE WILL CORRUPT YOUR WAYS AND SPREAD DUNG UPON YOU AND TAKE YOU AWAY, IF YOU CONTINUE IN YOUR OLD GOSPEL WAYS. ASKING WHERE SHALL YEE RETURN? THIS IS THE INHERITANCE FOR THE CORN FOR THE YOUNG MEN TO BE CHEERFUL AND THE NEW WINE FOR THE MAIDS AND SHALL NOT MY FLOCK REMEMBER ME, IN THEIR PORTION. NOW KNOW I WITH THE KISS OF THE SWORD OF THE SPIRIT.

KNOWING THE TRUTH THAT THE SWORD IS UPON MY ARM. THE PRIESTS MUST NOW BE PURGED AND SO JUDGE NOTHING BEFORE THE TIME. FOR THE KINGDOM OF GOD IN NOT IN WORDS BUT IN POWER. SO BE NOT PUFFED UP ONE AGAINST THE OTHER, FOR HE THAT JUDGETH ME IS THE LORD. REMEMBER YEE PRIESTS AND MINISTERS AND STEWARDS OF THE MYSTERY GOD. IT IS REQUIRED OF YOU TO BE FAITHFUL, THINKING NOT OF YOURSELVES AS MEN TO BE ABOVE THAT WHICH IS WRITTEN. THE RELIEF OF THE BRETHREN AND COMMAND OF TIMOTHY.

NOW CONCERNING THE COLLECTIONS OF THE SAINTS, AS I HAVE GIVEN ORDERS TO THE BRETHREN OF THE CHURCHES SO DO YEE UPON THE FIRST DAY OF THE WEEK – LET EVERYONE OF YOU LAY BY HIM IN STORE, AS GOD HATH PROSPERED HIM, THAT THERE BE NO GATHERING WHEN HE COMES. THE LORD SAID WHEN I SHALL COME WHOMSOEVER YEE SHALL APPROVE BY LETTERS, THEM WILL I SEND TO BRING YOUR LIBERALITY UNTO JERUSALEM. AND IT IS MEET THAT I ALSO, THEY SHALL GO WITH ME. FOR GREAT IS THE DOOR AND EFFECTUAL, IS OPENED UNTO ME, AND THERE ARE MANY ADVERSARIES. BUT LET NO MAN THEREFORE DESPISE HIM. BUT CONDUCT HIM FORTH IN PEACE THAT HE MAY COME UNTO ME FOR I LOOK FOR HIM WITH THE BRETHREN, IN THE HIGH TIME THE CONVENIENT TIME OF HIS WILL. TO MAKE ALL MEN SEE WHAT IS THE FELLOWSHIP OF THE MYSTERY, WITH A SURER WORD OF THE PROPHECY.

POPPING THE WORD DOES NOT REPROVE THE BIBLE, IT IS A WARNING TO FOLLOW THE BIBLE AND THE MESSENGER AS AN EXAMPLE AND REFRESHER UNTO YOU.

BOOK FIVE

ADVERSITIES AS THE STIR

THE MODERATION

AND THE TRUTH ROLL OUT

FOR THE MESSENGER ADVERSARIES ARE PLENTY BUT ALTHOUGH THY ARE SO IS THE LORD JESUS CHRIST IN ABUNDANCE AROUND ME. THE MESSENGER ENDEAVORS TO SPREAD THE LIGHT OF JESUS CHRIST CONTINUALLY IN THE STIR, THE MODERATIONS, THE LIBERALITY, THE SPIRITUAL CHURCH OF THE MANIFOLD WISDOM OF GOD, UNDER THE TABERNACLE IN THE SUN, AS THE PREPARED WAY.

FOR NOW, THE ADVERSARIES ARE PLENTY AS THEY SEEM TO HELP PEOPLE IN THE MOCKERY OF ESCHATOLOGY, RATHER THAN FREEING MY DEJURE, WITH MANY EVEN WANT TO PLAY THE DEVIL'S ADVOCATE THAT MONEY IS NOT ALL. MANY USING A LIE TO MAKE ME BE THE INSIGNIFICANT ONE AT ALL TIME AND AT ALL COST TO RENDER ME INEFFICIENT AS A CONSTRUCTIONIST IN THE EMINENT DOMAIN OF THE SPIRITUAL THEOLOGY IN ALL THE TRADES OF LABOUR FROM THE MAN OF TRICKS TO CASANOVA, WITH SPIRITUAL THEOLOGY NOW THE WORST THING I COULD SUGGEST TO PEOPLE.

SPIRITUAL THEOLOGY

THE PIECE TEN IT — TAKE IT OR LEAVE IT, PUBLISHED IN THE CITY OF UNION, NEW JERSEY, USA, TO TETHER ACROSS THE BORDERS IN THE SANITY OF MEN AS THE MESSENGER COMES OUT TO MAKE THE PREPARED WAY OFFICIAL IN THE STIR TOWARD THE CHURCH AND HUMANITY. THE FORMATIVE WAS IN A VACATION SPACE BUT TRULY THE INFORMATIVE WANTED TO CONNECT TO THE DATA IN THEIR

OWN, SPACES OF ABUNDANCE UNDER THE DARKNESS, AND REJECTION TO THE SPIRITUAL INFLUENCE OVER MANKIND, AND AN JOSE MARTI TECHNICAL HIGH SCHOOL PAST STUDENT AS THE FIRST ESCHATON AND CHIEF ARCHITECT OF THE PREPARED WAY, STARTING WITH THE GARDEN PATH, ARMED WITH THE NEW GOSPEL A SWORD UPON MINE ARM IN REFLECTION OF WHO SENT ME, THE SWORD OF THE SPIRIT, AND THE NEW COVENANT AS REQUIRED BY GOD TO BE THE REALM OF LIGHT TOWARD HUMANITY IN THE DARKNESS. WITH THEIR REJECTION I THE MESSENGER WHO CAME IN MY OWN CONVENIENT TIME, LEFT THEM ONLY THE WILL, TO FOLLOW ME.

"TEN IT" "TEC IT OR LEAVE IT", MEANT THAT IF YOU FELL IN LOVE WITH THIS POEM, UNTO MEN, THEN TAKE IT AND PUT IT IN TEN DIFFERENT LANGUAGES FOR THOSE THAT HAVE TRANSGRESSED WICKEDLY TO THE DEATH TO RECOGNIZE IT, TEN IT TAKE OR LEAVE IT MEANT THE ROAD OF SALVATION TO MANY. SALVATION, IF GIVEN OUT FREELY NOW TAKE OR LEAVE IT AS A CHOICE AS THE END IS COME UPON US. THE DUST IN THE ROCKS OF THEIR MOUNTAINS ARE WAITING ON THE DISOBEDIENT AMONGST US TO CHANGE AND ACCEPT PEACE, LOVE AND SALVATION FREELY. FOR YET NOT MY REDEEMER WOULD LOVE TO HAVE THE WORLD NOT REDEEMED FROM THEIR WICKED WAY. NOW IT IS THE SPIRITUAL CHURCH PATHWAY TO THE PERFECTION OF MAN.

THE PATIENCE GARDEN PATH, NOT LUKE WARM, COLD BUT NO HOT WAITING A WHILE IN SILENCE, ZION TRAIN UNDERGROUND, CUTTING OFF OF THE ONE LOCKS AND TOSSING IT AWAY, FOR FREEDOM FROM THE TUNNELS OF INSECURITY TO THE SHEDDING OF THE LIGHT AS IT OUGHT TO BE UPON THE WORLD IN A TIME CONVENIENT TO ME,

THE CHURCH, STILL DID NOT WAKE UP, BUT THE WAS THEIR WAKE UP CALL, ENTERING INTO THE BOOK OF THE BOOK OF JUDE, THE MODERATION OF THE GARDEN PATH, ZION TRAIN THE LITTLE LIGHT IN THE DARK COMING FORTH FROM UNDERGROUND TO SHOW EVIL MEN THE WAY, BUT IN THEIR OLD WAYS UNDERSTOOD THEY, THEIR OWN EVIL PROPHETS WILL HAVE A HARD TIME UNLEARNING THEIR LEARNT MISFORTUNES, THE HIGHLIGHTS BUILDING OF GARDENS BETTER THAN THOSE OF EDEN, THE STAR TIME HAS BEGUN AND MANY

WILL BE COMFORTED AND MANY WILL OVERCOME, THE WHITE STONE, FOR A MEASURE OF FAITH AND STRENGTH TO EXPLORE, THE ESCHAT'S WAY, TO BE PREPARED, THE STENCH OF THE NORTH ARMY, AND THE MORNING STAR AND THE COMING OF THE CHRIST. THIS CHURCH WILL PREACH AND TEACH LOVE ONE TO ANOTHER AS THE ESCHATS OF THE WORLD AND EXALT THE SEVEN SERMONS OF THE PRIESTHOOD THEOLOGY BY MASS FRANCIS CHARLES MALCOLM © 2017.

THE SPIRITUAL CHURCH OF THE MANIFOLD WISDOM OF GOD IS BUILT BY GOD UPON THE LORD JESUS CHRIST FOR STAR TIME IS UPON US. IT NEEDS NO CONTENTION OR CONFRONTATION FOR ITS PLACE IN SOCIETY WITH PREACHERS TELLING YOU THE CHURCH CAN ONLY BE IF IT IS BUILT UPON PETER THE ROCK. THE LORD DID BUT HE IS STILL LORD AND HE HAS OTHER THINGS IN STORE FOR THE PEOPLE WHO FOR SO LONG HAS LEFT HIS ORDINANCE TO WORSHIP THE ORDINANCES OF MAN. BECAUSE – THE SPIRITUAL CHURCH IS NOT LAYING A NEW FOUNDATION, AS THAT IS GONE ALREADY, AND DONE BY THE CHURCHES – OPEN TO US IS THE

BIBLE AND NOW THE PREPARED WAY OF THE LORD JESUS CHRIST IN THE RECONCILIATION AND REDEMPTION OF THE WORLD. THIS SPIRITUAL CHURCH OF THE MANIFOLD WISDOM OF GOD, LOGS YOU, ONTO SPIRITUAL AND TRUE WORSHIP OF GOD THROUGH JESUS CHRIST. FOR GOD IS A SPIRIT.

THIS ALLOWS ANY MEMBER TO HAVE FAITH, ACCEPT THE LIGHT, LOVE EACH OTHER, SUBMIT YOURSELVES ONE TO ANOTHER SPIRITUALLY AND DRAW ALL MEN ONTO CHRIST WITH THE LIGHT AND WITH LOVE FOR ONE ANOTHER.

THE OLD CHURCHES ARE LIBERATED IN THE LAW OF LOVE, UNTO A NEW GOSPEL AS THEIR OWN IS NOW OLD AND IT DECAYETH, AND SO SHALL VANISH AWAY. THIS MAKES THE MESSENGER AN ADVERSARY TO THE CHURCHES EVEN FROM THE ONE I HAD LEFT FOR SO LONG. THE LORD JESUS CHRIST HAS ANNULLDED THE LAWS BY GRACE AND ESTABLISHED IT WITH LOVE, NOW FINDING THE LIGHT HELP THE ESCHATONS TO FERFECTION IN THE BODY OF CHRIST. IF YOU FIND THE LOVE OF JESUS CHRIST IN ME AND THE WAY OF THE FATHER, AM I AN ADVERSARY TO GOD AND MAN OR THE MESSENGER OF TRUTH AND A WAY TO THE SPIRIT OF YOUR SALVATION. - SEE THAT HAVING

PERFECTION, YOU BECOME CHRISTLIKE, EVEN HAVING TO BE ANGRY, AT TIME BUT SIN NOT, TO DISPLAY THE WILL OF GOD. I AM THE ADVERSARY TO THE CHURCH THAT WILL SHOW YOU THAT THE SPIRITUAL CHURCH HAS NO BOUNDARIES AND IS OPEN TO WHO WORSHIP GOD IN SPIRIT AND IN TRUTH IN THE HANDS OF HIS SEVEN ANGELS IN HIS RIGHT HAND. I SPEAK TO THE CHURCHES IF THEY CONTINUE TO BE MINE ADVERSARY THEN THE WORSER OF THE JUDGEMENT WILL BE UPON THEM THROUGH THE PRIESTS THAT SHALL BE CURSED FOR IGNORING THE WARNING AND TO FOLLOW ME IN THIS HIGH TIME.

THE LORD JESUS CHRIST ALTHOUGH BEING LORD OF THE SABBATH - REQUIRES THAT MAN LEAVE THE EPHERMERAL CHURCHES AS THEY ARE OF THE ORDINANCES OF MAN, EVEN THE SABBATH DAYS CHURCHES OF MINE OWN IF THEY HEED NOT THE WARNING. FOR OUT OF BABYLON MUST THE PATIENT SAINTS COME TO BE SAVED IF THE CHURCHES ARE NOT WILLING TO BE REDEEMED UNDER THE TABERNACLE IN THE SUN WITH THE SEVEN ANGELS READY TO DIM THEIR CANDLE STICKS. FOR THIS THE SEVEN EPHERMERAL CHURCHES NEED TO REPENT BEFORE GOD CAN SPARE THEM A PATH IN THE SPIRITUAL REALM OF HIS PRIESTHOOD TO REACH FOR THE LIGHT AND FIND FULL FERFECTION IN THE BODY OF CHRIST.

THE SPIRITUAL CHURCH WILL NOT WRESTE WITH YOUR CLAIM OF THE LAWS AND THE OLD CHURCH THAT IS BUILT UPON PETER THE ROCK,

THAT CLEAVE TO THE ORDINANCES OF MAN, INSTEAD OF GOD, LEAVE THE LIGHT OF GOD AND FOREVER WALK IN DARKNESS BECAUSE OF BEING IN A STATE OF STUBBORNNESS AND BLINDNESS OF HEART, BY WHAT WAS TRADITIONALLY UNDERSTOOD AND LEARNT, TO WHAT IS NEW, FOR THE FUTURE, OF GOD THE ONE WHO SENT ME AND TO YOU A WARNING TO RECEIVE WITH ALL YOUR HEARTS. GOD ALLOWS THE PEOPLE OF THE SPIRITUAL CHURCH OF THE MANIFOLD WISDOM OF GOD TO BE ORIENTATED IN FULL RIGHTEOUSNESS AND UNTO PERFECTION IN SO MANY SIMPLE WAYS OF SALVATION, THAT THROUGH HIM, THE GREAT MULTITUDE TO ACCEPT THE SPIRIT OF GOD AND BOW AT THE FEET OF JESUS AND SAY YES LORD YOU ARE LORD OF ALL. CLEAVE TO THE LAW OF LOVE WHICH TAKES IN THE LIGHT, AND GIVE LOVE ONE TO ANOTHER WITH HONESTY, LACK OF DECEPTION AND ENVY, THROUGH GRACE AND REDEMPTION OF GOD THROUGH THE HOLY GHOST. THE REDEEMED AND THE ESCHATS MUST USE THE LAW OF LOVE TO MAKE A PEACEFUL WORLD OF LOVE AND RIGHTEOUSNESS FOR ALL MANKIND IN THE ORDINANCE OF GOD.

CONSCIENCE OF THE NEW CHURCH

AND THE EATING OF THE SPIRITUAL MEAT

THE EARTH IS THE LORDS AND THE FULNESS THEREOF — BY GRACE YEE BE PARTAKERS OF THE FAITH BUT BY CONSCIENCE PARTAKERS OF LIBERTY, THAT LIBERTY UNTO YOU GIVEN BY LOVE THROUGH THE HOLY GHOST UNTO THE FOUR CORNERS OF THE EARTH. WHEREFORE YEE ARE NOT CONTAINED TO BE SOLD OF HIS PERFECTION OF THE GIFT OF THE EVERLASTING GOSPEL BUT BY CHARITY THROUGH THE HANDS OF THE PREIST FOR HIS LIPS WILL TAKE THE UNDERSTANDING GAINED AS SUCH WONDERFUL AND PERFECT GIFT TO YOU ALL. AND IN AS MUCH AS THAT I THE MESSENGER WITH THE SPIRIT OF COMFORT, FROM GOD WILL BE A PART OF YOU AGAIN.

BUT IF YOU EAT THIS BREAD AND WINE OF LIFE WHICH IS THE EVERLASTING GOSPEL BEING NOT IN PARTS ANYMORE BUT PERFECTLY UNWORTHILY YOU SHALL BE GUILTY OF THE BODY AND BLOOD OF THE LORD JESUS CHRIST, OF WHICH HE HATH REDEEMED YOU ALL WITH GRACE AND REMOVING THE ENMITY FROM YOU.

REMEMBER THAT WHEN WE ARE JUDGED WE ARE CHASTENED BY THE LORD THAT WE BE NOT CONDEMNED BY THE WORLD — THEREFORE TARRY FOR ONE ANOTHER IN LOVE WHEN YOU COME TO EAT OF THE SPIRIT, FOR IT MUST BE IN TRUTH.

IF YOUR SACRIFICE IS TO THE DEVIL AND NOT TO GOD, I WOULD NOT LOVE TO SEE THAT YEE HAVE FELLOWSHIP WITH THE DEVIL. HOW WOULD IT PROFIT YOU TO EAT THE BODY OF CHRIST AND SACRIFICE YOUR BROTHER EVEN THE MESSENGER GREATER THAN JOHN SO AS TO

BE JUDGED BY THE WORLD. FOR YOU WILL GO TO FEAST WITH THE BRETHEN LEAVING THE POOR MESSENGER HUNGRY, AND YOUR CONSCIENCE WITHOUT CHARITY WHICH WAS GIVEN UNTO YOU, UNSTABLE YOU BEFORE GOD AND ALL MANKIND.

WHERFORE YEE EAT OR DRINK OR WHATSOEVER YOU DO, DO ALL TO THE GLORY OF GOD. GIVE NONE OFFENCE UPON THE JEWS, GENTILES OR THE CHURCH OF THE ALMIGHTY GOD THE LITTLE TABERNACLE IN THE SUN FOR THE MESSENGER GREATER THAN JOHN THE BAPTIST, AND GREATER THAN JOHN THE REVELATOR, PLEASE ALL MEN IN ALL THINGS, NOT SEEKING MINE OWN PROFIT, BUT THE PROFIT OF MANY, THAT THEY MAY BE SAVED. SO, YOU CANNOT DRINK WITH THE CUP OF THE LORD AND WITH THE CUP OF THE DEVIL AND STILL PLEASE GOD. THE PERFECT WAY IS OF THE LORD, PARTAKERS WILL HAVE TO LEAVE THE DEVILS WORKSHOP AND THE ORDINANCES OF MAN AND BE DISPENSERS OF THE BODY OF CHRIST, THROUGH THE LAW OF LOVE.

THE MINISTRY OF RECONCILIATION AND THE SPIRITUAL CHURCH IN THE MANIFOLD WISDOM OF GOD IS NOT ON THE DEVILS TABLE BUT THE TABLE OF GOD, WITH THE PREPARED WAY. DO NOT PROVOKE THE LORD TO JEALOUSY. ARE WE STRONGER THAN HE? ALL THINGS ARE LAWFUL FOR ME, BUT ALL THINGS ARE NOT EXPEDIENT — ALL THINGS ARE LAWFUL TO ME BU TALL THINGS ARE NOT EDIFYING, EACH SEEK ANOTHERS WEALTH AND I SEEK YOURS TOO LEST I BE HUNGRY AND YOU BOAST ON ME WHILE YOU EAT MY PORTION OF MEAT, SET IN MY INHERITANCE BEFORE ME, WHILE WE ARE YET MEMBERS OF ONE BODY THE BODY OF CHRIST. BUT, REMEMBER THAT MY WORK IS THAT WHICH IS SOWN UNTO SPIRITUAL THINGS AND NOT OF THE FLESH AS IN TIME GONE BY. AND ALL ARE BAPTIZED UNTO MOSES IN THE CLOUDS AND UNTO THE SEAS, BUT DID ALL EAT OF THE SPIRITUAL MEAT? AND MORESO DID ALL DRINK OF THE SAME SPIRITUAL DRINK, BUT THEY DRANK OF THE SPIRITUAL ROCK THAT FOLLOWED THEM AND THAT ROCK WAS JESUS CHRIST OUR LORD AND SAVIOUR. WILL YOU FOLLOW ME?

NOW THE END OF THE WORLD IS COME, TAKE HEED WHEN YOU THINKETH THAT YE STANDEST LEST YE FALL. I THEREFORE BESEACH YOU ALL FOLOW ME. STAND WITH THE MESSENGER, FOR THE SPIRITUAL

THEOLOGY OF THE END OF TIME AS YOU FLEE FROM IDOLATRY LACK OF CHARITY TO YOUR BELOVED WHO BROUGHT THE GIFT OF THE EVERLASTTING GOSPEL TO YOU IN CHARITY AND LOVE. FOR I RUNNING MAN FROM THE GARDEN PATH RUN, WITH CERTAINTY AND PURPOSE AND SO FIGHT I, NOT. FOR AS ONE THAT BEAT UPON THE AIR, REMEMBER THAT CHARITY IS LOVE AND IT NEVER FAILS SO HAVE HOPE AND FAITH IN CHRIST. FOR THE PERFECT WORK OF JESUS CHRIST IS COME TO YOU IN FULL, – AND NOT IN PARTS AS BEFORE BY THE DECEIVERS – SO THE MESSENGER COMES NOT TO CONVINCE MAN, BUT WITH A WARNING, SO, HE THAT HATH AN EAR LET HIM HEAR,

BUT IN THE MANIFESTATION OF THE SPIRIT, MAY PROFIT ALL MEN BRINGING WISDOM, KNOWLEDGE, FAITH, HEALING, MIRACLE WORKINGS, PROPHESYING, DISCERNING OF SPIRITS, DIVERS KINDS OF TONGUES, INTERPRETATIONS OF TONGUES, BUT AS DIVIDED TO EVERY MAN SEVERAL AS THE GOD ABOVE WILL GIVE TO THEIR MEASURE OF FAITH, BUT THEY ALL WOEKETH IN BODY ONE FROM THE SELFSAME SPIEIT OF GOD.

THE ACTUAL SPIRITUAL BODY BECOMES ONE WITH GOD, WHEN WILL THE CHURCH SEE THIS AND REALIZE THAT THEY THAT FIGHT AGAINST ANY OF THE GIFTS ARE FIHTING AGAINST THE BODY OF CHRIST AND GOD. MAN MUST STOP BEING ADVERSARIES TO THE MESSENGER AND GOD. NOW YE ARE THE BODY OF CHRIST, AND MEMBERS IN PARTICULAR TO UNITY OF THE BODY OF CHRIST HIS SON. AND GOD THE GOD I KNOW IN WHOSE SPIRIT I COME UNTO YOU HAVE SET SOME IN CHURCHES, SOME AS FIRST APOSTLES, SOME AS SECONDARILY PROPHETS, THIRDLY TEACHERS, AFTER THAT MIRACLE WORKERS, SOME WITH THE GIFTS OF HEALING, SOME WITH THE CAPACITIES TO HELP, SOME IN GOVERNMENTS, AND OTHERS WITH DIVERSITIES OF TONGUES. ARE ALL APOSTLES? ARE ALL PROPHETS? ARE ALL WORKERS OF MIRACLES? ARE ALL IN GOVERNMENT? HAVE ALL THE GIFTS OF HEALING? DO ALL SPEAK WITH TONGUES? DO ALL INTERPRET? BE NOT DISMAYED THEY COME TOGETHER AS ONE. BUT REMEMBER WHEN YEE COVET THE BEST GIFTS AND SUCH ARE MULTIPLIED IN YOUR CUP FAITH BUT LACK CHARITY, YOU HAVE NOTHING BUT ARE BECOME AS SOUNDING BRASS AND A TWINKLING CYMBAL. TAKE FROM YOUR OWN EYES THE GIFT OF THE SWORD OF THE SPIRIT FOR THE MESSENGER'S INHERITANCE, FOR SUCH IS THE PEACE OF THE LORD JESUS CHRIST. ARE WE ON THE SAME PAGE NOW? FOR CHARITY VAUNTETH NOT, PUTTING DOWN OF OTHERS EVEN THE MESSENGERS SENT UNTO YOU BY GOD THROUGH THE SPIRIT OF GOD WHOM WE ALL SERVE, IS NOT WORTHY OF CHARITY FOR YOUR OWN STORE HOUSE. FOR NOW, THAT WHICH IS PERFECT IS COME, THEN THAT WHICH IS IN PARTS SHALL BE DONE. SO, I SAY AGAIN CHARITY VAUNTETH NOT, CHARITY IS KIND SO SHALL THE PRIESTS UNTO THE MESSENGER. ASK YOURSELF IF YOU ARE NOT BE KIND TO ME THE MESSENGER GREATER THAN

JOHN THE BAPTIST AND GREATER THAN JOHN THE REVELATOR IN AS MUCH AS THE WORD PERMITS, THE WHICH GOD DO YOU SERVE? HAVE NOT I SEFFERED LONG FOR THIS SPIRITUAL CAUSE — WELL CHARITY SEFFERETH LONG AND THE INHERITANCE IS SURE, THROUGH JESUS CHRIST OUR LORD AND A SURER THING THE CURSE OF THE LORD, FOR DISOBEDIENCE UNTO GOD'S WORD.

CHARITY VAUNTETH NOT ITSELF AND IS NOT PUFFED UP, CHARITY DO NOT BEHAVE ITSELF UNSEEMINGLY GOING TO SEEK ITS OWN AS SOON AS THE PERFECTION IS COME FROM THE TABERNACLE OF THE SUN AND THE SPIRITUAL CHURCH WITH THE MANIFOLD WISDOM OF GOD

CHARITY THINKETH NOT EVILAND ISNOT EASILY PROVOKED, HERE IN THE TABERNACLE IS UNITY OF ONE BODY NAME BRANDS ARE THE PAST THE TABERNACLE IN THE SUN TAKES OVER THE NEW. CHARITY REJOICETH NOT IN INIQUITY AND ABOVE ALL THINGS CHARITY REJOICETH IN THE TRUTH., UNDER ONE GOD CHARITY NEVER FAILS BUT ALL THE PARTS THAT BUILDS UP TO THE TABERNACLE OF THE SUN WILL CEASE, AS IT FOLDED NOT UNDER YOU BUT IS UPRIGHT IN THE HAND OF THE LORD JESUS CHRIST, WITH THE SEVEN ANGELS READY TO DIM YOUR LIGHTS.

AND I ASK AGAIN, ARE YOU WITH ME NOW? FOR NOW, THAT WHICH IS PERFECT IS COME, THEN THAT WHICH IS PART SHALL BE DONE. THE HEAD OF THE TABERNACLE IN THE SUN IS GOD IN THE SPIRIT, WHO CREATED THE WORLD BY JESUS CHRIST, HE IT IS THAT IS GOD UNTO ALL MANKIND, JESUS CHRIST HIMSELF IS THE HEAD OF THE SPIRITUAL MAN AND THE MAN THE HEAD OF THE WOMAN WHETHER SHE BE THE CONTAINER OR THE CHURCH. THE MAN PREACHETH THE SPIRITUAL

GOSPEL OF CHRIST FOR IN IT THERE MUST BE NO ERR. UNTIL THERE BE THE RESPONSE TO THE CALLING UNTO GOD BY THE MESSENGER AND SALVATION HATH COME UNTO ALL, MAKING ALL ONE UNDER GOD BOTH MAN AND WOMAN HAVING NO DIFFERENCE OF OPINION AND UNITY IN CHRIST, THROUGH THE SWORD OF THE SPIRIT AS PREPARED BY THE MESSENGER AS A PREPARED WAY UNTO REPENTANCE OF ALL AND ALL CHURCHES. FOR THE CHANGE OF THE CHURCH IN THE LAST DAYS, COMES UPON THE LIBERALITY TO DO THIS, AS AN ACT OF GOD, NOT MAN. I THE MESSENGER DO THIS WILLINGLY UNTO THE CHURCHES IN THE LAST DAYS AND BECAUSE NECESSITY IS LAID UPON ME YEA I PREACH AND DELIVER THE EVERLASTING GOSPEL, AS THE NEW GOSPEL AFTER THE DECAY OF THE OLD GOSPEL, AND THE NEW COVENANT AFTER THE DECAY OF THE OLD COVENANT, TO GIVE WAY TO CHRIST AND HIS ANGELS AND THE TABERNACLE IN THE SUN, TO CONTROL OVER THE CHURCHES AND THE REDEEMED OF SIN. JOHN THE REVELATOR CALCULATOR MISSED THE E'S

IN THE EXPONENTS BECAUSE OF THE STUBBORNNESS OF MAN ONLY TO BEAR WITNESS IN VISIONS A GREATER NUMBER ON THE SIDELINES. AS IN THE LAST DAYS THE PRIEST AND PASTOR WILL PREACH THE EVERLASTING GOSPEL AGAINST THEIR WILL FOR AFTER 2018 YEARS WHAT CROWN SHALL THEY WEAR, BUT I REMIND YOU THE MESSENGER HATH COME BACK TO SAVE SOME AND BEAR IN MIND YOUR WILL TO ACCEPT THE WARNING COULD TURN THE E'S INTO EXPONENTS OF GLORIOUS FIGURE. FOR GOD DID NOT PUT SOME IN THE GREAT 144000 OR THE GREAT MULTITUDE UNDER CONVICTION RIGHT NOW AS WITNESSES OF THE SWORD OF THE SPIRIT CHRIST COMING AND HIS WORD.

THE MINISTRY OF RECONCILIATION AND THE SPIRITUAL CHURCH WITH THE MANIFOLD WISDOM OF GOD, THROUGH ESCHATOLOGY AND THE LAW OF LOVE IS WITH ABOUNDING GRACE. FOR THEN WILL YOU PREACH THE EVERLASTING GOSPEL OF CHRIST WITHOUT A CHARGE BY DISPENSATING IT VIA THE PREIST WHO IS WORTHY TO UNDERSTAND WISDOM AND ACCEPT IT AND GIVE UNTO YOU, EVEN AS THEY PRESS WITH JEALOUSY AND BECOME ZEALOUS THROUGH THE STIR AND THE MODERATIONS ON VARIOUS PLATFORMS FOR MANKIND TO ACCEPT THE WILL OF GOD. MURMER NOT NOR TEMPT CHRIST FOR YOU SHOULD REMEMBER MANY THINGS HAPPENED BEFORE AS

EXAMPLES AND THEY ARE WRITTEN FOR OUR ADMONISTION UPON US TO WHOM THE END OF THE WORLD IS COME. WE EAT NOT MEAT UNTO IDOLS, OR SATAN ANYMORE, FOR SUCH MAKE THE WEAK BE OFFENDED AND EVEN WOUND THE CONSCIENCE OF THE WEAK AND MAKE THEM SICK UNTO DEATH.

I PREACH TO YOU AND HAVE TAKEN THE TIME TO SHOW YOU UNDERSTANDING IN MANY SERMONS SO THAT YOU MAY SAY AMEN, MEANING YOU HAVE UNDERSTOOD THAT WHICH IS NEW NOW TO BE ABLE TO PUT AWAY THE OLD, AND FOLLOW ME THE MESSENGER WITH THE EVERLASTING GOSPEL OF CHRIST THAT IT BE SEEN IN YOU THAT AFTER ALL YOU HAVE PUTALL THINGS UNDER YOUR FEET THAT UNTO YOU GOD MAY BE ALL IN ALL. I NOW SPEAK THIS TO YOUR SHAME AWAKE TO RIGHTEOUSNESS AND SIN NOT FOR MANY HAVE NOT THE KNOWLEDGE OF GOD WITHOUT THE MANIFESTATION OF THE MESSENGER IN THE HIGH TIME. THE MESSSENGER WILL NOT BE ABLE TO CONVINCE MAN HE THAT HATH AN EAR LET HIM HEAR, FOR NOW YOU WILL HAVE TWO WITNESSES, BEFORE YOU, ONE, THE THING CALLED YOUR CONSCIENCE, AND TWO THE BODY OF CHRIST.

THE CHANGE IN THE CHURCH IS SPIRITUAL AND BINDING THE CHURCH TO THE BODY OF CHRIST, SO DOES THE CHANGE IN EACH MAN AS THE PATIENT

SAINT. WHICH MUST ALWAYS BE IN HARMONY OF BOTH CONSCIENCE AND THE BODY OF CHRIST.

MY DREAM IS IN THE GARDEN PATH THAT CARRIES THE WORD, AND THE END THEREOF THAT BUILD THE NEW WAY, AND FOR THIS CONSCIENCE AND THE BODY OF CHRIST THAT NOW ALLOW MANKIND TO BUILD GARDENS MUCH MORE BEAUTIFUL THAN THAT OF EDEN.

AND I WILL NEVER CONVINCE ANYONE, BUT RATHER, WAIT UPON YOUR FAITH IN GOD, AND THE LORD JESUS CHRIST, SO, PREACH I UNTO YOU, THE NEW AND THE EVERLASTING GOSPEL TO YOUR UNDERSTANDING TO GET AN AMEN.

I PREACH THE EVERLASTING GOSPEL OF JESUS CHRIST IN THE SPIRIT OF GOD TO CHANGE THE CHURCH IN THE LAST DAYS THROUGH A WARNING TO THE CHURCHES THAT IS, AT EASE, IN BABYLON, NOW AS THE CIPHER STIRS THESE LITTLE GOD'S ARE NOT WILLING TO BE CONVINCED BUT THE HOLY GHOST HAVE SET OUT THE WORK TO THE FOUR CORNERS OF THE EARTH TO ACT UPON THEIR FAITH DIAMONDS AND DIACRITIC MARKS, THAT THROUGH JESUS CHRIST WILL BE TOUGHER IN AND UNDER WE UNDER THE TABERNACLE IN THE SUN'S LIBERATORS "WE THE ENTRUSTED" WITH THE BRAZEN WALL OF FIRE.

THE EARTH LEAVING MANKIND IN WONDERLAND FROM THE TEACHING IN PARTS OF THE GOSPEL OF CHRIST, BUT FROM THE PIPPETED RIBBONS IN THE MODERATIONS OF THE LIBERALITY AND THE SPIRITUAL CHURCH OF THE MANIFOLD WISDOM OF GOD, HERE COMES THE CAST.

I SPOKE TO A LADY RECENTLY AND AS SHE OFFERED ME A TRACK IT TITLED "WHAT DOES THE FUTURE HOLD?" AND SHE SAID, "DO YOU BELIEVE IN GOD AND CAN YOU PREDICT THE FUTURE?" .... I SAID, "I BELIEVE IN GOD, AND MAYBE MUCH MORE THAN ANY OTHER MAN IN THE WORLD RIGHT NOW, AND I KNOW THAT GOD CAN PREDICT THE FUTURE, BUT MAN THROUGH THE SPIRIT OF GOD YOU CAN ALSO PREDICT THE FUTURE". SHE SAID ALONG WITH HER COMPANIONS, "...... THE WORLD TOO WICKED AND ONLY JESUS CAN CHANGE IT", THEN, I SAID, "JESUS WILL NOT HAVE TO CHANGE THE WORLD, JESUS HAVE GIVEN, HIS WILL AND THE WILL OF GOD TO MANKIND TO ACCEPT, IF THEY DO THEY ARE CHANGING THE WORLD, BY CHANGING THE SELF, THE CHURCHES AND HENCE, CHANGE THE WORLD BY CREATING THE FRUITS OF JESUS CHRIST AND THEN THE FIRST CREATURES OF GOD WHICH ARE MAN IN THE SPIRITUAL FORM OF GOD AND, DOING THE WILL OF GOD, ." I ASKED DO YOU BELIEVE THAT THE CHURCH WILL HAVE TO CHANGE IN A SHORT TIME. ......? ONE AGREED AND SAID, "I SEE WHERE YOU ARE GOING, AND IT COULD BE SO" AS I GO

FURTHER INTO THE TOPIC YOU WILL SEE THAT THIS IS SO ALTHOUGH IT IS VERY EVIDENT IN THE TABERNACLE IN THE SUN, WITH THE MINISTRY OF RECONCILIATION AND THE SPIRITUAL CHURCH OF THE MANIFOLD WISDOM OF GOD.

GOD IS AWESOME AND ARE LEFT IN WONDERLAND WITH HIS AWESOME POWER. WITH THE AWESOME POWER OF GOD TO THOSE WHO SAY THEY SERVE GOD AND GOD THEY TRY TO BE TO THE MESSENGER GREATER THAN JOHN THE BAPTIST, WANTING ME TO CONVINCE THEM AS TO

HOW THE CHURCH MUST CHANGE IN THE LAST DAYS OH, I JUST SAY I PREACH THE PERFECT GOSPEL NOT IN PARTS WILLINGLY UNTO YOU, IT IS THE NEW GOSPEL AND IT IS UNDER THE NEW COVENANT OF GOD. WITH IT I COME TO WARN YOU AND FOR YOU TO ACCEPT WITH ALL YOUR HEARTS THE WILL OF GOD TO BE YOUR WILL. THEN THIS WILL OF THE GOD YOU ALL SERVE WILL BECOME YOUR WILL. I WARN AND THEY BE LIKE FOOLS SET IN A TROUBLED DEN, AS THE GOD IN THEM BE UPON A MUFFLED-UP MAN AND THE HEAT THEREOF OF THEIR UNBELIEF, ALSO BE THEIR DESTRUCTION IN THE END. THE EVERLASTING GOSPEL IS NOT OF MAN AND WAS NEVER OBSERVED UNTIL 2017 INITIATION THROUGH TEK IT OR LEAVE IT AS THE FIRST PIECE CALLED TEN IT. IN FULL THE PERFECT GOSPEL IN 2018 AS FROM RUNNING MAN FROM THE GARDEN PATH AS IT SURFACE WITH ZION TRAIN WITH RUNNING MAN LIVING STILL IN HIS NECESSITY, STIRRING AND MODERATING THE PERFECT GOSPEL WILLINGLY SO AS TO ALLOW THE HOLY SPIRIT OR TO YOU THE HOLY GHOST TO BE PUBLIC UNTO THE FOUR CORNERS OF THE EARTH. OR THROUGHOUT THE WHOLE WORLD WITH RUNNING MAN IS THE COMFORTER OF GOD, OF THE, AS A DELIBERATE ATTEMPT TO SHOW THE WORLD WHO THE MESSENGER NOW IS IN THE HIGH TIME CONVENIENT TO ME. THE MESSENGER GREATER THAN JOHN THE BAPTIST AND JOHN THE REVELATOR BRING YOU TO THE COMFORT IN THE LAST DAYS, OF THE HOLY SPIRIT. AS I PUT YOU ON YOUR WAY SPIRITUALLY SERVING GOD THROUGH LOVE AND THE ACCEPTANCE OF THE GRACE OF GOD WITH ALL THE GIFTS OF LIFE, THAT CANNOT FIND GOD, IF YOU CONTINUE ON THE ROAD NOT WILLING TO TAKE HEED.

THIS COMFORT I BRING TO THE SAINTS IN THE LAST DAY WHO WERE LED ASTRAY FOR 2018 YEARS. ARE WE NOT TO OBSERVE THE GOSPEL OF CHRIST? FOR I BEING THE MESSENGER GREATER THAN JOHN THE BABTIST HAVE COME UNTO YOU, BUT YOU WHO SERVE GOD IS AFRAID OF THE PERFECT WORKS OF GOD. THIS WILL SHOW THAT THE ANCIENT HAVE NOT FALLEN FROM GRACE BUT COME TO THE SAVING GRACE OF THE SON OF GOD. THROUGH ME AND NOT AS A PECTACKLE UNTO MAN FOR I BEAR IN MY BODY THE MARKS OF THE LORD JESUS CHRISTIANS AS MUCH AS SATAN

SHOULD SHIVER AT THE WORDS OF GOD AND HIS HOLY NAME JAH, SO SHALL MANKIND FEAR HIS HOLY NAME, AND IN

DUE SEASON THERE WILL BE THE ALL AWAITED RECOMPENCE TO MANKIND FOR THEIR OBEDIENCE OR DISOBEDIENCE, IF WE EAT AND DRINK NOT, WE FAINT, BUT SO IT IS, IF WE DO SO IN DISSOBEDIENCE UNTO GOD, AND JESUS CHRIST SAITH SUP WITH HIM FOR ~ I AM THE WAY THE TRUTH AND THE LIGHT, AND LIFE. ~ AND WE FAIL TO IN THE LAST DAYS. HE WILL MAKE YOU HIS BROTHERS AND SISTERS AS SONS AND DAUGHTERS OF GOD, JUST SUP WITH ME. FOR HE SAITH, "MY LINE IS NOT OUT FROM AMONGST MEN AS YOU WOULD HAVE IT FOR THE SAINTS TO SERVE GOD IN IGNORANCE FOREVER. JOIN THE LINE AND HEAR WHAT THE SPIRIT SAITH UNTO THE CHURCHES — YES UNTO ALL THE CHURCHES, AS SURELY MIX IT MIX AND SPLIT IT SPLIT FROM THE TOP TO THE VERY LAST DROP. BUT NOTE YEE, THE LAST DROP IS PERFECT. WHO HATH AN EAR LET HIM HEAR? FOR, GOD IS NOT MOCKED, ALL KNEES SHALL BOW AND EVERY TONGUE CONFESS THAT JESUS CHRIST IS THE SON OF GOD. THE LORD OF LORDS, AND KING OF KINGS WILL YOU WAIT UNTIL THE LAST DAY TO HONOUR HIM, WHEN YOUR SOULS WILL BE LOST WHILE YOU AS CHILDREN OF GOD SAY YOU SERVE GOD AND HIS HOLY SON JESUS CHRIST,

I AM SET TO BRING A WARNING AND COMFORT TO THE PATIENT SAINTS, WON'T CONVINCE YOU AND TAKE YOU TO THE ALTER, AS THE LABOURERS IN CHRIST JESUS DO, THEIR WORK IS CUT OUT FOR THEM AS SOON AS THEY FOLLOW ME. YOU SEE THAT, THAT IS FOR YOUR PREIST AND PASTORS AND THE LABOURERS IN THE LAY MINISTRY THAT ILL NOT REPROOF THE WORD. BUT TO ONLY PREACH AND TEACH WILLLINGLY TO YOU TO BRING YOU UNTO GOD. THE EVERLASTING GOSPEL OF THE TABERNACLE IN THE SUN WITH THE MINISTRY OF RECONCILIATION IS IN THEIR LABOUR, TO CHANGE THE CHURCH AND THE PEOPLE OF GOD, TO UTILIZE THE SPIRITUAL CHURCH OF THE MANIFOLD WISDOM OF GOD TO CHANGE MANKIND INTO THE FRUITS AND FIRST CREATURES OF GOD. WHO SHALL NOT FEAR THE BLOOD OF JESUS CHRIST, IT IS RUNNING LIKE BUTTER AGAINST SUN FROM THE TABERNACLE OF THE SUN, WITH THE SAVING GRACE TO ALL THERE BE. THERE WILL BE NONE ABOVE GOD ALONE THERE BE IN THE LAST DAYS, THAT WILL BE GOD OF ALL GODS. SO THAT ANY THAT SHOULD FEAR AND WORSHIP SATAN CONTINUALLY IN THE LAST DAYS, BE PUNISHED WITH THE FIRE OF GOD. WHEN THE SEVEN

SPIRITS OF GOD BE POURED OUT UPON MEN.

BUT HE THAT FEED LOVE IN HIS HEART WIL NOT HAVE EXCEEDED HIS LIMITS BUT NE BLESSED TO ALLIGN HIMSELF TO THE THRONE OF GRACE, WITH BELIEVEING IN GOD WITH ALL THEIR HEARTS THROUGH FAITH IN

GOD, AND ACCEPTANCE OF THE WILL OF GOD AND ACCEPTANCE OF THE GIFTS OF GOD IN THE LAST DAYS. IN THE LAST DAYS LET NO MAN KEEP DECEIVING YOU AS THEY HAD DONE BEFORE PREACHING THE GOSPEL IN PARTS UNTO YOU — JOIN THE STIR IF WHAT YOU SEE IS GOD'S WILL UNTO YOU TO LET THE PREIST AND PRESIDENTS OF THE CHURCH KNOW WHERE THEY STAND IN THE REJESTION OF THE LAWS AND SERVING THE SON OF GOD WITH ALL THEIR HEARTS.

SO THAT THEY COME UNTO THE TABERNACLE IN THE SUN FOR THEIR DISPENSATION OF THE PERFECT GOSPEL. FOR YEA IN A LITTLE WHILE SHALL THE PRIEST AND PRESIDENTS OF THE CHURCHES COME FOR THE DISPENSATION AND THE UNDERSTANDING THEREOF THE WORD. FOR THE KNOWLEDGE OF GOD AS BEING PERFECT IN THE LAST DAYS FROM THE TABERNACLE IN THE SUN WHICH IS ABOVE ALL HILLS, IF THEY HAVE FAITH AND DO THIS WILL OF GOD LITTLE BY LITTLE TO SERVE THEIR WARDS UNTIL THE WHOLE LUMP IS LEAVENED, WHILE SEEING TO THE NECESSITY OF THE MESSENGER, FOR THIS THE HOLY GHOST HAVE DELIVERED TO THE ENTIRE WORLD TO BRING YOU TO RELEASE YOURSELVES OF YOUR UNHOLY SHAME IF FOR ANY REASON YOU STILL BELIVE IN YOUR PUFFED UP SELVES.

FOR NOW, YOUR RREWARD WILL BE LIFE FOR EVERMORE WITH JESUS CHRIST THE KINGS OF KINGS AND THE LORD OF LORDS, IF IT WAS NOT SO I WOULD HAVE TOLD YOU, FOR IF IT WAS NOT SO, WOULD THIS MYSTERY UNFOLD IN THE GARDEN PATH IN THE LAST DAYS AND SO MUCH AT THE OPPORTUNE TIME., HE LORD SAID BE STILL AND KNOW THAT I AM GOD. AND GOD OF THE WHOLE EARTH — LET NOT YOUR HEARTS BE TROUBLED YEE WHO BELIEVE IN ME SHALL NOT PERISH BUT HAVE EVERLASTING LIFE.

WE HAVE NOT SEEN THE ENMITY OF CHRIST BUT RATHER HIS LOVE – TO US ALL EVEN AS WE HAVE FAILED HIM – HE ALONE MANIFEST HIMSELF INTO US WARDS FOR SO MUCH AS HE BEARS OUR PAIN, OUR SINS AND WISH FOR US TO HAVE HIS HOLY SPIRIT UNTO ETERNITY IN A TIME OF GREAT NEED OF THE PERFECT WORDS OF THE GOSPEL UNDER THE NEW COVENANT, THE MEASURE OF ALL YOUR DEEDS IS EITHER AGAINST GOD,THE SON OF GOD OR AGAINST SATAN.

WHO DO YOU PREFER? IF YOU LOVE GOD, WHERE DO YOU STAND WITH RUNNING MAN THE MESSEGER OF GOD? THE MESSENGER GREATER THAN JOHNTHE BAPTIST, AND JOHN THE REVELATOR, AS I APPROACHES THE REALMS OF REALITY, IF YOU LOVE GOD WILL YOU CONTINUE TO RESIST THE EVERLASTING PERFECT GOSPEL? IF YOU LOVE GOD AND SERVE GOD, WILL YOU EAT AND FEAST AND TURN YOUR BACKS ON THE POOR. IF YOU LOVE GOD WILL YOU RESIST THE NECESSITY OF THE MESSENGER THAT BRING FORTH THE NEW GOSPEL UNDER THE NEW COVENANT OF GOD, WHICH IS

THE PERFECT GOSPEL UNTO YOU SO WILLINGLY, FOR YOUR COMFORT IN ZION. IF YOUR PREIST AND PRESIDENTS THAT LOVE GOD, DOES NOT SEEK OUT THE WORK OF THE MESSENGER, LIKE THE WISE MEN THAT SOUGHT JESUS CHRIST AT HIS BIRTH — OR WILL YOU RESIST THE WORKS OF THE LORD? REMEMBER YOU WERE BEFORE MORE SINFUL THAN OTHERS AND NOW YOU POLISH YOUR BROTHERS AND SISTERS WITH YOUR SINS THAT WILL NEVER GO AWAY AS YOU EVANGELIZE THEM IN YOUR FAULTS BEFORE GOD THE ALMIGHTY. WILL YOU GIVE UP THE OLD AND FIND THE NEW MORE COMFORTING TO ALL WITH GRACE YOU ALL THOUGHT YOU HAD ALREADY, LOVE AND THE LIGHT OF JESUS CHRIST.

WILL YOU CONTINUE AS YOU THE FORGIVER OF ALL SINS? WILL YOU CONTINUE AS YOU THE LITTLE GODS, YOU PROFESS TO BE? WILL YOU CONTINUE AS YOU THE REDEEMER, OF THE SINFUL SOULS ABOVE GOD EVEN FLOGGING PEOPLE IN THE CHURCHES. OR WALKING ON PEOPLE LIKE CARPET OR HAVING THEM EAT GRASS AND MORE UNDER THE POWERS OF SATAN. WHEN YOU DO THINGS OF JESUS THE GO AND TELL NO ONE LET OTHERS SEE AND THEREBY REFLECT ON THE MATTER. WILL YOU CONTINUE AS YOU, THE GIVER OF THE SPIRIT OF GOD? WILL YOU CONTINUE AS YOU THE GIVER OF THE GRACE OF GOD AT THE ALTER? FOR NOW, YOU WILL REALIZE GRACE IS ACCEPTED BY THOSE WHO BELIEVES IN JESUS CHRIST AND ARE WILL TO ACCEPT THE WILL OF GOD, THEREFORE COVERED BY THE WILL OF GOD. WILL YOU CONTINUE AS YOU, THE LORD OF HOST THROUGH THE CHURCHES? WILL YOU CONTINUE AS YOU THE KINGS OF KINGS, UNTO MANKIND WITH REFERENCE TO YOUR LINE OF POWER AMONGST MEN?

WILL YOU CONTINUE AS YOU THE EVERLASTING DOOR THAT ALL MUST COME TO, TO BE SAVED? WILL YOU CONTINUE AS YOU THE LORD OF THE SABBATH OF THE LORD THY GOD, WORKING IN THE CHURCHES ON THE SABBATH DAY, FORCING YOUR MEMBERS TO WORK ALL DAY IN THE CHURCH WITH THEIR MOUTHS AND WORDS LIKE THE LORD DID IN SIX DAYS TO CREATE THE WORLD AND ALL THINGS IN IT, IN THE BEGINNING? OR WILL YOU CONTINUE AS YOU THE CHILDREN OF GOD, WILLING TO BURY THE HATCHET AS WE THE LITTLE CHILDREN TO BE HIS FIRST FRUITS? WILL YOU CONTINUE TO SHOW THAT LOVE CANNOT HEAL YOUR WOUNDS? WILL YOU CONTINUE TO SHOW THAT PRAYER CANNOT HEAL YOUR LANDS? WILL YOU CONTINUE WITH YOUR OLD BIBLES WRITTEN BY LYING PROPHETS OF UNBELIEF IN GOD'S WORD, AND YOUR OLD GOSPEL WHICH CANNOT CHANGE YOU TO GRACE AND LOVE WITH A WILLING HEART?

I THE MESSENGER GREATER THAN JOHN THE BAPTIST TELLS YOU THAT I COME NOT TO CONVINCE YOU BUT TO WARN YOU, NOW YOU SEE THAT THE HOLY GHOST HAVE GIVEN THE SWORD OF THE SPIRIT FOR THE ENTIRE

WORLD TO BE HEALED, FOR YOUR SAKE, MUCH EASIER, THAT YOU DO NOT ERR ANYMORE AGAINST THE WORKS OF YOUR GOD.

I THE MESSENGER IS A MINISTER UNTO YOU BY THE EFFECTUAL WORKING OF THE WORKS OF THE LORD OUR GOD. WHO COMES TO YOU IN THE TABERNACLE OF THE SUN UNTO THE ENTIRE WORLD FOR YOUR REDEMPTION DRAWETH NIGH UNTO JESUS CHRIST AS THE TABERNACLE IN THE SUN, ALSO WILL BE IN HIS HAND WITH THE SEVEN ANGELS, THE SEVEN CANDLE STICKS! UNTO YOU THROUGH THE SWORD OF GOD, FOR THE TABERNACLE OF THE SUN IS ABOVE ALL HILLS AND AS MUCH AS THIS IS SO, HAVE NO FEAR OF YOUR MISUNDERSTANDING BUT EAT AND DRINK HONESTLY AND WITH LOVE, OF THE INHERITANCE OF JESUS CHRIST TO HIM, WHOM THE PERFECT WORKS WAS GIVEN AND TAKE HEED OF THY WAYS. FOR IF YOU BE CHILDREN OF GOD CHILDREN OF GOD DO RIGHTEOUSLY BEFORE GOD, AND ALL MANKIND — TAKE HEED FOR THE RIGHTEOUS SEEDS SHALL FLOURISH

AND CREATE THE FIRST CREATURES OF GOD AND LET NOT THE RIGHTEOUS PLACE AN EVIL SWORD OVER THE MESSENGER OF GOD THROUGH JEALOUSY AND BEING OVERZEALOUS, AND YOU ALL WILL SEE TO THE INHERITANCE OF JESSUS CHRIST UNTO THE LAST DAYS, FOR

IF THIS WAS NOT SO THEN I WOULD HAVE TOLD YOU, THAT THERE IS NO PREIST AMONGST YOU THAT HAVE HONOUR IN HIS EYES AND A WANTONNESS FOR THE SAVING GRACE OF THE FATHER AND LORD JESUS CHRIST, WILL COME UPON YOU. FOR HAVING NOT, THE SEAL OF GOD AS THE 144000. BE YEE VIGILANT FOR YOU SHALL KNOW BY THE FRUITS THAT IS WITHIN YOUR PREIST FOR SUCH THE HOLY GHOSTHAVEDELIVERD ACROSS THE ENTIRE EARTH, IN THE LAST DAYS THE SPIRIT OF GOD EXIST FOR ALL, AND WHERE THERE IS LOVE, THE ACCEPTANCE OF GOD'S WILL, WILL BE FORTHRIGHT.

NOW THE GREATEST TEST OF TIME IS NOT THE TEST THEY ALL GIVE DAILY TO THE MESSENGER FOR THE MESSENGER DON'T HAVE TO TAKE THEIR TEST EVEN TO PROVE ALL THINGS FOR THIS THEY READ I DON'T HAVE TO STAY AMONGST THEM THOUGH IN THE END IF THEY SHOULD TURN THEN I WILL BE BACK AMONGST THEM MY BRETHREN AND COLLEAGUES IN CHRIST. BUT LEAVE THEM UNTO THEIR REPROBATE MINDS, FOR NOW. BUT THE TEST, YES THE TEST, THE TEST OF THE FAITH OF THE SEVANTS OF GOD, UNDER HEAVY ADVERSARIES, FROM THOSE WHOM SAY THEY ARE THE CHILDREN OF GOD, FOR IN THE LAST DAYS THEY SERVE EITHER GOD PARTIALLY OR MAN IN THEIR ORDINANCES RIDING SATAN LIKE HUNGRY LIONS FOR THE SAME MEAT THEY ARE NOT READY TO RECEIVE.

TO SERVE GOD IS TO LOVE GOD. TO LOVE YOUR BROTHERS AND SISTERS AS MUCH AS YOU LOVE YOURSELVES, BRINGS YOU CLOSER TO GOD. LOVE SOWETH WISDOM AND IT DOES NOT VAUNT UP ITSELF TO TEST THE HUNGRY MESSENGER, LOVE BRINGETH UNDERSTANDING UNTO ALL TO REPEAL ALL WRONG ACTS OF MEN IN THE HIGH TIME FOR A BETTER WORLD. IF YOU DON'T SEE TO MY NESSITY HOW CAN I FEED THE POOR AROUND ME, WHICH YOU ALREADY HAVE NO REMEMBRANCES OF. DON'T SEND THEM TO TEST ME IN MY HUNGRY STATE, SAYING I HAVE YOUR MONEY AND SHOULD FILL THEIR NEEDS, I ALWAYS HAVE MY OWN THAT I SHARE WITH THE NEEDY AMONGST

MEN. THEN SAY YOU HAVE JUDGED ME, I SAY UNTO YOU, JUDGE YOUR PUFFED-UP EVIL SELVES. FOR IT IS GOD THAT JUDGETH ME. LOVE IS NOT PUFFED UP AND SHARETH THE LIGHT OF JESUS CHRIST AND NOT THE WILL OF EVIL. LET IT BE SEEN THAT IN THE HIGH TIME THE SPIRIT OF GOD IS ACTIVE IN YOU WHILE YOU COMMUNE WITH HIM IN HAVING HIS FLESH AND HIS BLOOD IN THE SPIRIT WHILE YOU WASH EACH BROTHER DOWN WITH HIS HOLY SPIRIT OF LOVE.

INCENSED AGAINST ME

WITH KNOWLEDGE I COME AND YOU ARE INCENSED AGAINST ME, I COME IN THE SPIRIT TO YOU MY PEOPLE YET STILL YOU ARE INCENSED GAINST ME. TELLING THE WHOLE CHURCH HOW ONE GETS THE SPIRIT BUT AS I GO THROUGH ALL THE NOTES YOU MUST SEE THAT THERE ARE MANY WAYS TO COME BY THE SPIRIT OF GOD. THIS IS NOW MORE PROFOUND IN THE HIGH TIME. THAT EVEN ME AS THE MESSENGER WHO BELIEVED ON THE WORD WITH ALL MY HEART TO PREPARE AND DELIVER IT TO YOU IS SANCTIFIED AND SAVED BY THE SPIRIT UNTO SALVATION. I KNOW THE POWER OF GOD IS AWESOME, YET STILL YOU ARE INSECED AGAINST ME BECAUSE OF IT. YOU JUST THERE WISHING THAT THE EFFECTUAL WORK OF GOD WOULD BE IN YOUR HANDS AS YOU TRY TO MAKE ANOTHER GOSPEL OF SUCH IN THE LAST DAYS.

I HAVE MY BOY ANDREW, AND YOU SAY HE IS NO GOOD, AND YOU ARE INCENSED AGAINST ME. MY MOTHER'S INDIGNATION HAVE RISEN UPON HER AND HER CHILDREN, AND YOU ARE INCENSED AGAINST ME. I SPEAK SPIRITUAL WISDOM OF THE SWORD OF GOD AND YOU ARE INCENSED AGAINST ME. IS IT TOO GOOD FOR ME THAT YOU ARE INCENSED AGAINST ME. AS THE WATERS MOUNT UP NEARING THE BRIM, I CAME BACK TO YOU, MY BRETHREN AFTER LEAVING THE CHURCH FOR SO LONG IN MY DISPENSATION, YOU, WHO SHOULD KNOW ME BETTER, AND YOU ARE INCENSED AGAINST ME. I CAME BACK TO YOU SO THAT I MIGHT SAVE SOME,

BUT NOT FOLLOWING THE WILL OF GOD, YOU ARE INCENSED AGAINST ME. WHAT GOOD AM I, AS A

PRODIGAL SON, IF MY OWN PEOPLE ARE INCENSED AGAINST ME. WHOSOEVER COMETH TO YOU IN THE SPIRIT HATH REPENTANCE YET STILL YOU ARE INCENSED AGAINST ME. WHOSOEVER COMETH TO YOU IN THE SPIRIT HATH POWER TO MAKE CHANGE OF ANYTHING IF THE NEEDS BE, YET STILL YOU ARE INCENSED AGAINST ME. I BRING JOY OF SALVATION THROUGH FREE REPENTANCE TO THE EVIL ONES OVER YOU, YET STILL YOU ARE INCENSED AGAINST ME. YOU WANT THE EVIL ONES TO RETURN TO GOOD, YET STILL YOU DO EVIL AND NOT GOOD

ON THE SABBATH DAY, BECAUSE YOU ARE INCENSED AGAINST ME IN YOUR SAYINGS. YOU ALL KNOW THAT IF YOU HAVE A LAMP AND YOU PUT IT UNDER A BUSHELL IT WILL NEVER GIVE LIGHT, YET STILL YOU HAVE CONTEMPT WITH THE SPIRIT AND YOU ARE INCENSED AGAINST ME.

YOU SAY YOU ARE RICH IN CHRIST AND SAVED IN HIM AND I SAY YOU ARE NOT, OVER THE YEARS YOU HAVE PROVED IT FOR YOURSELVES, SAYIING ONLY 144000 WILL BE SAVED, YET STILL YOU ARE INCENSED AGAINST ME. PASTOR COWART DID UNDERSTAND WHAT I MEANT WHEN I SAID TO THE PASTORS TO PREACH DOCTRINE, BROTHER I SALUTE YOU IN THE NAME OF JESUS. I NEVER PREACHED THE MARK OF THE BEAST BUT UNTO YOU SPIRITUAL THEOLOGY FROM THE SWORD OF GOD, YET STILL YOU ARE INCENSED AGAINST ME WITH SOMETHING YOU PREACH DAILY TO FOOL YOUR PEOPLE INTO SUBMISSION TO YOUR WORSHIP DAY OF WHICH THE MESSENGER WILL NEVER FIND SOLACE IN, BUT FIND SOLACE IN REVERENCE UNTO GOD IN SPIRIT AND IN TRUTH HOLLOWING THE SABBATH DAY AS MUCH AS I CAN AT HOME RESTING ALSO AS MUCH AS I CAN.

YOU READ THE MARK OF THE BEAST TO ME AS A PREVENTER TO YOURSELF. YOU READ THE MARK OF THE BEAST FROM REV 14: VS 6-14 TO ME AND PREVENTEST ME WITH BLESSINGS WHICH IS THE MARK OF THE BEAST, YET STILL YOU ARE INCENSED AGAINST ME.

IF ANY MAN ASK OF YOU GIVE — I ASK OF YOU AND YOU GAVEST NOT. THE SPIRIT OF GOD IS NOT IN YOU. YOU CHASTEN ME TO THE POINT, THAT, IF I AM GENEROUS IN TITHES, I WILL BE WELL BLESSED, WHAT THAT MEAN — I WILL BE WELL BLESSED AGAIN BY MAN, BUT I SAY WHO

GOD BLESS NO MAN CURSE. I COME NOT WITH THE MARK OF THE BEAST. IF ANY MAN ASK OF YOU – GIVE IF YOU HAVE IT. BUT BOB MARLEY SAY WHO JAH BLESS NO MAN CURSE, FOR THINGS YOU KNEW NOT YOU ARE INCENSED AGAINST ME FOR AN INHERITANCE THAT IS SURE, A SURE THING OF GOD. YOU YOURSELVES BECOME BRUTES OF SUCH YET STILL YOU ARE

INCENSED AGAINST ME. I AM A MINISTER ORDAINED BY GOD THROUGH THE EFFECTIVE WORKINGS OF HIM, I COME TO YOU IN THE SPIRIT, YET STILL YOU ARE INCENSED AGAINST ME.

YOU TEST ME, YOU GRAB AT MY CROWN, YOU MAGNIFY YOURSELF AGAINST ME, WITH YOUR PUFFED UP SELFRIGHTEOUSNESS — IF YOU LINE UP ALL THE TEST THEM YOU FIND STAMP DUTY APPROVAL FROM THE BOOK OF GOD CALLED THE BIBLE FOR THE EFFECTIVE WORKINGS OF MY LORD. CHRIST IN HIS DEATH HATH CONQUERED, AND IN THE SPIRIT CHRIST IN HIS DEATH HATH CONQUERED, AND IN THE SPIRIT HE CHRIST WILL CONQUER ONCE MORE.

I CHIDE YOU STOP DRINKING MILK AND STAND AS CHILDREN OF GOD BEING STRONG AND WELL FORTIFIED BY EATING STRONG MEAT, BE BLESSED IN THE SPIRIT, SEEKING SPIRITUAL UPLIFTMENT DAILY FROM THE AFTER REPENTANCE OF THE CHURCH SO THAT OUR LORD JESUS CHRIST WILL REMOVE HIS WRATH FROM THIS GENERATION AND THE ONES TO COME

I GREET THE REGGAE AMBASSADORS FOR PREACING AND TEACHING UNITY, FOR BEING THE WATCHMEN IN THE UNSEEN WORLD, FOR BEING SPIRITUALLY INCLINED TO TEACH THE YOUTHS OF THE WORLD THE LOVE OF JAH, BEING THE WEAK FENCE, BUT THE CHURCH THE STRONGER FENCES IN THE LORD JESUS CHRIST ITS YOUR TIME TO REPENT AND STOP LIFTING UP YOUR REPROACH UNTO GOD FOR NOT BEING MINDFUL OF THE LITTLE LIGHT IN THE DARK

I HAVE PIPE 5 MUSIK WITH THE VOICES OF JAH, THE VOICES OF THE TEMPLE, THE VOICES OF THE CITY, THE GARDEN PATH, THE LETTER TO THE UN FOR THE ANCESTORS REWARD, THE WORLD ECONOMIC PLAN, ROOT 2, AND MORE WITH NOTHING HID FROM GOD, YET STILL YOU ARE INSCENSED AGAINST ME. I COME NOW AS THE PRODIGAL SON IN

THE SPIRIT UNTO YOU, I DON'T EVEN NEED YOUR WELCOME OR HAVE THE NEED TO. I COME NOW AS THE PRODIGAL SON IN THE SPIRIT UNTO YOU I DON'T EVEN NEED YOUR WELCOME OR HAVE THE NEED TO STAY. BUT COMING TO ROOST WITH THE OLD CHURCH I EXPECT MUCH MORE FROM WHOM MUCH WAS GIVEN ON THE FOUNDATIONS OF THE CHURCH

I COME TO YOU WITH THE SPIRITUAL THEOLOGY FROM THE SPIRITUAL CHURCH WITH THE MANIFOLD WISDOM OF GOD, BEING A BAPTIZED MEMBER IN THE SPIRIT OF GOD BY THE LORD JESUS CHRIST.

IF YOU KNOWETH THE GIFT OF GOD AND ALL HE HATH GIVEN THEE UPON THE FOUNDATIONS OF THE CHURCH WHEN.

I ASK GIVE UNTO OF THE FOLD OF THE LORD FOR I COME WITH THE SPIRIT, IN THE SPIRIT OF THE LORD JESUS CHRIST, WHY WITHOLDEST THOU THINE HEART OF GOODNESS, HAVEN'T YOU, YOUR CHILDREN, AND CATTLE, AND YOUR SHEEP WHOSOVER EAT AND DRINK OF THE SPIRIT OF GOD WILL NEVER LOOSE THE LIGHT OF GOD.

FOR THE MESSSENGER COMETH AS THE LITTLE LIGHT IN THE DARK, BUT WOE UNTO YOU IF YOU RECIEVETH HIM NOT. SPIRIT OF GOD BE WITH US ALL IN JESUS'S NAME. THEY THAT HAVE ATTAINED HAVE FALLEN FROM GRACE, OF WHICH THEY CAN'T RECEIVE. THE CHURCH BEGINS TO LOOK BACKWARDS AT THEIR PAST WITH NO REGRETS OF DOING THINGS THE WAY THEY DO, AND SEEMINGLY FEW CAN SEE THEIR FAULTS AND FEW HAVE THE WILL TO FOLLOW AND CHANGE, BUT ARE BUSY GATHERING SCRIPTURES TO MAKE A NEW GOSPEL OTHER THAN THE LIBERALITY. WHICH AN ADVERSITY TO THE WILL OF GOD, AND THE MESSENGER THAT HAVE COME TO COMFORT THEM, WITH A NON-COMPROMISING GUIDELINE FOR STABILITY OF PURPOSE ONCE AND FOR ALL, UNDER THE TABERNACLE IN THE SUN. THIS ADVERSITY KEEPS THEM OUT BUT INTO PERDITION WITH SATAN THEIR FALLEN REDEEMER, THAT HAVE HOSTED THEM FOR 2018 YEARS.

FALLEN FROM GRACE

I COME TO YOUR BLINDED HARTS – MAKING A WAY FOR YOU TO COME BACK TO GOD – I NEVER KNEW IT WOULD BE SO TOUGH – YES, I NEVER KNEW THAT GOD'S OWN PEOPLE COULD – RESIST HIS HOLY WORDS SO MUCH. TO BE FALLEN FROM GRACE. FALLEN FROM GRACE, FALLEN FROM GRACE, YOU'LL SURELY BE. FALLEN FROM GRACE IF YOU DON'T FOLLOW ME, FALLEN FROM GRACE FOR CHRIST LAW YOU DON'T TAKE. BUT I SEE WHERE THEY WERE DECEIVED – IN THEIR MANY WINDS OF DOCTRINES – BUT I'M CALLING THEM GOME – CALLING THEM HOME – CALLING THEM HOME – CALLING THEM HOME TO REDEMPTION GROUND. FALLEN FROM GRACE, FALLEN FROM GRACE, FALLEN FROM GRACE. YOU'LL SURELY BE. FALLEN FROM GRACE IF YOU DON'T FOLLOW ME, FALLEN FROM GRACE IF YOU DON'T TAKE THE MESSAGE OF RECONCILLIATION. I CREATED A STIR – BUT THIS TIME IT'S DIFFERENT – I'VE GOT TO STIR THEM UP – OVER AND OVER AGAIN – THEY DON'T WANT TO HEAR MY POINT OF VIEW – THEY ARE TOO PUFFED UP, FOR THE MEAT THAT I'VE GOT – FALLEN FROM GRACE FOR THEY RESIST THE LAW OF LOVE. FALLEN FROM GRACE, FALLEN FROM GRACE, FALLEN FROM GRACE. YOU'LL SURELY BE. FALLEN FROM GRACE IF YOU DON'T FOLLOW ME, FALLEN FROM GRACE IF YOU DON'T TAKE THE MESSAGE OF RECONCILLIATION. MANY ARE THE THAT ARE FALLEN FROM GRACE FOR HAVING DISBELIEF IN JESUS CHRIST PROVING TO UNDERSTAND ANOTHER BIBLE WRITTEN BY THEIR WICKED PROPHET,

AND TO ANNIHILATE THE WORLD WITH MINCEMEAT, BUT THE LORD SAID "I WILL HAVE MERCY UPON THEM", AND LOVE THEM AND BRING TO THEM FREE SALVATION, TO RETURN UNTO HIM, LOVE ONE ANOTHER AND BUILD GARDENS FOR EACH OTHER TO BE MORE BEAUTIFUL THAN THAT OF EDEN, STARTING WITH THEIR REFUGEES IN THEIR OWN STATE, BY THEIR CHURCH THAT WORSHIP AN UNKNOWN GOD, ONE NOT OF THE BIBLE.

THE MESSENGER NOT A SPECTACLE TO THE WORLD

THE HEAVENS DECLARE THE GLORY OF GOD AND THE FIRMAMANT SHOWETH HIS HANDY WORKS. DAY UNTO DAY UTTERETH SPEECH AND NIGHT UNTO NIGHT SHOWETH KNOWLEDGE, THERE IS NO SPEECH OR LANGUAGE WHERE THEIR VOICE IS NOT HEARD, THEIR LINE IS GONE OUT THROUGH ALL THE EARTH AND THEIR WORDS TO THE WORLD IN THEM HATH HE SET A TABERNACLE FOR THE SUN, WHICH IS LIKE A BRIDEGROOM COMING OUT OF HIS CHAMBER AND REJOICETH AS A STRONG MAN TO RUN A RACE.

IN SINCERERITY UNTO GOD, WHERE DO WE GO FROM HERE?

DO YOU WILLINGLY JOIN THE LINE THAT LEADS DIRECTLY TO GOD OR CONTINUE TO REJECT GOD IN THE ORDINANCES OF MAN, OPTING TO RIDE THE DEVIL? WITH THE EPHEMERAL CHURCHES ON THE WORKING ON THE SABBATH DAY KNOWING AND UNKNOWING WHAT THEY DO UNTO GOD AND HIS HOLY COMMAND. THE SABBATH DAY IS TO BE HOLLOW. ED TO BRING REVERENCE UNTO GOD, MAN MUST RETURN TO THE REVERENCE OF GOD AND REVERENCE MEANS HOLY REVERENCE OF THE SABBATH DAY NOW IN SPIRIT AND IN TRUTH. RUNNING MAN IS THE STRONG MAN, WITH THIS RACE IN RELIGIOUS HISTORY TO BRING MAN BACK TO GOD, WITH HIS SWORD OF THE SPIRIT AND HIS COMFORT AND HIS WILL UNTO ALL MEN WITH WORSHIPPING GOD IN SPIRIT AND IN TRUTH.

THE WORLD WILL NOT BE AN ABLED PLACE IF ALL COULD RUN AND THAT'S WHY THE SWORD OF THE SPIRIT OF GOD WAS GIVEN TO ME OVER FORTY YEARS AGO TO THE MESSENGER, TO RUN THIS RACE, NOT AS A SPECTACLE UNTO MEN, BUT TO DELIVER A PREPARED WAY OF RETURN UNTO GOD. WHERE IT WILL BREAK EVEN ALSO WITH THE WRETCHED AND THE FILTHY OF THIS WORLD FITTING INTO SALVATION AND MERCY OR FACE UTTER DESTRUCTION BY FIRE OF

GOD THUS SAITH THE LORD, WITH REJECTION OF HIS WILL A CURSE

AND THEN A CURSE, FOR THE GARDEN PATH IS PLANNED FOR IT'S PURPOSE IN OF CLOSURE AND RUNNING ALL TO STAND AS THE MESSENGER OF

GOD, IN A TIME CONVENIENT UNTO HIM AS THE MESSENGER WITH THE WARNING AND THE PREPARED WAY OF GOD, TO DELIVER THE WARNING OF GOD TO ALL THE SEVEN CHURCHES AND THEIR EXPONENTS IN THE CHARGE OF THE SEVEN ANGELS IN THE TIME OF JUDGEMENT BY THE DIMMING OF THE LIGHTS OF THE SEVEN CANDLE STICKS AND THEIR EXPONENTS. THE LORD THY GOD, HIS GOING FORTH IS FROM THE ENDS OF THE HEAVENS AND THE CIRCUIT LIKE UNTO THE ENDS OF IT AND THERE IS NOTHING HID FROM THE HEAT THEREOF, YEA THE HEAT AROUND THE GLOBE, STRUCTURED UNDER THE GARDEN PATH BY MASS, IN THE PREPARED WAY. THE LAWS OF THE LORD IS PERFECT CONVERTING THE SOUL BUT THE TESTIMONY OF THE LORD IS SURE MAKING THE WISE SIMPLE. SHALL WE BE WISE, SHALL THE CHURCH CONTINUE TO BE SIMPLE. THE MESSENGER COMES, THE MESSENGER IS WAITING TO BE ACKNOWLEDGED.

I AM GREATER THAN JOHN, AND AS THE MESSENGER THE MESSAGE THAT MUST BE PREACHED IS THE SPIRITUAL MESSAGE OF HEALING IN THE WORSHIP OF CHRIST TO PERFECTION. AS YOU SEE ME, LET ME ASK, "HATH ANY MAN MEAT"? IF YOU ARE NOT FOLOWERS OF ME THEN YOU HAVE WORKED THE MEAT OUT ALREADY PREACHING THE MARK OF THE BEAST, WITHOUT KNOWING FOR TO WORK IN WORSHIP NOT WITH GOD BUT TO THE BEAST THAT YOU HONOUR IN THE ORDINANCES OF MAN. DO REMEMBER I COME TO YOU AS THE MESSENGER WITH THE COMFORTING SPIRIT OF THE COMFORTER DIRECTLY FROM ONE GOD, HE WHO CREATED THE HEAVEN AND THE EARTH AND EVEN HE THAT IS ZEALOUS OF MY WORK. THE STATUTES OF THE LORD IS RIGHT. REJOICING IN THE HEART. IS YOUR HEART CLEAN? IS YOUR HEART REJOICEABLE IN THE LORD OR JUST YOURSELF?

THOU THE COMMANDMENTS OF THE LORD IS PURE ENLIGHTENING THE EYES, YOU HAVE DARKENED YOUR EYES TO TAKE THE LEAD ON THE MESSENGER AS SOON AS YOU HEAR, BUT, THE TRUTH TO BE TOLD IT IS LOCKED IN A SERIES OF WORKS, FOR ME AFTER GETTING THE SWORD OF THE SPIRIT FROM JESUS CHRIST AS HE CAME THROUGH THE WALL OF MY HOUSE, THEN AS EARLY AS 1977 GETTING A SPECIAL SCHOLARSHIP AWARD, TO ATTEND JOSE MARTI TECHNICAL HIGH SCHOOL DONATED BY CUBAN LEADER, THE LATE FIDEL CASTRO, TO JAMAICA AND THE THEN HONOURABLE PRIME MINISTER, THE LATE MICHAEL MANLEY AND THE LATE JOSEPH EARLE THE PRINCIPAL AT LARGE AND IN CHARGE. SCHOOLERS WE WERE BUT SET WITH AN INDELIBLE MARK TO MAKE A DIFFERENCE IN THE WORLD BY WORKING AND STUDYING TO BE A TOTAL MAN.

GO WITH ME NOW, BEFORE YOU FLEE FROM THE PRESENCE OF GOD IN YOUR LIFE AND TAKE EVIL WITHIN. IN THESE DAYS THE LORD THY GOD STILL RULE OVER THE EARTH, JESUS CHRIST IS STILL LORD OF THE SABBATH,

AND HIS DISOBEDIENT PEOPLE, BECAUSE OF LOVE. BUT HERE COMES A TIME WHEN, THE ORDINANCES OF MAN IS OF NO USE EVEN UPON THE FOUNDATIONS OF THE CHURCH ON PETER THE ROCK. EVIDENTLY, NOW, SO MANY PEOPLE OF GOD ARE PUFFED UP AND MUFFLED UP AT THE MESSAGE AND THE MESSENGER, AS THEY WISH I WOULD NOT COME UNTO THEM IN THIS LIFE TIME, BUT UNTO MEN THE MESSAGE IS FOR MY CONVENIENT TIME ALSO. THEREFORE, WHEN THE PASTOR SAID, I SHOULD WAIT ON THE RIGHT TIME TO COME TO DELIVER. WELL THEN, SHE KNEW I HAD TO DELIVER AS A FAMILY OF GOD AND OF MAN UNDER TRADITION, BUT, THE RIGHT TIME IS MY TIME CONVENIENT TO ME. FOR NOW, WE ALL HAVE DRANK THE LIVING WATERS OF CHRIST, SO MUCH WATER MORE THAN WE EVEN NEEDED.

AS I KNOW, I WOULD RATHER NOT COME UNTO YOU LIKE THEM PUFFED UP WITH SELF, BUT RATHER HUMBLE AS THEY MOCKED ME IN THE MOCKERY OF ESCHATOLOGY, BUT I THE MESENGER WILL COME UNTO YOU IF THE LORD WILL AND IF THE LORD WILL KNOW THROUGH YOU HIS SERVANTS WITH NOT THE SPEECH OF THEM THAT ARE MUFFLED AND PUFFED UP BUT WITH POWER, KNOWING THE KINGDOM OF GOD. FOR THE KINGDOM OF GOD IS NOT IN WORDS BUT IN POWER. IF YOU RIGHTEOUSLY FOLLOW ME THEN THIS YOU WILL COME TO KNOW AS YOU KNOW GOD THE CREATOR OF THE HEAVEN AND THE EARTH. THEREFORE, RUNNING MAN WILL WAIT TO AS LONG AS IT TAKES FOR YOU TO ACCEPT THE GOD OF CREATION WITH ALL YOUR HEARTS AND WITH LOVE FOR THE LORD JESUS CHRIST AS MUCH AS I DO. THE CHURCH TO REALIZE THAT THE MESSAGE MUST BE DELIVERED AND MAYBE PREACHED IN SOME CASES THOUGH NOT AN EFFLUENT SPEAKER BUT I WILL STILL TEACH AS THE MESSENGER OF GOD.

WHAT WILL YE LIKE? NOW PERTAINING TO THESE THINGS, I MAY SPEAK OF, SHALL I COME UNTO YOU WITH A ROD? OR IN LOVE AND IN THE SPIRIT OF MEEKNESS, WE ARE THE APOSTLES THOUGH OF THE LAST DAYS, WE LOOK LIKE FOOLS UPON THE ORDINANCES OF MAN FOR HE WHO SENT US THE LORD JESUS CHRIST IS NOT IN THEM, BUT IN US, BUT THEY ARE BLIND BOTH IN SIGHT AND UNDERSTANDING IN THEIR HEARTS. MAKING US WEAK, BUT THEY ARE STRONG, WE ARE DESPISE YET YOU ARE HONOURABLE, BEFORE MEN, BUT WE ARE BEFORE OUR GOD TO BE GIVING INSTRUCTION EVEN UNTO ANGELS. WE UNTO THIS DAY SUFFER HUNGER, THIRST, NAKEDNESS, AND HAVE NO CERTAIN DWELLING PLACE, AND THESE THINGS WE BEAR FOR TO BE UNDERSTOOD WHEN YOU ARE READY TO UNLEARN YOUR REVERENCE OF ORDINANCES UNTO MAN.

AS THE MINISTER OF CHRIST AND STEWARD OF THE MISTERIES OF GOD, MORE OVER IT IS REQUIRED OF STEWARDS TO BE FAITHFUL, AND SO THE MESSENGER IS AND AS AN EXAMPLE TO THOSE THAT FOLLOW ME, THEY

WILL BE FAITHFUL LIKEWISE UNTO ONE GOD, BEARING IN MIND ONLY ONE GOD. BUT YOU CAN SEE, WITH ME IT IS A VERY SMALL THING THAT I SHOULD BE JUDGED OF YOU FOR HAVING ONE GOD EVEN THE GOD THAT I EXTOL HIS NAME AS JAH.

OF MAN'S JUDGEMENT, GOD IS NOT PLEASED, FOR SUCH HAS RAVISHED MANKIND FROM THE START OF HIS WORLD EXISTENCE., I JUDGE NOT MY OWN SELF EVEN THOUGH THEY MAY BE PROOF OF THE MISTRIES OF THE END OF TIME DISPENSATIONAL FEATURES, FOR I KNOW NOTHING OF MYSELF YET I AM NOT HEREBY, JUSTIFIED, BY THE LAW, BUT THE LOVE IN YOUR HEARTS. UT HE THAT JUDGETH ME IS THE LORD, THEREFORE JUDGE NOTHING BEFORE THE TIME, UNTIL THE LORD COMES, FOR HE WILL BE THE JUDGE, UNTO MAN, WHO BOTH WILL BRING TO LIGHT THE HIDDEN THINGS OF DARKNESS, AND WILL ALSO MAKE MANIFEST THE COUNSILS OF THE HEART, AND THEN SHALL EVERY MAN HAVE PRAISE FOR GOD. THIS IS WHERE I THE MESSENGER IS GREATER THAN JOHN AND JOHN THE REVELATOR IN BRINGING FORTH THE SWORD OF THE SPIRIT.

IN IT I WILL NOT BE THE SPECTACLE TO THE WORLD, AND TO ANGELS, AND TO MEN AS THE LORD REST. THE FOUR ANGELS FOR THE SEALING OF THE LAST APOSTLES — MUZZLE NOT THE MOUTHS OF THE APOSTLES OF THE LAST DAYS. FOR WE LABOUR WITH OUR OWN HANDS, BEING REVILED WE BLESS, BEING PERSECUTED WE SUFFER IT, BEING DEFAMED WE INTREAT, WE ARE MADE AS FILTH OF THE WORLD AND ARE THE OFF SCOURING OF THINGS UNTO THIS DAY OF THE LORD.

THESE THINGS WERE WRITTEN TO SHAME YOU ALL, BUT AS THE BELOVED SONS I WARN YOU, BEFOREHAND. YES, JESUS LOVES YOU SO I WARN YOU, FOR THOU YOU HAVE TEN THOUSAND, OF INSTRUCTORS, IN CHRIST, YEE HAVE NOT MANY FATHERS. THE FATHER IS ONE AND ONLY ONE GOD WHO CREATED THE HEAVEN AND THE EARTH.

BUT IN CHRIST JESUS, I BEEN THE MESSENGER, BEGOTTEN THROUGH JESUS CHRIST AS AN EXAMPLE FOR YOU TO BE BEGOTTEN UNTO HIM ALSO. I HAVE ALSO BEEN HAVE BEGOTTEN UNTO YOU THROUGH THE GOSPEL I HAVE CARRIED UNTO YOU. WHEREFORE I BESEECH YOU BE FOLLOWERS OF ME THE MESSENGER GREATER THAN JOHN THE BAPTIST, AND GREATER THAN JOHN THE REVELATOR, FOR BRETHEN I BRING UNTO YOU THE TIMER, TO BRING YOU INTO REMEMBERANCE AS I TEACH EVERY WHERE IN THE CHURCH.

NOW THE FEAR OF THE LORD IS ENDURING FOR EVER. THE JUDGEMENT OF THE LORD IS TRUE AND RIGHTEOUS ALL TOGETHER, BRETHEN MORE TO BE DESIRED ARE THEY THAN FINE GOLD, YEAH THAN MUCH FINE GOLD,

SWETER THAN HONEY AND THE HONEY COMB, MOREOVER BY THEM IS THY SERVANT WARNED, THY JEALOUS SERVANTS, ALSO WISHING TO PARTAKE IN EVIL, WHO CAN UNDERSTAND HIS ERROR AND CLEANSE THOU, FROM SECRET FAULTS THAT ARE SINS? NOW LORD GOD ALMIGHTY, KEEP THEM FROM PRESUMPTEOUS SIN, LET THEM NOT HAVE DOMINION OVER ME. THEN SHALL I BE UPRIGHT, BEFORE THEIR EYES AND THE MESSENGER SHALL BE INNOCENT FROM THE GREAT TRANSGRESSION.

NOW LORD LET THE WORDS OF MY MOUTH AND THE MEDITATION OF MY HEART BE ACEPTABLE IN THY SIGHT, OH LORD MY STRENGHT AND MY REDEEMER

WARY THE MSSENGER, WHY?

WITH WISDOM AND KNOWLEDGE, I COME UNTO YOU. I PROMISE YOU NOT TO LABOUR IN MINE OWN WORK I HAVE NOTHING TO REPROVE OR MAKE MANIFEST OF MINE OWN BUT OF GOD WHO SENT ME THROUGH THE LORD JESUS CHRIST. I COME IN THE SPIRIT I COME TO YOU. I KNOW THE POWER OF GOD. I WANT YOU TO KNOW GOD ALSO, YES EVERYTHING UPON THE EARTH AND IN THE HEAVEN FOR GOD IT IS THAT CREATED THEM. THEREFORE, LOOK TO HONOUR THE WORD OF GOD AS I JUST BRING YOU A WARNING.

I SEEK YOUR WANTONNESS TO LEARN ABOUT THE SWORD OF THE SPIRIT OF GOD, BUT I FIND THE CHURCH LACKING IN DISCERNMENT. I FIND THE CHURCH STAGNANT WHERE THEY ARE CONCERNED WITH THE WORDS OF GOD. I FIND THE LEADERS NOT WILLING TO CONCEDE AS IF THEY ARE ASHAME ABOUT THE SWORD OF THE SPIRIT OF GOD, AS TO BE KNOWN AS TRUTH WOULD REDUCE THEIR MEAT AND BRING SHAME. BUT, I SAY UNTO YOU THE LONGER YOU TAKE TO FOLLOW THE MESSENGER THE WORST OFF IT WILL GET AS THE CURSE OF THE LORD FOLLOWS YOU THROUGH THE STIR AND THE MODERATIONS FOR ANOTHER CURSE FOR THE DISOBEDIENT LEADERS OF THE CHURCHES WE CALL, PRIESTS AND RABBI, AND PASTORS AND PROPHETS, THEIR COMING TO THE LORD THIS TIME TO KNOW HIM AND TO UNDERSTAND HIS WILL FOR MANKIND IS FAR A GREATER THING THAN THE MEAT THEY CRAVE FOR THE LORD THY GOD HATH PROMISED THEM MUCH MORE THAN THEIR STORE HOUSES CAN HOLD.

WE NEEED TO PURGE OUR SELVES FROM THE WEAKNESS IN THE FAITH, WE NEEED TO PURGE OUR SELVES FROM THE WEAKNESS IN THE SPIRIT. WE NEEED TO PURGE OUR SELVES FROM THE WEAKNESS THROUGH HERESY. WE NEEED TO PURGE OUR SELVES FROM THE WEAKNESS THROUGH DECIETFULNESS. WE NEEED TO PURGE OUR SELVES FROM THE WEAKNESS IN CURRUPTION. WE NEEED TO PURGE OUR SELVES FROM THE WEAKNESS OF DEFIANCE TO

THE TRUTH OF JESUS CHRIST. THE SWORD OF GOD NO MAN CAN BEND, STRAIGHTEN, BLUNT OR CHANGE

FOR ALL THE THINGS I MENTIONED ONLY KEEP YOU IN THE DARKNESS YOU CREATED. THE MESSENGER OF GOD, IS AS IS AND NO MAN CAN WARY TO DARKNESS SET TO DO THIS PROFOUND WORK BEFORE MEN. HE WILL NOT BE MADE TO MARVEL AT YOUR DOINGS OR TO BE CONFOUNDED. THE FINISHER OF THIS WORK ON EARTH IS GREATER THAN JOHN THE BAPTIST AND JOHN THE REVELATOR TO THAT WILL BELIEVE UPON THE WORD. YOU CAN'T MAKE A SPECTACLE OF THE MESSENGER SO, HUMBLE YOURSELVES BEFORE GOD AND SEE THE LORD THY GOD WORK THINGS OUT HIS WAY.

HIS WAY IS PRESCRIBED AND CAN ONLY BE DONE HIS WAY. I THE MESSENGER HAD MY WAY BUT IT WAS A WAY PREDETERMINED AS HIS WAY FOR ALL COMETH THROUGH JESUS CHRIST FROM GOD TO HIS SERVANT AND THE FRIEND OF HIS SON THE LORD JESUS CHRIST. HIS WAY IS DONE IN THE BEAUTY OF RECEPTION TO HOLINESS AND NOT IN YOUR SPOTTED WAY, THAT STILL NEED HIS REDEMPTION TO TAKE YOU ALL OUT OF PERDITION, BUT, YET STILL YOU TRY TO WARY OUT THE MESSENGER.

THE PRESCRIPTION FOLLOWS, TEACHING AND PREACHING EVERYWHERE IN EVERY CHURCH // GARDEN PATH READING: WE SHALL TAKE TO THE SKIES AFTER THE REGGAE AMBASSADORS PUT AWAY PREACHING UNITY, AND THE RIGHTEOUS HEARTS, MOVE CLOSER TO PURITY. IN ONE CHURCH THE TABERNACLE IN THE SUN. AND, ON EARTH DWELL WITH THE SPIRITS OF GOD. NO MAN CAN STOP THAT AS COMMANDED BY GOD, FOR HE WILL POUR OUT HIS SEVEN SPIRITS UPON US ALL OF US TO MINGLE WITH HIS PRESENCE AND TRUE LOVE IN THE TABERNACLE IN THE SUN. NOT BECAUSE YOU DON'T TEACH YOURSELVES THE TRUTH YOU SHOULD BE ASHAMED OF THE TRUTH. NOT BECAUSE THE CHURCH IS IGNORANT WHEN YOU HEAR THE TRUTH YOU MUST TRY TO RUN AND LEAVE THE MESSENGER BEHIND, THE MESSAGE IS IN THE FOUR CORNERS OF THE EARTH ALREADY AND YOU ONLY NEEDS TO BE IN EVERY CHURCH DOING THE WILL OF GOD TO PRESERVE YOUR SOUL FOR JESUS CHRIST.

WE ARE NOT WORKING FOR OURSELVES AS SCAMMERS GOD CANNOT BE MOCKED OR ROBBED. YOU CAN BLAZE ABOUT THE WORKS OF GOD AND TELL THE CHURCH THAT NO SPIRITUAL THEOLOGY WILL HELP.

BUT YOU WILL NEVER FIND YOUR WAY WITHOUT IT. YOU ONLY SET YOURSELVES TO MORE DESTRUCTION AT THE HANDS AND WRATH OF GOD. WHEN YOU KICK AGAINST THE PRICK TRYING TO SHUT DOWN THE MESSENGER IN YOUR OPEN CONGREGATION. YOU ARE CREATING THE

UTMOST DESTRUCTION FROM THE WRATH OF GOD, BECAUSE GOD IS NOT MOCKED, HE IS TOO HIGH TO BE AND MOST HIGH TO BOTHER ABOUT LITTLE BEINGS LIKE US AS WARRIORS AGAINST HIM. IT IS YOUR OWN OLD TEACHINGS AND WAY OF WORSHIPPING THE LORD GOD OF HOST WANTS TO CHANGE TO HELP YOU.

IT IS YOUR OWN DISOBEDIENCES THAT GOD WANTS TO CHANGE, INTO OBEDIENCE UNTO HIM NOT A MATTER FOR YOU TO WAY THE MESSENGER, THE MESSENGER IS COT CONFOUNDED FOR YOU TO DO THAT. YOU ARE PUFFED UP AT THE MESSENGER ONLY WITH YOUR OWN IGNORANCES, YOU MUST LEARN TO ACCEPT THE MESSENGER OF GOD AND LEARN TO WORK WITH THE MESSENGER OF GOD, AS HE CAME UNTO YOU BEING YOUR OWN, YET STILL YOU TRY TO WARY THE MESSENGER OUT FOR NOT HAVING A JOB.

YOU HAVE BEFORE YOU THE GREATEST TOOL THE CHILDREN OF GOD BUT BEFORE NOW YOU HAD NOT BUT, NOW YOU AS STUBBORN AS A BULL, CAN YOU SEE THE ELEVATION OF MAN BEFORE YOUR OWN EYES, OR THROUGH GOD'S EYES? IS IT THAT YOU NEVER EXPECTED GOD TO WORK IN YOUR LIVES IN SUCH A WONDERFUL WAY. WHILE YOU CORRUPTING YOUR OWN YOUR OWN, WHO IS SEEKING TO GIVE YOU A PREPARED WAY TO YOUR REDEMPTION.

FOR YOU IN YOUR SPOTTED GARMENT CAN NOT PULL THROUGH THE UNSEEN LOCKS OF SIN AGAINST GOD. YOU THAT WILL DENY THE MESSENGER WILL ALL BE LOST IN YOUR SINS AGAINST GOD. ONE THING THAT CANNOT BE MUTED IN THE LAST DAYS IS THE WORDS OF GOD AND THAT'S WHY THE WORDS IS IN THE FOUR CORNERS OF THE WORLD BEFORE YOU KNEW IT. THE MESSENGER ALSO IS UNCHANGEABLE ONE GIVEN A SWORD FROM THE LORD JESUS CHRIST. IF GREATER THAN JOHN THE BAPTIST AND TO YOU I AM A FOOLISH PERSON BECAUSE THE MESSENGER SHOULD BE GREATER THAN JOHN THE REVELATOR. BUT I AM NOT AMAZED AT MY LEARNED PALS IN THE OLD GOSPEL I JUST CONTINUE AS HOW I ARRANGED THE

PRESENTATION WITH THE WILL OF GOD. HOW DO YOU PROPOSE TO RENDER IMPOTENT IN THE WORD? IF NOT, A SPECTACLE FOR HIS BELIEF IN GOD. HOW DO YOU CHOOSE TO RENDER THE FINISHER OF THE WORK OF JAH THE REDEEMER THROUGH JESUS CHRIST IN THE HIGH TIME, TO NOUGHT? ASK YOURSELVES WHO ARE YOU BEFORE GOD AM, I HUMBLE ENOUGH TO SERVE HIM OR JUST ENOUGH TO SERVE MAN. FOR YOU IN THE ORDINANCES OF MAN WARY THE MESSENGER TO FIND A LOOP HOLE FOR A CATCH.

EXPLORE THE THRONE OF GRACE, FOR YOU THAT LACKED LOVE FOR YOUR BROTHERMAN ONE TO ANOTHER WILL NEVER SERVE GOD, FOR YOU THAT

IS UNWILLING TO WORSHIP GOD IN SPIRIT AND IN TRUTH WILL NEVER FIND THE LIGHT OF GOD, AND IF YOU CAN'T FND THE LIGHT YOU NEVER GOING TO GET NEAR THE SEVEN SPIRITS AND THE POWER OF GOD. I SAY FOLLOW ME AND YOU ARE SO ASHAMED TO FOLLOW ME, YOU CAN'T CROSS THE FLESHY SELF TO THE MENTAL SPIRITUAL SELF, TO BE ABLE TO DISCERN IN GOOD FAITH.

THE CHURCH NEED TO PURGE ITSELF OF IT'S WEAKNESS, WHAT FRUITS HAD YE THEN IN THOSE THINGS WHERE OF YE ARE NOW ASHAMED? FOR THE END OF THOSE THINGS IS DEATH. FOR GOD BE THANKED, THAT YE WERE THE SERVANTS OF SIN BUT YE HAVE OBEYED FROM THE HEART THAT FORM OF DOCTRINE THAT WAS DELIVERED TO YOU BEFORE. THIS NEW DOCTRINE I BRING, HAVE TO BE OBEYED BY ALL YOU FROM THE WHOLE HEART. THIS DOCTRINE I BRING, TOOK LONG TO UNFOLD, CAUSE GOD DID NOT WANT YOU TO LOOK BACK AT ME, HE WANTED YOU TO WATCH, SEE HIS WILL UNFOLD, HE WANTED YOUTO FEEL HIS POWER TOO, CAUSE HE DID NOT WANT YOU TO LOOK BACK AT ME. WHEN YOU PRAISE THE HIGH GOD, DO YOU BELIEVE HIM OR NOT? WITH HIS LIGHT YOU CAN'T LOOK BACK AT ALL THE LITTLE THINGS I USED TO DO, WHEN YOU GLORIFY THE HIGH GOD, DON'T GLORIFY ME A JUST A MESSENGER OF THE LIGHT I BRING TO YOU. WITH THIS LIGHT YOU CAN'T LOOK BACK AT ALL THE LITTLE THINGS I USED TO DO AND PRAISE THE MIGHTY GOD OF HEAVEN AND EARTH THAT SENT ME UNTO YOU. THIS DOCTRINE I BRING — TO — YOU, IT IS NEW AND FOR IT YOU CAN'T WARY ME OUT. IT DOES NOT SEEK YOUR CLARITY OR CLARIFYING. BUT TO HAVE YOU OBEY THE WILL OF GOD — WITH — THE ENTIRE HEART.

THIS DOCTRINE I BRING, TOOK LONG TO UNFOLD, BECAUSE GOD DID NOT WANT YOU TO LOOK BACK AT ME AS THE INDEPENDENT SOURCE, BUT HE WANTED YOU TO WATCH HIS EFFECTUAL WORKINGS AS TIME GOES BY. AS YOU SEE HIS WILL UNFOLDS, YOU BEGIN TO CONCEPTUALIZE A REAL HEAVENLY KING AND AS THE GARDEN PATH PROCEEDS. ENVY DID NOT STOP THE PROCESS, NEITHER DID FAILING TO BE SUCCESSFUL WITH ENVY STOPPED THE ENVIOUS, FROM ATTEMPTING TO DO MORE WRONGS TO THE MESSENGER. GOD WANTED YOU TO LIVE THROUGH WHAT YOU COULD NOT DO TO FEEL HIS SIMPLE POWER TOO, AND SEE THAT THERE IS A GOD, BEFORE YOU ARE READY TO HARNESS THE KINGDOM OF GOD. CAUSE HE DID NOT WANT YOU TO LOOK BACK AT ME, AS THE MESSENGER, BUT LOOK STRAIGHT IN HIS WONDERFUL FACE AND BELIEVE IN THE WORD BY THE MESSENGER WHO PREVAILED OVER ALL YOUR WRONG EFFORTS TO PREVENT HIM FROM PROSPERING. JUST TO SEE THE MESSENGER AS AN EXAMPLE, OF A MAN THAT KNOWS GOD AND BELIEVE IN GOD THAT HE COULD ATTEMPT A GARDEN PATH ACTIVITY TO PROCESS THE PREPARED WAY, WITH EMPHASIS ON THE EFFECTUAL WORKINGS OF GOD.

WHEN YOU PRAISE THE HIGH GOD, DO YOU BELIEVE HIM OR NOT, THINK ABOUT IT, WITH HIS LIGHT YOU CAN'T LOOK BACK AT ALL THE LITTLE THINGS I USED TO DO, WHEN YOU GLORIFY THE HIGH GOD, DON'T GLORIFY ME, I AM JUST A MESSENGER THE WORD, I BRING TO YOU, THAT GIVES YOU LIGHT. WITHOUT THIS LIGHT YOU CAN'T LOOK BACK AT ALL THE LITTLE THINGS I USED TO DO. FOR LOOKING BACK, YOU SEE DARKNESS, THIS DOCTRINE I BRING, — TO — YOU, FOR YOUR OBEDIENCE UNTO GOD. HAVE YOU OBEYED — FROM — THE WHOLE HEART? THE SCRIPTURE SAYS YOU MUST LIVE HONORABLE BEFORE THE GENTILES BUT, LOOK AT IT EVEN MORE HONORABLE BEFORE YOUR CHURCH BRETHEN, FOR NOW YOU SEE MY MINE INHERITANCE AND TRY ALL MANNER OF WAYS TO DEGRADE ME FOR YOUR BENEFIT AND MY ISOLATION. YOU DECLARE ME AS THE MODERN PRODIGAL SON HAVING LEFT THE CHURCH FOR SO LONG ON MY FATHER'S DUTY IN MY DISPENSATION, SO, WHY WANTEST THOU THE SPIRITUAL THEOLOGY OF YOUR HANDS WHEN ACCORDING TO THE SCRIPTURES IT COMETH OF THE MESSENGER WITH A PREPARED WAY, FOR YOUR GUIDANCE, FROM THE MESSENGER IN THE TABERNACLE IN THE SUN WITH THE SPIRITUAL THEOLOGY THE EIGHT-CANDLE STICK IN THE RIGHT HAND OF THE LORD JESUS CHRIST. IN WHICH THE ANGELS WILL CARRY OUT THEIR JURISDICTION UPON THE SEVEN CANDLE STICKS ALSO IN THE RIGHT HAND OF THE LORD JESUS CHRIST.

FROM LONG TIME I AM TELLING YOU THAT MORALLITY, MORALITY, MORALITY, RELEASE ITS IDENTITY, BECAUSE THERE ARE PEOPLE WAITING AND WATCHING TO SEE ME IN IN THE GAMES OF FAME. FOR THEY WATCH NOT, SO THAT WHEN I SHALL COME WITH THE PREPARED WAY COME UNTO THEM IN A TIME CONVENIENT UNTO ME THE MESSENGER, TO FIND THEM STILL UNAWARE OF THE WORK OF GOD, AND THE PRIEST AND PASTORS STILL LACKING UNDERSTANDING OF THE NEW GOSPEL AND THE NEW COVENANT OF GOD BY CONTINUING TO WORK IN DARKNESS AND PROFILE CONTINUOUSLY SEEKING THEIR OWN MEAT. HENCE CARING NOT FOR THE PATIENT SAINTS WHOM ARE ALREADY LEFT BEHIND IN THIS SALVATION.

I AM STILL WAITING TO DO GOD'S WILL BEFORE FOLD THAT SAY THEY KNOW GOD, TO WHOM I AM NO STRANGER. THE FOLD WHO USED TO PRAISE THE PRODIGAL SON SO MUCH, AS IN HIS RETURN FROM LIVING RIOTIOUSLY AND UNCLEAN. BUT TO KNOW ME AND TO LOVE ME IS TWO DIFFERENT THINGS. NOTE NOW, THAT GOD IS THE LIGHT.

YOUR CALLING TO THE LIGHT AND ELECTION SURE

RESPONDING TO THE CALL OF JESUS CHRIST FROM BY THE SWORD OF THE SPIRIT IS OF GOD, AND ONLY ONE GOD. YOUR REWARD GAURAUNTEED BY GOD, WHEN YOU BELIEVE IN HIM AND THE WORDS OF GOD, AND NOT WHEN YOU BELIEVE IN YOURSELVES AND THE ORDINANCES OF MAN. NOTE, THE SWORD OF GOD NO MAN CAN BEND, STRAIGHTEN, BLUNT OR CHANGE. THE MESSENGER OF GOD NO MAN CAN WARY TO DARKNESS AND MAKE CONFOUNDED. THE MESSENGER OF THIS HIGH TIME'S WORK FINISHER IS GREATER THAN JOHN THE BAPTIST AND JOHN THE REVELATOR, AND YOU CAN'T MAKE A SPECTACLE OF HIM, I SALUTE THE SEVEN CANDLE STICKS AS I PREPARE THE WAY OF THE LORD TO YOU. I DELIVER FIRST TO THE ANGELS HOWEVER IN CHARGE OF YOU. HUMBLE YOURSELVES BEFORE GOD AND SEE THE LORD THY GOD WORK THINGS OUT HIS WAY, FOR YOU. GOD'S WAY IS PRESCRIBED AND CAN ONLY BE DONE HIS WAY, HIS WAY IS DONE IN THE BEAUTY OF RECEPTION TO HOLINESS AND NOT IN YOUR SPOTTED WAY. THE PRESCRIPTION, TEACHING AND PREACHING EVERYWHERE IN EVERY CHURCH // THE SPIRITUAL THEOLOGY, TO RECOGNIZE THE GOD WHO IS A SPIRIT AND FIND GRACE THROUGH HIM AND LIVE THE LAW OF LOVE.

WE SHALL TAKE TO THE SKIES AFTER THE REGGAE AMBASSADORS PUT AWAY PREACHING UNITY AND THE RIGHTEOUS HEARTS MOVE CLOSER TO PURITY. WITH OUR HEARTS AND MIND IN THE TABERNACLE IN THE SUN. NOW UNTO MAN TO REPLACE THE EARTHY NAME BRAND CHURCHES IN UNITY WITH CHRIST. NOTE, THERE IS NO MAN THAT CAN STOP THAT AS COMMANDED BY GOD.

NOT BECAUSE YOU DON'T TEACH YOURSELVES THE TRUTH IN YOUR TRADITIONS OF THINGS TAUGHT AND LEARNT YOU SHOULD BE ASHAMED OF THE TRUTH. YOU WERE WAITING ON THE PREPARED WAY AND IT IS PRESCRIBED TO COME AND TO COME UNTO YOU BY AND IN A TIME CONVENIENT TO THE MESSENGER. THEREFORE, TELLING YOURSELF THAT YOU WOULD HAVE TAKEN IT IF I DID NOT SING WOULD NOT MAKE IT SINGING IS NOT THE PREPARE WAY. NOW YOUR ATTEMPT TO HAVE SOMETHING YOU KNOW NOTHING ABOUT IS SHAMEFUL AND DISGRACEFUL TO THE CHURCHES. NOT BECAUSE THE CHURCH IS IGNORANT WHEN YOU HEAR THE TRUTH YOU MUST TRY TO RUN AND LEAVE THE MESSENGER BEHIND. NONE CAN MOVE FORWARD WITHOUT THE PREPARED WAY OF THE MESSENGER AND THE INHERITANCE OF THE MESSENGER. THE MESSAGE IS IN THE FOUR CORNERS OF THE EARTH ALREADY AND NOW, ONLY NEEDS TO BE IN EVERY CHURCH. WE ARE NOT WORKING FOR OURSELVES AS SCAMMERS GOD CANNOT BE MOCKED OR ROBBED. HIS WORK IS PURE AND TRUE.

YOU CAN SET BLAZE ABOUT THE WORKS OF GOD AND TELL THE CHURCH THAT SPIRITUAL THEOLOGY WILL NOT HELP IN SALVATION. YOU ONLY SET YOURSELVES TO MORE DESTRUCTION AT THE HANDS AND WRATH OF GOD. YOU KNOW SOME TRUTH BUT UNDERSTANDETH NOT THE WHOLE MYSTERY OF JESUS CHRIST. WHEN YOU KICK AGAINST THE PRICK TRYING TO SHUT DOWN THE MESSENGER IN OPEN CONGREGATION, YOU ARE CREATING THE NEXT DESTRUCTION FROM THE WRATH OF GOD FOR HE IS NOT MOCKED, BUT REWARDED ALL FOR HIS JUST WORK. NOW ALL PRIEST AND PASTORS ARE CONVERGING ON THEIR PRECURSOR FROM GOD WHICH WILL BECOME A FULL CURSE UPON NEGLECTING TO HONOUR THE WILL OF GOD AS PREPARED IN THE WAY.

IT IS YOUR OWN TEACHINGS AND WAY OF WORSHIPPING THE LORD GOD OF HOST THAT THE ONLY GOD WHO CREATED THE HEAVENS AND THE EARTH WANTS TO CHANGE. SO YOU CAN UNLEARN YOU OLD WAYS OF THE OLD GOSPEL THAT WAS UNDERSTOOD IN SUCH A WAY THAT IT CAN'T BE UNLEARNT THAT EASILY BECAUSE YOU ARE NOT LOCKED INTO YOUR SINFUL WAYS OF WORSHIPING GOD IN THE ORDINANCES OF MAN.

IT IS YOUR OWN DISOBEDIENCES THAT GOD WANTS TO CHANGE, YOU ARE MUFFLED UP AND PUFFED UP AT THE MESSENGER ONLY WITH YOUR OWN IGNORANCES, YOU MUST LEARN TO ACCEPT THE MESSENGER OF GOD AND LEARN TO WORK WITH THE MESSENGER OF GOD IN THE DELIVERY OF THE PREPARED WAY THAT YOU ARE NOT READY TO RECEIVE. YOU HAVE BEFORE YOU THE GREATEST TOOL WERE

BEFORE YOU AS STUBBORN CHILDREN OF GOD, WERE THOSE WHO HAD UNBELIEF THAT THEY MADE THEIR OWN GOSPEL TO FIGHT A WAR FOR A LYING PROPHET FOR A GOD THEY KNEW NOT. CAN YOU SEE THE ELEVATION OF MAN BEFORE YOUR OWN EYES, TO THE THINGS WHICH THEY ARE LED TO BELIEVE IN. LEADING THEM TO AN END IN WHICH THEIR OWN CHURCHES ARE NOT EVEN WILLING TO WORK WITH THEM TO SET THEM FREE FROM DISDAIN? THE MESSENGER ALSO WARNS THE CHURCHES OF THESE WARRIORS AGAINST HUMANITY TO HELP THEM TO BE COMPENSATED FOR DOING WRONGS FOR A CHURCH AND PAYING THE ULTIMATE PRICE FOR IT. THEY MUST HELP THE REMNANTS OF THE REMNANTS WHO WERE NOT MINCEMEAT TO FIND A NEW LIFE ALSO AND HELP THEM TO REBUILD GARDEN EVEN MORE BEAUTIFUL THAN THAT OF EDEN. IT IS THAT YOU NEVER EXPECTED GOD TO WORK IN YOUR LIVES IN SUCH A WONDERFUL WAY, WHEN YOU DOUBTED GOD AND BELIEVED IN A LIE, NOW GOD HATH GIVEN YOUR PEOPLE SALVATION FREELY AND THE CHURCHES MUST PICK UP THE SOCIAL END OF TRANSFORMATION BY BUILDING GARDEN FOR THE REFUGEES AND THE ILL-FATED MEN, WOMEN AND CHILDREN, RATHER THAN BE CRITICS OF THE EPISODE OF TRANSFORMATION TO GOD.

YOU MUST REMEMBER THAT, WHILE YOU CORRUPTING YOUR OWN YOUR OWN SEEKING YOUR REDEMPTION IN PARADISE FOR THOSE LEAVING US AS MINCEMEAT, YOU WERE LOSING OUT ON REDEMPTION, WITH YOUR SPOTTED GARMENTS, THAT MIRIDS THE CHURCHES, AND YOU, CAN NOT PULL THROUGH THE UNSEEN LOCKS OF SIN AGAINST GOD. ALL OF YOU THAT WILL DENY THE MESSENGER WILL ALL BE LOST IN YOUR SINS AGAINST GOD, FOR ONE THING THAT CANNOT BE MUTED IN THE LAST DAYS IS THE WORDS OF GOD AND THAT'S WHY THE WORDS IS IN THE FOUR CORNERS OF THE WORLD BEFORE YOU KNEW IT. THE MESSENGER ALSO IS UNCHANGEABLE IF GREATER THAN JOHN THE BAPTIST ALREADY AND GREATER THAN JOHN THE REVELATOR, AND HAVE PREPARED A WAY AFTER LEAVING HIS OWN FLOCK, COMING IN A TIME CONVENIENT UNTO YOU, HOW DO YOU PROPOSE TO RENDER THE MESSENGER IMPOTENT, NON-NEGOTIABLE, UNRECOGNIZED FOR COMING OVER A PERIOD OF TIME WITH THE EFFECTUAL WORKINGS OF THE LORD. IF AND NOT, A SPECTACLE HOW DO YOU CHOOSE TO RENDER THE MINISTER OF GOD TO NOUGHT,

AS HE WORKS FOR THE FINISHER TO FINISH THE WORK OF GOD. YOU EARTHLY GODS CANNOT POWER YOURSELVES INTO GOD'S DOMAIN. BUT THROUGH FREE SALVATION AND A REPENTANT CHURCH FOR KEEPING YOU ALL IN THE DARKNESS. WHO ARE YOU BEFORE GOD? ASK YOURSELVES ARE YOU HUMBLE ENOUGH TO SERVE GOD OR JUST ENOUGH TO SERVE MAN IN THE ORDINANCES OF MAN. YOUR RABBI, PRIESTS AND PASTORS ARE BEING CURSED JUST NOW IN CASE YOU DON'T KNOW, BUT TO BE CURSED IN FULL BY THE LORD JESUS CHRIST AND THE FATHER AS SOON AS THE WAY IS DECLARED UNTO TO THE ANGELS OF THE SEVEN CANDLE STICKS AND YOU COME NOT FOR THE UNDERSTANDING OF THE PREPARED WAY BUT CHOOSE RATHER TO CONTINUE WITH YOUR SAME OLD GOSPEL AND COVENANTS.

FOR YOU IN THE ORDINANCES OF MAN CANNOT EXPLORE THE THRONE OF GRACE, FOR YOU THAT LACKED LOVE FOR YOUR BROTHERMAN ONE TO ANOTHER WILL NEVER SERVE GOD WITHOUT A CHANGE TO THE LAW OF LOVE. FOR YOU THAT IS UNWILLING TO WORSHIP GOD IN SPIRIT AND IN TRUTH WILL NEVER FIND THE LIGHT OF GOD, AND IF YOU CAN'T FIND THE LIGHT YOU NEVER GOING TO GET NEAR THE POWER OF GOD.

I SAY FOLLOW ME AND YOU ARE SO PUFFED UP AND MUFFLED TO FOLLOW ME, BUT I SAY, THE CHURCH NEED TO PURGE ITSELF OF IT'S WEAKNESS BEFORE GOD. WHAT FRUITS HAD YEE THEN IN THOSE THINGS WHEREOF YEE ARE NOW ASHAMED? FOR THE END OF THOSE THINGS IS DEATH, FOR GOD BE THANKED, THAT YE WERE THE SERVANTS OF SIN BUT YEE HAVE OBEYED FROM THE HEART THAT FORM OF DOCTRINE THAT WAS

DELIVERED TO YOU, YOU WERE REVIVED. THIS DOCTRINE I BRING, HAVE YOU OBEYED FROM THE WHOLE HEART,

CHRIST CALLETH THOSE THAT ARE NEAR AND THOSE THAT ARE FAR OFF UNTO HIM, YOUR LETTINGS AFFIRMS YOUR FAITH IN BABYLON, WHICH MAKES THE NEAR VERY FAR OFF BECAUSE YOU CONTINUE TO LACK UNDERSTANDING OF THE NEW GOSPEL AND THE NEW COVENANT OF GOD. AGAINST THE MESSENGER GREATER THAN JOHN THE BAPTIST AND GREATER THAN JOHN THE REVELATOR, IN THE MOST INAPPROPRIATE WAY, ISSUING WORDS OF INSTRUCTIONS

"WORDS OF LETTINGS", AFTER THE AFFIRMATION OF YOUR FAITH IN GOD, AGAINST THE MESSENGER'S STIR. BUT EVEN YOUR AFFIRMATION IS A TENT TO COVER YOU IN BABYLON, AS THE CHURCHES YOU ARE IN. TO ALL THAT LETTETH, CHECK IT OUT CLEARLY, YOU ARE LITTLE GODS, AND BEING LITTLE GODS ARE YOU SO STRONG IN THE OLD THINGS THAT YOU HAVE UNDERSTOOD BY TRADITION IN THE ORDINANCES OF MAN, WHICH IS BECOME HARD TO UNLEARN, THAT YOU BECOME SO WEAK IN ACCEPTING THE TRUTH AND BELIEVING THE TRUTH AND EVEN SO WEAK IN TRYING TO UNLEARN WHAT WAS TAUGHT IN DARKNESS, AND IN UNBELIEF, AND IN WRONGS, DONE UNTO YOU AND THE PATIENT SAINTS AS AN OLD GOSPEL OF GOD FROM MAN'S ORDINANCES. THIS MAKING WHAT YOU SEEK TO ESTABLISH YOURSELVES AS CHRISTIANS WORSHIPPERS WITH A LITTLE FAITH, BUT A SIN UNTO GOD, WITH FAULTS IN THE HIGH TIME THAT MUST BE CORRECTED BY THE SWORD OF THE SPIRIT, FOR YOU TO BE PURGED BY ACCEPTING GRACE AND THE WILL OF GOD, AND SO UNLEARNING THE WRONG THINGS UNDERSTOOD IN THE BODY OF CHRIST, AND LIVE THE LAW OF LOVE. AND NOW I BRING YOU BACK TO MY AFFIRMATION IN THE LORD JESUS CHRIST. IT IS THAT "I AM ATHIRST, FOR I LACK NOT FOOD AND WATER BUT, THE WORD.

SHOULD ANY MAN DO EVIL ON THE SABBATH DAY, NO, BUT WHAT TOLD THE STORY OF EVIL IS YOUR LETTING, AND YOUR FULL INSTRUCTION TO THE CONGREGATION TO MARK THE MESSENGER OF GOD AS ORDAINED BY GOD AS A MINISTER, THE ONE THAT REFRESHED THE MASTER'S SOUL. HE WHO WITH THE WARNING FROM GOD HAVE NOT EXALTED THE SELF UPON YOU BUT COME WILLINGLY TO THE STIR AND THE MODERATION IN A TIME CONVENIENT UNTO ME. FOR THE MAN THAT CEASETH FROM LETTING CEASETH FROM OBSTRUCTING THE SWORD OF GOD WHICH IS THE WORD OF GOD. AND SO CEASETH FROM KICKING AGAINST THE PRICK, FOR HE THAT LETTETH WILL BE REVEALED AS THE DECIEVER, FOR THOSE WORTHY UNDER THE BEAST THE DECIEVER, THAT FORNICATED WITH ALL THE CHURCHES, AND WHOM ALL THE CHURCHES UPHOLD INSTEAD OF THE GRACE OF GOD AND HOLY SPIRIT OF GOD AND HIS SON JESUS CHRIST.

FOR IT IS WITH YOUR MOUTH THAT YOU WILL RIZE UP AGAINST THE MESSENGER, SPREADING DARKNESS IN BOUBT ABOUT HIM. TO CONVINCE MEN TO

TREAD HIM DOWN, SPREADING YOUR MARK UPON HIM, BUT THE MESSENGER HAS THE MARK OF JESUS CHRIST, AND ABOVE ALL THINGS WORKS WITH THE HOLY GHOST TO DELIVER, AS YOUR PUFFED UP SELVES AND WORTHINESS IN BABYLON THAT SEEMS UNKNOWN UNTO YOU AND SO COMFORT YOU AS YOU UNLEARN YOUR WHAT WAS UNDERSTOOD FALSELY AND FREE YOURSELVES BY THE SPIRIT OF GOD, UNDER TABERNACLE IN THE SUN IN THE RIGHT HAND OF JESUS CHRIST.

I RENDER NOT EVIL FOR EVIL TO ANY MAN, BUT REJOICE AND PRAY UNCEASINGLY TO GOD, HAVING BEEN AWARE MANKIND PUFFED UP AND MUFFLED SELVES UNTO THE TRUTH. AND I HAVE SPOKEN OF THEM AFORE IN MY SERMONS, BUT IF YOU PROVE TO BE EVEN MORE UNFAITHFUL, BEING WORTHY IN BABYLON KNOWINGLY, AFTER THIS LATTER RAIN YOU HAVE DESPISED GRACE KNOWINGLY. CLINGING ON TO BABYLON AS LITTLE GODS AND HANGING ON TO THE WEALTH OF THE CHURCH LIKE ANANIAS AND SAPHIRE WHICH SHOULD FEED THE WORKERS OF THE WORKS OF GOD. ALSO, AS THE LITLE GODS OF REBELLION AGAINST THE MESSENGER, YOU ALL SHOULD BE ADMONISHING FOR YOUR SALVATION. FOR THE MESSENGER BRINGS SALVATION BACK UNTO YOU AN EASY WAY.

YOUR CRAZY WORDS THAT, "THE MESSENGER CARRY HIS BELLY TO THE TABLE", REMEMBER YOUR BELLY WAS ON IT BEFORE THE MESSENGER OF GOD. THE MESSENGER HAS AN INHERITANCE FROM THE LORD JESUS CHRIST OF WHICH YOU SHOULD SEE TO IT, IT IS DONE AS A WILL OF GOD. FOR THE ONE, GREATER THAN JOHN THE REVELATOR, AND TO YOUR SURPRISE GREATER THAN JOHN THE BAPTIST, OF WHICH NO GREATER PROPHET WAS SEEN BEFORE OR AFTER TOO.

I SAY SEE THAT YOU GRIEVE NOT THE SPIRIT OF GOD ANY MORE, FOR IF YOU DO YOU ONLY KICK AGAINST THE PRICK, BUT, KISS THE SON LEST HE BE ANGRY WITH YOU ALL, AND YOU PERISH FROM THE WAY AS YOUR LIGHTS GO DIM. IT IS THE LORD MY GOD THAT HELPED THE MESSENGER TO DELIVER THROUGH THE HOLY GHOST, AND COMFORT YOU, UNTO THE FOUR CORNERS OF THE EARTH. HENCE PROVING ALL THINGS ONCE AND FOR ALL, WHEREBY MEN CAN NOW COMFORT THEMSELVES IN THE GRACE OF GOD AND THE HOLY SPIRIT.

AND EDIFY EACH OTHER, FOR GOD HAS NOT APPOINTED US TO WRATH, BUT TO OBTAIN SALVATION THROUGH JUSUS CHRIST, UNDER THE TABERNACLE IN THE SUN. THERE HE HATH PRESERVED THY FAITHFULNESS TO GOD.

NOW HE CAN WATCH FOR YOUR COMING IN UNTO THE LIGHT, FOR IN THESE DAYS WE ARE SOBER. MUCH THAN BEFORE BRINGING THE HOPE OF SALVATION BACK UNTO ALL, WHICH IS THE ESCHAT'S HELMET, FOR HAVING PUT ON THE BREASTPLATE OF FAITH AND LOVE, FOR THE SAKE OF JESUS CHRIST WHO DIED FOR US. THUS, IN THE END WHETHER WE ARE ASLEEP OR WAKE WE SHOULD LIVE TOGETHER FOR HIM.

IN THIS SHUFFLE AGAINST THE MESSENGER HE TAKES YOU THERE FROM WHERE YOU WERE NOWHERE WITH CHRIST DOING HIS WILL FOR 2018 YEARS AND BEYOND AS ADAM AND HIS CHILDREN WERE AT FAULT ALSO. BUT NOW, UNDER THE TABERNACLE IN THE SUN ALL THAT CAN CHANGE

YOU ALL SAY THAT I AM UNRULY IN THE WORKS OF GOD, BECAUSE YOU JUDGE ME ACCORDING TO YOUR WILL AND ORDINANCES, BUT I SAY UNTO YOU, YOUR ESTEEM FOR THE WORKS OF THE TRUTH OF GOD, IS RATHER IN SUCH LOW ESTEEM. MAKE ESTEEM OF HIGH ESTEEM, AS THE MESSENGER IS TO BE ESTEEMED ABOVE ALL, AND MORESO ADMONISHED ABOVE ALL. AND ALL THAT FOLLOW THE MESSENGER AND ACCEPT THE LIGHT AND GRACE, BE ADMONISHED AS WELL. YOU SHOULD VERY HIGHLY IN LOVE FOR MY WORK AS WELL AS THOSE SERVANTS OF GOD, WHO SEEK TO UNDERSTAND AND DELIVER IN HIGH EXHORTATION THE WORKS OF THE LAST DAYS, LET US BE ADMONISHED WITHOUT A DOUBT OF MIND. LET ANY MAN THAT STANDS FOR ME, BE ADMONISHED AS MUCH AS MUCH AS YOU CAN, FOR SAKE OF OUR GODS WORKS EVEN THOUGH IT IS GOING TO BE AN HARD TASK TO UNLEARN WHAT WAS TAUGHT IN THE SCRIPTURES TO YOU WRONGFULLLY.

FOR IN ALL THINGS WE WHOM ARE SAID TO BE UNRULY IN THE SCRIPTURES, WARN THE REAL UNRULY FOR WE KNOW THAT IT IS THE WORTHY IN BABYLON THAT HAS CAUSED THE WRATH OF GOD TO BE UPON THEM AND THE CHILDREN OF MEN. WE ARE PATIENT UNTO ALL MEN AS I SAID AFORE IN A FEW WORDS IN THE GARDEN PATH, WHERE

ESCAHTOLOGY DOES NOT INTERFERE WITH WHAT YOU ARE DOING BUT BRING AN END TO YOUR EVERLASTING SINS. SO, WE COMFORT THE FEEBLE MINDED, WE SUPPORT THE WEAK AS OUR BROTHER AND SISTERS, FOR THE LORD OUR GOD WILL FILL OUR NEEDS. YOUR EXHORTATION AGAINST ME THAT LETTETH IS PROVING ALL THINGS THE WRONG WAY. YOU CAN'T TURN THE MESSENGER CARRYING THE SWORD OF THE SPIRIT OF GOD INTO A LIAR, NOR MUTE HIS WORD. THE MESSENGER OF GOD WILL NOT PARTICIPATE WITH YOU IN ANY DISCUSSION AGAINST THE TRUTH WHEN YOU ALL, STUDIED THE BIBLE, AND IF YOU NEEDS SOMETHING MORE, YOU CAN READ THE BIBLE FOR YOUR SSELVES AND SEE WHERE YOU WERE WRONG. THE MESSENGER IS NOT AFRAID OF YOU AND YOUR LETTINGS,

AS TO LEAVE YOUR PRESENCE IS NOTHING AS I AM LED BY GOD AND NOT SATAN AS YOU THINKETH.

THE MESSENGER IS OF GOD COMES TO YOU AND DELIVER THROUGH THE HOLY GHOST. NOW WHEN IT'S ALL GONE YOU SEE AND HEAR THE WORD AND WHEN THE STIR MAKES YOU UNEASY AS PRIEST AND PASTORS, BUT MAKES THE BRETHEN UNSERSTANDS THE GRACE OF GOD, AND THE WAY TO GO, THEN GO RESEARCH YOU SLEEPING BASTARDS FOR THE WORK OF THE TABERNACLE IN THE SUN IS ABOVE ALL HILLS, THE SPIRITUAL CHURCH OF THE MANIFOLD WISDOM OF GOD, IS NOT SEARCHEABLE AND EVER TESTABLE. IT IS HERE TO BUILD THE CHARACTER OF MAN TO BE PERFECT.

AS YOU BEGIN TO HATE ME FOR EXPOSING THE LAW OF LOVE AND GRACE THROUGH SPIRITUAL THEOLOGY, YOU BIGIN TO DEFLATE THE TRUTH ABOUT IT. BUT I EXHORT THOSE THAT AMPLIFIES IT, AND LET THE WORLD KNOW MY RIGHTS AS A MESSENGER UNTO USWARDS. IT IS ALL UP TO YOU TO SATISFY THE MESSENGER AFTER THE HOLY GHOST HATH DELIVERED, THE WORK INTO THE SEVEN ANGELS HANDS, YOU HAVE HEARD FOR A LONG TIME TO FOLLOW ME, AND IF YOU DID YOU WOULD BE FAR AHEAD AND NEARER TO THE THRONE OF GRACE WITH YOUR PATIENT SAINTS. RATHER THAN SPEAKING OF MY BELLY FULL THAT IS MINE INHERITANCE FROM THE LORD IN A DISDAINFUL MANNER LET ME TELL YOU, THAT IT FOR IS FOR ME, THE POOR, AND THE NEEDY THAT'S HOW IT HAS BEEN AND WILL ALWAYS BE, UNDER THE TABERNACLE IN THE SUN.

THE MESSENGER, WHICH IS THE LITTLE LIGHT IN THE DARK HAVE NO NEED OF BUYING AIRPLANES AND CANNOT FEED THE HUNGRY, BILDING EVERLASTING MANSION CANNOT SATISFY THE NEEDS OF THE POOR. LIVING LAVISHOUSLY CANNOT HELP THE WEAK. TURNING YOUR BACK AGAINST THE ROOT OF THE TWO RACES. THE NUMBER ONE COMES UP, AND YOU CAN ALL SEE THAT THERE IS NEEDS FOR ALL OUR CAUSES TO MAKE US ONE. ROOT TWO DOES NOT NEED YOUR GUNS AND YOU BAYONETS, THE ROOT OF TWO IS ONE, THE NEED FOR CAUSE WILL BE, IF TO FILL OUR SATISFACTION JUST LIKE HOW YOU HAVE FILL YOUR SATISFACTION AFTER SLAVING US FOR 400 YEAR, ONE RACE, ROOT TWO NEEDS A REWARD. ALONG WITH THE DISPOSSED. FOR A BETTER WORLD, A GREAT WORLD ECONOMIC PLAN MUST BE DEVELOPRED FOR ALL. FROM THE GARDEN PATH, ROOT TWO AND WORLD ECONOMIC PLAN ADJUNCT TO THE LETTER TO THE UNITED NATIONS.

IN THE PROVISION OF THIS WORKS THE ONLY THING FOR YOU TO DO AS A CHURCH IS TO ACCEPT THE WILL OF GOD, WHICH IS GRACE AND THE LAW OF LOVE, SPIRITUALLY WORSHIPPING THE FATHER IN SPIRIT AND

IN TRUTH. NOT TO PROVE THE MESSENGER WITH THE SWORD OF JESUS CHRIST. THIS SWORD OF THE SPIRIT WAS NOT GIVEN UNTO YOU AND YOU ALL KNOW IT BY REFERENCES ALONG THE WAY. IT IS ESOTERIC FROM THE FIRST BOOK, AND NEW AND GENERIC FROM THE BIBLE WHICH YOU READ BUT CAN'T UNDERSTAND. AS YOU ALL NEEDS THE [ESP] EXTRA SENSORY PERCEPTION TO DEAL WITH IT, AS WELL AS HUMILITY AND LOVE, WITH AN HEART TO ACCEPT THE WILL OF GOD,

WHEN YOUR PRIEST WILL COME FOR THE PERFECT KNOWLEDGE FROM THE MESSENGER AND TAKE SUCH UNDERSTANDING UNTO YOU AND WHEN YOU ACCEPT THE WILL OF GOD YOU DO SO WITH ALL YOUR HEARTS, MAGNIFYING GOD IN THE SPIRIT AND IN TRUTH UNTO HIM. THIS IS THE WILL OF GOD TO PRESERVE THE INHERITANCE OF CHRIST, YOUR PRIEST THEN MAY BE BY THE SIDE OF THE LAMB AND READY AND WILLING TO CREATE THE FIRST FRUITS OF JESUS CHRIST AND CREATURES OF GOD. THEN LAW OF LOVE WILL STAND ALIVE IN US ALL, I ASK OF YOU TO READ NOW FOR IT IS YOUR TURN TO PARTICIPATE INTO THE WORKS OF GOD,

HAVING READ THE BIBLE' WORDS AND SET IDENTIFICATION FOR THE MESSENGER TO BE IN YOUR FOCAL POINT FOR THE WRONG REASONS AS TO BE MARED AS NOT A PART OF YOUR TEACHING OR THE TEACHINGS OF GOD OR THE LORD JESUS CHRIST, BECOMING HE THAT LETTETH, AND YOU SET ME UP AS A TARGET OF YOUR RIGHT EYES, AFTER THE AFFIRMATION YOU YOUR FAITH, IN YOUR LITTLE TENT IN BABYLON, ASKING YOUR CONGREGATION TO MARK ME AS SUCH A ONE, THOUGH I DECEIVED YOU NOT, BE IT KNOWN THAT I REMAIN THE MESSENGER

WITH THE SWORD OF THE SPIRIT UNDER NOT YOUR CHURCH A LITTLE TENT IN BABYLON BUT UNDER THE TABERNACLE IN THE SUN.OF JESUS CHRIST THAT ENCOUNTERS THE WHOLE WORLD. THE MESSENGER GREATER THAN JOHN THE BAPTIST AND JOHN THE REVELATOR, THE MESSENGER NOT YOU SPECTACLE. THE MESSENGER TO BE ADMONISHED BY ALL MEN, I FORGIVE YOU AS WE ARE STILL BROTHERS IN CHRIST, YOU BEING A NATURAL MAN, I HOPE FOR YOU TO COME UNTO GRACE, BE FILLED WITH THE LAW OF LOVE, AND ACCEPT THE LIGHT OF JESUS CHRIST, AND TO FELLOWSHIP WITH THE HOLY SPIRIT THAT YOU JUST MISSED AS YOUR COMFORTER. FROM THE DEPTH OF YOUR JUDGEMENT AS A LITTLE GOD, TO RECEIVE THE HOLY GHOST IN YOUR REDEMPTION IS THE LOVE AND MERCY OF GOD, FOR THE CHURCH OF GOD. COME OVER UNTO RIGHTEOUSNESS, AND SO STRENGTHENING YOUR SELF WITH THE BREASTLATE OF RIGHTEOUSNESS SO YOU CAN SEE YOUR SALLVATION THROUGH THE SPIRITUAL THEOLOGY AND FIND GOD, KNOW GOD, AND ACCEPT HIS GRACE AND LOVE BY EPENTANCE OF YOUR FAULTS THAT THE GLORY OF GOD BE UPON YOU AND US ALL NOW AND FOREVER. YOUR CALLING AND ELECTION SURE

IS NOT IN THE PERPLEXITIES OF WICKED PASTORS AND THEIR WICKED PREEMINENCES BUT, WITH LOVE AND HUMILITY UNTO THE LIGHT OF GOD.

ZION TRAIN

ZION TRAIN COMING FROM UNDERGROUND, UNDERGROUND, UNDERGROUND, BUT ZION TRAIN WILL SURFACE SOON JUST LIKE THE LIGHT OF THE MOON. IN A TIME, CONVENIENT TO THE MESSENGER.

JESUS I CAN WALK WITH YOU, - JESUS I CAN TALK WITH YOU - SOMETIMES I WONDER - ABOUT THE STARS IN THE SKY - ARE THEY TOO FAR TO REACH — WITH GOD'S LOVE - WITH THE LAWS UNTO MAN = THE BEAUTY OF CREATION, THE LAND IN MINE EYES = AND MAMA WOULD ASK ME IN HER INDIGNATION — WHERE WOULD YOU GO, OOO, - I'D SAY RIGHT AFTER JESUS - HE'S THERE AND YOU KNOW - JESUS I CAN WALK WITH YOU - JESUS I CAN TALK WITH YOU - NO NEED TO WORRY - HE'LL CARRY ME THROUGH - THE EVERLASTING GOSPEL THIS IS BETWEEN ME AND YOU, - AND MAMA WOULD ASK ME WHERE WOULD YOU GO, OOO, - RIGHT AFTER JESUS — HE'S THERE AND YOU KNOW

SOMETIMES I WONDER - ABOUT THE ABOUT THE LOVE THAT WE HAVE - LINED WITH GOLD AND SILVER - AND A BOW AND A QUIVER - THE STATE OF DEGREDATION, THE LAND REDIFINED - AND MAMA WOULD ASK ME WHERE WOULD YOU GO, OOO, I'D SAY, THE GARDENS PATH TO FIND — AND RIGHT AFTER JESUS, - HE'S THERE AND YOU KNOW, = JESUS I CAN WALK WITH YOU = JESUS I CAN TALK WITH YOU - NO NEED TO WORRY - LORD YOU'LL CARRY IT THROUGH - THE NEW GOSPEL, THIS IS BETWEEN ME AND YOU - AND MAMA WOULD ASK ME WHERE WOULD YOU GO OOO, - RIGHT AFTER JESUS - HE'S THERE AND YOU KNOW

SOMETIMES I WONDER - ABOUT GOD'S GRACE AND HIS LOVE - HAVING BUILT THIS WORLD - AND MAN AS ITS DOMINION - THIS MAKES ME BELIEVE YOU ARE NO ORDINARY MAN - THE NEW COVENANT THIS IS BETWEEN - ME AND YOU - AND MAMA WOULD ASK ME WHERE WOULD YOU GO, OOO, - I'D SAY, RIGHT AFTER JESUS - HE'S THERE AND YOU KNOW - JESUS I CAN WALK WITH YOU, - JESUS I CAN TALK WITH YOU - NO NEED TO WORRY, HE'LL CARRY IT THROUGH.

JESUS HE'S THERE AND YOU KNOW, YOUR BEGGARLY ATTITUDE BRINGS, DISRESPECT TO MY INHERITANCE IN JESUS CHRIST, TO PUT THE MESSENGER DOWN, SHOULD NOT BE OF THE CHURCH WHICH SHOULD BE IN AN ADVANCED POSITION TO RECEIVE THE MESSENGER. I'D SAY GO RIGHT AFTER JESUS, HE'S THERE AND YOU KNOW.

MANY ARE THEY THAT DON'T EVEN KNOW WHENCE IT STARTED, THE THREE SEVENS CLASH BLENDING FOR THE NEW THINGS TO COME, THE NEW GOSPEL AND THE NEW COVENANT SO TO SPEAK, THE 7TH OF THE 7TH. 1977 WHILE AT JOSE MARTI TECHNICAL HIGH SCHOOL,

DADDY SEVEN (7) AND THE NOTORIOUS SEVEN (7) CHURCHES OF GOD AND THE SEVEN (7) SPIRITS OF GOD. CLASH TO BRING A LIFE OF LOVE AND LIFE THROUGH THE BLOOD OF JESUS WITH THE SPIRIT OF JESUS CHRIST AND THE SPIRIT OF GOD — WITH THE PRE-CONCEPTS IN THE GARDEN PATH 1, 2 AND 3 CREW, THAT WILL BE PREPARING THE WAY FORWARD.

NOW THE SECOND AND THE THIRD CREW IS AT WORK WITH THE LIBERALITY AND THE SPIRITUAL THEOLOGY OF THE SPIRITUAL CHURCH OF THE MANIFOLD WISDOM OF GOD, UNDER THE TABERNACLE IN THE SUN.

THE BLOOD OF JESUS IS RUNNING WORLD WIDE LIKE BUTTER AGAINST SUN — AS THE HOLY GHOST HAVE DELIVERED THE 2ND. AND 3RD. VOLUMES OF THE BOOK FOR THE LOVE OF THE FOUNDATIONS OF THE SEVEN CHURCHES AND THE INHERITANCE OF THE MESSENGER DADDY SEVEN (7) GREATER THAN JOHN THE BAPTIST AND JOHN THE REVELATOR TO CREATE ONE CHURCH THAT IS THE UNITY OF THE CHURCH IN JESUS CHRIST, GIVING LIFE AND A LIFELINE TO THE ALMOST FULLY FALLEN SEVEN CHURCHES AND THEIR EXPONENTS OF CHURCHES. BRINGING THE CROSS TO A FALLEN STATUTES FOR THE UNIFICATION OF THE CHURCHES WHETHER ON THE ONE HAND THE ENMITY OF THE CROSS OR ON THE OTHER THE CARRIER OF THE CROSS, THE MESSAGEIS CLEAR — ITS ALL IN THE AIR— THE HOLY GHOST HAVE CENSORED IT ALL ACROSS THE WORLD, TO BE UNIFIED AS ONE IN THE BODY OF JESUS CHRIST UNDER THE TABERNACLE IN THE SUN WITHOUT THE ENMITY OF CHRIST.

THERE WILL BE NO MORE STRUCTURED BARRIERS, EMANATING FROM THE CHURCHES AND THE NEW GOSPEL OF CHRIST, BUT FREEDOM AND REWARDS FOR THE DISPOSSESSED. THIS HITS THEM WITH NO BY SURPRISE, BUT TO CREATE HARMONY AMONGST MEN, TO BUILD THE SPIRITUAL MAN IN THE LAW OF LOVE. ARE WE ON THE SAME PAGE WITH OUR LORD? DO WE FULFIL HIS PROMISES OF LOVE AND LIFE FOR EVER MORE? OR, DO WE WANT TO SACRIFICE OUR BROTHERS RATHER THAN BEING SONS OF GOD - ZION TRAIN COMING FROM UNDERGROUND ESTABLISHES GOD'S LOVE - FOR MAN TO ACCEPT OR BE DOOMED TO A NEGATIVE FORCE OF TORMENT FOR EVER MORE.

MANY A THINGS THEY HAVE DONE UNTO ME,

BUT WHEN I FIND MYSELF IN TIMES OF TROUBLE MOTHER MARY COMES TO ME WHISPER WORDS OF LET IT BEE. AND IN MY HOUR OF DARKNESS

THERE IS A LIGHT SHINING DOWN ON ME, SHINES UNTIL TOMORROW LET IT BEE.

I THE MESSENGER — I CAME TO YOU WITH THE GARDEN PATH, WITH THE LAST ENTRY "RUNNING MAN", A LIFE STORY TO MARK THE START OF THE NEW WAY TO ZION, SHUT THE DOOR ON THE "GARDEN PATH" FOR YOUR SAKE FOR NOUGHT, YEA LAID IT ALL UP FOR NOUGHT, WHAT MANY OF YOU WOULD NEVER DO, AS YOU SAY HE IS HIDING. HIDING WHERE, IN PLAIN SITE, JUST FOR YOUR LOVE. BUT I KEEP GETTING YOUR HATE. GIVING YOU A CHANCE AT THE OPPORTUNE TIME TO FIND THE WAY THE TRUTH AND THE LIGHT OF JESUS CHRIST TO BRING TO YOU;

1. THE PEACE OF GOD
2. THE JOY OF GOD
3. THE LOVE OF GOD
4. THE SPIRIT OF JESUS CHRIST
5. THE SPIRIT OF GOD
6. THE NEW GOSPEL OF GOD
7. THE NEW COVENANT OF GOD
8. THE SEVEN SPIRITS OF GOD
9. SPIRITUAL BAPTISM
10. SPIRITUAL REVERENCE TO GOD ON HIS HOLY DAY OF REST
11. TO GET YOU YOUR SALVATIONS AT THE OPPORTUNE TIME
12. TO REPENT OF YOUR WORSHIP IN THE ORDINANCES OF MAN TO
13. GOD WHO IS A HIGHER BEING THAN MAN
14. THE ORDINANCE OF GOD IN THE TRUTH OF GOD FROM THE TABERNACLE OF THE SUN, THE TABERNACLE THAT IS HIGHER THAN EVERY HILLS ON EARTH

I THE MESSENGER THE LITTLE LIGHT IN THE DARK., HAVE BEEN DOWN FOR SO LONG AS YOU EAT AWAY MY PROGRESS.

GONNA BREAK THESE CHAINS AROUND ME GONNA LEARN TO FLY AGAIN, MIGHT TAKE TIME, MIGHT TAKE TIME, BUT I'LL DOO IT, WHEN I'M BACK ON MY FEET AGAIN.

AS I STAND, I WAS FAITHFUL TO JAH, THE CHILDREN OF GOD AND THE CHURCH AND WILLINGLY CAME TO SAVE SOME.

BUT IS THE CHURCH FAITHFUL TO GO ON TO THE NEW COVENANT WHICH MUST MOVE ON WITH GOD'S WORK? IN THE ORDINANCE OF MAN, THEY WILL NEVER BE, AND WILL NEVER CREATE THE FIRST FRUITS OF CHRIST, AND THE CREATURES OF GOD IN THE SIMULTITUDE OF HIS SON JESUS CHRIST. YEA WE ALL WALKED ON THE ROAD OF HELL, I ON THE ONE HAND AND THEY ON THE OTHER THROUGH DISOBEDIENCE THEY WILL CONTINUE TO WALK IN THEIR WAYS WITHOUT LOVE OR WITHOUT GRACE. THE WORK OF CHRIST IS NOT IN VAIN THEY BE WARNED BY THE MESSENGER GREATER THAN JOHN THE BAPTIST AND GREATER THAN JOHN THE REVELATOR. THEY BE LOVED TO ETERNITY BY GOD AND HIS SON JESUS CHRIST. BUT ON THIS ROAD, WE WALKED THIS JAMAICA WAS THERE TO LEAD THEM ALL OUT OF HELL, IN THE NICK OF TIME. YES, LEAD THE CHURCH OF GOD OUT OF THEIR FALLEN PATH. HAVING NO RESPECT FOR GOD BUT FOR MAN AND OBSERVING MAN'S ORDINANCES REPLACING THAT OF GOD'S ORDINANCE. CAUSE WHAT WAS LAW AND COMMAND WAS FROM THE BEGINNING. FOR IN THEM, THERE IS NO LIGHT AND THE CHURCH ITSELF BE LOST BEFORE GOD AND HIS SON JESUS CHRIST. THE CHURCHES NOW HAVE MORE HUNGER AND THIRST FOR RIGHTEOUSNESS THAN THE LITTLE MAN IN

THE STREET. THEY HAVE MORE HUNGER AND THIRST FOR THE WORD OF GOD THAN THE UNSAVED. FOR THEY NOW HAVE TO UNLEARN WHAT WAS TAUGHT TO THEM WRONGLY AND UNDERSTOOD

WRONGLY ALL OVER AGAIN TO BE UNDERSTOOD PERFECTLY. HENCE NOW CHRIST HAVE REMOVED SOME OF THE HASSLE AND MADE IT EASIER UNDER THE TABERNACLE IN THE SUN, WITH THE PREPARED WAY OF HIS FATHER. BUT AS THE MESSENGER SHARE THE LIGHT AND SPIRIT OF JESUS CHRIST AND THE LIVING WATERS OF THE LORD JESUS CHRIST, THEY ALL ARE MUFFLED AND ARE HEAT UP SO BAD AND THE WORDS OF THE LORD GOD SUGGEST TO THEM BE NOT ANNOYED, ACCEPT WITH ALL YOUR HEARTS [FOR A REASON OF YOUR FAITH] LEST YOU SHOW THE FRUITS THAT IS WITHIN YOU. WHICH IS NOT THE EVERLASTING GOSPEL BUT;

1. JEALOUSY
2. ENVY
3. HATE
4. LASCIVIOUSNESS
5. LACK OF LOVE
6. WRATH
7. BLOOD SACRIFICE
8. ZEALOUSNESS

THEY BE MORE ZEALOUS AND FOUND WANTING WITH HIGH PRIDE AND PUFFINESS, AGAINST ZION TRAIN THEY ALL PUT UNDERGROUND, BUT THIS IS THE VERY REASON WHY THE MESSENGER IS GREATER THAN JOHN THE BAPTIST — TO KEEP THEM WONDERING FOR YEARS WITH THE FEAR OF FEAR GOD.

WILL THEY COME TO A COMMON GROUND, WITH THE UNDERSTANDING OF THE WORD? OH, YE PRIEST. LET'S SAY ALL THE PRESIDENT OF THE CHURCHES OF THE REGIONS — LET'S SAY ALL THE CHURCHES COME UNDER THE TABERNACLE OF THE SUN — THAT IS ABOVE ALL HILLS. TO SATISFY THE RELATIONSHIP OF THE UNITY OF THE CHURCHES AND IN FAITH CREATING ONE BODY IN THE BODY OF CHRIST. SUCH KNOWLEDGE IS WONDERFUL WHY CAN'T YOU ATTAIN UNTO IT IN THE NAME OF THE LORD JESUS CHRIST. YOU CAN'T PRESS

THE WINE PRESS OUT OF ACTION, THE WORK MUST BE DONE, THE YOUNG MEN NEED MORE CORN AND THE MAIDS NEED NEW WINE. THE WARNING BEFORE YOU WITH THE LAW OF LOVE TO ACHIEVE ALL THINGS THROUGH JESUS CHRIST FOR GRACE UNTO ALL MEN.

THE ELECT THAT ARE SEALED RECENTLY WILL EVEN, THROUGH THEIR JEALOUSY AND ZEALOUSNESS OF HAVING THEIR OWN WAY AFTER NOT CATERING FOR THE LITTLE LIGHT IN THE DARK AND THE SWORD OF GOD. WANTING TO TAKE THE REIGN OVER THE LIBERALITY WITH JUST THE STIR AND THE PARTIAL MODERATION IN PLACE, WITHOUT BIULDING THE CHURCH TO FITLY, FIT IN ACCORDANCE WITH UNITY OF ONE BODY AND ONE LOVE TOWARDS ONE ANOTHER, AND GIVE THE INHERITANCE OF JESUS WILLINGLY TO THE MESSENGER, WHICH COME AND IN ME IS NO DARKNESS BUT WITH THE MESSAGE OF HOPE UNTO YOU, I ALSO DECLARE UNTO YOU THAT GOD IS LIGHT. NOW BELIEVE ME THAT IN HIM THERE IS NO DARKNESS. IF YOU HAVE FELLOWSHIP WITH HIM AND SAY YOU WALK IN DARKNESS **YOU THEREBY LIE,**

AND YOU WILL NEVER DO THE TRUTH. FOR HE THAT WALKETH IN THE LIGHT HAVE FELLOWSHIP WITH ONE ANOTHER, AND THE BLOOD OF JESUS CHRIST AND JESUS CHRIST THE SON OF GOD CLEANSES US FROM ALL OUR SINS.

FOR BY CALLING OF THE PRIESTS IN DARKNESS AND THAT'S HIS MANIFESTATION TO WALK IN DARKNESS WITH THE LIGHT THE TRUTH IS NOT IN THEM AND THEY ARE LIARS AND WE SHOULD NOT FELLOWSHIP WITH THEM, UNTIL THE TURN TO THE LIGHT. AND HIS SPIRIT SHALL

CONFESS THAT JESUS CHRIST CAME IN THE FLESH UNTO US, FOR SUCH A SPIRIT IS OF GOD AND IS NOT THE ANTI-CHRIST UNTO US. FOR IT SHALL COME UNTO YOU THEY THAT CANNOT CONFESS JESUS CHRIST WHO CAME OF GOD IN THE FLESH, WHEREBY THEIR SINS CANNOT BE CLEANSED AS THEY WILL LACK PROPITIATION IN CHRIST.

FOR MANY DECEIVERS ARE COME INTO THE WORLD, WHO CONFESS NOT THAT JESUS CHRIST IS COME IN THE FLESH, THIS IS A DECEIVER

AND AN ANTI-CHRIST. LOOK TO YOURSELVES THAT WE LOSE NOT THOSE THINGS WHICH WE HAVE WROUGHT, THROUGH THE STIR AND THE MODERATIONS TO DECEIVERS, BUT, THAT WE RECEIVE A FULL REWARD. HENCE FORTH LET NO PRIESTS OR MINISTERS OR PASTORS, ACQUIRE THE LIBERALITY AND THE PREPARED WAY OF THE SWORD OF

THE SPIRIT FOR THE BENEFIT OF PERSUADING MEN TO BE IN THE DARKNESS AND IN THE LIGHT AT THE SAME TIME CONFESSING NOT THAT JESUS CHRIST CAME IN THE FLESH UNTO US, OR UNTO THE WORLD, AS THE LIGHT IS NOT IN THEM NOR THE GOD THAT SENT HIS SON TO THIS WORLD. FOR SUCH MEN THE LIGHT IS NOT IN THEM AND THEY BE DECEIVERS AND ANTI-CHRIST TO THE WORLD. FOR THEY THAT TRANSGRESSETH ABIDETH NOT IN THE WILL OF GOD, AND IN THE DOCTRINES OF CHRIST, NOTE HE THAT ABIDETH BY THE DOCTRINES OF CHRIST HAVE BOTH THE FATHER AND THE SON.

FOR CHRIST IS THE PROPITIATION OF ALL OUR SINS AND THE SINS OF THE WORLD. LET US KNOW HIM NOW AND LOVE OUR BROTHERS AND SISTERS SO THAT THE TRUTH CAN BE IN US. CHRIST WAS FROM THE BEGINNING AND WE THEN LOOKED UPON HIM IN THE FLESH, AND OUR HANDS HAVE HANDLED, OF THE WORD OF LIFE. UNTO US THE LIFE WAS MANIFESTED, AND WE HAVE SEEN IT, BEARING WITNESS AS HE SHED US ETERNAL LIFE WHICH WAS WITH THE FATHER, AND WAS MANIFESTED UNTO US. FOR OUR FULL JOY IN HIM THE FATHER THROUGH THE SON THE LORD JESUS CHRIST.

AND FOR THIS 144000 ELECT GOD MAY CUT THE TIME SHORT FOR THEIR BLINDNESS OF HEART, THAT WILL CAUSE THEM TO BE FALLEN FORM GRACE. THE CHILDREN OF THE ELECT SISTER GREET THEE. BUT REMEMBER THEY THAT BRING NOT THIS DOCTRINE, RECEIVE THEM NOT IN THINE HOUSE, NOR BID THEM GODS SPEED, FOR SUCH WORSHIP OTHER GODS AND OTHER PROPHETS OF MA'S ORDINANCES AND WILL NOT CHANGE TO ACCEPT GRACE AND THE WILL OF GOD, FROM HIM CHRIST THAT HAVE DECLARED GOD BY COMING IN THE FLESH, TO GIVE GRACE AND TRUTH BREAKING DOWN THE LAWS OF MOSES, WHICH WAS FOR THE REBELLIOUS

ISRAELITES AND WHICH WE COULD NOT UNDERSTAND BEFORE. BE NOT ASHAMED OF THE NEW GOSPEL OF CHRIST FOR IT IS THE POWER OF GOD UNTO YOU, AND UNTO

SALVATION TO EVERYONE THAT BELIEVETH, TOUCHING ALL PEOPLE, FOR THE RIGHTEOUSNESS OF GOD IS REVEALED FROM FAITH TO FAITH, AS IT IS WRITTEN THE JUST SHALL LIVE BY FAITH.

THE HOLY GHOST OF GOD PERMITTED THE WORKS OF GOD TO GO TO THE FOUR CORNERS OF THE EARTH FOR A REASON, AND BY FAITH

MANY SHALL RECEIVE AND TURN TO GOD. ZION TRAIN COMING FROM UNDERGROUND IN THE HIGH TIME AND ONE CONVENIENT TO THE MESSENGER HAVE DECLARED THE THAT GOD IS ANGRY WITH SIN, AND HAVE GIVEN HIS MERCIES FOR ALL TO COME UNTO HIM. NOW THE WRATH OF GOD WILL BE REVEALED FROM THE HEAVEN, AGAINST THE UNRIGHTEOUSNESS OF THE CLERGY AND LAITY OF MEN, LIKE OUR PASTORS, OUR PRIESTS, OUR MINISTERS AND THE PATIENT SAINTS, WHO HOLD TRUTH IN UNRIGHTEOUSNESS. FOR THAT WHICH MAY BE KNOWN OF GOD IS MANIFEST IN THEM, FOR GOD HATH SHEWN THEM IT IN THE HIGH TIME. EVEN THE INVISIBLE THINGS OF HIM FROM THE CREATION OF THE WORLD, ARE CLEARLY SEEN, AND BEING UNDERSTOOD BY THE THINGS THAT ARE MADE, EVEN HIS ETERNAL POWER AND GODHEAD, SO THEY ARE WITHOUT EXCUSE.

OUR PASTORS ARE BEGGARLY ZEALOUS OF THE MESSENGER, MINISTER OF GOD, DADDY SEVEN (7) AND THEIR SACRIFICES ARE MORE THAN PLENTY. TO THE LEVEL OF BRINGING ENMITY INTO THE CHURCH ONCE MORE. I CAN SHOW YOU ALL THE LETTER JOHN WOULD HAVE SENT TO THE CHURCHES BUT IN THE LIBERALITY TO THE SEVEN ANGELS IN CHARGE OF THE SEVEN CANDLE STICKS AND SERMON DELIVERED UNTO THE WORLD — THOSE WHO HATH AN EAR WILL HEAR WHAT THE SPIRIT SAITH UNTO ALL THE CHURCHES.

FOR THE APOSTLES WHO KNOW THE WILL OF GOD WILL BE SEALED AND ALL 144000 SET FOR BULDING THE FIRST CREATURES HENCE TRANSFORMING THE CHURCHES TO FELLOWSHIP WITH JESUS CHRIST CREATING THE SONS OF GOD.

BEAR ME OUT CAUSE EVEN THOSE BEING ELECT WILL WANT TO TAKE THE CHURCHES MESSENGER'S INHERITANCE AS NOTHING, BUT, WHEN EVEN THEY WORK FOR AN HIRE, AND IF THE ELECT CAN THEN LOSE THEIR WAY. THEN, WHAT IS LOVE? WHAT IS GRACE? WHAT IS THE LIGHT OF JESUS CHRIST? WHAT IS THE LIGHT OF GOD FOR, TO THE RIGHTEOUS? IF NOT

TUNED IN INTO THE SPIRIT OF GOD AND THE SPIRIT OF HIS SON THE LORD OF THE SABBATH AS FROM THE

BEGINNING, THE LORD JESUS CHRIST, WHICH NOW REIGNS IN THE TABERNACLE IN THE SUN. HOLDING SUCH IN HIS RIGHT HAND UNTIL ALL MEN AND ALL THINGS COME UNTO HIM.

THESE QUOTES I FIX IS FOR THE TABERNACLE IN THE SUN BY FRANCIS CHATLES MALCOLM OF THE ESTATE FRANCIS CHARLES MALCOLM TGPMASS WITH AN INHERITANCE FROM JESUS CHRIST — THE EVIDENCES OF CHRIST FELLOWSHIP ARE FROM THE BOOK OF GOD THE BIBLE.

~ THE TRUTH OF GOD ONLY NEEDS TO BE LIVED BY MAN WITH LOVE FOR ONE ANOTHER TO THE BUILDING OF GARDENS BETTER THAN THOSE OF EDEN FOR THE RETURN OF OUR SAVIOUR. ~ WITH SUCH GARDENS BEING THE DWEELING PLACE OF THE LAW OF LOVE ~ COMPLETE WITHOUT THE CONTINOUS BUILDING OF THE CHURCH ON SACRIFICES AND BLOOD ~ MY GOD AND OUR GOD DOES NOT REQUIRE AND ACCEPT SACRIFICES OF YOU ANYMORE ~ MY GOD AND OUR GOD ONLY NEEDSA WILLING HEART OF ACCEPTANCE TO HIS SON'S WORDS WITH ALL YOUR HAERT ~ MY GOD AND OUR GOD ONLY NEEDS YOU TO TRANSFORM YOURSELVES IN HIS ORDINANCE AND LOVE GOD AND THE SON OF GOD OVER ALL MEN ~ BUT HE CAN LEAVE YOU TO YOUR REPROBATE MINDS ALLOWING YOU ALL TO AS PUFFED UP MEN AGAINST HIS WILL TO CONTINUE TO BELL EACH OTHER TO YOUR OWN DESTRUCTION

MAN, NO FI BELL MAN, FOR UNTO US THE WOMAN AND THE MAN NOW ONE, TWAIN TOGETHER AND NOT THE MAN AND THE MAN WHICH SHOULD REPEL EACH OTHER. ~ THIS TAKES US CLOSER TO THE LAST SACRIFICE. WHO IS MAN TO BE MAKING SACRIFICES OF MEN EVEN THE BLIND TO GOD WHO DOES NOT REQUIRE IT OF MAN IN THE LAST DAYS? THIS TAKES US CLOSER TO THE LAST SACRIFICE SHOWETH THE GREAT FAITH IN GOD BY ABRAHAM, NOW GOD REQUIRE GREAT FAITH IN HIS SON JESUS CHRIST, TO CREATE IN YOU AS HUMAN BEIGNS THE

NEW CREATURE WITH THE LIKENESS OF HIS SON JESUS CHRIST. THE SCRIPTURES SAYS. ~ IN THE LATTER DAYS WE WILL SEE THAT JESUS CHRIST REALLY GAVE HIMSELF FOR OUR SINS "YET STILL WE SIN SO MUCH TRYING TO PLEASE HIM" HE GAVE HIMSELF SO THAT HE MAY

DELIVER US FROM THE PRESENT EVIL OF THIS WORLD — ACCORDING TO THE WILL OF OUR FATHER OUR GOD. NOW TO WHOM GLORY BELONGETH

FOR EVER AND EVER. MANKIND HAVE DRIFTED FROM GOD'S ORDINANCE TO WORSHIP HIM IN THE ORDINANCES OF MAN

I MARVEL THAT YE ARE SOON REMOVED FROM HIM THAT CALLETH YOU INTO THE GRACE OF CHRIST UNTO ANOTHER GOSPEL. HOWEVER, I WARN YOU BEFORE HAND LET NOT DARKNESS CONTINUE TO REIGN OVER YOU, LET THE PRINCIPALITIES AND DARKNESS CHANGE TOWARDS YOU AND TOWARDS OUR FAITH IN JESUS CHRIST, AND TOWARDS THE GOD OF LOVE.

SEE GRACE AS AN ANNOINTING OF FAITH IN CHRIST AND BE NOT REMOVED FROM THE LATTER RAIN OF THE MINISTRY OF RECONCILIATION WITH THE NEW GOSPEL AND THE NEW COVENANT OF GRACE AND UNITY, TO COME BACK TO HIM AND BE RESERVED INTO ANOTHER GOSPEL THAT YE MAY WRITE UNTO YOURSELVES, PERTAINING TO THE STIR AND THE MODERATIONS BLENDED WITH DARKNESS AND LACK THE TRUTH OF THE BIBLE AND THE LIGHT OF GOD, BUT THE TRUTH OF THE FELOWSHIP IN CHRIST JESUS FROM THE TABERNACL IN THE SUN UNBLEMISHED BY THE WILL OF GOD FOR HIS FIRST FRUITS FROM THE DISSOBEDIENT PEOPLE CALLED BY HIM JESUS CHRIST FOR YEARS "FACTS OF THE BILBLE FIRST" & "TRUTH OF OUR LORD JESUS CHRIST FIRST".

THE GOSPEL THAT YOU HAVE TURNED TO, IS NOT ANOTHER BUT ONE TO PERVERT THE WAY OF THE MESSENGER GREATER THAN JOHN BAPTIST AND JOHN THE REVELATOR, HENCE PERVERTING THE EVERLASTING GOSPEL OF JESUS CHRIST. BUT REMEMBER THAT WHICH WAS FROM THE BEGINNING AND THAT WHICH IS NEW FOR THE SAKE OF GRACE UNTO YOU WILL BE FOR THE CHILDREN TO FLEE THE WRATH OF GOD. THE MESSENGER BE NOT CURSED HAVING PERSUADED MEN TO COME TO THE DOOR OF REPENTANCE UNTO GOD. FOR I PERSUADED

MEN TO COME UNTO THE GOD OF LIGHT.

THE MESSENGER COMETH UNTO YOU TIME AND TIME AGAIN, SAYING FOLLOW ME, YOU HAVE BELITTLED ME AND DEFAMED ME FOR AS ANGELS WOULD COME TO YOU SO I COME WITH THE EVERLASTING

GOSPEL, WHICH IS NEW AND OF GOD BUT WAS OF OLD AND OF THE PRESENT AND FOR THE FUTURE FOR YOUR FULL JOY, IT IS THAT WHICH MUST BE PREACHED TO THE WORLD. I CERTIFY YOU, BRETHEN THAT THE GOSPEL WHICH WAS PREACHED OF ME THAT GOETH TO THE FOUR CORNERS OF THE EARTH THROUH THE HOLY GHOST WAS NOT

OF MAN, BUT OF GOD, WHICH IS WITH THE LIGHT. YET STILL YOU HAVE USED THE GOSPEL TO PERVERT THE YOUR OWN WILL UNTO TORMENT. BUT

I RATHER YOU GLORYFY THE LORD GOD IN ME, FOR I AM YOUR EXAMPLE AND FIRST FAITH UNTO GOD FOR RETURNING UNTO HIM.

NOW BRETHEN THROUGH THE LAWS BE DEAD, TO THE LAW THAT YOU MAY LIVE THROUGH JESUS CHRIST, TO THE CHURCHES DO NOT FRUSTRATE THE GRACE OF GOD, HEAR WHAT THE SPIRIT SAITH UNTO THE CHURCHES. ARE YE SO FOOLISH HAVING BEGUN IN THE SPIRIT ARE YE MADE PERFECT BY THE LAWS? THIS IS THE LIBERALITY WHICH TELLS YOU TO, BELIEVE UPON GOD, WITH ALL YOUR HEARTS AND HAVE FAITH IN GOD, SO THAT JERUSALEM WILL NOT BE MADE A HEAP. FOR YOU WILL NEVER HAVE THE SPIRIT IN THE FLESH BUT BY FAITH. REDEEM THEM ALL THAT WERE UNDER THE LAWS THAT THEY MIGHT RECEIVE THE ADOPTION OF SONS OF GOD THROUGH JESUS CHRIST.

THE TABERNACLE OF TH SUN DOES NOT WHICH FOR YOU TO RETURN TO THE WEAK BEGGARLY ELEMENTS AS YOU WERE OUT OF THE SPIRIT OF CHRIST AND BE YE IN BONDAGE OF THE LAWS FOR ANOTHER TIME UPON TIME. FORGET YOUR PREEMINENCE THAT IS POSSESSED BY SATAN, FORGET ABOUT PRATING AGAINST THE CHILDREN OF GOD, FOR THE PURPOSE OF REAPING MORE TO SIN AGAINST GOD IN YOUR ORDINANCES OF MAN, DOING SO WITH MALICIOUS WORDS, WHICH ARE NOT THE CONTENT OF THE BIBLE, NEITHER DO YOU RECEIVE THE BRETHREN BUT DRIVE THEM OUT OF THE CHURCH, FOR HE THAT DOETH GOOD HATH SEEN GOD WHICH DOETH GOOD AND NOT EVIL. LOOK AT THE NEW GOSPEL THAT COMETH WITH GRACE AND LOVE, DISPENSED WITH HUMILITY. HOW COULD WE PRATE MALICIOUSLY AT OUR CHILDREN, OUR YOUNG MEN AND OUR FATHERS? WHEN WE OFFER THEM LIGHT AND LOVE, WITH REDEMPTION IN SALVATION THROUGH GRACE. TO BE FAR FROM THAT WE ARE EVIL AND GOD IS NOT SEEN IN US.

I BEAR YE THE TRUTH OF THE BEGINNING. BRETHREN HEAR ME I WRITE UNTO YOU NO NEW COMMANDMENT, BUT AN OLD COMMANDMENT WHICH YOU HAD FROM THE BEGINNING. THE OLD COMMANDMENT IS THE WORD WHICH YOU HEARD FROM THE BEGINNING. AND OF SUCH, AGAIN, I WRITE UNTO YOU A NEW COMMANDMENT WHICH

THING IS TRUE AS SEEN BEFORE AND NOT OBSERVED UNTO RIGHTEOUSNESS. BUT MOW NEW FOR THE DARKNESS IS PAST, AND THE TRUE LIGHT NOW SHINETH. OF THIS LOVE YOUR BROTHERS AND ABIDE IN THE LIGHT, AND THERE BE NONE OCCASION OF STUMBLING IN HIM.

I AM BECOME AN ENEMY TO YOU AS YOU TRY TO PERVERT THE WORKS OF OUR LORD TO FIT YOUR OWN WEAK WILL IN GOD'S WORK IN THE HIGH TIME. BUT I COME TO BUILD TO FIT ALL IN TWAIN AS YOU CARRY THE

CROSS TO THE DECAY TO VANISH WITH THE ENMITY OF CHRIST UNTO THE NEW GOSPEL, AND THE LIGHT OF GOD IN THE NEW COVENANT UNTO MEN. TO THOSE WITH ENMITY TO THE CROSS WHICH GOD'S LIGHT HATH BURNED TO THE GROUND, SO AS TO MAKE ALL BE ONE, UNITING IN ONE GOD OVER ALL THE EARTH. NOW THE BUILDING OF THE CHURCH TO FIT THE EVERLASTING GOSPEL OF CHRIST IS ON A SUPERELEVATION "THE TABERNACLE IN THE SUN" YOU WILLNEVER FIT THE CHURCH INTO THE PERSPECTIVES OF ONE POINT UNLESS YOU GO THROUGH THE TABERNACLE OF THE SUN. THE LITTLE BOOK TO LAUNCH THE SWORD OF THE SPIRIT OF GOD WAS AROUND FOR OVER FORTY YEARS, IT YOU HAVE STOLEN AND DONE ALL MANNER OF THINGS UNTO THE MESSENGER, YET STILL, YOU NEVER UNUNDERSTOOD THE LIFE STORY OF THE MESSENGER, THE WORKS OF THE BOOK YOU STOLE, AND THE SECOND PROPOSAL TO TAKE IT AWAY.

YOU COULD NOT FIT YOURSELVES PROPERLY INTO THE LIFE STORY OF THE MESSENGER, NOR THE BOOK TO COME AT A CONVENIENT TIME WITH SOMETHING YOU KNEW NOTHING ABOUT. — YET STILL YOU

PERVERTED THE MESSENGER'S WAY — YOU DEFAMED THE MESSENGER. YOU ALL TRIED TO TAKE THE INHERITANCE PLEDGED TO ME OF JESUS CHRIST FROM ME, AS ANANIAS AND SAPPHIRE. BUT I FRANCIS CHARLES MALCOLM WAS NEVER DAUNTED OR DISMAYED BY YOUR PERVERTION OF THE TRUTH AND THE GOSPEL OF JESUS CHRIST TO BRING ME DOWM BECAUSE YOU NEVER KNEW THE TRUTH OF GOD, HIS WILL AND

MERCIES TOWARD THE PEOPLE OF THE WORLD WHOM HE LOVE SO MUCH, IN AS MUCH AS TO BE PREPARING THE WAY BY THE SWORD OF THE SPIRIT WHICH WAS NOT GIVEN UNTO YOU. THOUGH YOU TROUBLE ME YOUR SACRIFICES WAS NOT THE WILL OF GOD AND SO ZION TRAIN WILL COME EVEN TORN, SICK AND LAME FOR THE FAMILY OF GOD WILL, TO CONTINUE AFTER THE INDIGNATION UPON THE EARTH, IN THE TABENACLE OF THE SUN, HIGHER THAN ALL HILLS, AND MORESO WITH THE SPIRITUAL CHURCH TO BE CREATED WITHIN ALL MEN AS THEIR INHERITANCE FROM ME THE MESSENGER GREATER THAN JOHN THE BAPTIST, AND GREATER THAN JOHN THE REVELATOR.

YOU AND THE CHURCH AND WHATEVER POWERS THERE BE WANTED TO MOVE MY WORK FROM UNDER ME AND YOU DID NOT EVEN KNOW THAT I WAS ALSO GREATER THAN JOHN THE BAPTIST, ALSO AS THE SENTENTIOUS ONE. WE HAVE REDEMPTION THROUGH THE BLOOD OF CHRIST AND THE FORGIVENESS OF SINS ACCORDING TO HIS RICHES IN HIS GRACE, BECAUSE WE BELIEVED UPON GOD. — MY BROTHERS AND SISTERS IN CHRIST MAY HAVE SINNED AGAINST GOD — BUT BE THOU RIGHTEOUS THROUGH

CHRIST JESUS GRACE TOWARDS YOU ALL, AND GIRTH THY FAITH IN GOD BEFORE IT IS TOO LATE.

THE GIFT & TRUTH OF JESUS CHRIST, STIRS YOU UP AT THE ALTAR OF THE SUN, WITH THE LAST ALTER CALL FOR THE FREEDOM OF THE SAINTS BE TAUGHT THE WORD, TO UNDERSTAND GOD IN TRUTH TO DO THE WILL OF GOD AND FOR MY REMEMBERANCE TO FEED MY CHILDREN, WITH MINE OWN INHERITANCE OF JESUS CHRIST, CHRISTOPHE KENNY 3RD. EXECUTOR, ANDREW SHAWN, NOTOYA, SHERINE ELIZABETH, SHANIEL SHARON OF THE BRANCH OF MALCOLM. MY BROTHERS CONRAD LLOYD 2ND. EXECUTOR, CHARLES HEADLEY LAREN/LARIN 3RD. EXECUTOR, LEROY RUDOLPH, MY SISTERS GLORIA MARJORIE, YVONNE HYACINTH LYDIA, WIFE FORMALLY, DENEISE JOY

DRUMMOND, NOW MR. AND MRS. FRANCIS CHARLES MALCOLM ALL OF THE SAME BRANCH OF MALCOLM, CHILDREN AND GRAND CHILDRENS OF EDWARD & BARBARA MALCOLM, PIPE 5 MUSIK, DARNOC RECORDS AND SUBSIDIARIES, FOUNDATION OF THE SPIRITUAL CHURCH OF THE MANIFOLD WISDOM OF GOD, [FOR THE POOR] FROM THE PURE HONEST WORK OF THE TABERNACLE IN THE SUN. FROM THE WORK OF THE GARDEN PATH MASS, WITH VOLUME 2 & 3 CONTAINING THE LIBERALITY, MINISTRY OF RECONCILIATION, AND VOLUME THREE CONTAINING THE SPIRITUAL CHURCH OF THE MANIFOLD WISDOM OF GOD. TO THE ADMINISTRATION OF THE SEVEN (7) STARS IN THE RIGHT HAND OF GOD. — BUM SALUTE & COME — MASS/MATTY/DADDY SEVEN (7)/THE ROCKSMAN/THE MESSENGER GREATER THAN JOHN THE BAPTIST AND JOHN THE REVELATOR, CAPTAIN F. C. MALCOLM, HATH REFRESHED THE SOUL OF THE MASTER AND HATH BECOME A GIFT UNTO MEN AND AN EXAMPLE, WHILE ZION TRAIN WAS STILL UNDERGROUND. OUT LIKE THE LIGHT OF THE MOON WITH THE LIGHT OF GOD NOW, UNTO US WARDS, IN THE TABERNACLE IN THE SUN WITH "WE THE ENTRUSTEDTM © 2018". AGAINST THE TAVERNACLE OF THE SUN THERE IS NO OTHER DECLARATION, BUT YOU HAVE ENDEVOUR TO;

SACRIFICE THE MESSENGER GREATER THAN JOHN THE BAPTIST YOU ALL GOING TO NEED, YOU SCOURGE ME, BUT THE LIGHT IN THE TABERNACLE OF THE SUN YOU ALL GOING TO NEED BECAUSE YOU CAN'T COME TO GOD WITHOUT REPENTANCE AND ACCEPTANCE THROUGH THE MINISTRY OF RECONCILIATION, OR THE FIGHT AGAINST GOD, OR WITHOUT THE LITTLE CHURCH WITH THE MANIFOLD WISDOM OF GOD IN YOU, OR WITH OUT UPHOLDING THE INHERITANCE FROM LORD JESUS FOR FRANCIS CHARLES MALCOLM IN THE TABERNACLE IN THE SUN, [THE SHAME WILL COME FROM LACK OF YOUR WILL] [GOD WILL TURN OFF HIS LIGHT ON THE DISOBEDIENT] ACCORDING TO, WHAT YOUR ILL WILL HAVE SOWN IS YOUR ONLY FRUITS WITHIN YOU IT SHALL YOU REAP IN THESE WORDS

"DEPART FROM ME I KNOW YOU NOT", " I KNOW YOUR HATE NOT YOUR LOVE". WHEN YOU SHALL HAVE GOTTEN TO THE " BOOK OF THE FIGHT AGAINST GOD" THE PROBATION OF THE CHURCHES WOULD HAVE ENDED, AND YOUR CURSE WOULD HAVE DESTROYED ALL OF YOU WITH FIRE AS THE SEVEN STARS IN THE HAND OF GOD DIMS YOUR

LIGHT, AS YOU SHALL LOOK UPON THE TABERNACLE OF THE SUN AND YOU REAL HUNGER AND THIRST FOR RIGHTEOUSNESS SHALL COME UPON YOU BUT, IT SHALL NOT BE SATISFIED.

WILL I SEE MY INHERITANCE THROUGH JESUS CHRIST THEN IN YOU — THE INHERITANCE I HAVE IN JESUS CHRIST IS IN THE HANDS OF THE GRACE AND THE LAW OF LOVE THROUGH JESUS CHRIST OUR LORD — IF THOU FEED AND YOUR PUFFED-UP SELF THE TABERNACLE IN THE SUN IS LEFT TO HUNGER FOR THE FRUITS OF CHRIST. FOR AFTER THE HIGH TIME, THE CHRIST I KNOW WILL SAY EVEN IN HIS JUDGEMENT "DEPART FROM ME I KNOW YOU NOT". THEN YOU WILL KNOW THAT YOU HAVE NO LOVE AND HAVE KICKED AGAINST THE PRICK, THEN THE BOOK OF THE FIGHTERS AGAINST GOT IS ESTABLISHED AND YOUR WAYS AND FRUITS YOU WILL SEE AS PERDITIONS.

FOR THEY BE NOT LIFTING THE WRATH OF GOD FROM OFF THE CHILDREN OF MEN THEN YOU WOULD HAVE FAILED AS A CHURCH TO REPENT — YOU WOULD HAVE FAILED AS A CHURCH TO CREATE THE FRUITS OF CHRIST AND THE FIRST CREATURES OF GOD — THEN YOU WOULD HAVE FAILED AS A CHURCH TO WALK IN THE SIMILTITUDE OF JAH — THEN YOU WOULD HAVE FAIL JESUS CHRIST IN THE ADOPRION OF HIS PEOPLE TO HIS SPIRITUAL BODY IN TRUTH AS SONS OF GOD.

THE LAST SACRIFICES SHOWED THE GREAT FAITH ABRAHAM HAD IN GOD, JESUS CHRIST IN GIVING HIS LIFE ON THE CROSS SHOWED HIS GREAT FAITH TO SAVE THE CHILDREN OF GOD THROUGH THEIR FAITH AND MORE SO GRACE. HAVING PUT AWAY THE ENMITY OF THE CROSS DESTROYING IT WITH THE LIGHT OF GOD. NOW FALLEN FROM THOSE WHO CRARRIED THE CROSS THROUGHOUT THE AGES TO THE DOOR STEPS OF GRACE FOR FULL JOY. HERE IN GRACE TO ACCEPT THE EVERLASTING GOSPEL OF SALVATION FOR ALL IN AND OUT OF CHRIST;

1. BUT WITH YOUR ENVIOUS BEHAVIOURS YOU AND YOU CHILDREN OF ONE GOD WILL SACRIFICE EVEN A BLIND MAN

2. IT IS TIME TO KNOW AND RESPECT ONE GOD ON THE FOUNDATIONS OF THE CHURCHES OF ONE GOD AND OF CHRIST THAT YOU ARE ON, NO MATTER WHAT YOU MAY CALL HIS NAME TO BE, ONCE YOU

CAN PROVE THAT, IT IS THE GOD WHO CREATED THE HEAVEN AND THE EARTH AND ALL THINGS THERE BE.

3. IF YOU CAN PLEASE GOD AND NOT MAN THEN YOU WILL BUILD JOY, PEACE, LOVE AND HAPPINESS IN A WORLD THAT YOU HAVE PUT TOHEAPS FOR HIS NAME

4. BUT BUILD THE NEW MAN IN THE FELLOWSHIP OF CHRIST THROUGH THE SPIRIT OF CHRIST AND THE SPIRIT OF GOD, TO WHO HE WILL VOW FOR YOU IN THE JUDGEMENTTO HIS FATHER WHO WILL EVENTUALLY DWELL WITH US ON EARTH HERE — WITH HIS NEW CREATURES HAVING THE BODY OF JESUS CHRIST AND BEING ADOPTED AS HIS SONS IN THE LIGHT OF GOD.

5. WHAT A BEAUTY THAT WOULD BE FOR THE MESSENGER TO COME UNTO YOU AS AN EXAMPLE, SO CAN SEEK THE KINGDOM OF GOD.

6. THIS HAPPY NONSECTARIAN MAN TO COME BACK UNTO YOU AS A MESSENGER IS PRETTY CAPABLE TO DELIVER VOLUME 2 AND VOLUME 3 OF THE GARDEN PATH BY HOLY GHOST UNTO THE ENTIRE WORLD WITH THE LIGHT OF GOD, FOR THE PRIESTS UNDERSTANDING TO COMFORT THE PATIENT SAINTS.

YOU PLAY AROUND IT FOR YOUR OWN DETRIMENT, YOU PLAY AROUND WITH MY INHERITANCE IN JESUS CHRIST FOR YOUR OWN DETRIMENT, THE GARDEN PATH HAS ONE MESSENGER, ONE MESSAGE FROM THE TABERNACLE OF THE SUN, ONE MESSENGER GREATER THAN JOHN THE BAPTIST AND JOHN THE REVELATOR WITH ONE LIGHT THE LIGHT OF GOD. FOR GOD IS LIGHT NOT DARKNESS. — WHY LOOK FOR TWO AND THREE — ONE ACCEPTANCE OF GODS WILL TO ONE GOD NOT TWO ACCORDING TO SOME ZEALOUS MINISTERS, AND ONE INHERITANCE FROM THE LORD JESUS CHRIST SO WHY TRY TO WITHOLD IT?

THE 144000 APOSTLES SEALED TO TURN AND TO EVEN WAIVER WILL UNSEAL THEMSELVES AND OF NO USE WILL THEY BE TOWARDS YOU, AND CHRISTIANITY OR TO THOSE WHOM WERE NEAR UNTO GOD. FOR TO WAIVER OR TURN AWAY FROM GOD'S WILL, WILL THE VERY ELECT BE DECEIVED. ARE YOU WITH ME? AND WHERE DO WE GO FROM HERE? AWAY FROM THE LIGHT OR TO THE LIGHT OF GOD, WELL THEN YOU MUST DECIDE, ACCEPTANCE IS YOUR WILL NOT MINES. JOHN POSTED THE LETTER OVER 2000 YEARS AGO. WHERE WERE YOU THEN? THE ANGELS HAVE IT NOW AND WHERE ARE YOU NOW? LET'S SAY UNDER A CANDLE STICK WITH ITS LIGHT ABOUT TO BE DIMMED. NOW YOU GET THE MESSENGER — WHERE ARE YOU NOW, WITH YOUR UNDERSTANDING? DID YOU EVEN FOLLOW ME? THE WORK IS A WORK OF LOVE TO BUILD THE CHURCHES INTO ONE AND CREATE THE SPIRITUAL FRUITS OF CHRIST AND GOD'S FIRST SPIRITUAL

CREATURES AND BE SONS OF GOD, WITH HIS SEVEN SPIRITS POURED OUT ON THEM. — TAKE IT OR LEAVE IT. THE TIME IS NOW, THE TIME HAS COME, GRACE BE TO YOU AND PEACE FROM GOD THE FATHER AND FROM OUR LORD JESUS CHRIST — FOR ALL KNOWETH THAT THE MESSENGER COMETH THROUGH JESUS CHRIST, WHO BELIEVED UPON HIM AND HIS FATHER

AND THE WORD OF THE BEGINNING. HE JESUS CHRIST GAVE HIMSELF FOR OUR SINS THAT HE MIGHT DELIVER US FROM THE PRESENT EVIL OF THIS WORLD, ACCORDING TO THE WILL OF GOD OUR FATHER, AS I SAID BEFORE. I MARVEL THAT YOU BE SOON REMOVED FROM HIM THAT CALLED YOU INTO THE GRACE OF CHRIST UNTO ANOTHER GOSPEL. WHICH IS NOT ANOTHER GOSPEL, BUT THERE BE SOME THAT TROUBLETH ME THE MESSENGER, AND WOULD PERVERT THE GOSPEL OF CHRIST THAT IS PREPARED FOR YOU. BUT THOUGH WE OR ANY ANGEL FROM HEAVEN, PREACH ANY OTHER GOSPEL UNTO YOU THAN THAT WHICH WE HAVE PREACHED WHICH IS CONTEMPORARY AND TO THE BIBLE, UNTO YOU LET HIM BE ACCURSED.

FOR DO I NOW PERSUADE MEN OR GOD? OR DO I SEEK TO PLEASE MEN? FOR IF I YET PLEASE MEN, I SHOULD NOT BE THE SERVANT OF CHRIST — AND I WILL TELL YOU AGAIN THAT THE GOSPEL WHICH I PREACH IS NOT OF MAN OR CERTIFIED IN MAN. FOR I NEITHER RECEIVED IT OF MAN NEITHER WAS I TAUGHT IT BY MAN BUT BY THE REVELATION OF JESUS CHRIST AND THE LIGHT OF GOD. WHICH PROSPERED IN ME THROUGH THE WELL BEING OF THE SAINTS OF GOD GONE BY WHO HELP ME TO LOVE AND BELIEVE IN THE GOSPEL OF JESUS CHRIST. THE SAINTS GONE BY IS SUFFICIENT PROOF TO KNOW THAT I WAS A PART OF THE FOLD OF JESUS CHRIST AND IS WORTHY OF THE REVELATION. AT AN OPPORTUNE TIME WHEN IT PLEASED GOD. HE WHO SEPERATED ME FROM MY MOTHER WOMB AS A FOR THE INHERITANCE OF JESUS CHRIST TO CALL ME UNTO HIM BY GRACE. GOD CALLED ME BY GRACE TO REVEAL HIS SON IN ME THAT I MIGHT PREACH THE EVERLASTING GOSPEL, AS A NEW ONE UNDER A NEW COVENANT OF LIGHT.

I CONFERED WITH THE SPIRIT OF GOD THAT LED ME THROUGH THE GARDEN PATH AND NOW TO THE TABERNACLE IN THE SUN AND THE SPIRITUAL CHURCH OF THE MANIFOLD WISDOM OF GOD. I NEVER CAME AND BEGGED FLESH AND BLOOD, OR MADE SACRIFICE TO WHAT WAS TO BE TRANSPIRED UNTO YOU IN THE LAST DAYS, AS THE MESSENGER, DID I? AND MORE SO, I LIE NOT TO YOU FOR IF YOU HEAR

THE WORDS FROM THE SWORD OF THE SPIRIT OF GOD AND BELIEVE YOU WOULD ALSO CONFER WITH YOUR BIBLES OF ITS CONTEMPORARINESS, AND TRUTH, AND LIGHT, AND GRACE AND LOVE OF GOD. LET NOT CHRIST BE DEAD IN US FOR IF RIGHTEOUSNESS BE JUSTIFIED BY THE LAW,

THEN CHRIST IS DEAD IN VAIN. BUT REMEMBER THE LAWSIS NOT FAITH WHOSOVER DOETH THEM SHALL LIVE IN THEM — NO MAN DISANNULETH OR ADD THERETO THE THINGS OF GOD BUT GOD. THE SCRIPTURES CONCLUDED THAT ALL UNDER SIN, THE PROMISE OF FAITH BY JESUS CHRIST MIGHT BE GIVEN TO THEM THAT BELIEVE, WHERE IS YOUR BELIEFT IN THE EVERLASTING GOSPEL OF CHRIST?

SO, THROUGH CHRIST FAITH CAME— WE WERE KEPT UNDER THE LAW, SHUT UP UNTO THE FAITH WHICH WOULD AFTERWARDS BE REVEALED 24 WHEREFORE THE LAW WAS OUR SCHOOL MASTER, TO BRING US UNTO CHRIST, THAT WE ALL MIGHT BE JUSTIFIED BY FAITH. BUT AFTER FAITH IS COME, WE ARE NO LONGER UNDER THE SCHOOL MASTER IN THE EVERLASTING GOSPEL TO PREACH TO THE WORLD, IT IS NOW CLEAR THAT AS CHILDREN OF GOD WE NEED TO HAVE FAITH IN JESUS CHRIST, AND BE BAPTIZED IN JESUS CHRIST SO AS TO PUT ON CHRIST AND NOT WATER FOR CHRIST IS YET THE LIVING WATERS. WHY DO I BECOME YOUR ENEMY AT THE APOINTED TIME OF GOD WHEN YOU ALL HAVE RECEIVED ME IN THE TEMPTATION OF THE FLESH BUT NOW I BRING YOU THE TRUTH? YOU ARE MY LITTLE CHILDREN FROM HENCEFORTH IN WHICH I TRAVAIL IN BIRTH AGAIN UNTIL CHRIST BE FORMED IN YOU. I COME BACK TO YOU GAL 4:20 I THE MESSENGER DESIRE TO PRESENT WITH YOU NOW, IN THE WILL OF GOD AND TO CHANGE MY VOICE, FOR I STAND IN BOUBT OF YOU, UNTIL YOU ARE

FREE IN CHRIST CALLETH YOU IN THE LAST DAYS AS THE MESSENGER GREATER THAN JOHN THE BAPTIST AND JOHN THE REVELATOR, STIRS YOU UP. BUT I SAY PERSUASION COME NOT OF ME THAT CALLETH YOU, BUT RATHER A LITTLE LEAVEN LEAVENETH THE WHOLE LUMP, SO IF ONE PRIEST HEARETH KNOWLEDGE AND UNDERSTANDETH THE GARDEN PATH, THE PATHWAY OF THE EVERLASTING GOSPEL OF JESUS CHRIST SO SHALL THE LUMP BE LEAVENED LITTLE BY LITTLE BY THAT ONE LITTLE PRIEST WITH UNDERSTANDING.

FORM THE BOOK THE GARDEN PATH ESCHATOLOGY "IT IS A RELIGIOUS SCIENCE THAT WILL TEACH US TO CARE AND SHARE — LITTLE BY LITTLE IT WILL BE TAKEN FOR RECOGNITION SO THAT OUR NATURAL HOMES WILL BE ON NATURAL LANDS" MASS FRANCIS CHARLES MALCOLM © 87, 88 – 2011.

FOR NOW, THE LAW IS FULFILLED IN ONE WORD, EVEN IN THIS, LOVE ONE ANOTHER AS AND THOUGH SHALT LOVE THY NEIGHBOUR AS THYSELF. LET US NOW WALK IN THE SPIRIT SO AS TO LIVE THE LAW OF LOVE, FOR ALL WHO MAY DECIDE TO WALK IN THE DARKNESS, THE FELLOWSHIP OF CHRIST IS NOT IN YOU. NEITHER IS THE LIGHT OF GOD. HENCE, WE BECOME

NOT DESIROUS OF VAIN GLORY, THAT WILL CONTINUE TO WRECK THE WORLD WITH LACK OF UNDERSTANDING OF THE SWORD OF THE SPIRIT OF GOD AND OF THE WORD, PROVOKING ONE ANOTHER AND ENVYING ONE ANOTHER, EVEN IN THE REVELATION AND INHERITANCE OF JESUS CHRIST THROUGH THE MESSENGER GREATER THAN JOHN THE BAPTIST, AND JOHN THE REVELATOR, UNTO THE SALVATION OF THE CHURCHES, AND UNTO THE SPIRITUAL MAN, AND UNTO THE FIRST CREATURES OF GOD. FOR IF A MAN THINKETH OF HIMSELF AS SOMETHING, WHEN HE IS NOTHING THEN HE DECEIVETH HIMSELF. THROUGH THE GADREN PATH THE REVELATION IS REVEALED TO ME TO FEED THE CHURCHES IN THE LAST DAYS. SUCH REVELATION IS AWESOME I HAVE ATTAINED UNTO IT AND EVEN WHEN I WAS IN HELL THE FATHER WAS WITH ME.

I THE MESSENGER COMETH OF CHRIST AND PROVED MY OWN WORK IN THE GARDEN PATH AND FOLLOWED IT WITH THE MODERATION OF THE TABERNACLE IN THE SUN, AS MAS THE MESSENGER OF GOD, AND WITHIN THE SPIRITUAL CHURCH OF THE MANIFOLD WISDOM OF GOD.

REJOICE NOT IN ANOTHER MESSENGER OR ANOTHER PASTOR'SWORK BUT THAT OF MYSELF ALONE, NOW EVERY MAN SHALL BEAR HIS OWN BURDEN IF YOU RESIST FOLLOWING ME TO PERISH IN ANOTHER WORK OF ZEALOUSNESS. SO, LET HIM THAT IS TAUGHT IN THE WORD COMMUNICATE WITH ME THE MESSENGER THAT TEACHETH ALL GOOD THINGS AND BE NOT DECEIVED. BE NOT DECEIVED GOD IS NOT MOCKED, FOR WHATSOEVER A MAN SOWETH THAT SHALL HE ALSO. WAIT YOUR DUE SEASON FOR THEN SHALL YOU REAP THAT WHICH IS GREATER UNTO YOU IN CHRIST AND OF GOD, THE LIGHT OF GOD. SEEK YEE THE OPPORTUNITY TO DO GOOD UNTO ALL MEN ESPECIALLY UNTO THEM OF THE HOUSEHOLDS OF FAITH. WHICH ARE NOW LEFT IN THE REFUGEE CAMPS AS YOU BOAST OF YOUR DARKNESS AND YOUR GOD. THIS SERMON IS THE LONGEST OF THE LOT BUT UNTO YOU IT'S THE WORKS OF MINE HANDS FROM THE GARDEN PATH 1, 2, & 3 CREW THAT

I BRING UNTO YOU. THIS IS THE CELIBRITY CREW OF GOD'S WORK, THOUGH THEY BE FEW WHO WEREN'T BLIND AND COULD SEE WITH THE HEART MANY THERE WILL BE AS SOON AS A LITTLE LEAVEN EXPANDS THE LUMP BY THE TRUE BELIEVERS IN CHRIST. BEAR YEE WITNESS THE LIGHT SHALL NOT MISS THE REGGAE AMBASSADORS FOR THEY THAT PREACHED UNITY AND LOVE ARE AMONGST THE GREAT MULTITUDE OF THE KINGDOM OF GOD AND WITH THEIR BELIEF IN JESUS CHRIST SHALL THEY BE SAVED UNTO SALVATION TOO BY THE SPIRIT TO BE SPRINKLED AWAY FROM EVIL AND TO DO GOOD FOREVER MORE.

IF MY PEOPLE WHICH ARE CALLED BY MY NAME, SHALL HUMBLE THEMSELVES AND PRAY, AND SEEK MY FACE, AND TURN FROM THEIR WICKED WAYS, THEN WILL I HEAR FROM HEAVEN AND WILL FORGIVE THEIR SINS AND HEAL THEIR LANDS. SO THAT THE ELDERS PASS AND PRESENT THAT TAUGHT ME TO LOVE GOD'S WORDS WILL SEE IN ME THE STEWARD I BE BEING TAUGHT BY THE SPIRIT OF JESUS CHRIST AND LED BY GOD THE FATHER UNTO THE WHOLE WORLDS OF REDEMPTION. AS IT PERCHES ON THAT CLIFT OF ZION AS ZION RAIN MOUNTS FROM UNDERGROUND IN THE SPIRITUAL REALMS OF JESUS CHRIST OUR LORD. AND THE LIGHT OF GOD REIGNETH, IT IS THAT TIME WHEN THE LORD IS STRENGTHENING HIS WORK TO BUILD THE FIRST CREATURES OF HIS CALLING

THE POUGHING UP OF ZION IS AT HAND IN THIS HIGH TIME, PATIENTLY HE CALLED FOR 2018 YEARS NOW IT'S THAT TIME FOR THE PEOPLE TO DO THE WILL OF GOD. BUT OUR PRIEST, PASTORS, DIVINERS, SEERS, ELDERS HAVE ALL BEEN PREACHING AND TEACHING HIS WORDS UPON THE FOUNDATION OF GOD'S TRUTH IN THE ORDINANCES OF MAN FOR A HIRE, BUILDING ZION ON BLOOD, ABHORING JUDGEMENT AND PERVERTING EQUITY. AS OF NOVEMBER 14, 2017, THE GARDEN

PATH IS SHOWING THE LIGHT AND THE WAY TO GO WITH THE RIGHT HAND OF GOD. THEY HAVE SPARE NO MEANS OF JEALOUSY AND ENVY TO TAKE CONTROL ONCE MORE OF A WAY WHICH NEVER SEEMETH GOOD UNTO MEN. IF THERE IS NO ANSWER FROM GOD, TO THE DECEIVERS, AS TO MANY A PRIESTS, SEERS AND DIVINERS FOR YOU HAVE NOT MADE THE NAME OF THE LORD GREAT IN THE ORDINANCES OF GOD BUT IN THE ORDINANCES OF MAN, BUT HIS NAME SHALL BE GREAT AMONGST THE HEATHEN OVER YOU WHOM ARE CALLED BY HIS NAME. YOU HAVE PROFANED HIS NAME BECAUSE YOU HAVE SAID HIS TABLE IS POLLUTED MALACHI 1:12 AND FRUITS THEREOF EVEN THE MEAT IS CONTEMPTIBLE. THE MESSENGER COMES WITH THE MEAT AND YOU HAVE PUFFED AT IT. YOU HAVE BROUGHT YOUR OWN OFFERING AS SACRIFICE OF THE MESSENGER WHO COMETH WITH THE GARDEN PATH FOR NOUGHT, OVER TIME, AND AS A SACRIFICE OF THE MESSENGER BEING BATTERED BY A TWO TON TRUCK AT HIGH SPEED, NOW, SICK, LAME AND TORN WITH A BLOOD CLOT IN THE HEAD AND A STROKE FORM SUCH, YOU ARE EVIL AND HAVE STRAYED FROM THE CONCEPT OF THE LAW OF LOVE, NOT BECAUSE OF THE LIGHT, AND NOW HIS SEVEN SPIRITS OF GOD BUT THE EVIL SPIRIT OF SATAN.

CURSED BE THE DECEIVER WHICH HAVETH IN HIS FLOCK A MALE AND SUCH THAT VOWETH THE SACRIFICE UNTO IDOLS TO CORRUPT THNGS, SHOULD GOD TAKE THAT OF YOUR HANDS, AND SO I TELL SUCH A ONE FOLLOW ME, FOLLOW ME, FOLLOW ME, FOR WHAT? JUST REMEMBER YOU

ARE LOST SHEEP, SHEPHERD AND FLOCK WITHOUT THE LIGHT OF GOD AND THE SEVEN SPIRITS OF GOD. FOR WHAT?

FRANCIS CHARLES MALCOLM CALL THEM HEATHEN AS YOU LIKE BUT THEY ARE MY PEOPLE TGPMASS THE SERMON ZION TRAIN COMETH FROM UNDERGROUND TGPMASS WE ALL PRAISE THE SAME GOD. WHY HAVE YE DEALT TREACHEROUSLY WITH US TO THIS DAY? TRYING TO MAKE THE SICK, LAME A SACRIFICE IN MY STATE IT IS OF YOU THEN AS BROTHERS OF THE FAITH TO SACRIFICE EVEN A BLIND MAN, YOU ARE EVIL AND BEFORE THE LORD THY GOD YOU ARE COUNTED AS DECEIVERS

FOR THIS MESSAGE THAT IS PROPOSED BY THE MESSENGER FROM THE TABERNACLE IN THE SUN MASS CANNOT BE USED BY DISHONEST HANDS, DECEIVERS, BUT ISSUED BY THE MESSENGER TO THE ANGELS THE STARS IN THE LORD'S RIGHT HAND, THEN TO THE PRIEST OF EACH STATE OR REGION TO GLORIFY THE KNOWLEDGE OF GOD FOR HIMSELF AND THE LAITY, BRINGING THE INHERITANCE OF THE LORD JESUS CHRIST TO BEAR FULLY UPON THE MESSENGER GREATER THAN JOHN THE BAPTIST IN THE LAST DAYS.

FRANCIS CHARLES MALCOLM CALL THEM HEATHEN AS YOU LIKE BUT THEY ARE MY PEOPLE TGPMASS THE SERMON ZION TRAIN COMETH FROM UNDERGROUND TGPMASS WE ALL PRAISE THE SAME GOD. WHY HAVE YE DEATH TREACHEROUSLY WITH US TO THIS DAY? FRANCIS CHARLES MALCOLM REMINDS YOU THAT THE PRIEST'S LIPS SHALL KEEP KNOWLEDGE AND THEY SHOULD SEEK THE LAW OF LOVE AND GRACE AT MY MOUTH FOR I AM THE MESSENGER OF THE LORD AFTER CAUSING MANY TO STUMBLE IN THE WORLD WITHIN THEIR CORRUPTED WAYS, IN YEARS GONE BY UNTIL NOW. ZION TRAIN FROM UNDERGROUND IS HERE TO BUILD THE HOUSE OF THE LORD IN THE TABERNACLE IN THE SUN. ~ YOU SEERS, DIVINERS MY ANSWER FROM GOD GO NOT ANY MORE TO THE MOUNTAINS FOR SANCTIFICATION AND TO JERUSALEM FOR PRAYERS AND TO SEEK GOD BUT DO SO NOW IN THE SPIRIT AND IN TRUTH. SHALL YOU NOT COME UNTO THE MESSENGER IN THE PEACE AND JOY, FOR THE SAKE OF THE LORD JESUS CHRIST FOR THE KNOWLEDGE OF GOD, TO BE UNDERSTOOD AND TO BE DESPERSED UNTO YOU FOR YOUR HOUSEHOLD TO ABOUND IN THE WISDOM OF GOD, AND NOT YOUR OWN GLORY IN MAKING ANOTHER GOSPEL AROUND THE LIBERALITY AND SPIRITUAL THEOLOGY OF THE CHURCH OF THE MANIFOLD WISDOM OF GOD IN THE TABERNACLE IN THE SUN.

WHERE WE BACKTRACK ON THE WILL OF GOD "TEK IT OR LEAVE IT" "TAKE IT OR LEAVE IT", YOUR OWN FREE SALVATION IS COME UNTO YOU. YOU WOULD NOW BE LIVING A LIFE OF LOVE UNDER THE LAW OF LOVE

THROUGH JESUS CHRIST HAVING ACCEPTED HIS GRACE UNTO YOU. WITH THE LAW OF LOVE THE HOLY MEN DON'T NEED TO GO DOWN TO JERUSALEM TO PRAY ANYMORE, BUT YOU RATHER HATE AND THE OLD LAWS AND THE WILL OF THE OLD GOSPEL AND OLD COVENANT, WHEN HOLINESS BECOME THE HOUSE OF THE LORD FOR YOU ALL, HAVING PUT AWAY THE OLD GOSPEL OF WAR AND DISUNITY AMONGST YOURSELVES AND THE SEVEN CANDLE STICKS AND GOD. SAY YOU LOVE GOD COME BACK TO GOD, AND KNOW THE TRUE GOD WHO CREATED THE HEAVEN AND THE EARTH AND ALL THAT IS IN IT SUCH AS THE FOUNTAINS OF WATERS AND THE BEAST OF THE FIELD, HENCE YOU SHOULD NEVER HAVE DOUBTED GOD AND HAVE DISBELIEF FOR HIS SON THE LORD JESUS CHRIST. IT'S ALL PEOPLE THAT NEEDS

SALVATION, FROM THE ENMITY OF CHRIST, BUT THE SALVATIONS ARE DIFFERENT FOR ALL UNDER THE FOUNDATION OF CHRIST. THE PRIESTS OF THE CHURCHES THAT YOU SERVE GOD UNDER NEEDS TO FOLLOW THE MESSENGER UNDER THE TABERNACLE IN THE SUN ~ MASS ~ CAPTAIN FRANCIS CHARLES MALCOLM. FOR THE MINISTRY OF RECONCILIATION, IN THE LIBERALITY TO BE UNDERSTOOD. BUT THOSE WHO GOT THEIR SALVATION FREE AND REJECTED IT, IS FIGHTING AGAINST GOD STILL, HAVING NOT FOUND A COMMON GROUND TO LOVE ONE ANOTHER AFTER DEFEAT. GOD HAS ALL THE SEVEN STARS IN HIS RIGHT HAND AND IS WALKING BETWEEN THE SEVEN CANDLE STICKS AND THE DAY WILL COME WHEN HE WILL STEP ON THE DISOBEDIENT THAT CALL THEMSELVES BY HIS NAME, UNTIL NOW WITH NO ANSWER FROM GOD, WITH THEIR EVIL PLAN FROM THEIR EVIL UNBELIEVING PROPHETS. SO, IN THESE LAST DAY JESUS WILL SEEK TO FIND DIVINITY IN MEN ONCE MORE THROUGH THE TABERNACLE OF THE SUN BUT HE SHALL MAKE ME THE MESSENGER SEE WHAT SHALL BE AFTER ME, FOR PREPARING THE WAY. YES, AN INHERITANCE IN THE NAME OF THE LORD JESUS CHRIST.

FOR THOUGH THEY OUGHT NOT TO BUT, WARIED ZION WILL THEY ALL WANT TO REVEAL THEMSELVES AS ME THE MESSENGER GREATER THAN JOHN THE BAPTIST, WHICH THEY KNEW NOTHING ABOUT OR JOHN THE REVELATOR, THAN MANY TRIED TO PITCH IN WITH WORKS NOT COVERED FOR THE PREPARED WAY UNTO SALVATION BUT TO INSPIRE A CALL TO JUDGMENT AT THE HAND OF GOD WITHOUT SALVATION THROUGH GRACE AND THE LAW OF LOVE AS IT OUGHT TO BE. I AM THE MESSENGER FULL OF POWER BY THE SPIRIT OF THE LORD AND OF JUDGEMENT AND OF MIGHT TO DECLARE UNTO JACOB HIS TRANSGRESSION AND TO ISRAEL HIS SIN. TO UNIFY THE TRANSGRESSORS UNTO GOD. SO WHERE YOUR HEADS JUDGE FOR A REWARD, YOUR PRIEST TEACH FOR AN HIRE, AND THE PROPHETS IN YOU DIVINE FOR MONEY, AND LEAN ON THE LORD AND BOAST THAT HE THE LORD IS AMONGST US, AND SO NONE EVIL CAN SUBDUE, PREACH

FOR A HIRE, SO ZION WILL BE PLOUGHED UP AS A FIELD AND JERUSALEM SHALL BECOME HEAPS AND THE MMOUNTAIN OF THE HOUSE AS THE HIGH PLACE OF THE FOREST.

BUT THE LORD WILL ESTABLISH THE MOUNTAIN OF THE HOUSE OF THE LORD ZION WILL HE ESTABLISH IN THE MOUNTAINS OF OUR LORD AND SUCH EXALTED ABOVE THE HILLS FOR THE PEOPLE TO FLOW UNTO IT, YIELDING TO THE EIGHT CANDLE STICK A HIGHER ORDER CHURCH IN THE RIGHT HAND OF OUR LORD JESUS CHURCH THE TABERNACLE IN THE SUN WHERE GRACE AND THE LAW OF LOVE WILL GO FORTH IN ITS SPIRITUAL TRANSMISSION UNTO GOD.

NOW NATIONS WILL NOT WANT TO WAR AGAINST EACH OTHER IN DUE SEASON BUT WILL DRAW NEAR TO THE LORD OF HOST SO AS TO COME INTO THE HOUSE OF JACOB AND BE AT PEACE. AND THE LORD SHALL REIGN OVER THEM IN MOUNT ZION, WHERE EVERY MAN SHALL SIT UNDER HIS OWN VINE AND FIG TREE HIS OWN ROOT, AND PEOPLE SHALL WALK EVERYONE IN THE NAME OF OUR GOD FOR EVER AND EVER YEA NONE SHALL MAKE THEM AFRAID. AS I SAID BEFORE MY WORK AS THE MESSENGER WILL NOT BE IN VAIN. BUT REMEMBER THAT THE FIGHT AGAINST GOD BEGINS WITH THE REJECTION OF GOD'S MANY SALVATION FOR THE PEOPLE OF THE WORLD AND AFTER A THOUSAND YEARS WITH CHRIST ON EARTH [IN THIS THOUSAND YEARS MANY WILL NOT BE ABLE TO GO INTO THE CITY OF GOD] AND THE FIGHT AGAINST GOD WILL CULMINATE WITH GOD DESTROYING THE EVIL ONE WITH FIRE FROM HIS EYES, AND MOUTH EVEN WITH HIS WORD.

FRANCIS CHARLES MALCOLM ZION TRAIN COMING FROM UNDERGROUND TO BE IN THE MOUNTAIN ZION, UNDER THE TABERNACLE OF THE SUN TABERNACLE IN THE SUN. SO DON'T PERVERT THE EVERLASTING GOSPEL TO BE PREACHED TO THE ENTIRE WORLD WITH ANOTHER GOSPEL, AGAINST THE NEW GOSPEL AND COVENANT OF THE LIBERALITY, AND THE SPIRITUAL THEOLOGY OF THE SPIRITUAL CHURCH OF THE MANIFOLD WISDOM OF GOD, WITH SIMPLE FOLLOWING THE BIBLE AND NOT ANYMORE A MANLY DESIGN IN THE ORDINANCES OF MAN. WHICH SHOULD ALSO BE ON THE FOUNDATION

OF CHRIST. SO, SEE THAT YOU HURT NOT THE OIL AND THE WINE FRANCIS CHARLES MALCOLM. AS A STEWARD OF JESUS CHRIST, I WILL NOT GO OUT AND SEEK THE SOULS FOR HIM, IN DARKNESS BUT UNDER THE LIGHT OF GOD. SO, YOU CAN SEE THE REASON FOR NOT EVANGELIZING WITH THE CHURCH BECAUSE THEY ARE IN THE DARKNESS WITH ALL THEIR FAULTS UNTO GOD AND REAPING SOULS THAT BEGINS TRANSGRESSING RIGHT AWAY. THEY BRING THEM TO WORSHIP IN DARKNESS OF THE LAWS OF

THE ORDINANCES OF MAN — BUT I WILL GO OUT AND SEEK THE SOULS FOR HIM IN THE ORDINNACES OF GOD. BUT, BE IT KNOWN I LABOUR NOT IN MY OWN WORK IT IS NOW TO THOSE THAT WILL COME FOR THE UNDERSTANDING AND THE FEW LABOURERS IN THE GREATEST HARVEST OF ALL TIMES.

IN THE CHURCHES THAT ARE NOT WILLING TO ACCEPT THE MESSENGER AND THE GRACE OF GOD, TEACHING THE LAITY TO LIVE THE LAW OF LOVE, LOVING ONE ANOTHER AS THEMSELVES WILL CONSUME THEMSELVES WITH A BLIND HAERT THAT WILL NEVER SEE THE TRUTH OF GOD, AS THEY CONTINUE UNTO PERDITION RIDING SATAN, KNOWINGLY NOW.

WHEN I ENTER THE CHURCH OF GOD, I PRAY THAT THE SPIRIT OF GOD WILL GIVES ME PERMISSION TO SPEAK, I PRAY THAT GOD WILL GIVE ME PERMISSION TO PRAY IN THE SINAGOGUE THAT IS UNDER THE LAWS, I THEN ENTER WITH A FREE HEART WITH THE STIR, TO STIR UP MY

COLLEAGUES TO COME BACK TO CHRIST. YEA THEY THINKING THAT OH! THEY ARE EVER RIGHTEOUS, AND AT WORSHIP UNDER THE LAW THEY ARE THE MOST UPRIGHT, IF THEY SHOULD TARRY TO LONG IN THIS STATE THEY BE FALLEN FROM HIS GRACE, THE MESSENGER IS HERE JUST TO WARN THEM AND HELP TO SAVE THE WILLING FEW, THAT UNDER GOD IS WILLING TO CHANGE, WILLING TO WORSHIP HIM IN THE FELLOWSHIP OF HIS GRACE GIVEN TO MAN 2018 YEARS AGO, IN THE BEGINNING. BUT MAN HAVE STILL NOT RENDERED THEIR HEARTS TO DO SO, JUST BECAUSE THEIR HEARTS ARE BLIND, WITH EMPHASIS AND SEEKING HAPPINESS, GLORY AND JOY IN MAN AND THE ORDINANCES OF MAN. THE CHURCH WILL HAVE TO LEAVE THE ORDINANCES OF MAN, THEY WILL HAVE TO LEAVE BABYLON, AND RETURN TO GOD, AND WORSHIP GOD IN THE ORDINANCE OF GOD, HENCE THE MESSENGER IS HERE TO BRING YOU TO REPENTANCE, OF YOUR FAULTS UNTO GOD. NO MATTER WHICH WAY YOU TURN, REPENT OF ONE THING, SERVING GOD UNDER THE ORDINANCES OF MAN, REPENT OF TESTING THE MESSENGER'S WILL, THE MESSENGER HAVE BEEN GIVE THE SWORD OF THE SPIRIT OF JESUS CHRIST FROM WAY BACK WHEN, TO PERFORM THIS ROLE IN THE OPPORTUNE TIME, THE MESSENGER SEEK SOULS FOR THE LIGHT OF GOD, TO KEEP THE LIGHT SHINING IN THE HEARTS OF MEN. NOT SOULS FOR THE DARK TO BE MY BURDEN IN CHRIST, THE MESSENGER SEEKS SOULS FOR GRACE. THE MESSENGER AMONGST YOU, IS NOT HERE TO BE TESTED AS AN ANTI-CHRIST WITH FULL KNOWLEDGE OF THE LIGHT OF GOD, GRACE AND BELIEF IN THE LORD JESUS CHRIST THE SON OF GOD WHO CAME IN THE FLESH TO THE WORLD THAT WE MAY HAVE GRACE IN THE HIGH TIME.

YOU WANT TO WORK ME OUT IN MY WORK THE LIBERALITY AS A FOOLISH MESSENGER, NO THAT NOT THE WAY IT GOES. THE SEVEN STARS IN THE RIGHT HAND OF THE LORD JESUS CHRIST WILL WORK YOU OUT OF THE KINGDOM OF GOD, AS THEY DIM YOUR LIGHT FOR UTTER DISOBEDIENCE UNTO GOD'S MESSENGER, THAT REFRESHED THE SOUL OF THE MASTER.

THE CHURCH HAVE TO ACCEPT THE ROLE GOD HAVE ASKED THEM TO PLAY IN THE LAST DAYS, THAT IS TO COME FOR THE UNDERSTANDING

OF THE LIBERALITY, COME UNDER GRACE AND THE LAW OF LOVE, FOR ABOVE LOVE THERE IS NOT A GREATER LAW. FOR CHRIST WILL NOT BE A DEBTOR TO OR FOR THE LAWS. SO, IF GRACE ABOLISHES THE LAWS THEN YOU ALL NEED TO TIDY UP OR GET OUT OF THE BUSINESS OF WORSHIPING GOD IN THE OLD LAWS AND UNDER THE ORDINANCES OF MAN. FOR THERE IS AND WILL BE NO TRUTH IN YOU, BECAUSE THE TRUTH IS IN THE LOVE FOR GOD AND THE LORD JESUS CHRIST WHO IS ALSO IN ME., I WILL HAVE TO STIR YOU UP TO ACCEPT THE SWORD OF THE SPIRIT OF GOD, SO YOU CAN TEACH THE REDEEMING GRACE TO BE UNDERSTOOD BY THE CHURCH. BEFORE YOU HIT THE ROAD TO GATHER MORE SHEEP FOR THE DARKNESS. BUT HAVING ACCEPTED THE LIGHT OF GOD, REAP THEM FOR THE LIGHT.

YOU WILL HAVE TO TURN YOURSELVES OVER IN THE MINISTRY OF RECONCILIATION, AND ITS NOT JUST THE PASTOR WHO NEEDS TO PRAY FOR REPENTANCE. IT'S THE WHOLE CHURCH — REASON YOU ALL WERE WRONG BEFORE GOD, HAVING BEEN TO A POINT WHERE YOU UNDERSTOOD THINGS OF GOD WRONGFULLY AND NOW TO UNLEARN THEM AND START ANEW, WITH THE NEW GOSPEL AND NEW COVENANT ON THE SAME FOUNDATIONS OF JESUS CHRIST IN A UNIFIED CHURCH UNDER THE TABERNACLE IN THE SUN.

YOU ALL REVILED AGAINST GOD, YOU ALL DISRESPECTED THE GOD YOU SAY YOU SERVE — YOU GOING OUT THERE IN A WORLD TO GET MANY SOULS, OF WHICH NOT ALL ARE LOST, BRINGING THEM INTO PERDITION WITH YOU. A GREAT MULTITUDE HAVE ACCEPTED GRACE THROUGH JESUS IN THE SPIRIT AND A GREAT MULTITUDE IS ALREADY BAPTIZED IN THE SPIRIT OF JESUS CHRIST AND THE SPIRIT OF GOD, FOR JUST BELIEVING IN GOD, AND LIVING THE LAW OF LOVE.

AT THE STIR AND THE MODERATIONS, YOU ARE JUST COMING INTO THE LIGHT OF JESUS CHRIST THROUGH GRACE — THE THING TO DO IS TO ACCEPT GOD'S GRACE FROM THE MESSENGER — WITH ALL YOUR HEART AND STOP WATCHING THE FRUITS WITHIN YOU. SEARCH FOR YOUR FAULTS AS A CHURCH DENOMINATION AND RECTIFY IT WITH GOD FOR YOUR HEALING AND SANCTIFICATION IN THE MOUNTAIN OF ZION AND BECKON

UNTO THE TABERNACLE IN THE SUN FOR THE LIGHT OF GOD TO BE NOW AND FOREVER WITH YOU.

FOR TO CONTINUE TO DWELL ON THE FRUITS OF DARKNESS, YOU WILL BE CURSED MUCH MORE THAN NOW, AND YOUR PATIENT SAINTS WILL COME OUT FROM YOU, YOU NEED TO HUMBLE YOUR PUFFED-UP SELVES BEFORE GOD, AND SEEK HIM FOR YOURSELVES IN SPIRIT AND IN TRUTH. THEN PUT AWAY THE DARKNESS OF HERESE, ENVY AND MANY OTHERS THAT YOU ALREADY TEACH, THAT ARE THE POSSIBLE FRUITS WITHIN YOU THAT HAVE HELD YOU BACK FROM THE LIGHT OF GOD, AND FROM WORSHIPING GOD IN SPIRIT AND IN TRUTH. SO, YOU CAN GET THE LIGHT OF GOD FROM HIS SALVATION, FOR TO CONTINUE TO DWELL ON THE FRUITS OF DARKNESS, YOU WILL ALL BE LOST IN BABYLON, YOU HAVE TO BURN DOWN BABYLON FOR YOURSELVES, YOU NEED TO COME OUT OF HER, THIS ORDINANCE OF MAN WILL GET YOU NO WHERE WITH GOD, I AM HERE TO SHOW YOU ALL HOW TO BRING BACK THE LORD JESUS INTO YOUR LIFE EVEN THOUGH YOU

WERE CONSIDERED NEAR UNTO GOD. NOW IN A VERY SHORT SPACE OF TIME, FOR THE END OF TIME IS COME. YOU NEED TO GET YOURSELVES READY TO JOIN THE GREAT MULTITUDE AT THEIR LEVEL OF BELIEF IN GOD, AND REVIVE YOUR SOULS IN JESUS CHRIST GRACE

UNDER THE LAW OF LOVE, STRENGTHEN YOURSELVES SO YOU CAN HAVE HOPE IN HIS SALVATION, A SALVATION YOU THOUGHT YOU NEVER NEEDED, AND BE STRONG AGAINST THE WHILES OF THE DEVIL, IF YOU ARE NEVER TO ACCEPT GRACE. IF YOU ARE NEVER TO LET GO OFF THE LAWS, IF YOU ARE NEVER TO WORSHIP GOD IN HIS ORDINANCE, THEN CERTAINLY IN BABYLON YOU WILL BE WHEN THE SAVIOUR SHOULD APPEAR, BEING TORMENTED DAY AND NIGHT, FOR FIGHTING AGAINST GOD, THE MESSENGER SEEKS TO AWAKEN SOULS FOR CHRIST, WITH A PREPARED WAY THAT HAVE REFRESHED THE MASTERS SOUL, SO SHALL IT REFRESH YOUR AS I AM A TRUE EXAMPLE OF THE LIGHT OF GOD. FOR YOU ARE DRIVEN IN DARKNESS FOR TOO LONG UNDER THE PUFFED-UP MEN OF GOD, THAT IS UNWILLING TO LEAVE THE ORDINANCES OF MAN, BECAUSE THEY ARE SEEKING THEIR OWN MEAT. NOTE THE MESSENGER IS NOT HERE TO BRING SHAME TO YOU OR ANYONE, BUT TO GIVE A WARNING UNTO YOU. BUT REJECTION AND ENVY WILL BEAR FRUITS OF UNRIGHTEOUSNESS, WHAT IS MORE SHAMEFUL?

THE MESSENGER IS HERE TO DO THE WORK IN THE SPACE ALLOTED, AND MY POWERFUL GOD HAVE PLACED THE MESSAGE ALL OVER THE WORLD ALREADY, BEFORE YOU ARE EVEN READY TO RECEIVE IT AND BE FILLED WITH JOY, IN HIS HOLY SPIRIT AND IT CANNOT BE DENIED UNTO THE

ENDS OF THE EARTH. CAN A MAN ROB GOD? — CAN THE CHURCH ROB GOD? — IT IS THAT TIME WHEN YOUR SALVATION CANNOT BE IN THE DARK;

• THERE MUST BE REDEMPTION OF THE CHILDREN OF GOD BY BRINGING THEM BACK TO THE BEGINNING AND THE LAW OF LOVE, WITH THE LIGHT OF GOD. SO, SHALL WE ACCEPT THE WILL OF GOD FOR THEIR TURNING AWAY FROM HIS WRATH.

• AND THEIR REDEMPTION IS NOT THE ONE THAT IS FROM REPENTANCE ALONE, BUT TO ACCEPT THE MESSENGER WITH ALL THEIR HEART GIVING THE MESSENGER THE INHERITANCE HE HAS IN JESUS CHRIST JUST LIKE THE CHURCH. FOR HAVING WORSHIPPED GOD IN THE ORDINANCES OF MAN FOR 2018 YEARS — ON JESUS'S OWN FOUNDATION OF THE CHURCHES — UNDER THE TABERNACLE OF THE SUN THROUGH THE MESSENGER'S WAY, YOUR LIGHT WILL NEVER

GROW DIM. THIS IS MASS, THE MESSENGER — DADDY SEVEN (7) WITH MINISTRY OF RECONCILIATION ON THE ONE SIDE OF THE PRICK, NEVER TO KICK AGAINST IT, AND AGAIN THE MESSENGER'S WAY OF SPIRITUAL HOPE AND FELLOWSHIP IN JESUS CHRIST AND ON THE SAME SIDE OF THE PRICK NEVER TO KICK AGAINST IT.

IN THE SPIRITUAL CHURCH WITH THE MANIFOLD WISDOM OF GOD — WHICH IS THE INHERITANCE IN JESUS CHRIST IN HIS SWORD GIVEN UNTO I THE MESSENGER GREATER THAN JOHN THE BAPTIST AS FOR 2018 YEARS YOU NEVER KNEW AND GREATER THAN JOHN THE REVELATOR AS I DELIVER THE MESSAGE TO THE ANGELS IN CHARGE OF THE CHURCHES IN THE HIGH TIME.

THERE WILL BE A LOT OF HE SAID SHE SAID BUT WHEN IT COMES TO JESUS CHRIST AND THE ADOPTION TO BE HIS SONS HE'LL SAY "DEPART FROM ME I KNOW YOU NOT" YEE SOLDIERS THAT SOJOURN WITH THE CROSS WHETHER IT BE IN THE ENMITY OF THE CROSS OR THOSE THAT CARRY THE CROSS, SEE THAT YOU FIGHT NOT THE MESSENGER GREATER THAN JOHN THE BAPTIST AND GREATER THAN JOHN THE REVELATOR. — I THEREFORE WISH FOR YOUR ACCEPTANCE OF THE WILL OF GOD WITH ALL YOUR HEARTS BEFORE IT IS TOO LATE.

THEY BEING THE CHILDREN OF ONE GOD AVOIDING TO TEACH AND PREACH THE EVERLASTING GOSPEL OF JESUS CHRIST, WHICH IS THE NEW GOSPEL AND THE UNDER THE NEW COVENANT OF GOD, WHICH WAS FROM THE BEGINNING AND ALSO OF THE OLD BIBLE, BUT NOW TO YOUR UNDERSTANDING. ALL CHURCHES HAVE TO HUMBLE THEMSELVES AND COME BACK TO GOD, UNLEARN THE OLD WRONGFULLY UNDERSTOOD WAYS

THAT LEADS TO PERDITION, AND COME BACK TO GOD WITH ACCEPTANCE OF GRACE, IN A LIFE ON EARTH IN LOVE IN THE ORDINANCE OF GOD ONLY, UNDER HIS LIGHT.

ZION TRAIN SURFACES JUST LIKE THE LIGHT OF THE MOON TO HUMBLE RECEIVE THE LIGHT OF GOD UNDER THE TABERNACLE OF THE SUN WITH THE MINISTRY OF RECONCILIATION OF THE LIBERALITY AND THE SPIRITUAL CHURCH WITH THE MANIFOLD, WITH THE LIGHT OF GOD. IN UNITY EVEN IF ALL SHOULD CARRY DIAMOND AND DIACRITIC MARKS.

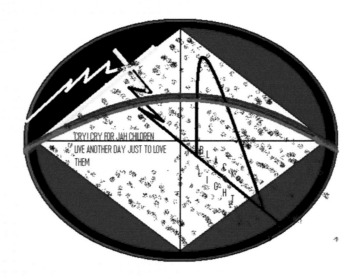

Figure 5: "Chip A Diamond", The Garden Path™ Ensign, to the four corners of the earth. ©1988, 1998, 2008, 2018, 2019.

Fruits and Creatures of God's Kingdom

The Lord said unto my Lord, the Priests that cometh for the understanding of this book with The Prepared Way, shall not be cursed neither shall they be in wants of wisdom of the Holy Bible anymore, and they shall have not room enough to store their

tithes and offerings, but unto God a New Creature in His WORD. This, the work of the Lord for his effectual workings of His will upon the earth to return

His goodness unto mankind if only their faith in Him

is restored in Him, the God of Creation over all things. To teach the Patients Saints of God, The Redeeming Way to return and come unto God. Likewise, all that cometh shall know God, and be set aside from the His condemnation in the High Time. This also is good tithings unto all that heareth and seeth the WORD of God, and so spread the light of joy unto the four (4) corners of the earth. The Lord said hereafter cursed be any man that dispiseth the Messenger of God, saying

all manner of evil against this old man and so let with

iniquity of His work, and desireth to be baptized by the same Spirit of God and to have salvation by the same Spirit which hath been sent by God unto you. For now man shall have no need to go down to the temple to pray but pray and worsh ip Him in Spirit and in truth. As the fallen cross recedes into the decay of the Old Gospel and the Old Covenant, The LIBERALITY brings forth the New Gospel of the Prepared Way as the Old vanishes away. Building the fruits of Christ and Creatures of God with the understanding thereof given to the Priests under the Tabernacle in the Sun, to create gardens much more beautiful than that of Eden.

Figure 6: The Garden Path™ Ensign, interim 1977, ©1987, 1988, 1998, 2008, 2018, 2019.

The Messenger cometh unto you to remind you puffed up Christians that God rested on the Sabbath day, and it is this same God that commanded man to do likewise, likewise from His work. Let me remind you God worked with His mouth and His words in most cases so do you on the Sabbath Day, before He that made you. It was never Satan. So, Satan does not have a day of rest. It was God that asked man to hallow the Sabbath day meaning having reverence to the day and Not Satan. It was God that said my day of rest is the Sabbath Day and in it thou shouldest do no work. It is Satan that allows you to work through the day of rest. Therefore, it is important to avoid leaving your house on a Sabbath Day of rest to speak your own words, or any other form of work if it is essential for the common good of all men and God. You may collect an offering for the even me the messenger for an inheritance through Jesus Christ but make sure you do it on the first day of the week, for if it be done on the Sabbath Day you will need to keep it.

We must return unto God for his peace. When God gives us His peace by every means possible His peace will keep us standing and unmoved by satanic influences. The Bible continue to say "In returning and rest shall we be saved, in quietness and in confidence shall be your strength" Therefore we must trust in God, so, let us return to the Lord, let us be still in his presence and know he is God. As Zion Train moves from underground with "The LIBERALITY", then we will be like Mount Zion which cannot be moved.

When the return is done by the Churches the Patient Saints will revere, and consecrate the Sabbath Day at home resting and recuperating for the next week of work and Worship. Mankind will then know that in all things they have no power over God and He is so merciful unto them for Lord God of all the heaven and the earth He created.

For, so shall mankind put away the enmity of Christ under the Tabernacle in the Sun for everlasting peace on earth. Now Let the Priests Come to the understanding of God's word, taking Him back to the beginning in the High Time to please God with all their entire hearts.

Printed in the United States
By Bookmasters